Customer Relationship Management

Getting It Right!

Terence Ip
2005

Hewlett-Packard® Professional Books

HP-UX

Fernandez	Configuring CDE: The Common Desktop Environment
Madell	Disk and File Management Tasks on HP-UX
Olker	Optimizing NFS Performance: Tuning and Troubleshooting NFS on HP-UX Systems
Poniatowski	HP-UX 11i Virtual Partitions
Poniatowski	HP-UX 11i System Administration Handbook and Toolkit
Poniatowski	The HP-UX 11.x System Administration Handbook and Toolkit
Poniatowski	HP-UX 11.x System Administration "How To" Book
Poniatowski	HP-UX 10.x System Administration "How To" Book
Poniatowski	HP-UX System Administration Handbook and Toolkit
Poniatowski	Learning the HP-UX Operating System
Rehman	HP Certified: HP-UX System Administration
Sauers/Weygant	HP-UX Tuning and Performance: Concepts, Tools, and Methods
Weygant	Clusters for High Availability: A Primer of HP-UX Solutions, Second Edition
Wong	HP-UX 11i Security

UNIX, LINUX, WINDOWS, AND MPE I/X

Diercks	MPE i/X System Administration Handbook
Mosberger	IA-64 Linux Kernel
Poniatowski	UNIX User's Handbook, Second Edition
Roberts	UNIX and Windows 2000 Interoperability Guide
Stone/Symons	UNIX Fault Management

COMPUTER ARCHITECTURE

Kane	PA-RISC 2.0 Architecture
Markstein	IA-64 and Elementary Functions

NETWORKING/COMMUNICATIONS

Blommers	Architecting Enterprise Solutions with UNIX Networking
Blommers	OpenView Network Node Manager
Blommers	Practical Planning for Network Growth
Brans	Mobilize Your Enterprise: Achieving Competitive Advantage Through Wireless Technology
Cook	Building Enterprise Information Architecture: Reengineering Information Systems
Lucke	Designing and Implementing Computer Workgroups
Lund	Integrating UNIX and PC Network Operating Systems

SECURITY

Bruce	Security in Distributed Computing: Did You Lock the Door?
Pearson et al.	Trusted Computing Platforms: TCPA Technology in Context
Pipkin	Halting the Hacker, Second Edition
Pipkin	Information Security

Customer Relationship Management

Getting It Right!

Judith W. Kincaid

Hewlett-Packard Company

www.hp.com/hpbooks

PTR
Prentice Hall PTR
Upper Saddle River, New Jersey 07458
www.phptr.com

Library of Congress Cataloging-in-Publication Data

A CIP catalog record for this book can be obtained from the Library of Congress.

Editorial/production supervision: *Mary Sudul*
Cover design director: *Jerry Votta*
Cover design: *DesignSource*
Manufacturing manager: *Alexis Heydt-Long*
Acquisitions editor: *Jill Harry*
Editorial assistant: *Kate Wolf*
Marketing manager: *Dan DePasquale*

Publisher, Hewlett-Packard Books: *Patricia Pekary*

Published by Prentice Hall PTR
Prentice-Hall, Inc.
Upper Saddle River, New Jersey 07458

Prentice Hall books are widely used by corporations and government agencies for training, marketing, and resale.
The publisher offers discounts on this book when ordered in bulk quantities. For more information, contact Corporate Sales Department, Phone: 800-382-3419; FAX: 201-236-7141;
E-mail: corpsales@prenhall.com
Or write: Prentice Hall PTR, Corporate Sales Dept., One Lake Street, Upper Saddle River, NJ 07458.

Printed in the United States of America
10 9 8 7 6 5 4 3 2 1

ISBN 0-13-035211-X

Pearson Education LTD.
Pearson Education Australia PTY, Limited
Pearson Education Singapore, Pte. Ltd.
Pearson Education North Asia Ltd.
Pearson Education Canada, Ltd.
Pearson Educación de Mexico, S.A. de C.V.
Pearson Education — Japan
Pearson Education Malaysia, Pte. Ltd.

CONTENTS

PREFACE

I've been asked the question "Why are you writing this book?" many times in the past several months. That question was easy for me to answer, but others were harder. Questions like "What will the book be about?" and "Whom are you writing it for?" have been more difficult, and I've been wrestling with them as I've sat staring at my blank computer screen suffering the agonies of writer's block. (I'm not sure it can actually be *writer's* block before I've ever written a page, but you know what I mean.) All these questions are important, and I want to answer them all.

So Whom Is This Book For?

This book will be helpful to anyone in any company that is planning to invest in a Customer Relationship Management program. It is primarily aimed at two key audiences: business managers in the customer-facing functions (marketing, sales, service, and support) and the IT managers who support these functions. Because these two groups must work in partnership as a single team, my intent is to provide a bridge that helps each understand his or her own concerns, issues, and responsibilities as well as those of the "other half," helping to close the communications gap that often exists between them.

Business function and Information Technology professionals often have different training and experience, different objectives and rewards, even different languages. CRM is information-based and technology-based. Good communication is imperative because responsibility for various deliverables switches back and forth between the business functions and the IT department. Responsibility for a CRM program is collaborative and joint. Each member of the team must be able to fundamentally understand how his or her efforts impact others on the team – even when they speak different languages. If you are an IT manager, give this book to the business managers responsible for your company's CRM program so they can learn and understand what you need from them and why. If you're a sales or a marketing manager, give this book to your IT team so they understand the critical transition points and the importance of using business knowledge to drive all technical decisions.

You probably chose this book because your organization has a problem with market share, profit, competitive pressures, organizational silos, product commoditization, or some other issue that you know has a negative impact on your company's ability to build strong customer relationships and loyalty. You know all the reasons why your company needs to become more customer-focused, and now you want to know how to get started doing it. My goal is to help business and IT professionals understand how to work together to build the infrastructure required to put a successful CRM program in place. Real business examples will be used to clarify key steps.

I spent the past 20 years at Hewlett-Packard working initially in Information Systems Management and data warehouse management roles. For many years, HP operated as a collection of independent divisions rather than as one company. These small business units operated like small companies. Year after year, we continued to see irrefutable evidence that neither size nor product changed the basics of the business problem (order processing, manufacturing planning, inventory control, etc.) or the basic approach required to address the problem. At the same time, some efforts had to be initiated across the entire enterprise. We were often asked to switch back and forth between the individual requirements of each of the business units and company-wide requirements. That experience showed us time and again that the business needs of the individual organizations involved all the same basics, no matter how "different" each thought it was. Of course, project scope and scale varied, but the basic tenets of managing relationships with customers are about *customers,* not about the *organization!*

Right now, you may be wondering "How is it that anything that worked for huge companies like HP would ever work for my company? We're nowhere near that size." This book isn't specifically about what HP *did,* but about the processes HP (and other companies) used to do it. Real-life examples and case studies are the best way to share information and illustrate concepts. We will use case examples from HP and other companies with whom I've worked since launching my career as an independent consultant. Finally, we'll use detailed case examples from XYZ Corporation, a mythical company founded in Chicago in 1992. XYZ's CRM program is a composite of experiences from several of my clients (mostly mid-size companies) and others whom I've met through my frequent speaking opportunities at national and international conferences. XYZ represents a broad spectrum of industries, including manufacturers, service organizations, business-to-business, and consumer. All of these companies, including HP, are looking to improve their customers' loyalty through improving the relationships they have with their customers.

What Is This Book About?

First and foremost, it's about making your business more successful. I am *convinced* that the only factor that will prove to be a sustainable differentiator in the marketplace as we enter the twenty-first century is customer loyalty. Certainly product superiority will always play a huge role in developing a loyal customer following, but product life cycles have become so compressed that there is often little time to capitalize on having a superior product. Products become commodities too quickly, and commodities are generally purchased for one reason, the best price.

Loyalty is the one factor that will keep a customer buying from you even when the competition is fierce. (I'm a prime example; I continue to buy HP toner for my LaserJet III printer even though knock-off products are available at HALF the price. Sure, my total HP experience isn't just about being a customer, but you get the idea.) Loyalty is built on trust, which results from the total experience that a customer has with your organization.

Many companies mistakenly think they can jump right into building customer loyalty and personalization programs. They can't, and neither can you. This book is intended to help you develop the strategy and build the infrastructure that absolutely must be in place before you can begin to understand your customers and start delivering effective loyalty programs.

The goal of this book is NOT to persuade you that customer relationships are important, nor is it my intention to convince you to become customer-centered instead of product-centered. I'll touch on the business imperatives and benefits as a way to set the stage, but many excellent books already address this part of the issue. We will look at the key components of a CRM infrastructure: information and knowledge management, business processes and organizations, people and change management, and technology (as an element, but not as the whole solution). This book gives you the tools you need to help define your company's goals and priorities. You'll also learn how to build the foundation to launch your CRM projects. CRM is about putting customers in the center of what your organization does. This book gives you an overview of the actions you have to take to make CRM happen.

How *do* you integrate systems, information, processes, and people's behavior across the enterprise? Why do you need to set a strategy first? What are the most common risks you should be aware of before launching a CRM program? What should you do about organizational politics? Is sponsorship important, and if so, how do you secure it? What are the special concerns of linking web data to non-web data? You'll be able to get answers to these questions and many others in this book.

Why Did I Write This Book?

During my early years at HP, information became my passion because it often was treated like something that just happens when a system is built. And yet my training as an industrial engineer responsible for making decisions based on information had taught me that this was a mistake. Bad information cannot enable good decisions. The "data happens" attitude invariably led to application software that provided little real benefit to the end user. After all, half of "Information Technology" is "information!" but that was seldom the focus for any software development project. The fun stuff was the nifty, whiz-bang technology. Information was an incidental. Because I felt that good information was critical to good business planning, I decided to take up the challenge. I always seem to be a champion of the underdog anyway.

For the past twelve years, I've managed Database Marketing and Customer Relationship Management organizations. As the environment has changed (HP, the marketplace, and technology), we continued to learn about the problems and opportunities involved in moving toward customer-centered, enterprise-wide treatment of our customers.

This journey has been filled with many successes and lots of not-so-successful lessons. I am passionate about the promise that increased customer loyalty holds for all companies whether they sell to consumers, business-to-business customers, or both. I'm also a fanatic about the role that high-quality customer information plays in improving customer loyalty. I'm proud of what HP accomplished. Long known as a very product-centric engineering company, HP has made tremendous progress in its efforts to create an excellent total experience for its customers. I hope you can learn from what we learned, what went well, and what didn't go so well, to aid you on your own journey.

Another reason for writing this book was to explore the ways that the Internet has affected how we interact with our customers and the resulting relationships. You probably have heard repeatedly that the Internet would change everything. Well, it didn't. But one thing did change dramatically. The Internet took the people you have been counting on for years *out* of the customer interaction equation.

Historically, as companies were founded and grew, they developed processes and systems that supported a single functional area. Unfortunately, this is still true even of companies who have started up in the last five years or less. All companies have depended on their people (e.g., sales representatives, sales support, and service representatives) to build relationships with customers. People provide the glue that links together disconnected organizational silos and hides the organization's complexity from the customer.

The need to build enterprise-wide customer relationships (not just for one function or one product line) has been growing for more than a decade. However, among the many other things the web has affected is a new urgency for many companies to build strong customer relationships and to build them quickly. Expectations of "Internet speed" seem to impact everything we do. Another change that the Internet has effected is that customers are learning to expect more from each company because they can easily surf the web and compare us to our competitors. The Internet has increased time pressure and raised the level of the playing field, but it hasn't changed **all** the rules. All this change leaves many of us unsure whether we love or hate the web, but we certainly all worry about it.

Even though the web is a new and important aspect of Customer Relationship Management (CRM), it's neither the whole problem nor the whole solution. For at least two decades, and probably longer, most companies have been collecting information about their customers and trying to use that information to better understand and predict what customers might want next. This was the promise of Database Marketing programs that many companies adopted ten to fifteen years ago. And, of course, people (vendors) have been building relationships with other people (buyers) for centuries.

What's so new about CRM? CRM involves using information you have about your customers and technology tools to deliver quality experiences to your customers. But it is not just about technology and information. Both business processes and people behavior often must also change to ensure a consistent and positive total customer experience. For the same reason, it must involve all customer interactions, on the web, off the web, and through third-party channels.

Maybe most important, CRM is about how your customers experience your company, not about how you look at your customers. Managing customer relationships today is almost like turning the management of the relationship over to the customer. One of my colleagues refers to this as *Customer Managed Relationships.* I like that term because it emphasizes that CRM is about making business decisions based on how it will look (feel, sound) to your customer. This is a CRM fundamental.

How Is This Book Organized?

This book is organized around a *CRM Program Life Cycle,* which covers all the work necessary to build a successful program. The term *life cycle* is appropriate because a complete cycle is repeated for each small project that will result in overall program success.

The first few chapters put CRM in the context of the marketplace and your overall business activities, and introduce a few key concepts and definitions. Part 2 describes the all-important planning and organizing steps that are required before you launch your program. In Part 3, we track the steps of a CRM infrastructure project development and implementation. In Part 4, we look at using the new infrastructure to deliver customer experiences. Finally, Part 5 talks about living with and caring for your new CRM tools.

A key to bridging the understanding and communications gap that often exists between the business functional team members and the Information Technology team members is creating clear definitions of important terms. It is equally important that you and I share a common vocabulary as you read this book. After all there's no guarantee that we have the same background and experiences. Key definitions are indicated by a *dictionary* symbol:

 DEFINITIONS

These definitions will also be summarized for quick reference in Appendix A.

Throughout the book, you'll find important points that warrant special attention. These key concepts are identified by a *key* symbol:

KEY IDEA

At the end of each chapter is a series of reflective questions that will help clarify your understanding of where your organization is today and the steps you need to take to develop a successful program.

Why Do I Want You to Enjoy This Book?

It's my hope that we will be able to build a relationship through my investment in writing this book and your investment in reading it. Because relationships are two-way, I hope very much that we can benefit from each other's experiences. I would be thrilled to hear about the risks you've taken, the new approaches you've tried, and the new solutions (or false starts) you've discovered. If you want to share your insights or experiences, please send me an email at jkincaid@jk-associates.com.

ACKNOWLEDGMENTS

With more thanks than I can possibly express...

To Bojana Fazarinc for her early sponsorship and for encouraging me to start this project and to Stephanie Acker-May for her current sponsorship—and the encouragement to finish it!

To Pat Pekary for pointing me in the right direction and to my editors Jill, Jennifer and Mary for teaching me the ropes.

To the many colleagues (and great friends) who have influenced my growth and understanding of customers, relationships and information management.

To my husband, Bob Carlson, and our exceptional children Jennifer, Christina, Andrew and Brian, for all the years of love and support.

Most of all, to my reviewers, Lee Bonds and Joe Podolsky. Thanks for the hours of reviewing, coaching, counseling, consoling and brilliantly phrased insights. This book would never be here without you guys.

CRM: Is It Right for Your Company?

CHAPTER 1

Commerce in the 21st Century

Today's marketplace isn't the same as the one we're used to, even though many of the basic principles haven't changed. Events in the external marketplace are forcing us to rethink what we have to do internally in order to remain successful. This book starts by taking a look at some of the internal and external factors that influence the way we will do business in the 21st century in order to remain competitive.

You are reading this book because you already know that Customer Relationship Management is important for your organization. Even so it's appropriate to start by building a common understanding: CRM isn't one total solution that everyone just plugs in and finds that all problems are solved. We need a framework for describing the different needs of different kinds of companies and for understanding the changes that are taking place in the world around us.

We also need to develop an understanding of how we are going to work together while you're reading this book. My goal is to give you the tools and knowledge you need to manage a successful CRM program for your own company. You don't need to hire one of my colleagues or me in order to be successful. You don't need us to "do CRM" for you. You just need to understand the basic principles and ground rules.

1.1 Understanding the Landscape

Yes, the environment in which we operate has changed. Both inside our companies and externally in the marketplace, many of our old working assumptions just don't look the same.

1.1.1 The Internal Landscape

Michael Treacy and Fred Wiersema are leading authorities on business strategy and corporate transformation. In their extensive study of highly successful companies versus those that are less successful, they identified some key differences in strategy setting and operational behavior between industry winners and losers. The value discipline model they developed is an important frame of reference for understanding how changes in the marketplace have affected all businesses and why requirements for success have changed for most, if not all.

Treacy and Wiersema showed that successful companies build their competitive advantage by focusing on and excelling in only one of three basic values: product leadership, customer intimacy, or operational excellence. In addition to having the discipline of maintaining this single focus, companies must be at least adequate in the other two; they cannot be failing (Treacy, et al., 1995). These values are outlined in Figure 1-1.

Figure 1-1 The Value Discipline Model (adapted from Treacy, et al.)

Treacy and Wiersema's business principle still holds true. These three value disciplines form an understandable and actionable model that describes the different ways in which companies can focus their efforts and build success. Understand what differentiates your company, know where your strength and unique value comes from, and maintain your focus. There is no one correct model that all companies must follow to achieve success. According to Treacy and Wiersema, the Value Discipline Model includes these three values, as were shown in Figure 1-1:

- **Operational excellence** involves building business processes that provide the best product quality, best price, and the best purchasing experience, yielding *the best total cost* to the customer.

- **Product leadership** involves focusing investment and energy into developing the product that is the newest or most revolutionary or most sought after, offering *the best product* to the customer.
- **Customer intimacy** involves building strong customer relationships, really getting to know your customers so you are sure to really understand their situation, which should yield the *best total solution* for the customer.

These value disciplines describe the way different companies build relationships with their customers, and they haven't changed. The importance of being able to pick just one to focus on while keeping the other two at an acceptable level also hasn't changed. What *has* changed is what it takes to be adequate or excel in each of the three disciplines. The Internet hasn't changed everything...but it has changed a lot!

1.1.2   The New (e)Marketplace

At first, we thought that the Internet was going to break all the rules. But painful as it was, it didn't take long to learn that business basics still count. No matter how many sales are made or how much traffic is generated, if a company cannot make money, it will not survive. In fact, no matter how much *value* a company provides to customers, if its business plan isn't sustainable, it can't continue to provide that value for very long.

We also now know that the Internet didn't destroy all the traditionally successful companies. In fact, it is the solid brick-and-mortar companies that have been able to combine their strong infrastructures with the new tools and capabilities that the Internet offers. These "bricks-and-clicks" companies have turned out to be the real winners.

So, what *has* changed? Let's take a closer look.

- **Access:** The Internet puts more information in customers' hands, at a faster rate, than was previously possible. Having all of this information at their disposal has given them the opportunity to evaluate alternatives and to make much more intelligent decisions about purchases.
- **Control:** The Internet also gives customers the opportunity to do business when and how they want to do it, not when we choose to be open for business. Customers have more power and control than ever. They aren't about to give any of it back; in fact, they want even more.
- **Speed:** Commerce on the Internet occurs at unheard of speeds. Information can be gathered, options compared, and transactions completed faster than a customer could drive down to the mall or get a call back from a sales rep. These incredible speeds are reshaping customer expectations of how quickly things can and should be done everywhere.
- **Globalization:** The Internet has opened up the entire world as a marketplace to everyone. We are no longer constrained by the neighborhood or even the borders of the

country we live in. Companies that have never sold outside of their own region may now have customers all over the globe. These global customers often have very different expectations from those they've always known. Everything from language to product features, from privacy to payment options and more can be (and probably should be) different.

- **Automation:** Finally, and maybe most important, the Internet has eliminated many of your employees (order administrators, call center support reps, sales reps, etc.) from the processes that you have moved online. Historically, human intelligence and knowledge have created a link between many of our internal disconnects. Now, just at the time that customers' expectations have risen regarding how quickly, easily, efficiently, and accurately commerce can take place, the Internet has removed the "glue" that has allowed most companies to mask all of their disconnected processes and systems.

This doesn't mean that an Internet experience has to feel "cold" or mechanical. Stanford University professor Clifford Nass showed that people actually react to computers as if they were human (Reeves and Nass, 1998). But computers don't (yet) have the human capability to make intellectual leaps or connect information that is not obviously linked. Computers are logical, but not intelligent.

1.1.3   The Impact

The Internet has affected companies that have chosen to focus on operational excellence in several ways. It has given customers more information and, thus, more control over their buying experiences and has raised customer expectations regarding speed and convenience. The speed at which transactions can take place affects expectations of how fast everything should be done. For many industries, it has leveled the operational playing field, but the level of play is much higher and more competitive! There is less differentiation today and less of a gap between the minimum acceptable experience and the best experience. It's harder to be excellent, and even the minimum standard has been raised.

The impact on customer-intimate companies is equally strong. The single global marketplace serves customers from many different cultures with different expectations and needs. This makes building relationships much harder. Of course, the biggest impact is removing the direct human contact from so many interactions. It's harder to be excellent when you don't understand your customers' expectations (or even their language) and even more so when the human interaction is eliminated.

Product-leadership companies have also been significantly impacted. More control in your customers' hands means less control in yours. With more information available to customers, they can easily compare products and prices and make buying decisions. All the information that's available on the Internet has contributed to another phenomenon in today's marketplace. Many products have become or are becoming commodities, and it's happening very quickly. Customers are better informed and can make better decisions about what they really need (and what they don't need). In addition, the Internet makes it much easier for competitors to access your product information and to quickly develop competitive products. Today, it's difficult to maintain product superiority for very long.

Almost overnight the marketplace has become truly global, and most of us haven't had enough time to learn who our new customers are. Most important, many customer interactions take place without a human being there to smooth out the rough spots and eliminate the disconnects in many of our processes.

Table 1-1 summarizes the Internet changes that have impacted the whole marketplace. You can use tools like this table to track the situation for your own company.

Table 1-1 Summary of Changes in the (e)Marketplace

Internet Effects	Operational Excellence	Product Leadership	Customer Intimacy
Access	Easier to compare and swap	Commoditization	Providing human contact
Control	Always on	Broader choice, less differentiation	Interaction preference
Speed	Process expectations	Products unique for shorter periods	Efficiency, not loyalty
Globalization	Language, localization	Localization of products	Unknown language, culture
Automation	Process disconnects	Distance from customer needs	Loss of human memory, connection

At the end of the chapter in the Questions for Reflection, you can refer back to this table to help you understand the specific impact of the Internet on your company.

1.1.4 The Result

As a result of all these significant changes, many people (including me) believe that customer loyalty is the single most important differentiator for ensuring competitiveness and success into the 21st century.

1.2 Defining "Customer Loyalty"

There is a very persistent barrier that comes up time and again whenever groups of people and organizations attempt to adopt new ideas or change the way they do business. This barrier is the simple fact that often there is no universal understanding of or common language for describing the issue and identifying the goals you want to achieve. People frequently use exactly the same words to describe very different ideas. And they use different words to describe the same idea. Generally the result is that no one really knows what has been agreed. This situation is even more common when the ideas are fairly new and not widely understood. Meetings arc concluded with great good feeling and nods of agreement all around, followed by months of conflict and rework because everyone thought they'd agreed to something different.

We are not going to accept this state of affairs. We're going to fight this barrier by developing a common language that we agree to use throughout this book. I'll present definitions of the critical terms that we'll be using, and ask that you agree with that definition while you're reading. Remember that when you're finished reading, you are back in control. For your own purposes or your own organization, you may want or need to create your own concepts and definitions. Just be sure that if you do so, you make your definitions very clear and very visible to those with whom you're working. And be sure that you get their agreement that they will use your definition for the duration of the time you're working together. Most important, watch for people using inconsistent terms or definitions, and educate these people right away. Don't let these inconsistent concepts take root.

So, for the duration of the time that we're working together (that is, while you're reading this book), I will ask you to suspend any current definitions you may have and use mine instead. This will ensure that for this time period, we're speaking the same language.

1.2.1 What Is a Customer?

To understand what is meant by *customer loyalty,* we first must define what a customer is.

1. A customer is a human being. Only human beings can make decisions and use products. I know this seems terribly obvious, but many companies that sell to businesses instead of consumers forget this.
2. A customer is a person who has acquired or is considering the acquisition of one of our products. Anyone who is involved in making a decision, from the financial decision maker to the decision influencer to the end user (and often they are one in the same), is a customer.

Note that people who are considering but have not yet acquired one of your products are included. You may not have gathered much information about these prospects, but the relationship starts as soon as you become aware of each other. What you do with this knowledge is a topic for future consideration as we discuss "valuing" potential customers. Also, product "acquisition" may be the result of a purchase, a lease, a gift, or any other means of getting a product into the customer's hands. After a customer has begun using or even considering one of your products or services, he has started a relationship with you. It's your job to be sure you know about each customer and to take care of those relationships.

For business-to-business (B2B) sellers, the concept of a "customer company" is also important. But its importance is as a label for and a set of facts about a group of customer people. The company represents additional interesting information about the set of customers who are employed there. Companies do not make decisions to buy things. Companies do play an important role in that they have certain cultures, certain sets of needs, certain standards and processes, and certain styles, all of which influence how the people who work there make decisions. We can identify a group of customers with characteristics in common by knowing that they work for the same company. We often identify the "value" of this group of customers by knowing the aggregate sales to their entire company. As discussed in the preface, a dictionary sitting beside a box of text will indicate these definitions. All the definitions will be summarized in the glossary in Appendix A.

 DEFINITIONS

A *customer* is a person (or a group of persons) who influences or decides on the acquisition of one of our products or services, or who uses one of these products or services.

A *customer company* is an organization (public, private, non-profit, or governmental) that has characteristics that influence the group of people who work there.

Through the remainder of this book, when you see the word *customer,* it will refer to people. If we're talking about a company as a whole organization, we will use the term *customer company.*

1.2.2   What Is Loyalty?

Loyalty is an emotion; it isn't rational. Loyalty occurs when an individual has a vested interest in maintaining a close relationship, usually resulting from a series of positive experiences that have occurred over time. These experiences can be either tangible (product quality, ease of use, prompt and effective service) or intangible (respectful communications, trustworthy company image).

Customer Loyalty, for our purposes, leads to the behavior we hope our customers will demonstrate. We hope our customers will continue to choose to purchase our products instead of our competitors' just because they would rather do business with us.

DEFINITIONS

> *Customer Loyalty* is a behavior, built on positive experiences and value. This behavior is buying our products, even when that may not appear to be the most rational decision.

Once established, there is momentum for a customer to remain loyal. All things being equal (or only slightly unequal), the loyal customer continues to buy our products. But if we stop delivering the tangible and intangible positive experiences to customers, their loyalty will be lost and they will surely disappear.

1.3   Loyalty in the New Marketplace

Loyalty is built on relationships developed through the customer's experiences when she interacts with your company. Of course, so is disloyalty! Loyalty, for our purposes, is the likelihood that a current customer will buy from you again, rather than from a competitor, whenever she needs new or additional products that you sell. The value of loyalty is well understood. A recent study by Bain and Company showed that when loyalty (customer retention) was increased 5 percent, profits within various industries (both consumer and B2B) increased from a minimum of 18 percent up to a high of 125 percent. The impact of customer loyalty on profits hasn't changed, nor has the way loyalty is created through a customer's experiences with our company. Positive experiences build strong loyalty, but so can prompt resolution of negative experiences. In fact, many people believe that reversing a negative experience is the strongest way to ensure loyalty (Vavra, 1992).

From the corner grocery store to the sophisticated telephone support organization, managing customer relationships has traditionally involved human interactions. But with so many of these interactions now taking place over the Internet and involving less (or no) direct human contact, how do we build relationships now? There is a simple (but not easy) solution. The answer lies in information. The knowledge about our customers that we collect and save, combined with our ability to use this information, will allow companies to build and maintain loyalty in the Internet age.

Information can make it possible for us to link together customer experiences across different interaction channels. Information can make computers appear to recognize a customer and thereby create a relationship with him. Information can be used to personalize and humanize electronic interactions. Information can be used to customize the best product or service for a customer.

Regarding the critical role that information plays in making the Internet successful, Pradeep Jotwani, president of Hewlett-Packard's Consumer Business Organization said in a presentation at an e-commerce summit in San Jose,

The Net has forever changed our world, and as a result, we can expect to be part of a continually shifting social and economic landscape. [...] Electronic sales to consumers passed $20 billion in 1999. U.S. online consumer retail revenue will exceed $184 billion by 2004. Business-to-business sales will surpass consumer sales at about the same time. You wouldn't be here today if you didn't believe this was true. The online opportunity is staggering, and the long-term success of almost every business will require some degree of online activity. Success in this New World will depend on creating new and inventive ways of doing business. Data is collected, mined, and analyzed to provide extremely high qualitative and quantitative information. As a result, we are in a position to provide levels of customized, personal services never before imagined. From New Delhi to New York to Newcastle, it's a New World.

The Internet has a big impact on how we do business. Let's look at these changes and consider how they relate to our ideas of what it will take to be successful in the future. Although this book certainly isn't a study of Treacy and Wiersema's Value Discipline theory, understanding their three basic operating styles allows us to form a good foundation for measuring the impact of the Internet on the way we do business. (If you do want to know more about Value Disciplines, please refer to Treacy and Wiersema's terrific book.)

Understanding the changes in measuring success or even maintaining the minimum standard for each of the disciplines will explain why managing your customer relationships must be an important component of your business strategy even if your company is not, and never will be, *customer* focused.

1.3.1   Loyalty and Operational Excellence

In an effort to streamline and focus on core competencies, most companies have found ways to outsource elements of their operating environments to third-party specialists at lower costs. Focusing just within the walls of the company hasn't been enough to achieve operational excellence for some time. Now, in an effort to streamline processes and further reduce costs, companies are moving many of their remaining internal processes to the Internet. Activities including order management, product delivery, product support, and fulfillment are taking on new forms.

We've already discussed how the Internet has impacted the customer's expectations across all types of interactions with your company. The Internet has caused customers' expectations for the operational performance of your company to be raised as well. Today your customers can easily experience and compare how your competitors do the very same things you do, so you must be at a level that is at least acceptable. It's also easy for your competitors to test and emulate your processes. You can continue to improve operations to maintain your operationally excellent position, but each improvement in your operational performance in effect challenges your competitors to match or exceed your performance. It's not as quick or easy for them to do as price slashing, but the resulting level of performance is now part of your competitor's operating environment and is sustainable (unlike a price war, which can't be sustained over the long haul).

You can provide this value by capturing and storing knowledge about your customers that only you have. Use that knowledge so that you can consistently recognize your customers. You can remember and understand what they really need, and respond to their specific requirements in the most efficient and cost-effective manner. Competitors can duplicate your processes, but they can't duplicate your knowledge. Use your knowledge to ensure that you are delivering what the customer wants at the best possible price.

This doesn't mean that your operationally excellent company must change its focus to become customer intimate. It does mean that, while you are focusing on operational excellence, you can't ignore the importance of your customers and their relationship with your company. We will look at how to build and manage these relationships.

1.3.2   Loyalty and Product Leadership

Product leadership also doesn't look quite the same as it did. It's becoming harder to sustain success based on product differentiation alone. Your competitors are able to copy you and catch up more quickly and without the heavy, initial product development effort or expense that your company incurred. This leaves a much shorter period of time during which a company can remain in a product-dominant position before the competition at least matches current offerings.

Because so many industries sell products that have already become (or are in danger of becoming) commodities, prices are being squeezed and product differentiation is becoming blurred. When profits are narrowed, it's more difficult to continue to invest in the development efforts that will keep your products out in front. As an example in the high-tech industry, PCs have become essentially ubiquitous. PCs are everywhere, and they all have basically the same capabilities because there is little customer demand for extraordinary features. Gone are the days when each manufacturer could claim (and charge for) a uniquely "best" product. The market is looking for basic, standard capabilities, and no one is willing to pay significantly more for any specific product. PCs and many other products from many different industries have become commodities. Price wars are common and continue to shrink margins painfully. This catch-22 cycle, as presented in Figure 1-2, makes product leadership riskier and more expensive to sustain.

How do you continue to be a successful product leadership company when so many products, maybe even yours, have become commodities? Customer loyalty can make the difference between successful and unsuccessful product leadership companies, because loyal customers will choose your products even if they aren't that much better than someone else's. Your customer's loyalty to you makes your product the best choice for him. You will undoubtedly continue to invest in those efforts that have always resulted in your superior products, but because you also recognize that return on investment may have shrunk, you also allocate resources toward managing your customer relationships. Loyal customers feel that your product is better and choose it over other similar products. Loyal customers seek out your products. The relationships you have with your customers are the only differentiators that your competitors can't

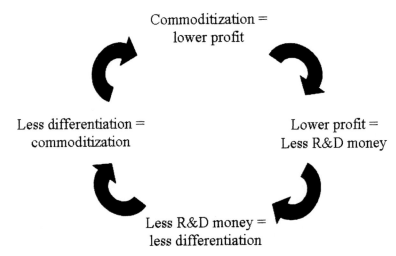

Commoditization =
lower profit

Less differentiation =
commoditization

Lower profit =
Less R&D money

Less R&D money =
less differentiation

Figure 1-2 A catch-22: Commoditization means less money for development, which increases commoditization

duplicate. Loyalty once created is extremely stable; it is hard for competitors to dislodge. Customer loyalty is based on developing and maintaining personal relationships with your customers and providing them excellent experiences, even when using the Internet means that many of these experiences will not involve people on your end.

This certainly is not to suggest that all product leadership companies need to change everything they do and make customer intimacy their discipline focus. It does mean that the luxury of having such a superior product that you can afford to ignore your customers and force them to do business your way is going, going, gone.

1.3.3 Loyalty and Customer Intimacy

The Internet has had a tremendous impact on both the numbers and types of interactions that customers have with your company. Customer intimacy is no longer just a matter of providing excellent call center support and a high-quality sales force. Only in rare cases is there one single person who has knowledge of all of a customer's needs and experiences. Many of these interactions are online and don't involve the customer's having direct contact with any one of your employees. Others involve isolated interactions with a large number of people who may never see or talk with each other.

Historically, it was the men and women in your sales and service organizations who built and managed relationships with customers. The most successful sales and service people **knew** intuitively that their relationships with their customers were the keys to their success. Sales people knew that PEOPLE make buying decisions, that keeping a customer for the long term is where you really make money, and that long-term loyalty is based on maintaining good relationships and providing consistently high quality experiences. Service people knew that heroic individual efforts could often overcome a negative situation, making the customer more loyal.

As other sales channels emerged, the customer could experience your company through many different avenues. Whether through a retailer, a reseller, catalog phone order, or telemarketer, people have been involved in building and managing the customer relationship. But these people operate in silos, and some aren't even your employees. They certainly don't work as a customer-centered team. The Internet has removed "people" from the product supplier end of the interaction. How can you build intimacy without consistent and direct human interactions? What information do you need? How do you get it? Where do you store it? How do you protect it? How do you use it? We'll explore the answers to these questions throughout the rest of the book. Soon, you will fully understand the discipline that uses information and technology to emulate human interactions and to bridge the organization's silos. You will learn how to build relationships between your company and your customer when there are either too many or too few (or zero) human beings responsible for the relationship.

1.4   Building and Managing Relationships in the New Marketplace

The Internet is here to stay. Customers like it because it puts them more in control. Companies like it, too; it's the most cost-effective way to enable most sales, marketing, and support activities. We will talk more about the Internet and building loyalty in Chapter 4. Throughout the book, we'll consider the impact of the Internet-generated issue: how to build trust and loyalty when there aren't at least two people directly involved.

This new marketplace requires that we substitute electronically stored and accessed customer knowledge for the customer knowledge held by sales people and others. We know that fewer and fewer of our customer relationships will involve interactions between two human beings. Information, history, memory, and knowledge are the elements from which we must build relationships. When there is no human interaction, knowledge must be collected and used electronically. We know that customer experiences can be vastly improved by better information. Information about the customer's needs, wants, behavior, experience, and expectations allows us to better understand our customers so that we can:

- Match our operational processes to known customer expectations tuned to meet specific needs at the best overall cost
- Build the products we know the customer needs and wants (and leverage customer loyalty to ensure ours are the products customers seek and buy)
- Build and customize our product and service offerings to meet specific customer expectations

We won't talk much more about product leadership, operational excellence, or even customer intimacy as business disciplines. There is certainly no implied message here that all companies should immediately change their focus to customer intimacy. The Internet has changed what it takes to maintain the minimum acceptable standard within each of the three disciplines. It has also changed, to a varying degree, what it takes to be successful in all of the disciplines. Customer loyalty is a key element of meeting the challenges of the new marketplace for all companies. (Reminder: Key Concepts for each chapter will be indicated by a key symbol.

KEY IDEA

No matter which of the value disciplines your company has chosen for its focus, your ability to manage customer relationships and build loyalty is critical to your success in the new marketplace.

Using our knowledge about customers will help us meet new customer expectations and new standards. Information and technology will help us manage our relationships with our customers and build the loyalty we need to maintain success. That success is dependent on our collecting meaningful information, remembering it and making it available, and developing tools and processes so that we can use information about the experiences and interactions our customers have had with us.

In the next chapter, we will discuss the approach your company should take to build strong customer loyalty so you can meet at least the new minimum standards for customer intimacy, product superiority and operational excellence.

Questions for Reflection

These questions will help you build a plan for how you'll get started moving your company's CRM program forward. These and other questions for reflection in subsequent chapters are included in the Company Self Assessment in Appendix C.

1. What is your company's value discipline focus? (Remember, the three disciplines are operational excellence, product leadership, and customer intimacy.)
2. How do you assess your performance in your primary discipline compared to your competition's performance?
3. How do you assess your performance in the other two disciplines compared to your competition's performance?
4. Which of these Internet-caused changes shown in Table 1-1 have had the biggest impact on your customers? Your company?

CHAPTER 2

The Case for Customer Relationship Management

Now that we have defined what a customer is, you are in a good position to identify which of Treacy and Wiersema's three value disciplines is the primary focus of your company. You are also better prepared to understand what approach to building customer loyalty will work best for you. Successful companies know that none of the value disciplines can be ignored, but that they must choose one of these as their primary focus. Companies relate to customers by providing either:

- The *best* products, or
- The *best* cost, or
- The *best* total solution.

These value disciplines (the ways in which a company delivers value to its customers) haven't changed. Most companies still have the same types of customers they've always had. What is different is what it takes to successfully *manage* relationships with those customers. Marketplace demands and customer expectations have changed, setting the bar for success at a higher level. Companies need to manage their interactions with customers in a way that delivers consistent and positive experiences. Sadly, most companies have intellectual, organizational, and cultural obstacles that make it more difficult for them to manage relationships effectively.

2.1 Understanding Common CRM Obstacles

Since the broad adoption of the Internet, customers have more information and more control over what they decide to buy and from whom. The Internet has significantly raised customer expectations; at the same time, its emergence has created obstacles to meeting these expectations. The Internet has generated a whole slew of new, online systems that are very difficult to integrate with our old, often fragmented system infrastructure. It has also eliminated the "human glue" that used to connect information across these legacy systems and processes.

Added to the Internet-created infrastructure barriers are several major internal obstacles. Too many companies believe that they merely have to wave a magic wand and all their customers will suddenly become loyal. This intellectual barrier – this wishful thinking – is supported by many purveyors of software and consulting "magic," and it really gets in the way of companies actually doing the work that it takes to develop customer loyalty.

There are also cultural barriers to delivering positive customer experiences created by the tendency of many companies to be internally focused when making plans, designing products, or defining processes. At a large, California-based medical clinic, a patient is required to fill out the same paper form for each new department visited. Is it possible that the information about next of kin is already on the clinic-wide computer systems? Companies like this are described as product-centered, even when the "product" they deliver is a service.

In addition to having a culture that is internally focused, many companies are organized into virtually autonomous business units and independent functional areas. These organizational silos don't share common strategies, plans, information, or practices, and they create a huge internal gap that makes it difficult to manage relationships consistently.

Wishful thinking, product-centricity, and organizational silos are significant sources of fragmented interactions and less-than-satisfactory experiences for customers.

2.1.1   Unrealistic Expectations

One of the most harmful barriers to building excellent customer relationships and strong loyalty is wishful thinking. Buying a piece of software or creating a customized web site cannot achieve loyalty. Loyalty is achieved by providing consistent, positive experiences over the long term. Building loyalty takes focus, effort, and patience. The potential payback is **huge.**

This barrier is so pervasive for two reasons. First, most companies are not patient. Results are measured by the quarter, not by the year, so patience is not a common corporate virtue. Second, few organizations really know which customers are loyal, why they're loyal, or how to develop more loyal customers. It's a complete mystery. Most companies don't have any actual experience in managing relationships with customers, so the belief in a magic wand or in someone who can just "do it" for them is very seductive. But then when results aren't perfect or immediate, everyone gives up!

2.1.2   Product-Centered Versus Customer-Centered Cultures

The defining difference between product-centered companies and customer-centered companies is purely the point of view from which the company operates. Product-centered companies take an inside-out point of view, defining customers by what company products they own. Customer-centered companies have an outside in or customer's viewpoint, and they define customers based on individual customer characteristics (Kincaid, 1999). Of course, these different operating styles produce many distinctions in results.

Product-Centered Cultures

Many companies, especially those in the high-tech sector, are product-centered. Of course, this is not particularly surprising. When a company is launched (or launches a new product), it must be product-centered. Frankly, if a company doesn't start out by making all its decisions around developing and delivering its product (or service), it has no future! In 1965, Everett Rogers first wrote his classic study on the adoption of innovative technologies, "Diffusion of Innovations." Rogers introduced the classification scheme that categorizes adopters into the five categories of "innovators," "early adopters," "early majority," "late majority," and "laggards." These categories form the Technology Adoption Life Cycle, which Geoffrey Moore describes in *Crossing the Chasm* [1991].

Moore identified a huge gap or "chasm" between the purchasing behavior of those in the early stages of the adoption life cycle where customers are innovative and visionary, and the mainstream customers who are more pragmatic and conservative. In the early stages, the early adopters who reinforce product-centric behavior drive the market. Companies often don't recognize the point when their product has crossed the chasm and moved into the mainstream market. This occurs partly because the early majority customers are still focused on product features (albeit for practical rather than visionary reasons). Given the rewards that companies receive from their early stage customers; it should be no surprise that it is easy for them to remain in their product-centered worlds. Figure 2-1, adapted from Moore [1991] and Norman [1998], shows how customer expectations change and how a company's product-centric culture may no longer be useful when selling into the huge, pragmatic majority market.

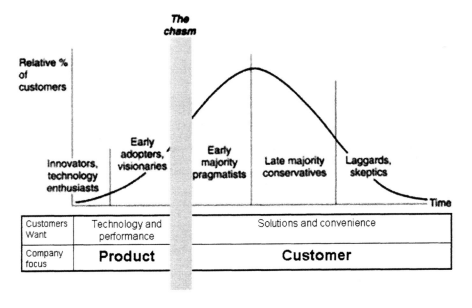

Figure 2-1 Technology adoption and product-centricity

Moore's Technology Adoption Life Cycle applies to more than just high-tech products; it applies to innovation in any industry. Any product or service that is new to the market, from tooth whiteners to hybrid automobiles, will go through the same adoption cycle, and companies will have to cross the chasm to be successful.

Being product-centered is not at all the same as being a Product Leadership company. Product Leadership is about building relationships with customers primarily through providing the best products. Product-centricity describes the viewpoint held when making strategic and operational plans and decisions; it is viewing the world from inside the company looking out. Any company can be product-centered, whether or not it is a Product Leadership company.

 ## DEFINITIONS

A *product-centered company* is one that makes plans and decisions based on an internal perspective (the impact inside the company).

Each of the product lines (sometimes, each individual product group) and each functional area sets strategy, plans, acts, and communicates according to its own unique viewpoint. Decisions are made, programs are launched, and even products are designed based on this inside-out view. Figure 2-2 illustrates the perspective of a company that views its customers from the inside out.

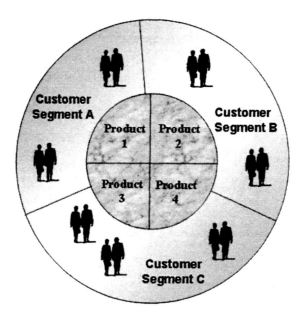

Figure 2-2 The product-centered company

Because product-centered companies define their customer segments based on what products the customer has purchased instead of his characteristics or needs, no one knows who else is communicating and interacting with the same customer. Product-centered companies are frequently unaware of how good and loyal many customers are because they have fragmented their knowledge into product-centered buckets.

Sadly for the customers of companies with these product-centered cultures, interactions look like the pincushion in Figure 2-3. And does he ever feel like he's getting shot full of arrows!

Product-centered companies are less effective in the mainstream marketplace. They don't look coordinated, organized, or competent. They certainly don't look like a single company to the customer, nor are they capable of providing a consistent set of positive experiences.

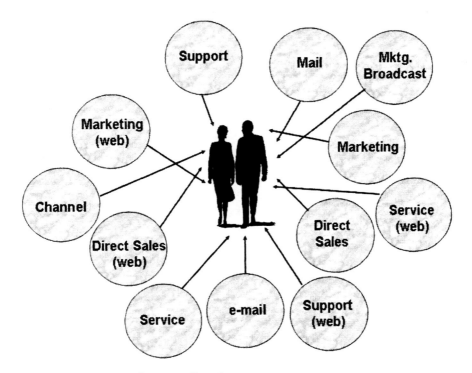

Figure 2-3 Fragmented Customer Experience

Customer-Centered Cultures

Customer-centered companies, on the other hand, really do look at their performance from the eyes of the customer, from the outside in. These companies make plans and decisions considering how those plans/decisions will impact the customer.

 DEFINITIONS

> A *customer-centered company* has an external point of view, making plans and decisions based on the anticipated impact on the customer.

This does **not** mean that product leadership or operationally excellent companies must change their value discipline and must all become customer-intimate. It does mean that when making product or operational decisions, the company will consider the customer's views and needs as valuable input. Plans won't be made, actions won't be taken, processes won't be defined, without taking into consideration how it will look to and impact the customer.

As shown in Figure 2-1, all innovative companies (not just high-tech ones) face the chasm separating early adopters from mainstream buyers and the different customer expectations that emerge in the mainstream market. To be successful with the pragmatic majority, companies need to start building relationships and value with customers beyond just the product itself. Failure to understand this lesson was a big factor in the collapse of many dotcom companies. Customer-centered companies have a huge advantage in building customer loyalty because they are set up to make plans and decisions keeping the impact on the customer in mind. They know that the customer neither has nor should have any understanding of their internal operational structure or their external partnerships. They work to deliver an integrated set of experiences and to interact with their customers as a single company. These companies look organized, in charge, and aware. They have eliminated the major barriers to loyalty and trust that develop through inconsistency and fragmentation. Decisions are made, programs are launched, and even products are designed based on this outside in view. Figure 2-4 illustrates the perspective of a company that that is customer-centered.

Customer-centered companies are more in tune with their customers, more aware of how the company is perceived in the marketplace, and much more likely to deliver consistent, coordinated, and positive customer experiences than product-centered companies.

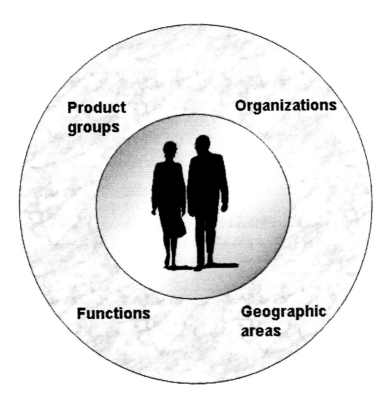

Figure 2-4 The customer-centered company

2.1.3   Infrastructure

Many companies have built and used their systems infrastructure for years. Over time, it has evolved in a very piecemeal and fragmented fashion for several reasons, including these:

- Systems have traditionally been developed to automate vertical processes within a single functional area. Data files were defined to support that specific use of the data.
- The moment a system is implemented, it becomes part of the infrastructure, dependencies are built, and it becomes difficult to make changes.
- Hardware and software evolve rapidly. New systems adopt the new technologies; old systems are stuck with what was available when they were built. Integration (e.g., exchanging information between an online order screen and an old, COBOL-based, finished goods system) is difficult, and often impossible.
- Information quality in older systems is suspect. This is especially risky now that we can let customers see what we know.

These fragmented systems make it almost impossible to understand a 360° view of the customer's interactions with a company, much less provide any kind of integrated experience.

2.1.4 Organization

Organizationally, there are significant internal sources of fragmented interactions because so many organizations have grown up with functional and geographic silos that have very different sets of objectives and measurements for success. Because "success" looks different to each of these organizations, their managers don't perceive a relationship to the other functions, so they don't coordinate their plans. Marketing and sales departments often deliver conflicting product messages to customers. Product support and customer services have different measures and may be delivering two more sets of messages. Internal Channel Management organizations don't even focus on the same "customer." To the channels function, your *partners* are the customers. Geographically, real differences such as language, currency, and culture are used to justify totally independent processes and systems. Siloed companies act like a loose confederation of functions, geographies, and product lines with little company-wide governance or coordination. (And because these companies are often product-centered too, they are completely unaware of the impact these organizational silos have on the customer.)

Of course, the multiple sales channels that many companies use to extend and enhance their capabilities in and of themselves add more fragmentation. Customers like to choose how to transact their purchasing and service activities. Companies like the benefit of outsourcing many of these sales and service activities to a lower cost "specialist." Channel partnerships are effective for many companies. If you use channel partner organizations as an extension of your company, they *are* part of your company. When a customer buys your product, he believes he bought it from you. Don't think that you're not responsible for the interactions that take place between your customer and your channel partners. While we won't discuss the pros and cons of alternative sales channels, we will look at how siloed channels impact the ability to know your customers and deliver reliable and consistent experiences. Later, we'll discuss this very important question that arises from partnerships with channel organizations: "Who owns the customer information?"

How do customers experience their interactions with your company: as an integrated whole or piecemeal and fragmented? Is their experience more like what you saw in Figure 2-3, or is it consistent and reliable as your customers expect?

2.1.5 Impact on Customer Experience

Product-centered organizations are inconsistent in their ability to deliver positive experiences to customers. Because the customer is not considered when plans are made and actions are taken, the resulting customer experience is piecemeal at best. Organizational silos create tremendous fragmentation in how customers are treated, because they are bombarded with so many disconnected and uncoordinated plans, disconnected processes, and conflicting messages.

The organizational and cultural disconnects within many companies are both aggravated and intensified because of the often inconsistent approach to how customers are identified. Each function and each business unit uses different schemes for identifying customers, making it impossible to recognize a customer consistently across multiple interactions. There is no capability for tracking all the interactions that a customer has had with your company or for understanding her total experience with you. There is even less chance that you can use this knowledge to improve a current interaction as it is taking place or those exchanges that will take place in the future. Lack of consistent recognition increases the fragmented feel of the customer's experience with your company and makes you look inept. You want to avoid having your customers pose questions like, "Why are you asking me that again, I just answered that question on your web site (or when I registered my product, etc.)?"

The product and functional silos that dominate product-centered companies combined with all the different means (internal and external) that companies have of touching the customer, add up to a significant barrier to a company's ability to successfully build customer loyalty. To be more successful, you don't need to switch your value discipline focus, but you may need to change the way your organization makes plans and decisions. If your company's products are largely in the mainstream, you may have to shift from a purely product-centered culture. Maintaining at least a balance with customer-centered perspectives will help you reach the early majority and especially late majority customers more effectively. A significant first step is simply to ask yourself, "What will this look like to the customer?" Delivering positive and consistent experiences also requires applying some level of coordination across the internal and external operations that directly touch your customers. Loyalty is based on the customer's total experience with your entire (extended) company.

2.2 Seeing the Total Customer Experience

The total customer experience is what a customer feels as a result of all the interactions he has had with your company, combined with other experiences and information he has gained from the external marketplace. It's not something you *do*, but it is the *result* of many things you do, combined with other influences that come from outside our direct control. We can certainly impact the total customer experience (for better or for worse), and we should definitely measure it to know how we're doing.

There are three major vectors that influence the customer's total experience: the external marketplace, your company's brand image, and all the different ways the company touches your customers. Total customer experience describes what the customer feels about the sum of her experiences with a company.

The customer's total experience is the result of matching experience to expectations. Meeting or exceeding expectations yields loyalty, while a negative match yields disloyalty. One of the most important yardsticks that we can use to measure how well we are doing is to monitor the customer experience. We can gather objective information through indices of customer loyalty such as retention rates versus turnover or brand awareness and value. Subjective data can be collected by asking customers to tell us how we are doing in all the important ways we impact them. Then we need to compare the trends these measurements against the trends in our financial results.

As illustrated in Figure 2-5, some of the influences that set customer expectations are external, and we have little control over these. But many are internal, under our direct control.

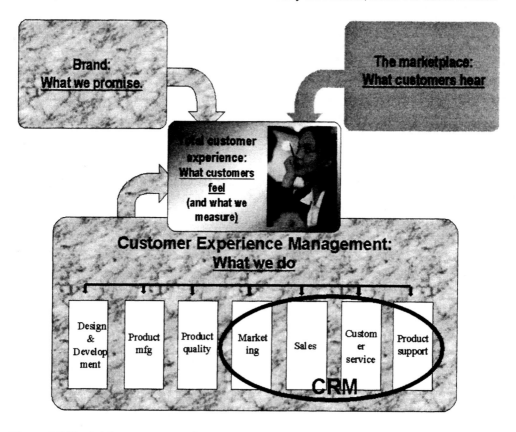

Figure 2-5 The total customer experience

We must understand what factors make up the customer experience and where we have control and can influence that experience.

2.2.1   What the Market Says (or Does)

What's happening in the market has a strong impact on setting customer expectations. We've already discussed that the Internet (access, control, speed, globalization, and automation) has changed customer expectations dramatically. Other strong external influences come from analysts and the media—what is being said about our industry as a whole as well as our company specifically. The media also set expectations about what's on the horizon for the types of products and services we sell. Of course, what our competition is saying and doing is another big factor in shaping customer expectations. Financial analysts, the stock market, and how the economy itself is perceived to be doing are also major influences, as illustrated in Figure 2-6.

Figure 2-6 What customers hear

We do have the ability to influence the marketplace with press releases and other forms of communication, but in general, this is the lever that is least available for our use in influencing the customer experience.

2.2.2 What We Say

One of the most important influences on the total customer experience is what we tell him he should expect from us. Our brand position, the image we establish in the marketplace, is a key element in setting expectations. Many think of a brand as simply a trademark, logo, company or product name, or visual identity. The problem with these traditional definitions is that they are too internally focused (product-centric, ignoring the importance of representing value to the customer), too superficial (just a graphic design), or too tactical (failing to recognize how brand must shape the strategic planning and direction of the whole company because of its influence on setting customer expectations).

DEFINITIONS

A *brand* is a pact between the company and its customers that makes promises, sets expectations, and defines agreements for their mutual benefit, which is symbolized by the "seal."

A brand is generally built on a small number of attributes that you have chosen to paint a picture of what your company is (e.g., high quality, good service, friendly, trustworthy, etc.). These brand attributes should support your company's chosen value discipline. You must then operate consistently with the promises you have made. For example, if "high quality" were one of the attributes of your brand, it would be suicidal to ship products with a high DOA (Dead on Arrival) or failure rate. Figure 2-7 shows the steps that build a brand.

A brand makes promises to customers. A successful brand makes meaningful promises—and keeps them! One of the worst things we can do to damage relationships with our customers is not keeping the promises we've made. Setting expectations with our customers that we can't or won't meet is a tremendous source of customer frustration. Although we do control and can change our brand image over time, this lever is not easy to move and it's certainly not quick to operate.

Figure 2-7 Elements of a brand

2.2.3   What We Do

The one area we can change on nearly a daily basis (of course, the Internet guys think daily is too slow), one that has a huge impact on the customer's total experience, is comprised of all the things our company does that directly touches the customer. These touches can be with any of the parts of the organization shown in Figure 2-8, and can occur through experiences with our products, interactions with our sales and service people, our channel partners, or our web site. Those touches also can be messages that we send out through any medium (broadcast advertising, mail/e-mail, etc.).

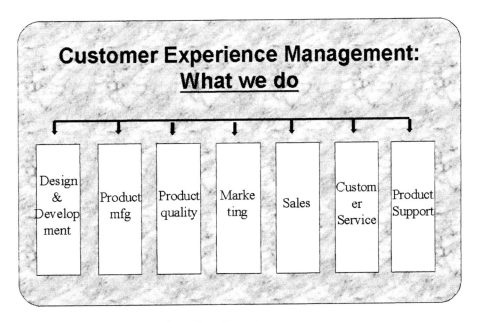

Figure 2-8 What we do must match our brand promise.

Managing and improving what we do *with the customer in mind* is where we have the biggest opportunity to impact the customer's total experience. This is the lever that allows us to impact the customer in a reasonable amount of time with a reasonable investment and a reasonable chance of actually making a difference. With the brand, we make promises. We deliver on our promises through the experiences we give our customers.

2.3   Defining Customer Experience Management

As you saw in Figure 2-5, the lever labeled Customer Experience Management is comprised of what you do; it is all the company functions that have a direct impact on the customer – generally the operational functions of your business. There are two major groupings of functions: the back office functions that contribute to the creation of products and services, and the front office functions that interact with the customer directly and often deliver the product or service. Many companies, for example IBM, prefer terms like "customer facing" and "product generation" to label the front office and back office processes. (Some people feel that a "back office" is a place no one would want to work.) For simplicity, we will use the more common (and shorter) terms throughout this book.

2.3.1 Back Office Functions

The back office, shown in Figure 2-9, is comprised of functions such as R&D, manufacturing, procurement, quality, etc., because these are all involved in the development, construction, and delivery of the product or service itself.

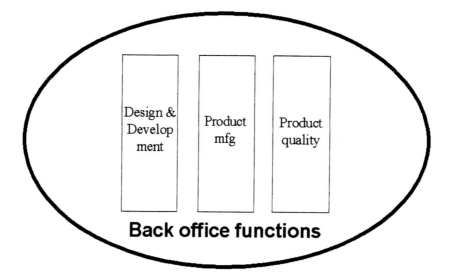

Figure 2-9 The back office delivers critical elements of the total customer experience.

For product manufacturers, the back office touches the customer indirectly through the product. A company's core product definitely has a huge impact on the customer's experience. Each time a customer interacts with your product/service he finds the answers to these questions for himself.

- Is it easy to set up?
- Does it make sense?
- Does it run?
- Does it do what I expect?
- Is it simple to use?

The product/service is created by our back office organizations, and they are responsible for this element of the customer experience. Lots of attention has been paid to the back office functions since the beginning of the industrial age. From the early days of Frederick Taylor's time studies and his system of "Scientific Management" through "Supply Chain Management" and beyond, we have continued to study and improve the way we design, build, and deliver products and services.

Many companies have invested heavily in reengineering their entire supply chain processes. Some of these efforts have been extremely successful, and unfortunately many have not. Reengineering the core of a company is difficult, time consuming, and often very expensive. The expected rewards are large, usually aimed at increased efficiency and cost reduction. Cost cutting keeps companies competitive on price and can increase margin and profit, but there is an absolute limit to the amount of money that can be eliminated from the cost. If we pass along the cost reduction by reducing price, we have sacrificed profit margin for sales volume – and not increased loyalty at all. Low prices do not build loyalty...ever. Low prices only influence buying behavior until someone comes along with a better price than yours.

Enterprise Requirements Planning (ERP) is the label that has been given to all the functions, activities, and processes that comprise the organization's back office. Unfortunately, the same label has been given to the software applications that automate these functions and processes. This has led many to think that ERP is the software, a primary cause of back office reengineering failures. Back-end activities are critical to business success, but they're not the whole story.

2.3.2 Front Office Functions

The front office organizations include marketing, sales, customer service, product support, and any channel partner organizations that perform any of these functions for you, as shown in Figure 2-10.

The front office functions directly communicate and interact with customers through various media such as face-to-face contacts, telephone, mail, the Internet, etc. The other major component of the customer's experience is formed when she interacts with our people and processes and finds the answer to these and similar questions:

- Are they competent?
- Are they respectful?
- Do they keep me informed?
- Do they play fair?
- Are they flexible?

The front office designs and delivers customer interactions. It is responsible for the relationship piece of the customer experience. Until recently, little attention has been focused on

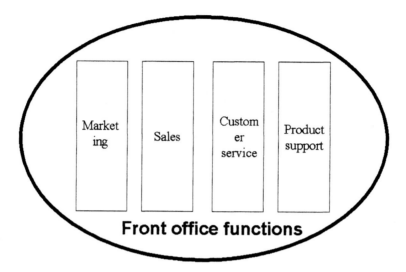

Figure 2-10 These four functions form the organization's front office.

organizing or automating the front office. Sales and marketing have been considered to be arts – not sciences that could be studied and measured and improved.

With the emerging understanding that loyalty is a key component of competitive success, interest in the front office has grown dramatically. The front office is thought to be ripe for automation and process improvements. Just as the software products automating the back office functions have been grouped together in the solution set called Enterprise Requirements Planning, the software that supports and integrates the front office has been grouped under the label Customer Relationship Management. It's critical that we not make the same mistake with automating the front office processes as we did with the back office automation efforts. We can't let ourselves think that the software tool is the whole solution. It's a very necessary enabler, as we'll discuss later, but only an enabler.

2.4 Ensuring Customer Loyalty

As we discussed, loyalty (retention) has long been known to have a significant impact on profit. Depending on the industry (and perhaps the statistician), it is somewhere between 5 and 17 times more costly to acquire a new customer than to keep the loyalty of a current one. The difference in revenue between the costs of selling to a new customer versus the cost of selling to an existing customer is pure profit.

2.4.1 Why Build Loyalty?

Frederick Reichheld of Bain & Company has studied the impact of loyalty on business profit extensively. He studied numerous industries (with both consumer and business end-customers) to understand the impact of customer loyalty on customer net present value.[1]

The Economics

Across all the industries studied, Reichheld found that a 5 percent increase in loyalty as measured by customer retention resulted in an increase in profits ranging from a minimum of 35 percent to a high of almost 100 percent. He found two reasons for this remarkable impact of a fairly small retention rate increase.

First, he studied the concept of changes in a company's customer "inventory." (Parallel to product inventory, customer inventory includes the number and value of customers.) All companies want to increase their number of active customers. Companies are continually in the process of acquiring new customers. This growth in customer inventory is offset when customers leave you to buy from other vendors. No matter the size of your current customer inventory or your current growth rate, just increasing your retention rate by 5 percent will result in your customer inventory doubling in size every 14 years.

The second reason for the strong impact on profits stems from the fact that loyal customers buy more and cost less to serve. In the first year of the relationship (Year 0), many companies actually spend more to acquire the customer than the base or average profit they can expect to make from each customer. Each year thereafter, each customer contributes at least the base average profit. Over time, loyal customers begin contributing to profit in a number of different ways as illustrated in Figure 2-11.

As you can see, purchase levels often increase because customers are more willing to trust your reputation on items they haven't purchased from you before. Customers who know and understand your products and processes actually cost less to serve; they don't need as much help. Very loyal customers are likely to refer their friends and colleagues. And as a result of introductory offers and other discounts they are not eligible for, they may even pay higher prices.

Loyalty and the Internet

Some people believe the Internet has made loyalty obsolete. We've defined customer loyalty as an emotion that produces behavior that may not be (or may not appear to be) the most rational buying decision. Loyalty was important when customers didn't have enough information to make rational decisions and had to rely on companies they trusted to do the right things for them. Of course, for some customers, this is still true. Some customers will simply never be comfortable online and will always rely on some form of human communication. (We'll discuss the power of combining two touch points in Chapter 4.) Other customers will use the Internet just for the convenience of the online purchase transaction, but still will visit a retailer to gather information or make comparisons in person.

---

1.   Net Present Value (NPV) is a measure of profit that you expect to get from customers over a period of years stated as if you received it all today. It considers the time value of money, which states that a dollar you get today is worth more than a dollar you get in the future. NPV is a useful tool for consistently evaluating future profit. We'll look at it again in Chapter 17.

Customer Profit Sources Over Time

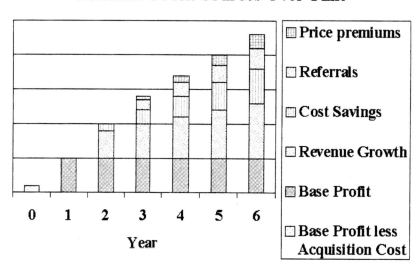

Figure 2-11 Why loyal customers are more profitable [Reichheld, 1996]

Other customers do use the Internet extensively to gather information so they can make truly informed and rational decisions. But loyalty still plays an important role in these situations. Even if your product, price, or operations are not quite equal to some competitors, loyal customers will not switch because they have an investment in the relationship. (It goes without saying that customers will not stay loyal if there are huge gaps between you and your competitors in the factors that form the total customer experience.) There is value to a customer in doing business with a trusted seller who already understands his situation and needs. Amazon.com will be a very interesting case to continue to watch. Amazon amassed a huge market share very quickly. By the loyalty measures of frequency and value of purchase (and even share of wallet), Amazon's customers have been extremely loyal. Will customers continue to be loyal now that Amazon has been forced to charge enough to cover all expenses? Is there enough value to customers in the relationship for Amazon to become profitable? The jury is still out.

Loyal customers continue to buy from you even when the product is not significantly different from, and may even cost more than, competitive products. Of course, the loyal decision may also be the most rational decision. Customers often become loyal because their experience over time has been that you have provided the best total value to them. For example, I prefer to buy HP toner for my printers even though it is more expensive than some other brands. I do this because I have been very happy with the results and believe this product produces higher quality documents. But I also have to confess that I even buy HP *paper,* and I'm not at all sure that it is much different from other manufacturers' paper!

How do we build loyalty? We do it by developing and using various tools and capabilities that help us deliver effective, coordinated, and positive interactions with our customers. Four elements make up the core of what it takes to build these tools and capabilities: information, process, technology and people. These four elements taken together will put your company in a position to effectively build customer loyalty. Choosing to pay more for paper that is probably no different from any other brand may appear irrational, but this type of behavior most often reflects the value of the relationship.

Building Loyalty

There are some misconceptions and partial truths about what it takes to create customer loyalty that produces the wonderful behavior of sticking with us over time and doing the following:

- Buying more
- Needing less expensive support (e.g., using online services)
- Referring friends
- Paying higher prices

We will discuss each of these partial truths so we understand what they can and can't do for us. We need to avoid depending on any one of them if we want to improve our chances of getting the full benefit of loyal customers.

Not Just Satisfying Customers

Many people equate customer satisfaction with customer loyalty. But satisfied customers are not necessarily loyal. In a Harvard Business Review article, Frederick Reichheld measured and showed the relationship between customer satisfaction and loyalty (see Figure 2-12).

We can learn several things from Reichheld's work. First, very dissatisfied customers (those who remain dissatisfied—we'll talk about that later) are never loyal. Not only will they not buy from you again, they are very likely to tell other people about their negative experience. These "terrorists" will actively hurt your reputation and your revenue.

However, it is important to understand that satisfaction alone is not enough to guarantee loyalty. Satisfaction and loyalty are independent factors. A customer can be very satisfied (4 or 5 out of 5) and still be indifferent as to which product he buys, shopping only for the best deal. Of course, some very satisfied customers are extremely loyal. Satisfaction is a necessary but not sufficient condition for customer loyalty.

Not Just Understanding Customers

Just as customers can be satisfied but not loyal, they can also be understood and still not loyal. Understanding customers in today's marketplace (where no one person really knows anyone personally) is largely based on collecting and analyzing information. But, in addition to understanding the customer, we must *use* the knowledge we gave gathered. We need tools and systems that let us access information and use it to deliver appropriate interactions based on

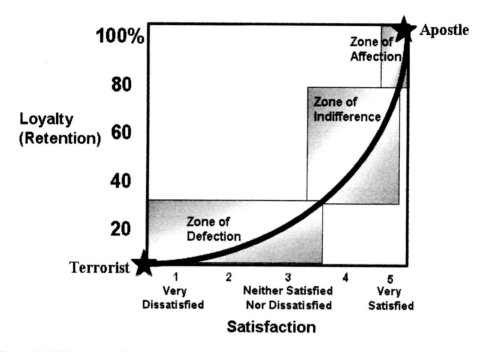

Figure 2-12 The Loyalty/Satisfaction Model (Reichheld, 1994)

what we know. Our people must be trained to do the right things for the customer based on having this knowledge.

Not Just Automating Processes and Customer Interactions

Loyalty is certainly not built on automating processes and interaction points alone. Automation can be a time and cost saver for companies. Many customers are choosing the flexibility and control they get over the web. But automated interactions can be pleasant or unpleasant; they can be appropriate to the customer or way off the mark. It takes more than flexibility, speed, and control to deliver positive relationships.

All These and More

By now, you realize that fostering loyalty is not just providing satisfaction or just knowing customers or just automating interactions that build loyalty. It is the sum total of the customer's experiences with our company's products, services, and people. The products and services developed and manufactured by the organization's back office have a major effect on loyalty, but we will focus on the front office functions of your organization: marketing, sales, customer service and product support, as well as any channel partner organizations that perform any of these functions for you. This is where we have the most cost-effective opportunity to impact customer loyalty.

2.5 Defining Customer Relationship Management

Customer Relationship Management (CRM) is a discipline that covers all the elements needed to build successful relationships with customers. CRM includes the following elements:

- The information needed to understand customers better
- The process management needed to deliver efficient and appropriate experiences to customers
- The software tools that allow us to use that knowledge
- The training and change management elements so our people and organizations understand and are capable of delivering experiences that build stronger relationships and increase loyalty

The back office reengineering efforts (Enterprise Requirements Planning) have focused primarily on increasing efficiency and reducing costs. CRM generally impacts the bottom line in a different way. The purpose of CRM is to increase revenue. Yes, some cost efficiencies should occur as well, and often these are more likely to get the attention of top management when you're starting, but that is not the real benefit of CRM. CRM increases revenue by enabling your company to meet and exceed customer expectations and by increasing loyalty. We're still talking about the bottom line, but the method to improve it is to increase income, not just cut costs. There is nothing new about the concept of building good relationships with customers and increasing their loyalty through positive experiences with your company. It's been going on for years.

What's different is that in today's marketplace, the emergence of the Internet, and the associated influx of global customers paired with a reduced number of human interactions, makes it impossible to build relationships in the traditional way. CRM is about using information, processes, technology and people to enhance relationships.

Most established and successful companies have learned that it is too expensive to try to build relationships based on human interactions alone. IBM is certainly the classic example of a company whose salespeople and account managers were closely engaged with and trusted by their customers. The "IBM Shop" was a well-known roadblock to its competitors. Many companies like IBM have had to change the way they do large parts of the sales and marketing for the reasons already discussed. They have outsourced the sales and marketing of lower-margin products and smaller customers to business partners.

Many smaller, but fast-growing companies have learned that it's impossible to scale manual processes to keep up with their growth. Peter Tait, Director of Internet Marketing for BEA Systems in San Jose, California, commented that BEA's huge success (as a Product Leadership company) was starting to create problems. As a small company, much of the company's success was accomplished through individual heroics. Everyone knew everyone else, and everyone took ownership for customers' needs. Relationships were managed through human effort. The problem was that heroics are not scalable and couldn't keep up with the tremendous growth that BEA was achieving. (BEA is the leading provider of the software that enables a company to transact business on the web. BEA reached a revenue run rate of $1 billion in less than five years from its inception.) BEA's great products put the company on the map. The commitment of its employees to providing personal help to customers using the products is what built the strong customer relationships that led to such dramatic growth. Growth made it impossible for employees to personally care for customers in the same way that helped the company to flourish.

Customer Relationship Management is more than customer satisfaction, customer understanding, or computer automation. It's about putting the four core elements (information, process, technology and people) together so you can provide your customers with a consistent and positive set of managed and personalized experiences to increase loyalty. In later chapters, we will learn about collecting, storing, managing, and using the customer information asset that is critical to your company's ability to implement a successful CRM Program. In Chapter 3, we will define exactly what we mean by CRM, the definition we will use for the rest of this book.

Questions for Reflection

Ask yourself these questions, which will help you to understand your organization's culture and the general relationship with your customers:

1. Is your company product-centered or customer-centered? How do you know?
2. How does your company segment your customers into groups?
3. Do customers experience their interactions with your company as fragmented or integrated? Why?

CHAPTER 3

What Is CRM?

People make buying decisions. People have loyalties. Relationships can only be developed between people. Your Customer Relationship Management program must be structured around this well-known fact. CRM is about people. CRM is an approach to organizing your company's interactions with customers that starts with a customer-centered point of view. It's an entire discipline, not a single activity. It's true that in the business-to-business marketplace, company descriptors such as size, industry, financial status, and purchasing power are critical to understanding and characterizing the people who work there. We will discuss the special case of B2B CRM later on in this chapter. In Figure 3-1, we begin to paint the picture of our CRM vision – a customer-centered organization.

This viewpoint ensures that the company's plans, activities, and communications that directly touch the customer will be seen as an integrated whole that supports your company's brand promise. We are now ready to establish our working definition for CRM.

3.1   Defining "CRM"

We're going to establish a definition of the term CRM that we will use throughout the rest of this book. Just before we do that, let's take a look at some of the misconceptions and partial truths that exist about CRM.

Creating a definition for CRM is both critical and dangerous. It is critical because your organization needs to have a common understanding of what you are doing. It is dangerous because so many definitions and misconceptions are already lodged in people's minds. One of the first things that any company should do when launching a CRM initiative is to test what the organization's current understanding of CRM is.

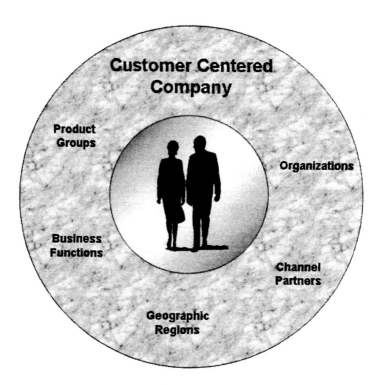

Figure 3-1 CRM provides a customer-centered view.

3.1.1   Common Misconceptions

Table 3-1 presents a series of quotes from a number of different individuals, all within the same company. These are great examples of the common misconceptions of CRM. (Conflicting statements often come from different individuals within the same company.)

Table 3-1 CRM Misconceptions

Misconception	Reality
"CRM is the solution that will solve all our customer problems; it's all the software tools that make it easier for a customer to do business with us."	Absolutely not. There is no magic, no sorcerer's stone, and no silver bullet. This effort takes vision, planning, investment, and patience. Software is certainly a necessary enabler, but not the total solution. The trouble with the magic software myth is that it allows business managers to think CRM is just an Information Technology problem. Application software vendors not surprisingly, abet this common misconception. If it were that easy, why wouldn't everybody be doing it already?

Table 3-1 CRM Misconceptions

Misconception	Reality
"CRM is the Internet."	The Internet has greatly increased the opportunity and need for better information, tools, and the processes that can take advantage of them. But relationships are built on understanding and trust. People who understand the customer's perspective must be the ones who design the web experience.
"CRM is just the latest name for Direct Marketing."	Using information and automation to understand and improve customer relationships has been practiced by Direct Marketers for years. CRM is a shift in focus from marketing (communicating "to") to relationship management (communicating "with").
"CRM means recognizing a customer wherever he interacts with our company, a 360° view of the customer."	This is a critical first step, but simple recognition isn't enough. We must learn to use the information we've collected in the past to interact effectively in each future interaction. Information about customers is critical to increased understanding and improved service. You also need tools and training so people know what to do with it.
"CRM means scoring and measuring Customer Value."	A very important use of CRM information is to be able to identify who our best customers are. We must have ways to use this knowledge to increase the number of loyal customers and the value of each.
"CRM is sales rep productivity tools."	Some companies still believe that the only way they can build relationships is through the sales force, so CRM must be about automating sales. The sales function is only one of those that directly touch customers and make up CRM.

None of these statements is totally wrong, but none tells the complete story. CRM is not just the Internet or just sales rep productivity; it is an entire discipline for interacting with customers that touches all the front office functions.

3.1.2 Definition

Here is the definition of CRM that we will use throughout the rest of this book. The definition includes all the elements that make up the CRM supporting infrastructure and all the functions that must be involved.

 DEFINITIONS

CRM is the *strategic* use of *information, processes, technology* and *people* to manage the customer's relationship with your company (marketing, sales, services, and support) across the whole customer life cycle.

This definition of CRM is quite broad and covers many, but not all, of your company's activities. CRM is limited to activities that take place in the customer-facing functions, including marketing, sales, customer services, and product support. CRM does not equal customer centricity. Frankly, although it's harder, you can implement a CRM program even in a company that is not customer-centered. CRM is not all-inclusive. Your company may choose to develop a customer-centered R&D process, but this new process would not be part of your CRM program. As we discussed in Chapter 2, CRM is limited to the front office functions. However, there is no doubt that the new R&D program would need customer information, which is generated by your CRM functions.

We are using this broad definition so that we can develop a framework that covers all the functions and components needed to build your CRM solution. Let's take a look at the key elements of the definition:

- CRM focuses on strategic impact rather than operational impact. Benefits are generally long term rather than immediate (future increased profit rather than immediate cost reduction). This doesn't mean that you shouldn't sell your program with some up-front cost-reductions proposals. It means that you need to understand where the benefits will really occur and set realistic expectations.
- CRM is a total discipline. To understand CRM, think of it as having the same components as any manufacturing business. It uses a machine (CRM technology) and power (your people) to turn raw material (customer information) into products (processes and interactions that build customer loyalty).
- CRM includes all the functions that directly touch the customer throughout his entire lifetime with your company. It touches multiple organizations and crosses boundaries. Functions usually included in a CRM effort are marketing, sales, customer services, and product support (whether internal or through a channel partner, whether on or off the web).

The components of the CRM total discipline are shown in Figure 3-2.

If you already hold a strong belief about what CRM means it may be hard to buy into a new one. Your brain will read "CRM" and automatically switch back to the definition you're familiar with. But please keep this definition in your mind as you're reading the rest of this book. The CRM that we're talking about is the CRM we've just defined. This definition covers all the important elements that you have to implement in a successful program. No matter what you call your effort or how you choose to implement the components within your own company, this is the definition that covers what customer relationship management really is. For example, maybe for you, as a dotcom company CRM *is* just about the web. Or maybe "CRM" has been tried before and failed, so you need a fresh term to rekindle enthusiasm. These kinds of special situations don't change the basic concept or what needs to get done, but you do have to make it your own.

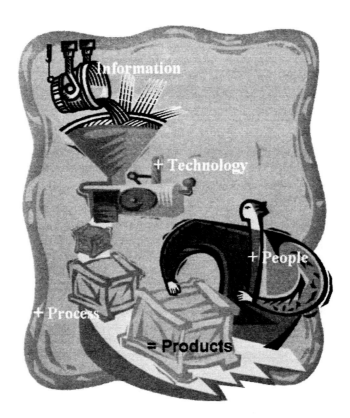

Figure 3-2 CRM is a total discipline.

Always remember that when you're getting started within your own company, you must have a clear understanding of what CRM is (even if it isn't this definition) and get universal agreement from everyone involved; otherwise, you will never get your company moving in a focused direction. You will have difficulty showing progress and measuring success without a universally understood goal and understanding. Lack of a clear definition puts any new program in a very high-risk position, and CRM is no exception. Also, don't forget that you'll likely have to repeat and reconfirm these terms and definitions frequently throughout the life of the program. Otherwise, you can't ensure that your management, your sponsors, and your team continue to understand and support your direction. I learned the hard way, so believe me when I say that it's almost impossible to repeat your purpose and goal too often.

It is also important to understand that your company does not need to implement a total CRM solution across your entire front office organization before you have succeeded at CRM. Because the CRM concept sounds so big and broad, we will look at ways to identify and prioritize small chunks that can yield quick success and build on each other to deliver your overall goal. CRM must be approached as an ongoing evolution in which the cost of each new project is weighed against the value for the customer (and, thus, the benefit for your company through increased revenue and reduced costs). Even though our definition of CRM is broad and complex, its goal is simple: to maximize the value of your company's *customer asset* including loyalty, revenue, and profit.

3.1.3   The Components of CRM

As our definition states, the CRM infrastructure is made up of four key components: information, process, technology, and people. Each of these components is critical to delivering a successful CRM program. These four components are described in Table 3-2.

Table 3-2 Components of a Successful CRM Program

Component	Description
Information	Information is the raw material of CRM. These types of information are useful to CRM: • Identification Data: Name/address/phone data collected from customers to complete a business transaction • Marketing data: Descriptors/traits/preferences collected from customers during a transaction (either by asking questions or tracking behavior) • List data: Names/addresses collected by a third party, which can be bought or leased • Overlay data: Customer profile data collected by a third party, which can be leased and appended to existing customer records
Process	Customer-centered processes are the "product" of CRM. Some examples are: • All current/future processes that directly touch the customer • Touch points, or means by which we interact with customers, such as phone, e-mail, etc. • Identifying and eliminating process disconnects and white space • Integrating and rationalizing processes from the customer's point of view
Technology	Technology is the machinery that enables CRM to work. These are examples of technologies that CRM may find useful: • Software products (process automation tools, analysis tools, web site development, and management tools) • Networking and integrating applications and databases • Databases, either purchased solutions or home-grown, central or distributed • Security features, such as encryption tools and firewalls
People	People are the power supply of CRM. The energy source must be set to the right voltage for the entire system to work. People are "reset" through various change management tools and support mechanisms, such as: • Training and education • New tools • Measurements and rewards

We will take an in-depth look at how to develop the requirements and plans for each of these components in Chapters 11 through 14.

3.2 Defining CRM Concepts

There are several important concepts that support the CRM definition. These concepts must also be commonly defined and understood, because they are critical to any successful CRM effort.

3.2.1 Customer Life Cycle

The CRM concept includes the definition of the customer life cycle. The customer life cycle is your customer's view of her relationship with your organization over the long term. The customer life cycle is NOT your company's view. For example, "Product Support" is not part of the customer life cycle. It is certainly a function that your company provides to help customers use your products or service. But from the customer's perspective, the perfect world is where everything always runs perfectly and she never needs any help from you while using your products.

 DEFINITIONS

The *customer life cycle* is the total time that the customer is engaged with your company from the customer's experience and viewpoint.

There is a high-level life cycle that is consistent for all customers, no matter the product or service and no matter how much time the customer spends in each stage:

1. **Consider:** Customer becomes aware of a need and investigates alternative solutions.
2. **Purchase:** Customer evaluates and chooses the best alternative and places an order.
3. **Set up:** Customer installs the product and learns how to use it.
4. **Use:** Customer operates and maintains the product and finally makes the decision to retire it or to upgrade, which starts the cycle all over again.

A typical customer life cycle covers these four major stages and includes a layer that you should make specific to your customers and your business. As an example, Figure 3-3 is the customer life cycle for a high-tech manufacturer in California.

Of course, there is no single life cycle that is identical for all companies and all customers. You'll need to determine the life cycle of your own customers. The basic framework is relatively consistent, but service companies, for example, are not likely to find the concept of "install" relevant to their customers' experience. We will look at the customer life cycle again in Chapter 8 when we take the customer's perspective in defining our overall CRM strategy.

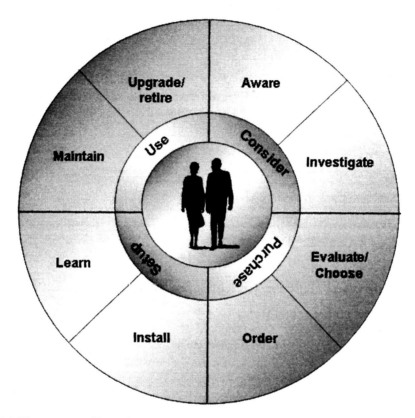

Figure 3-3 The customer life cycle

3.2.2 Business-to-Business CRM

CRM in the business-to-business (B2B) marketplace is plagued by all the same misconceptions listed in Table 3-1. But B2B CRM suffers from one additional misconception, as shown in Table 3-3.

Table 3-3 B2B Misconception

Misconception	Reality
B2B customers are <u>companies</u>	Although it is true that company information is an absolutely critical element of any B2B CRM effort, B2B customers are still human beings. We build relationships with the people who work at customer companies. Company information is very important because it helps us describe and understand the people who make up that company, but the company is not a customer!

There are some differences between how consumer and B2B CRM programs are implemented (information requirements) and managed (multiple contacts at the same business), but the basic definition of what CRM is remains the same. We look at some these implementation differences in Chapter 11 where we consider what data we need to deliver and manage customer relationship-building programs. The important thing to remember in all this is that basically CRM is CRM and the Internet is a new and powerful tool.

3.2.3   Customer Asset

The concept of the customer being one of your company's assets is just now beginning to be widely accepted. This concept is a very important one because investing in customer relationships often does not generate short-term gains, and we know that most companies today are focused on the short term.

CRM delivers value because it focuses on lengthening the duration of the relationship (loyalty). We learned from Reichheld's work (refer to Chapter 2) that loyalty does deliver increased profit. CRM makes good business sense because loyal customers buy more product, buy more often, cost less to sell to and support, and often pay a premium. Loyal customers continue to buy our products because they perceive value in the relationship itself. Based on the experiences (with our people, products, processes, etc.) that they have had over time and on the relationship we have been able to establish because of our knowledge of their situation, preferences, and needs, these loyal customers continue to buy from us. Of course, even the most loyal customers must be willing to pay enough that there is some profit on each sale. A company can't stay in business just by having loyal customers if they lose money on every transaction. This was one of the lessons from the dotcom bust.

Customer Information

Customer information is a tangible company asset that can (and should) be inventoried and managed. It is a critical component for building loyalty because it's impossible to build strong relationships if you don't know who your customers are and you don't know what their needs and experiences have been. It is an asset that must be protected and maintained. Asset management requires money and resources because poor data won't support any of the goals of CRM; in fact, it will probably make things worse. Data is the raw material that goes into building relationships and should be valued the same way you value the raw materials that go into building your products. We talk more about information and the resources required to maintain it in Chapter 20.

Just like raw material in a manufacturing environment, information has a value. That is becoming clearer as customer databases are beginning to be offered for sale as part of a company's assets. Of course, this has raised all kinds of privacy issues, such as the recent situation where bankrupt retailer Toysmart.com tried to auction off its customer database even though it had promised never to do so. The Federal Trade Commission (July 2001) did finally approve the sale of this asset, but under very limited conditions. The company acquiring Toysmart's customer information could not change any of the original privacy policies without notifying and asking permission from every customer.

How do you put a value on this kind of asset, especially considering the legal limitations? The difficulty with valuing the information asset is that, like all assets, its value is based on what the marketplace is willing to pay for it. We don't have enough experience yet on a standard definition of the precise value of customer information. There are no Generally Accepted Accounting Practices that cover customer information. We have the feeling that customer data is valuable, but we don't know how valuable. The value of customer information is related to the largely intangible concept of the loyalty the customers themselves.

You may be able to sell your customer database, but you don't control and therefore can't sell your customers' loyalty. The most a buyer can be assured of is receiving an accurate and up-to-date list of people who have bought your products. Of course, any customer list is made up of both happy and unhappy customers. And the unhappy customers aren't valuable at all!

Customer Value

One key benefit of collecting and saving customer information is that it allows you to measure and identify who your most valuable customers are. Much to the surprise of some, CRM is not about treating all customers the same. Everyone knows that not all customers are alike, so why would we want to treat them all the same?

CRM is about identifying and rewarding your most loyal customers so they remain loyal and their value to your company increases. CRM is also about moving the next tier of customers up to loyal (and, therefore, higher value) behavior. In Chapter 17, we learn more about measuring customer value.

Knowing which customers are the most valuable allows us to follow the important customer-centered concept outlined by Peppers and Rogers (1993) of achieving increased share of *customer* instead of increasing share of *market*. This means that we want our very best customers to buy more of what they need from us. This is much more profitable than the price manipulation and discounting that usually occurs to increase market share. Who cares where the low value customers are shopping? CRM is about being able to recognize your most valuable customers and doing everything you can to deliver high value experience and to ensure that they remain (or become) more loyal.

By the way, value is another place where managing consumer and B2B customers are different. Consumer value is calculated based on the purchases made by an individual. In the B2B marketplace, value is based on the purchases of the entire customer company. Each individual generally has the same "value" as the company account has. In either case, CRM helps you identify your best customers so that you're in a position to treat your *best customers best.*

3.3   Understanding the Goal of CRM

Maximum customer loyalty, the goal of CRM, cannot be achieved overnight. In Figure 3-4, we see that, much like Maslow's self-actualization pyramid, you cannot jump right in at the top designing loyalty programs unless you have already addressed all the lower levels of the pyramid.

As we discussed earlier, CRM is definitely not a sorcerer's stone that will instantly change everything and make all your customers delightfully happy and loyal. CRM usually requires significant changes in your systems, information management practices, business processes, and organizational and employee behavior in order to be successful. Achieving the goal of loyal customers and increased profit takes time. You must move through the levels of the CRM hierarchy one at a time. Like Maslow, you must first satisfy basic needs such as integrating your customer information and application silos, redesigning processes (and maybe even organizational structures), and educating your employees. If the task looks overwhelming, remember that you will be dividing this work into small, achievable steps based on the priorities of your company and your customers. Each project will yield measurable benefits, so you don't need to wait until your company is *customer actualized* before reaping any rewards.

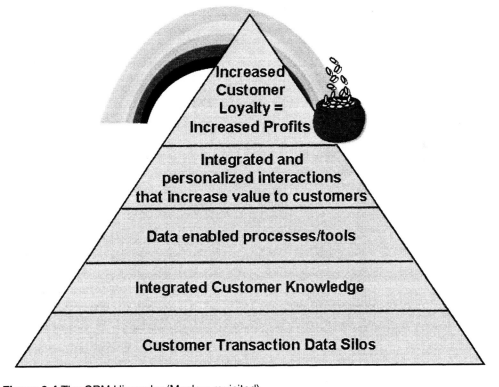

Figure 3-4 The CRM Hierarchy (Maslow revisited)

3.4   Using Customer Touch Points

Touch points are all the different means we use to interact with our customers, from general broadcast advertising at the lowest cost per touch up to human face-to-face interaction, which is the most expensive.

 KEY IDEA

Touch points are the means (media) that we use to interact with our customers. Touch point interactions must be targeted to a specific customer or customer company, and/or they must allow for a response (a conversation, a transaction, a reply, and so on).

All the following media types, except broadcast, can be targeted at a specific customer or customer company. Because a broadcast message may actually generate individual customer responses, it is included as a touch point. Table 3-4 lists and describes the most common touch points. Other touch points are being used today in some industries. For example, electronic kiosks have been set up in retail stores for shopping and ordering; in some senses, an automatic teller machine at an airport or mall is a kiosk for a bank. These other touch points are not as universally applicable as the ones listed in Table 3-2.

Table 3-4 Customer Touch Points

Medium	Cost per Touch (low-high)/Impact of Touch (low-high)	Characteristics
Broadcast		Message distributed to untargeted audience via any one of the broadcast media. Generally not considered part of CRM because it isn't directed at an individual. However, there may be a request for a customer response (call 1-800), so it is included.
E-mail		Message/interaction via electronic mail with a specifically identified customer. Does not include spam, which is untargeted and should never be used.
Systematic		Interaction with a customer through computers that communicate directly with each other. There may be no people involved in the transaction itself, but humans are required to set up the system communication.
Internet		Interaction with a specific customer over the Internet who may or may not be individually identified.

Table 3-4 Customer Touch Points

Medium	Cost per Touch (low-high)/Impact of Touch (low-high)	Characteristics
Mail		Interaction with a specific customer via hard-copy mail, usually an identified individual.
Event		Interaction with a customer at a seminar, trade show, training event, etc. Customer may or may not be identified.
Phone/ Fax		Interaction with a specific customer via telephone, cellular phone, or facsimile machine. Customer may or may not be identified.
Personal		Face-to-face interaction between two people such as a sales rep, a product support engineer or a clerk in the retail channel.

Let's continue building our CRM vision. Figure 3-5 illustrates the ideal situation in which all messages and touch point interactions are integrated across the entire front office organization. All these different media are coordinated to deliver consistency. This picture is beginning to look much better for the customer than the "archery range" we saw in Chapter 2. A customer-centered company looks and sounds like a single entity to its customers.

Will looking and sounding consistent guarantee customer loyalty? Of course not! We won't have loyal customers if we produce useless or low-quality products or if can't integrate our products with others to meet the customers' requirements for a total solution. But if we can't even produce consistent messages, we haven't a chance of looking like a company on which our customers can depend.

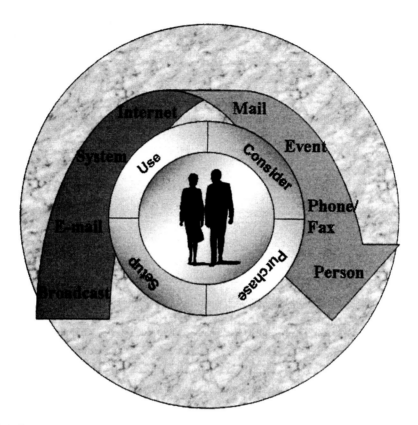

Figure 3-5 Seamless touch-point interactions

3.5   Deciding Who Should Lead the CRM Functions

As we've discussed, CRM covers the activities of the four functions normally labeled Market-ing, Sales, Product Support, and Customer Services. It also covers any third-party organizations you have contracted to perform any of these activities for you. Of course, we know that the cus-tomer's total experience is also governed by product and other back office experiences. But we have to set boundaries on our program scope somewhere.

These CRM functions are part of the organization's front officeand directly interact with the customer. One of the biggest roadblocks to effective management of customer relationships is that these functions rarely would come together under one senior executive below the CEO level in the company. As a result, goals, strategies, plans, actions, and communications are rarely coordinated, and customer interactions are often fragmented and uncoordinated.

3.5.1   Marketing

Marketing is the function most often associated with CRM, and indeed marketing must take on expanded responsibilities for your company to play successfully in the new marketplace.

Marketing has traditionally focused on branding and messaging strategies and broadcast communications. But this is no longer enough. The demands of the new marketplace require marketers to take on new skills and knowledge.

Because CRM is the discipline that ensures consistent, integrated communications and experiences for your customers that are all in support of your company's brand image, the marketing department is a logical home for the championship of CRM.

3.5.2 Sales

The sales function rewards selling and closing a deal. Sales reps are rewarded and paid according to how well they close.

When CRM is championed within sales, it usually takes the form of sales rep automation and productivity. While these tools don't help much in moving the organization to becoming more customer-centered or improving the customer experience, they should make sales reps more productive and, thus, increase sales. Sales force automation helps generate customer information, too. And sales reps interact frequently with customers. So the sales department is critically important to your company's overall CRM strategy and must be tightly integrated.

3.5.3 Customer Services

Service organizations are usually profit centers in companies that provide customer services, such as consulting and integration, in addition to products. If the entire organization is a service company, "services" are not a separate function. A customer service organization is treated and behaves like a product organization with most of the typical functions represented, even Research and Development (R&D) and production. Customer services is measured on traditional profit results, just like the organization's back office functions, but because it is so heavily involved in direct customer interactions, it must be included in your overall CRM program.

Service organizations must be very customer-centered to be successful. However, because service companies must be focused on their profitability, it is difficult for these organizations to take leadership across the other CRM functions and truly become the customer advocate. The experiences delivered and potential for information collection by customer services organizations require that they also be fully integrated into your CRM efforts.

3.5.4 Product Support

The product support department (which is often and preferably called customer support) focuses on helping customers answer questions or solve problems with your products and services. Unfortunately, product support is often treated purely as overhead, a cost to be minimized—so support people are measured on how quickly they can "close" (not necessarily solve) an incident. They are seldom measured on how well the incident was resolved or how happy the customer is.

Thus, when the customer support department champions CRM, the effort is usually focused on call centers and the systems and telephony that make support more effective while reducing costs. Technologies such as automated phone trees and timers that encourage quick call resolution do reduce the cost of support. But if these enhancements are not carefully implemented with the impact on the customer in mind, they can be very frustrating to customers and VERY costly to the bottom line.

In Chapter 1, we discussed the phenomenon that dissatisfied customers who get their problems resolved often become extremely loyal. Customer support is clearly a critical part of your customers' experience. Additionally, the customer support department has constant direct interactions with customers, and the employees are an invaluable source of customer information. Cost reduction concerns that create pressure to shorten phone calls and other support interactions must be balanced against the value of the customer knowledge that can be obtained, as well as the impact that being rushed off the phone has on the customer. Support is also a critical element of your overall CRM efforts that must be tightly integrated into the overall program.

3.5.5   The Channel and Other Partners

CRM partners are an extension of your organization that may perform any of the front office functions, from sales through the reseller channel to customer services and product support. These partners often have significant interactions with your customers and are a tremendous source of customer knowledge and information. If you do use any channel partners, you undoubtedly have an organization dedicated to managing the channel. This group thinks that these channel partners are the customers. That is not true. Channel partners (such as resellers, distributors, and retail outlets) are not customers. Actually, they are logically part of your CRM organization itself. Yes, of course, they're not really part of your company, and of course, we want to build great relationships with our channel partners. After all, we need great partner relationships so that they value our partnership and represent us well in any customer interaction. Sure, they aren't direct employees and may not have exactly the same business priorities that we have, and even though partners technically place purchase orders with us, they are not customers. They are not the people who purchase and use our products. We certainly need to include partners as constituents our CRM program efforts, but not as targets of our CRM program.

We need all the messages from each CRM function (including our partners) to our customers to be consistent and to be delivered though a seamless set of touch points. Figure 3-6 adds the CRM front office functions to our CRM Vision.

One of the obvious difficulties facing any CRM program effort is that few (if any) companies actually have an organization that comprises these four functions (much less the channel). This is where the marketing department has a great opportunity to leverage its communication and brand expertise and its broad customer perspective to provide CRM leadership within the organization. Where else in the organization does this kind of focus on and understanding of customers exist?

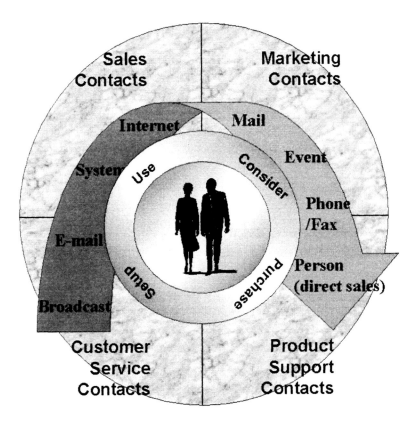

Figure 3-6 Successful CRM programs require integration across functions and touch points.

3.6 Creating a New Role for Marketing

Most companies aren't ready for (and are not even thinking of) a cross-functional department that is responsible for all CRM functions and activities. Some are trying to do CRM in a piecemeal fashion; each part of the organization is launching a CRM effort independently. This may get some tools up and running fast, but at best, a piecemeal approach will have no impact on the customer. At worst, this uncoordinated approach will actually cause the customer's experience to be more fragmented. On the other hand, some companies understand the value of a having an overall strategy and governance even if projects are actually implemented in organizational silos. These companies have established cross-functional management bodies whose members represent each of the core CRM functions and who oversee the company's CRM efforts. This can be a very effective means for ensuring an integrated program with little direct impact on the organization's structure.

But there is still a risk. When everyone is responsible, no one is responsible. For all significant organizational change efforts, there must be a single focal point that is responsible for leading the charge and encouraging and directing the team. In the new world, the marketing organization is in a great position to take on the leadership for CRM. We discuss this new role for marketing when we study organizing for CRM success in Chapter 7. The opportunities are great, but so are the challenges caused by all this change. We need to approach this challenge with a solid plan.

Before we start to develop our plans, we take a quick look at the additional impact of the Internet on CRM in Chapter 4.

Questions for Reflection

These questions help you understand how your CRM functions are organized. You may not call them Marketing, Sales, Customer Services, and Product Support, but somewhere in your company and/or business partners, all these activities are performed.

1. What functions in your company directly interact with the customer?
2. Where does each of these functions report?
3. Where (at what level in the organization) do these functions come together under a single manager?
4. What touch points does your company currently employ and which function manages them (broadcast, e-mail, systematic, Internet, mail, event, phone/fax, personal)?
5. What are the basic steps in *your* customers' life cycles (consider, purchase, set up, use)?

e-CRM—What's the Difference?

Now that we've created our working definition of Customer Relationship Management, we are ready to take a look at the special case of CRM on the Internet. We will also take a closer look at what has changed about CRM because of the Internet and what hasn't changed. As we discussed earlier, the Internet provides a new set of tools for interacting with customers. It is not a new way of life or even a new business function, but it is a new touch point medium with some new challenges and some great new opportunities. One of the major changes the Internet has brought to the marketplace is putting more information and control in the hands of customers. Customer expectations have been raised with the result that we all now have new requirements for and measures of success.

4.1   Merging CRM and the Internet

In Chapter 1, we discussed many of the changes in the marketplace and the impact of those changes on business success. The Internet has certainly been one major source of change. Now that customers are so much more in control, the importance of building strong customer relationships has greatly increased. This impacts all companies, no matter which value discipline they focus on. CRM impacts both operational excellence (using information and automation to improve performance and reducing the cost of providing products and services to customers) and customer intimacy (to improve customer experience and build loyalty). But even for companies focused on product superiority, the Internet has raised the bar for what is considered *acceptable* in the two other disciplines. Customers get to choose, and we want them to choose us!

4.1.1   New Customer Expectations

There are five key areas in which the Internet has impacted the way we do business. Increased access, control, speed, and globalization have raised customer expectations both on and off the Internet. Elimination of direct customer interaction by automation has changed the way we deliver experiences, but customer requirements about the quality of that experience haven't changed.

- **Access:** The Internet provides an unprecedented ability to deliver information, goods, and services to businesses and consumers. Customers are able to get information and do business whenever they want from wherever they can get connected. The Internet has made more information available to customers, giving them much more knowledge than they've ever had before. Although it is possible for companies to get information about customers surreptitiously over the Internet, this is **not** CRM! Building loyalty depends on building trust. Abusing customer privacy is not the way to achieve trust. We discuss this further in Chapter 22.

- **Control:** Additional knowledge gives customers an unprecedented opportunity to review all available products and select the one that has the most value for them. Customers have never had so much power before. As a result, customers' expectations are higher than they ever have been. Access to more information, more choices, and increased control are part of the baseline that customers now expect. It may sound like we're in an arms race where companies rush to implement the latest and greatest Internet and CRM solutions. This is why the CRM strategic planning step (discussed in Chapter 8) is so critical. Does your company need CRM to improve intimacy, to improve operations, or just to make sure that you meet the minimum new standards that customers expect? You will not find a one-size-fits-all CRM program. You will have to decide what's right for you.

- **Speed:** The Internet has impacted the speed at which business happens. We get an email acknowledgment of an order within seconds; a company is born—and sometimes dies—within a few months; products and services are delivered at breakneck speed. "Internet time" has dramatically changed customer expectations of how quickly *everything* should work (wait times at call centers, responses to e-mail inquiries, answers to questions).

- **Globalization:** The Internet has effectively eliminated country boundaries. Companies that are already dealing with global customers, but often interacted with them in fragmented geographic silos, have felt the impact of globalization most significantly. Before the Internet, customers usually had access only to local products, terms, and pricing. A company's geographic business silos weren't visible and didn't cause many problems. Most global companies knew that geographic fragmentation caused internal operational problems and expense. But that didn't become a big issue until customers could go online themselves and see all the internal disconnects. We know that customers now know about the fragmentation affecting many of our companies, and they have begun taking advantage of our silos. A large Internet infrastructure provider that sells online business- and customer-relationship management solutions recently discovered that many of its global customers were shopping around the company's web site to find the cheapest "country" price. The customer would then place all of its global orders in that country. Not only was the company losing money, they knew that this practice actually made them look stupid and ineffective to their customers. They weren't "practicing what they preached."

- **Automation:** Finally, and maybe most important, the Internet has eliminated the *people* component from processes that have been moved online. For most companies that have been in business for any length of time, it has been the employees who have shielded and protected customers from the complications and disconnects of the company's business processes. People can know how to link a customer's order to the relevant discount information (like a purchase agreement or a special offer) even when the customer or discount has not been identified the same way in the two systems. If there is no common identification scheme (which, sadly, most companies don't have), there is no way for a computer to know where to look for the right piece of information.

Not all these changes affect all companies to the same degree. Very small companies that target a particular country market may not be heavily affected by the globalization of the marketplace. They may force customers from other regions to do things *their way* or *go away*. As long as the volume of international purchasers remains small, this might be perfectly acceptable for some. However, turning away customers isn't a very appealing strategy for most companies, certainly not for those that are committed to growing and expanding their businesses.

For most of companies, the fact that the Internet has increased customers' expectations for access, control, speed, and service is a big deal. If customers are more in control, then loyalty (preferring us over competitors) is even more critical. Loyalty is built on strong relationships and positive experiences. Because the Internet has eliminated much of the direct employee-customer interactions, companies must find different ways of building customer relationships on the web.

4.1.2   Why e-CRM Is So Important

With all the changes brought about by the Internet, isn't it just too much trouble to deal with? The Internet gives customers more control and takes control away from us, so why should we bother? Of course, ignoring the Internet is not really an option for most companies for these reasons:

1. Customers want and expect the benefits that the Internet gives them. They get more information and more control, and they like that. If your competitors are using it, so should you—to maintain parity if nothing else. After all, in this book we're talking about making business decisions based on positive impact on the customer and becoming more customer-centric.

2. The Internet is an extremely cost effective medium for delivering customer interactions. Employees are almost always the most expensive element of most companies' front office activities. Automating elements of sales, order-taking, and customer service and support make great economic sense. Don't forget that even though we want to make decisions considering the customers' viewpoint, CRM is not about being so focused on the customer that we no longer make money! In other words, decisions should be made considering mutual values: the benefits the customer gets from the relationship and the profits that the vendor gets.

The Internet is a fact of life in the new marketplace. There are huge potential economic benefits, and customers expect it. It's our job to figure out what e-CRM is, how it's different from the relationship-building activities we've been doing for years and how to integrate it in to our current activities. We need to identify the risks that the Internet adds to managing customer relationships and pay special attention to those risks that we can reduce with extra strategy and planning. It's important to remember that just like traditional CRM, e-CRM is not a silver bullet. As you know, you can't hire a consultant or go to the store and buy the solution to all your problems.

4.2   Delivering CRM On and Off the Internet

In Chapter 3, we discussed CRM as a discipline that depends on people, process, information, and technology. It is not magic. There are no differences in the way we define CRM and e-CRM. But there are differences in the way we implement them that must be noted.

Lots of hype has surrounded the concept that e-CRM is a completely new approach to delivering customer experiences. In fact, e-CRM has exactly the same definition as traditional CRM: the strategic use of information, processes, people, and technology to manage the customer's relationship with your company across the whole customer life cycle. The Internet provides a new channel for customer interactions that we call e-CRM, much as we call customer interactions over the telephone telemarketing or telesales. The technology is new, but the basic rules are the same.

As we've seen, the Internet has significantly changed customer expectations for access, control, speed, and globalization that carry over to all areas of doing business. But the key change to CRM implementations that the Internet has caused is automation: changing the way that people are involved in customer interactions online. As shown in Table 4-1, each of the four elements is critical to CRM, whether the interaction takes place on or off the web. e-CRM uses the same raw material (customer information) and delivers the same end product (loyalty) as other CRM channels.

Table 4-1 CRM versus e-CRM

Business Concept	CRM	e-CRM
Raw Material	Customer *information*	Customer *information*
Manufacturing Process	CRM *interactions* (such as support centers and database marketing campaigns)	Online *interactions*
Energy or Power	People	Internet *technology* (infrastructure designed and implemented by *people*)
Machinery and Equipment	CRM *technology* (application systems)	Internet *technology*
Product	Improved relationships and loyalty	Improved relationships and loyalty

Process and technology differences are usually found in any new touch point medium. By far, the most significant difference between e-CRM and the other CRM touch points is that technology (based on the knowledge of your people), not the people themselves, powers the relationship development.

4.2.1 Information

Both CRM and e-CRM depend on electronic information that has been collected about customers, in place of human knowledge, to build and manage relationships. Although many CRM touch points (product support call centers, for example) involve direct human interaction, the interaction is probably with an individual who does not actually know the customer. Still, people can read between the lines and create intuitive linkages and conclusions. Because no human being is actually involved in the e-CRM process, there is no one to make interpretations. This means that complete and accurate information is even more critical to e-CRM. Whatever the future promises, there is no practical example of a computer that can actually think.

Unfortunately, many customers are not comfortable giving their personal information online. They are concerned that their personal data won't be protected and that companies will invade their privacy. Because customer information is so critical to e-CRM success, companies must have the trust of their customers to be successful. Companies can capture and analyze every click that a customer makes without letting the customer know. Instead of building trust, that type of behavior destroys it. We can ignore customer privacy and let it be done to us, or we can take control, actively participate in self-regulation efforts, and grab the opportunity to build trust and loyalty. We discuss privacy options and approaches in detail in Chapter 22.

"On the Internet, nobody knows you're a dog."

Figure 4-1 *"Unless they trust you enough to tell you."*

As Figure 4-1 so aptly illustrates, we do not know anything about customers who interact with us on the web unless they tell us. For e-CRM, this cartoon needs a subtitle! We will spend considerable time determining our information needs in Chapter 11.

4.2.2 Process

One of the most important things to do before moving processes to the web is to really understand what you are trying to get done. Don't just automate what you've got. Technology can do some things better than humans can, but there are some other things it can't do well at all. We need to evaluate our processes from the customer's viewpoint (how it will look to them) before we put the process online.

Amazon.com is perhaps the poster child for excellent online processes that integrate well into the back office logistical infrastructure of the company so that the overall experience for the customer is extremely positive. It's interesting to notice that Amazon.com has done such a great job of building easy-to-use and reliable online services that they have created a core of extremely loyal customers for themselves. These customers entrust all kinds of personal information to Amazon, from credit card information to family member birthdays, and trust that

Amazon will do the right things with their information. This allows Amazon to provide many special services, like a personalized web experience targeted to the customer's taste, birthday gift reminders, and instant checkout. Of course, Amazon also allows for those who don't want to share their credit card information – they just have to go through the tedious process of reentering all those numbers each time they make a purchase.

We'll discuss more about the process component and how to document and plan processes in Chapter 12.

4.2.3 Technology

For e-CRM, technology plays both the operational role and the role normally played by a human being. This is not necessarily so surprising. Research suggests that people actually treat their computers as if they were social beings. Stanford University professors Byron Reeves and Clifford Nass have completed more than 30 studies in the area of human responses to technology. Their research shows that people react to computers, televisions, and other communications media the same way they react socially with humans. Based on their research results, they have defined the media equation: "Media equals real life" (Reeves and Nass, 1996). Figure 4-2 shows what Reeves and Nass mean by this equation; there is real human emotion that people feel for the technology equipment with which they interact.

Figure 4-2 A man (or woman) and his (or her) computer

Though maybe not intuitive at first, Reeves and Nass found that these results were really not that surprising. Only humans are able to interact socially. When our televisions talk to us or our computers respond to a question, our brains expect and react to these interactions as if the source were another person.

The importance of recognizing that people have relationships with their computers is that we take responsibility for the kind of interaction that our web sites deliver. It is critical that we design online systems that deliver the kinds of experiences we want for our customers (that support our brand and strengthen relationships). In fact, to many customers, the web site is our company! Manners, personality, and emotion must be designed into the web experience. Here are some examples to consider:

- **Manners:** The experience should be polite, respectful, and helpful. It would be unlikely for any web site have an insulting error message (though I did once actually see "Invalid selection, dumb%$*!" on a screen – a little programmer humor?). But a message that is confusing or offers no help is almost as bad as one that's insulting.
- **Personality:** Remember, one size does not fit all. A great example of computer personality is Microsoft's Office Assistant. Personally, that little paper clip drives me crazy; I prefer the genius – somehow he seems smarter and better able to answer questions than a piece of bent wire. To others, he may be completely unappealing.
- **Emotion:** People prefer positive emotions. Look at the Lands End web site to see the smiling and helpful person you are talking to. Who wants to ask a grumpy curmudgeon for help?

People know about these rules, but computers must be taught. This is why people remain such an important part of e-CRM. Your sales reps, service reps, and marketers must take on the responsibility of specifying what the automated interaction will look like. Of course, your ever-important technology people must be able to understand what experiences you want to deliver to your customers and develop the online systems that deliver them. We have long understood that business process owners and technologists often speak a totally different language. For years, we've encouraged programmers to focus on the business, not technical bells and whistles. A newer concept is that business people must become savvier about technology. We will discuss this new role for marketing in Chapter 7. Good communication between business functions and Information Technology has never been more important, because information and technology underlie all aspects of CRM, but especially e-CRM.

4.2.4   People

CRM is about building and managing relationships, but where is the relationship for e-CRM? Common sense tells us that relationships must be between people. On the Internet, people normally aren't interacting directly with other people. Does that make e-CRM impossible by definition? Of course not. But we must make sure that when our customers are interacting with us online, they feel like a person is there. We can create this feeling using photographs and animated characters that display human behavior. Another effective method is to create "chat groups" and "chat" e-mail links that simulate face-to-face human communication. Of course, we know from Reeves and Nass that all these simulated human interactions must meet expected standards for good manners, wonderful personality, and positive emotion.

Another great technique is to provide your customers with a way to talk to live service representatives while they are shopping online. The Lands End web site, shown in Figure 4-3, is a great example of how one well-known company has implemented a live telephone option to its web site. (Don't overlook the friendly Customer Support Representative shown at the top of the page.)

Although your employees do not actually interact with most customers who visit your company's web site, they are still instrumental in delivering these interactions. What your people must do instead of directly touching your customers is to make key decisions like what kinds of relationships we should have with what kinds of customers. Those decisions will govern how your e-CRM processes and systems will be designed. We will discuss the appropriateness of providing experiences through different levels of human and technology interactions in Chapter 13. Again, there is no single right answer that applies to all companies.

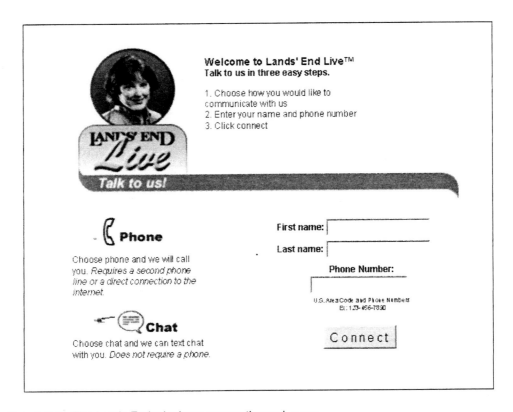

Figure 4-3 The Lands End telephone connection web page

4.3   Recognizing Barriers to Internet Adoption

Adding the Internet to our CRM efforts makes lots of sense. But it's not necessarily clear sailing ahead. Pricewaterhouse Coopers LLP found the top three concerns would need to be addressed to persuade those not currently using the Internet to participate in e-commerce: They are privacy, security, and ease of use. Table 4-2 lists the objections most often cited by customers as reasons they do not shop online and gives some strategies for counteracting them.

Table 4-2 Barriers to Customer Adoption of the Internet

Barrier	Customer Concerns	Strategies	Comments
Customer Confidence			
While many customers are eager to shop online, many are not.	The processes seem unfamiliar and confusing.	Design and build your e-CRM systems so they are simple, helpful, and friendly. Understand and prepare for what automation does well and where it is weak.	Look for ways to mimic the best of your company's offline interactions with your customers, while eliminating disconnects and bottlenecks.
	No real person is there to answer questions. We may treat our computers as if they are real people, but they aren't. So we cannot prepare for all possible questions a customer might have.	Weave in human contact where possible, such as a call center direct link from your web site. Of course, it's up to you to determine if the cost is outweighed by the value to your customers.	How complicated are your products or your online processes? What are your competitors doing? In Chapter 8, we will learn how to do a strategic analysis that will help you answer these questions.
	Interactions can be cold and unfriendly.	Make your key managers visit your web site and act like customers for a day.	This will teach them what your customers go through and ensure that you get the funding that you need to build an effective e-CRM program.
Customer Trust			
Customers don't trust us with their data, especially online.	Openness of the Internet makes it appear hard to secure data.	Don't ask for more information than you really need. Build relationships over time and get more information as you build trust.	If you require too much information, customers will fill in garbage. How many customers named Mickey Mouse (or worse) are in your database?

Table 4-2 Barriers to Customer Adoption of the Internet (Continued)

Barrier	Customer Concerns	Strategies	Comments
	Internet privacy issues sell more newspapers than credit card piracy or stories about what's right. Customers perceive that there is no safe place online.	Be open about what data you collect and why you need it. Be clear and simple in your expectations. Say it loud and often!	Give customers good reasons (benefits) to share their data with you, and use it for their benefit in the future.
	Customers don't understand what the real dangers are, and they don't have consistent expectations.	Use consistent terms and language. Join privacy education consortia and privacy seal programs.	Help educate your customers so they can understand what should concern them and what to look for. I hope that will be you.
Legislation			
Some legislation threatens the Internet's ability to grow as a medium for transacting business.	Legislation may limit the information that can be collected online and how it can be used.	Make your Privacy and Security policies part of your customer loyalty and relationship-management program.	Use your privacy policy to support your brand image and build trust. It's good business! (We'll discuss privacy more in Chapter 22.)
	Trading restrictions, such as imposing state sales tax on out-of-state transactions, negatively affect sales.	Join involved with trade organizations such as the Direct Marketing Association (DMA).	The Direct Marketing Association lobbies for open markets, postal rate limits, and limited privacy regulation.

The Internet is a fantastic new tool for helping us manage relationships with our customers in a cost-efficient and effective way. That's not all there is to CRM, but it is a very important and effective medium with incredible promise for strengthening loyalty.

In Part 2, we will plan and prepare for our integrated CRM program. We will start with an overview of the formal methodology and steps needed to build a successful CRM program in Chapter 5.

Questions For Reflection

These questions will help you understand the advantage your company may be taking of the Internet and what it might be missing.

1. Does your company currently have a web presence?
2. Is your web site integrated into your overall CRM initiative?
3. Do you use your web site to gather information from your customers and build relationships, or just as a way to present company and product information?
4. Have you ever been a customer on your own web site? How do you rate the experience?
5. Have you ever been a customer on any of your competitors' web sites? How do you rate the experience of your competitor's web site?

PART 2

CRM: Planning It Right

CHAPTER 5

Understanding the Method

Part 1 set the stage for our CRM efforts. We discussed how changes in the marketplace have made building customer loyalty and Customer Relationship Management imperatives. We developed a common understanding of what we mean by CRM and what it entails both on and off the web. We also discussed the following:

- The marketplace has changed for all companies. The Internet has dramatically raised customer expectations, but it hasn't changed the basic business rule that in order to be successful you have to run a profitable business. Competitive pressure on product and service uniqueness and cost has made commodities of many products, so it is even more difficult to be profitable.
- Customer loyalty (preferring to buy from us over competitors) is a key differentiator for companies, no matter which value discipline (product superiority, customer intimacy, or operational excellence) they focus on. Because of the ease with which customers can now get information and compare products, the level of acceptable performance in the other disciplines has been raised for everyone.
- CRM on and off the Internet is the discipline aimed at building customer loyalty. It combines information, process, technology and people to build strong relationships with customers.
- CRM is not just buying a piece of software to automate some of your current processes and then plugging it in. If it were that easy, more companies would have had CRM success already.

Now we will prepare for a successful outcome of our CRM program. CRM is no silver bullet. CRM program success is achieved by completing small, focused projects that add up to a big victory over the long run. We have been and will continue to use the terms *CRM program* and *CRM project* throughout the book. They are not interchangeable. Let's start by clarifying CRM program.

 DEFINITIONS

A *CRM program* is the sum of all the work your company does to improve the customer experience and increase loyalty. Your program can be as long or short as appropriate to your business needs.

A CRM program is made up of all the individual CRM projects. Each project will follow the same basic method. We define and use a standard method because that is the only way we can successfully tackle a program as large as CRM.

We will repeat the method steps as long as projects remain to be completed and they make sense for the organization. We'll deliver quick wins along the way to achieve visible success before the notoriously short corporate attention span wanders. Let's review the methodology steps and who is responsible for what. Both a formal method and formal responsibilities required for building a CRM program that is successful.

5.1   Understanding the Formality of CRM

Methodologies are alien to many sales reps and marketers who depend on creativity and intuition. They often achieve success through their own inspiration, intuition, and experience. Technology experts are equally creative people. They just use different instincts, tools, and experience in their drive to build the most original and elegant solution to a problem. It is very important to recognize that while the business functions and Information Technology must work together to build a successful CRM program, they have such different backgrounds that they have a hard time even understanding each other. Methodologies and defined roles are the bridge between various perspectives.

5.1.1   Methodology

Because CRM covers so much territory, we must tackle it a step at a time. A method that starts with an overall strategy and uses past results to deliver integrated capabilities on subsequent projects ensures that we continue to move toward our end objective. The only way to ensure successful integration of all these projects is to follow a well-defined method. Methodologies also allow us to learn from previous experience and to get better and faster at what we do. This is another very important consideration in delivering CRM programs. Figure 5-1 shows the entire methodology that is necessary to ensure delivery of a CRM program that achieves your business goals.

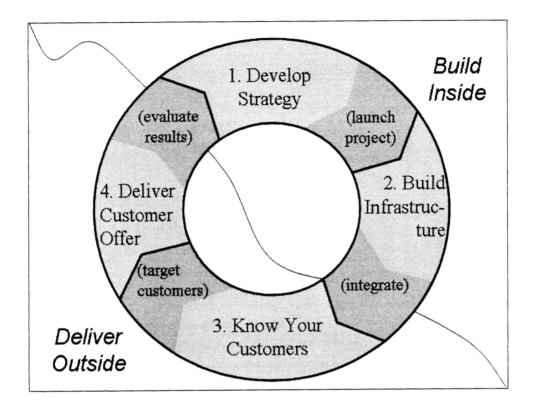

Figure 5-1 The CRM program life cycle

There are four phases in the CRM life cycle with four well-defined transition steps connecting them. Just like all other disciplines, planning is everything in CRM. The first phase begins by creating a vision and a strategy so that you know what you want to achieve. The process also helps you understand your business, your priorities, and your competitive position so you can pick the best place to begin. The second phase is to create the supporting infrastructure, remembering that CRM is more than just technology. After you have done the necessary work internally, it is time to take the new capability or new campaign to your customers. In Phase 3, you will identify the specific customers to include in the new capability; in Phase 4, you will actually deliver the benefit to these targeted customers.

The life cycle is shown as a circle specifically because this method is not linear. The steps are repeated until you have achieved the level of CRM implementation that is appropriate to meet your company's needs. At the end of the first project, you will evaluate your results and reassess your strategy based on those results, and then begin planning for the next highest priority project.

By the way, if you already have a methodology that works, is well understood, and is widely used within your company, use it. Just check to be sure that it covers all the elements in

Figure 5-1. If not, add them to your existing process. The most important point is that you use a defined methodology.

5.1.2   Define Responsibilities

Although methodology may be a foreign concept to many of those most closely involved, we must use standard, repeatable methods in order to achieve success. Another huge benefit from following a process is that it helps the key participants understand what needs to be done and who is responsible for what. For all the parts of the organization to be aligned and working together throughout the life of the program, we must develop a formal structure and set of rules that help everyone understand their responsibilities in the overall CRM program.

 KEY IDEA

> The business function is responsible for defining the business requirement, and the IT department is responsible for specifying the technical solution.

It just doesn't work the other way around. It is useless for Information Technology to try to define the business objective; they haven't been doing that job. It is equally ridiculous for business to come to the IT department requesting a solution, as if to say, "We need a sales rep automation tool." After the business function has identified its needs, let the IT professionals identify alternatives and present you with alternatives (including pros and cons) to consider. Figure 5-2 shows the different phases of the CRM program life cycle and who is primarily responsible for each.

We are going to spend most of our time on the two internal phases of the methodology because those companies rushing to grab hold of the CRM golden ring so often ignore strategy and infrastructure development. Many companies just jump right into a project such as building "personalized" web sites or running a "one-to-one" campaign without knowing what they hope to achieve or having the infrastructure to accurately target customers, measure results, or refine and repeat the effort.

By focusing on the internal planning and implementation, we prepare the foundation on which effective CRM capabilities are delivered to customers.

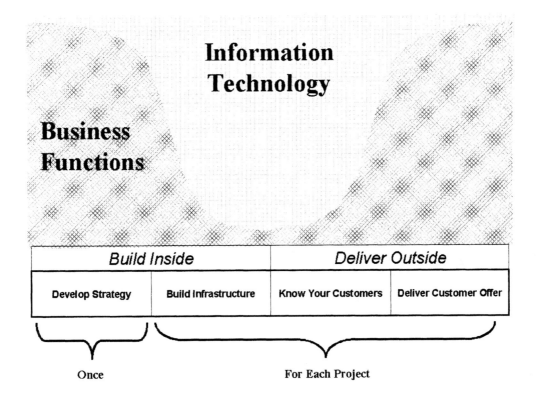

Figure 5-2 Program life cycle responsibilities

5.2 Developing Your CRM Strategy

The first major step in building a successful CRM program is Phase 1:

PHASE 1—DEVELOP A STRATEGY

There is no clearer early indicator of failure than starting (or maybe worse—finishing!) a CRM project without knowing where you are heading. This is the number one reason that CRM projects do not succeed. The no-plans approach usually results from the "quick-fix" or "silver bullet" mentality that is so common. Remember, it doesn't work that way—not for anybody—no matter what anyone promises you.

A strategic plan allows you to take the small steps that are more likely to be successful, while ensuring that each one takes you in the direction of your ultimate goal. Like sailing, we may have to tack in one direction or another, not always directly toward port. But at least we know we're continuing to sail in the right direction and not steering a course that is taking us away from where we want to be. This plan is like a civil engineer's design for a railroad. Unless we have a plan, we're going to end up like the two characters in Figure 5-3, and our customers will be just as sorry as the first engineer who tries to drive a train down this track!

Figure 5-3 Here's what happens without a strategy.

This is exactly the result if different parts of your organization begin independent CRM projects one piece at a time without an overall strategy. Without this clear and common understanding of what you want out of your efforts, you'll end up with fragmented bits that don't fit together. Then you'll have to tear down some or all of what you built in order to deliver a truly integrated customer experience.

It is the strategic plan that, like a blueprint, allows you to implement in small, manageable chunks because it ensures that the chunks will fit together. The plan allows you to identify what's most important, get started, have a success, and benefit from what you have already built while continuing to add functionality another chunk at a time. CRM is using processes, information, people, and technology to manage and improve relationships with your customers. There is no predetermined "right" set of chunks that you must build.

Another important outcome from your strategic planning effort is getting widespread participation, input, visibility, understanding, and support for both the long-term strategy and immediate priorities. Every functional area has different needs and priorities. If the stakeholders know the reasons why their requirements aren't the first to be addressed and when their requirements are scheduled to occur, they will be more supportive of your entire plan. Of course, visible progress is also necessary, or all the underground projects will certainly start up again. This is the reason we will undertake small projects leading to quick successes, and why we must make our progress visible through continuous communication.

Some organizations shy away from strategic planning because they think it will slow things down. They just want to get started. Yes, it does take time and effort. But if you spend too much time, you are wasting resources and probably getting stuck in *analysis paralysis*. The purpose of a strategic plan is to develop a fairly high-level view of your goals and objectives that lets you get started quickly but with a commonly understood goal in mind. The benefits far outweigh the time invested.

KEY IDEA

Even for the largest companies, the strategic planning methodology should never take more than a few months. With good tools, a good methodology, good participation, and good support, it should take no more than six to eight weeks.

The strategy and planning phase of the CRM life cycle encompasses surveys of key internal and external stakeholders. It produces a set of documents much like architectural blueprints.

5.2.1 Process Steps

As always, we must start with an understanding of the company's current business situation. No CRM effort can ever be successful if it is not aligned with your company's top strategies and priorities. Also, be sure to look outside the organization. Understanding customer expectations and your relative position against your competitors is critical. Why would you tackle an area in which you're already as good as or better than your competition, and your customers don't care very much anyway? Table 5-1 shows the main steps for the strategic planning phase.

Table 5-1 The Strategic Planning Process

Step	Purpose	Participants
Collect Data	• Ensure that the CRM program is aligned with company strategy. • Discover what customers think about your current performance. What do they want more of? What makes it difficult to do business with you? How do you compare to competitors? • Understand all the customer project and functional silos that currently exist.	Company Executives and Sales, Marketing, Service, and Support management Employees who interact directly with customers Customers
Assess Findings	• Identify business strategies, risks, and opportunities that will influence your CRM program. • Identify gaps between the goal and today's reality. • Define high-level customer segments.	Project team Impacted business function representatives Information Technology

Table 5-1 The Strategic Planning Process (Continued)

Step	Purpose	Participants
Create a Proposal	• Define a common vision and language about what CRM is for your company. • Ensure that key constituents understand and support the strategy.	Project team Sign-off from sponsor, key executives, and business managers
Transition: Launch Project	• Select the best project to tackle first (or next). • Determine scope, schedule, and resources.	Project team Sign-off from sponsor, key executives, and business managers

We also need to get an idea of what CRM efforts are already going on in the various CRM functions. What are the official and unofficial projects already underway to support sales, marketing, customer service, and product support organizations? Finding this out is critical because money is often limited and must be focused on the organization's key priorities. But it can be a political nightmare because many people fear that their pet project will be taken over or canceled. In fact, this may happen for many good reasons. In Chapter 8, we will discuss ways to get this information without causing projects to go deeper underground; at that time, we will also cover the strategic planning phase in detail.

5.2.2   What You'll Get

At the end of Phase 1, you will have completed the strategic plan as the blueprint for building your project. You will have defined a high-level view of the information, process, technology, and people requirements of your program. You will know how the overall program will be organized and supported, and you will have determined a consistent view of your CRM vision as well as a language to describe it that everyone understands. You will also have identified the priorities that will determine which projects to do next, the timing of future projects, and the risks you face so you can prepare for them. Time and again throughout each project life cycle, you will need to refer to these key documents.

At the end of each project, you will start the next cycle by evaluating the current blueprints, which allows you to enhance and refine them based on what you've accomplished, what's changed for your business, and what you've learned.

5.2.3   Transition: Launch Project

In Phase 1, we take a high-level look at the overall organization, marketplace, and technology situation and identify the project with which we'll begin. In the transition step to Phase 2, we focus on one small area—that business problem, issue, or opportunity that is most important to address first. Because the CRM program sounds so big and broad, we will be looking at ways to identify and prioritize small chunks that can yield quick success and build on each other to deliver your overall goal. These projects will:

- Be completed in a matter of months (before anyone can lose interest)
- Move the organization toward the desired goal (not in the wrong direction)
- Yield a visible and measurable result (which must be communicated widely)
- Build on previous success (show continuous progress and avoid rework)

We defined CRM program earlier; now let's understand what we mean by CRM project.

 DEFINITIONS

A CRM project is a well-defined effort with specific deliverables, due dates, and cost. To ensure success, a project must produce valuable and measurable results, but it must also be small enough to complete within a business sponsor's attention span.

We are about to launch our first project. The business functions that own or are affected by the project are the primary participants and contributors, but it's important for Information Technology to be involved also. When the IT department participates in the launch, they learn lots of information that will enable them to understand what really needs to be done to deliver a successful project.

Now, we will dig into much greater detail than we did during Phase 1. We must really understand exactly what the business problem is that we are solving and what the real business needs are, identify specific risks and critical success factors, and so on. This is the reason we can afford to spend just a short time getting a rough idea of our end goal during the strategy phase (thus, completing it quicker). We delve into much more detail as we plan and launch the project. Completing agonizingly detailed studies of all your possible CRM requirements as part of the strategic plan is really a waste of time. So much of the detailed requirements would change by the time you got to them that you would have to do it all again anyway. Worse yet, it's likely to keep you from ever getting started doing the real work. So we move to the infrastructure development phase by digging deeply into the true business needs and defining the project scope, time line, and resources.

5.3 Building a CRM Component

CRM is neither a silver bullet nor a magic wand. It takes careful planning and management to be in a position to successfully.

PHASE 2—BUILD THE INFRASTRUCTURE

Many quick-fix specialists believe that you can just "do CRM"! Just get Information Technology to build a web site personalization capability. Forget that you don't have any customer knowledge to decide what to do for whom. Part 3 of this book is devoted to understanding in detail what it takes to develop the infrastructure that is a required to enable an integrated and successful CRM program. Here, we will just review the method.

5.3.1 Process Steps

The development process steps will be used to manage efforts in each of the components of the infrastructure (process, information, people, and technology). All infrastructure development projects follow the same basic and well-understood method.

- Launch
- Analysis
- Design
- Construct/Test
- Implement

As we just saw, the project launch is the transition from CRM lifecycle phases 1 when we determined the business need and developed the project plan. The focus of Phase 2 is the analysis, design and construction of all the infrastructure elements required to meet the project objective. Implementation (integration) occurs during the transition to Phase 3. These steps, which describe the "waterfall" method of software development but can be applied to all components, are described in Table 5-2.

Table 5-2   Building Infrastructure Steps

Step	Purpose	Participants
Gather and analyze requirements	Identify business needs for information, process, technology and people Analyze and compare to existing infrastructure	Project Team Business function experts
Design component	Develop a detailed design	Business function experts Information Technology
Construct solution	Code and test information and technology solutions	Information Technology
	Develop process and people change solutions	Business function experts
Transition: Integrate Capability	Information Integration (consistency) Process Integration (continuity) Technology Integration (compatibility) People Integration (congruity)	Information Technology Business Function

We use this same waterfall method for each of the small projects we launch, learning from previous results as we start the next project. Barry Boehm, a professor at the University of Southern California's Center for Software Engineering, named this evolutionary development approach the *spiral model* in his 1986 paper "A Spiral Model of Software Development and Enhancement," as shown in Figure 5-4.

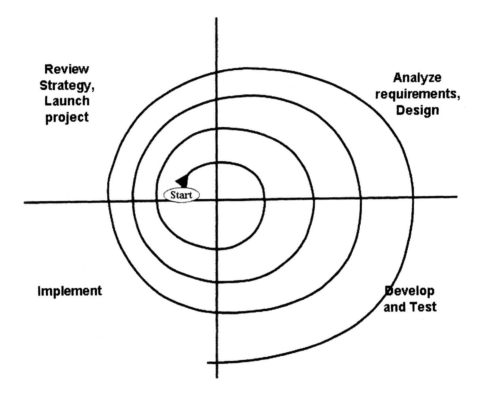

Figure 5-4   The Spiral Development Model

We will discuss this phase in more detail for each piece of the infrastructure so that we understand exactly what we need to get done.

5.3.2   What You'll Get

Not surprisingly, the major deliverable of this phase is the infrastructure itself, one piece at a time, of course. At the end of Phase 2, we are likely to have new or modified processes, improved customer information, additional technical tools, and the training, education, metrics, and rewards necessary to ensure that the new capabilities are adopted throughout the organization.

As soon as we have delivered the first piece of infrastructure, we also need to be prepared to manage the new capabilities. In particular, customer information is extremely volatile, and it is virtually worthless if the quality deteriorates without check. We will take a very detailed look at what is required to manage customer information quality in Chapter 20.

5.3.3   Transition: Integrate Capability

In the transition to Phase 3, we do the actual work of pulling relevant information together, merging new processes into existing workflows, etc. Unless we actually follow through on our strategy of integration, we will remain in disconnected operational silos that have no impact on our ability to improve the customer experience.

Sadly, because legacy customer data has generally been so poorly managed, this is the area that can take the most work and yet is so often overlooked. You may be thinking, "it's just names and addresses, so how hard can it be?" I am amazed at the number of companies that spend lots of money building a complex and expensive customer analysis capability that it then applies to lousy data. The only result is the companies' ability to make bad decisions more quickly!

It's time to take our efforts outside. We have completed all the necessary internal effort (information, process, technology and people change management) and are ready to give our customers the benefit of all our hard work.

5.4   Analyzing and Segmenting Customers

Whatever project you have chosen to work on, it's time to specifically identify the customer or group of customers for whom the result is intended.

PHASE 3—KNOW YOUR CUSTOMERS

If you've established web-based support to provide customer assistance and replace expensive call centers, you may want to target the effort at lower-value customers as you roll it out and refine it. On the other hand, if the new capability is expensive to build and roll out, like a detailed tool for a customer to view and manage all of his orders, you may want to start with the most valuable customers. But how do you know who they are?

5.4.1   Analyze Customers: Steps

You don't begin a project without any idea of who the target audience is. You might have even selected a few representative individual customers for interviews or focus groups. The steps shown in Table 5-3 will help you determine what other customers match the criteria you've identified.

Table 5-3 Assess Customer: Steps

Step	Purpose	Participants
Getting Down and Dirty with the Data	Determine customer profiling and scoring model Optimize profile coverage	Product Team Database Marketing Team Customer Information Management Team
Segmenting Customers	Define most predictive segmentation strategy Create Groups of customers "like one"	Product Team Database Marketing Team
Transition: Selecting Target Segments	Select customers profile values most likely to deliver the best response to the project offer. Identify specific customers who match that profile	Business Team Database Marketing Team

All customers are not alike, and CRM does not suggest they be treated all the same. CRM requires that all customers be treated appropriately to their needs and their value to the company. In Chapter 17, we will cover more of what's required to target customer segments.

5.4.2   What You'll Get

When finished with the customer analysis phase, you will have identified the types of customers who should be targeted to receive the new offer. You may also have identified some additional customer information sources that will improve your ability to send your offer to the right customers.

5.4.3   Transition: Select Target Segments

As a result of this transition, you will have identified the actual customers who fit the profile you intended this project to benefit. Depending on the offer medium, this list can be made up of mailing labels, e-mail addresses, phone numbers, or simply a list of companies you intend to sign up for a new capability.

5.5   Taking It to Your Customers

It is now time to take your program outside and deliver it to the customers you've targeted.

PHASE 4—DELIVER THE OFFER TO THE CUSTOMER

For the target customer audience, register them for personal web sites, offer information and access about your new online support capability, or run a one-to-one campaign.

5.5.1   The Process to Take It to Your Customers

Use everything that you've developed for this project (information, process, technology and people) to deliver a successful offer. The steps to get the offer out the door and into the arms of your customers are outlined in Table 5-4.

Table 5-4 Deliver Customer Offer: Steps

Step	Purpose	Participants
Design the offer	Maximize offer return on investment Optimize expected responses	Business Offer Sponsor and/or manager
Prepare the offer message(s)	Develop message that matches each segment value proposition Prepare to measure results	Depends on offer: Project team Business Offer Sponsor IT Department
Present the offer	Install new capability, and train customer to use it; release marketing communication Minimize cost of offer delivery	Depends on offer: Project team Business Offer Sponsor IT Department
Transition: Measure Results	Evaluate performance metrics Evaluate value metrics	Project Team

We will take a closer look at segmentation in Chapter 17 and delivering the offer to customers in Chapter 18. We'll learn about the tools that support these efforts and introduce several resources referencing some of the excellent work that has been done on analyzing customer information, segmenting and valuing customers, and delivering personalized customer experiences on and off the web.

5.5.2   What You'll Get

This is where you should really see the result of your efforts in terms of increased loyalty and business benefit. Measuring results is critical (another way to keep support for the project). I hope you defined the expected customer result at the beginning of the project. If there was no planned customer benefit, then (dare I say it again) it's not CRM! Sales rep productivity is a fine objective, but if it's not aimed at benefiting the customer, it's not CRM.

5.5.3   Transition: Evaluate Results

Along with measuring the performance impact of your changes on customer relationship and business results, you must assess changes to strategy or customer expectations as a result of this project. A key element of the success of your overall CRM program depends on learning from what has gone before and using all the experience and information you've gained to refine your methods going forward. This will feed back into the beginning of the methodology, where you will revisit your strategy and priorities, and test that there are no major changes resulting from the overall business direction or your previous efforts. Then you will begin the process again. Obviously, you won't spend another four to six weeks in the strategy-setting phase, but it's important to review where you thought you were headed and make any adjustments that are necessary.

5.6   Getting Ready for the Next Project

As we've discussed, the benefit that all companies get from using this method is that it can be repeated. Your project team will do these same steps over and over until your company's specific CRM needs and objectives are met. The world will not suddenly recognize that you have "done CRM." Instead, you will repeat these steps as long as the value of adding a new CRM capability outweighs the cost of the additional effort. At every step along the way, you will show benefit and value, and you will be aware of where you are going next.

As you begin the cycle again, that's the time to decide whether you have done enough. You don't have to implement every possible CRM capability. You should work only on the pieces that are most important to your business situation. There is no ideal CRM state that we should all be striving to reach.

Just as there is no perfect CRM state, there is no ideal size of a program or project. For a small company with few people to involve, it may take no more than a week to pull together a plan: You may need only a few days to complete internal interviews and talk to a couple of customers, and another day or two to summarize the results into a plan. Table 5-5 provides a gauge that will help you judge the size of your effort for each project phase. I've used number of employees to estimate size and complexity. A large, global company will need more time to gather information to build its strategy and to deliver results. Another factor to consider is the size and complexity of your customer base. Note that for all size companies, a project should be scoped small enough to be developed in six months or less. This probably will mean that a large company must bite off smaller chunks to be successful.

Table 5-5   Estimated Project Duration Target

Number of Employees	Strategy	Develop	Analyze/Target	Deliver
< 100	1 week	3-6 months	1 week	1 week
> 10,000	8 weeks	4-6 months	4 weeks	4 weeks

Following these guidelines, no individual project should be undertaken that is more than nine months from strategy setting to customer delivery. Answer the questions at the end of the chapter, and find where you fit on the continuum.

Now that we've learned the basic steps of the methodology, we will go on to Chapter 6 and learn how to overcome some of the most common barriers to CRM success.

Questions for Reflection

These questions will help you set realistic expectations for the length of each CRM projects. Based on your answers to Questions 1 and 2, plot your company's position on the chart shown in Figure 5-3. What size is your company: number of employees, locations, countries where located?

1. How complex is your customer base in terms of number of individuals, companies; type of customers (consumer, B2B); number of industries engaged in?
2. What is your position on the following chart? You should limit the scope of each project such that you believe the entire project can be finished in no more than this amount of time.

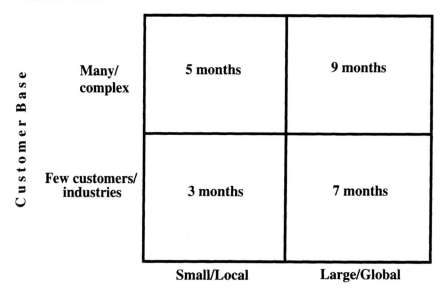

This chart gives you a rough idea of the maximum length of time that you should target for each of your company's CRM projects.

CHAPTER 6

Get Ready: Avoiding Common Barriers

Now that we understand the basic methodology we will follow, we need to understand the critical CRM barriers that can prevent success. Of course, every company has specific potential barriers within its culture and organization, which you will discover during the strategy phase we'll tackle in Chapter 8. But there are several universal barriers to success, like organizational silos, that almost all companies run into in one way or another. We'll take at look at these common barriers and discuss ways to prepare to reduce or remove them.

Figure 6-1 shows the three most common barriers:

- **Expectations:** Many companies fall victim to unrealistic expectations; they are looking for a silver bullet to fix customer relationships.
- **Culture:** Product-centered cultures discourage support and funding for customer-centered programs.
- **Operational Infrastructure:** Most customer-facing systems (order administration, call center support) automate a single process and do not integrate across all functions.

Let's look at these barriers more closely and consider some of the ways we can eliminate them or at least reduce their impact.

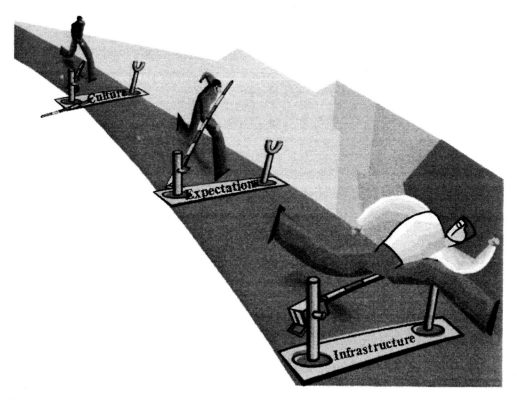

Figure 6-1 Common barriers to CRM success

6.1 Creating a CRM Culture

Many companies have cultures that don't support CRM. Entrepreneurial-style companies usually promote a high degree of organizational independence (read "separate silos"). Product-centered cultures virtually ignore customers and make decisions based on what they have bought
instead of who they are. These cultures create difficulties for building cross-organizational and
customer-centered programs like CRM. Changing the whole culture of an organization is far
beyond the scope of a CRM program. But we can hope to change some behaviors through training and education and by creating new metrics and rewards.

6.1.1 Change Management

Hey, change happens! We all understand that we have to adapt to change or we'll end up in
the same gas tank as the dinosaurs. While examining management challenges for the new mil-
lennium, Peter F. Drucker said,

> We do not hear much anymore about overcoming resistance to change, which 10 or 15 years
> ago was one of the most popular topics of management books and management seminars.
> Everybody has accepted by now that change is unavoidable. But that still implies that change
> is like death and taxes—it should be postponed as long as possible.

That's just the problem. Many companies are doing quite well to recognize change when it happens; they cannot anticipate and prepare for it. Change can't just be left to happen, because people must make the change, and many are generally resistant, even fearful, of the unknown. Without support and encouragement, the cultural and behavioral changes that will make or break your CRM program success will not happen. Drucker suggests that managing change doesn't guaranteed success. But ignoring the need to manage change guarantees failure. If your organization refuses to pay attention to the basics of change management, you have little chance of delivering a successful CRM program.

For those companies, like yours, who have recognized the need for changing your relationships with your customers, change management is key to changing culture and behavior. But few companies have the in-house expertise to manage change to a successful outcome. Change management is another area in which a consulting organization may play a big role.

When management wants to know how other companies have approached CRM, a consultant can bring external perspective and broad experience. A consultant can help you get the attention of top management because they're being paid so much more than you are. Consultants also bring an outside perspective that can be help keep the program externally focused, skill sets you don't have time to develop for yourself, and processes and tools that support your success. We will learn more about change management in Chapter 14.

6.1.2   Metrics and Rewards

You get the behavior you reward. No exceptions! Years ago, psychologist B.F. Skinner and his rats introduced us to this concept of behaviorism. Whether or not you like some of the implications of Skinner's approach, it is how animals (including humans) learn to change. If you want your employees to adopt new customer-focused goals and consistently deliver excellent customer experiences (the behavior), you have to have a way to recognize the new behavior and reward it when it happens. Here's an example:

> Straight commission rewards selling specific products. We want our sales reps to focus on
> understanding the customer's situation and to offer solutions that solve their problems,
> whether or not every piece of the solution earns commission. Sales reps aren't in this for the
> karma; we need to be able to measure this behavior (customer satisfaction with solution) and
> reward it (some percentage of the total value of the solution).

When you track the customer experience and measure loyalty (along with the normal financial measures, of course) you can use the information to build reward systems that will create an organizational culture that is better prepared for CRM. Measuring individual efforts to improve the customer experience and rewarding it will have a big impact.

Think of the service at a Ritz Carleton Hotel. Any request for anything (even the time of day) is responded to with a smile and the words, "My pleasure." Employees are trained to respond to guests in this way; their performance is measured and so is the resulting customer experience and loyalty. It may sound hokey, but even though we know it's almost a gimmick, it feels great. Guests report that they do feel welcome and honored and that the employees treat them as if it's a pleasure to assist them. What an incredible difference a small behavior change like this might make for the customers calling your support line!

6.1.3 Sponsorship

We know that unless we have the critical support of the executive sponsor, we have virtually no buffer between our program and the unexpected roadblocks that always occur. We're going to learn about how to find and "manage" a sponsor in Chapter 7. Here, we just want to emphasize how important a sponsor is to leading you past the cultural barriers that you run into. First, you need an executive sponsor who understands and believes in what CRM can do for your company. It's even better if the sponsor is the person who initiated CRM in the company. Second, your sponsor must carry enough clout to influence other parts of the organization through leadership and example.

 KEY IDEA

The closer your sponsor is to the top of the company, the better his or her ability to influence executive understanding and support. Even more critical, your sponsor will actually have the clout to remove cross-functional obstacles.

In small companies, the CEO or one of his direct reports may be playing the CRM sponsor role and will actively participate in the program steering committee. In larger organizations, if the sponsor is high enough to have the influence you need, it's unlikely that he or she will actually play any active role in the program. Still, it's essential that you actually have some direct time together, or you really don't have sponsorship.

6.2 Creating Realistic Expectations

With apologies to J.K. Rowling, there is no sorcerer's stone! No CRM software comes equipped with magic wands. Figure 6-2 is a reminder that there is no magic that will turn our customers into the loyal and profitable ones. That takes planning, time, and focused effort.

If your company and your team members are looking for a miracle, they're going to be disappointed; there's absolutely no way around it. No matter how much you do or how well you meet your project goals, if people expect something different, they'll consider the program a failure. Because there are so many voices making unrealistic promises in the marketplace, it's no

Figure 6-2 There is no CRM sorcerer's stone.

wonder that expectations are high. It's sort of like the latest diet fad that everyone jumps on. No one really wants to hear that losing weight means cutting calories and increasing exercise. There is no magic pill for CRM either. It takes work, and it takes time. *But it can be done.*

You can successfully lose weight as long as you don't expect to lose 50 pounds the first week; you can succeed at CRM, too, if you set realistic expectations over time. You might be asking yourself how you'll ever get your organization to have patience and be satisfied with only a pound or two per week. Most companies are set up to value immediate results, not long-term ones. That's why we'll be concentrating on quick wins to keep progress visible, with a plan that delivers the total program in the long run. In Chapter 8, as part of our strategic plan, we will develop a roadmap. The roadmap is a high-level plan with specific projects that we plan to deliver based on our CRM goals and priorities.

A large part of the strategic planning effort is aimed at developing realistic and well-understood expectations because they are so important. As part of the strategic plan, you will develop a common vision, shared goals, and realistic expectations across the organization. Although you will undoubtedly uncover some breakthrough ideas on what CRM can do for your company, the most important outcome from the internal interviews, meetings, and communication that occur during the planning phase is to build this consistency of vision and expectation.

You already know what needs to be done, don't you? If you didn't have any idea, you wouldn't have picked up this book in the first place. The vision and roadmap will help you communicate your vision throughout the organization.

6.2.1   Vision and Roadmap

There are several tools that will help you to set realistic expectations. You need a vision of where you want to be--objective means for setting priorities about which steps along the path to take first and a roadmap of when you'll get to these steps.

A vision should paint a picture that clearly illustrates where you want your CRM program to end up. What will your company look like to your customers when you have achieved your vision? Having a clear vision firmly planted in everyone's mind helps keep the organization focused. It enables you to take small steps that will steer your company toward its goal. Objective priorities take lots of the emotion out of various decisions and help different groups understand reality. A roadmap allows you to stage development and give everyone a realistic plan about when different projects will be completed. We will learn how to use these tools in Chapter 8.

6.2.2   Internal Communications

The second weapon we have for managing expectations is communication, and I don't just mean putting together a summary of your strategic plan and e-mailing it to everyone in the company. CRM impacts so much of the organization that it is essential to get this initial information out, but that's only the beginning.

Ongoing communication throughout the life of the program is imperative. One lesson that many of us (okay, me at least) continue to learn over and over is that you cannot repeat key messages too often. Get over the idea that after you've published the plan and objectives, you can stop worrying and get down to the real work. No! Each time you repeat your message, new people will start to get it, and those who got it before will be reassured of the continued direction.

Another important reason for continuous communication is that almost all project plans change during the life of the project. Keep everyone informed about these changes—what they are and why they are necessary. If people aren't aware how and why the target has shifted, they will not consider the project a success.

Communication is critically important to any major change initiative, but many of us have little communication experience or are too busy working to have time to communicate. CRM is a particularly sensitive area because vendors have been so grandiose in their promises to deliver a fully operational sorcerer's stone. The technology is important, but it actually is the easiest part. The most critical and most difficult element of the CRM infrastructure is changing people's behavior so that they use the new processes, information, and tools to improve the customer experience. Use your internal communications to start the education and change-management process.

To do all this, you must have an employee communications program outlining your internal communications goals and strategies. The goal of such a program is to elicit very specific changes in behavior from employees. The success of your CRM program depends on sending clear and precise messages outlining the expected changes. Warren Egnal, Vice President at Porter Novelli Convergence Group, which assists client companies with their internal and external communications, says, "Motivating change is the critical driver, for without new behaviors, real change is impossible and reorganizing, reinventing, or re-branding simply becomes a new way of doing old things, rather than doing things differently." Warren uses a five-step program to effectively reach employees with messages critical to organizational success:

- **Inform:** Build awareness.
- **Educate:** Set expectations and offer information/guidance/training to reach success.
- **Motivate:** Recognize behavior, and reward and publicize achievements.
- **Enable:** Provide tools needed to succeed.
- **Respond:** Incorporate interactive response to listen and adjust the program.

This process is not simple to do, and it's one that many companies have ignored because they are so ill-equipped to manage it. But it is critical to the success of your program, so if you don't have the experience or time you need, this is one area in which it's a good idea to get some help. No one has to be great at everything!

Not only must you be sure to set realistic expectations, but you also must **keep** expectations realistic. This is done by frequent communication of the project status. By the way, this means honest communication, not spin! Tell it like it is. Report issues and slowdowns, but don't dwell on them. Talk about how you plan to address the issues. Keep communications short, to the point, and clear. If the rumor mill reports a story that doesn't match your project communications, your employees will quickly lose all confidence in the project and your credibility will suffer as well. Sadly, like the emperor in Figure 6-3, after your program gets the reputation of "having no clothes," you may not be able to regain confidence, even if you can recover and get back on track.

Use every means possible for communicating: company newsletters and magazines, e-mail, bulletin boards, coffee talks, whatever. If you have an employee portal, make sure that you have a CRM page, and keep it up to date and interesting.

6.2.3   Customer Communications

Of course, our CRM program will impact and make changes for our customers as well. Even though these changes are for the better, it is still important to have a plan for bringing about changed behavior for customers. We will address customer communication in Chapter 18 when we take our offer to the customer.

Figure 6-3 The emperor's new clothes

6.3   Building an Operational Infrastructure

The operational infrastructure within most companies was developed to support and/or automate a specific business function. Because companies grew up in functional silos, they developed their computer systems and other infrastructure along the same functional lines. There exists little ability to connect information or processes across these silos.

A key to real CRM success (i.e., making life better for your customer, not just implementing a CRM capability) is that customers expect seamless integration across all your company's touch points. It's really not rocket science. Who wants to have one customer identification number while talking to the call center, and a different customer ID for logging on to the Internet? Who wants to be treated like a top customer when you make an airline reservation, but treated like a dog when you were too late to get an upgrade so you have to sit in the back of the plane? Nobody! In Part 3 of this book, we will examine specific methods of integrating pieces of the infrastructure across the entire organization.

Each of these common barriers is manageable. There are no quick fixes, but with planning and organized effort, these barriers can be overcome. Now that we've talked about how to minimize these three barriers, let's look at how to overcome our organizational silos and gaps. We will learn in Chapter 7 what it takes to set up a CRM organization that has the best chance of driving success.

Questions for Reflection

For the three barriers listed, what is your company's current situation and what actions could you take to address any issues you have identified?

1. Is the culture product or customer centered?
2. Does management have realistic expectations or are they counting on computer magic?
3. Is your company's infrastructure well integrated and cohesive or fragmented and disconnected?

CHAPTER 7

Get Set: Organizing for Success

W e've just learned how to deal with the most common barriers to CRM success. Now we will look at the gap created by organizational silos. We need to learn to work together across functions and organizations to bridge this gap so we can deliver CRM results. We need to answer these questions:

- **Organization:** What parts of the organization need to be involved, and how?
- **Sponsorship:** How do we find a sponsor and keep him/her engaged?
- **Leadership:** How do we govern a program that crosses so many independent functions?
- **Partnership:** How do we strengthen relationships and build partnerships between functions and between the business team and IT?

Unless your CRM program includes all the organizations that face customers, their experience will not be integrated. If it's not cross-functional, it's not CRM. If you just want to implement sales rep automation, you may not need to involve other functions. But the most that you'll get is sales representatives who are a little more organized and productive. It doesn't become CRM until it starts to affect the customer experience and until the sales reps can actually do a better job because they have more knowledge and understanding of the customer's total experience than ever before.

7.1 Defining the Organizational Scope

In Chapter 3, we defined CRM as the strategic use of information, processes, technology and people to manage the customer's relationship with your company (marketing, sales, service, and support) across the whole customer life cycle. Each of these functions has a traditional role in the organization, but the introduction of CRM into the organization means that each function must take on additional responsibilities. Table 7-1 shows the new CRM role of each of the CRM business functions and IT.

Table 7-1 New Organizational Roles

	Traditional Role	New CRM Role
Marketing	Communication and branding	Customer advocate
Sales	Selling products	Selling customer solutions
Service	Delivering services	Delivering customer partnership
Support	Supporting products	Supporting customers
IT Department	Enabling business activities	Enabling customer activities

Information Technology has a key role to play. The partnership between Information Technology and the business functions is critical to CRM success. We will discuss some of the methods for ensuring effective communication between business and IT team members later in this chapter. We will learn more about the specific roles that each function must play in delivering a successful CRM program.

These five functions make up the core of your CRM Team. Of course, many small companies don't have all these individual functions within their organization; still, all of these roles must be filled. Whether or not your company actually has a department called Marketing, you must have someone who manages your company's customer communications for consistency, brand image, etc. These are the people who are concerned with the customer experience. The role of experience enabler (Customer Advocate) will be filled by one of these individuals. You may not have an in-house IT organization. If you don't plan to develop that function internally, you will need to find someone to provide those services (such as an IT consulting organization).

7.1.1   The Marketing Department's Role in CRM

Traditionally, the Marketing Department has been responsible for communications and branding. Brand management makes a promise to customers, and customer satisfaction and brand equity measure how well the company meets its promise. Marketing has long been concerned with influencing and measuring customer awareness and satisfaction, and Marketing is the organization that should lead (but not own) your CRM program. As we discussed earlier, when everyone is responsible for a program, no one is really accountable. CRM needs a champion.

KEY IDEA

As a customer advocate, Marketing is responsible for leading the overall CRM program and keeping it focused on the customer.

Marketing's role as customer advocate doesn't mean owning all the customer interactions; rather, it means that Marketing is responsible for managing and monitoring the overall plan that governs how the various touch points work together to influence the total customer experience. For all significant organizational efforts, there must be a focal point for encouraging the team and leading the charge. In today's new world, the Marketing organization must step up to the plate and take the leadership for CRM. But this has several implications for the marketing community:

1. CRM has a significant technology component. It really is no longer acceptable for marketers to be technophobes. They certainly needn't learn to write computer code, but they will need a general understanding of what kinds of things computers are good for, what tools are available and how well they fit the business needs, and what pieces are most important or most broken (and should be addressed first).
2. CRM requires a shift in marketing resource allocation. Industry averages show that the percentage of marketing budgets spent on CRM has more than doubled in the first few years of adoption. Now at about 12 percent of budget, companies are faced with even more tough decisions about the types of investments that will produce the best returns.
3. Marketing must both spearhead the effort and model the behavior of being customer-centric. One way that Marketing can demonstrate customer focus is to initiate efforts to measure profit by *customer in addition* to the company's current performance metrics.

7.1.2   The Sales Department's Role in CRM

What do you think the role of Sales is in CRM? It's selling, of course. Selling is and always will be the primary role of a sales rep. And yes, sales interactions are critical to building positive customer relationships. And yes again, many salespeople understand the importance of the overall customer experience in generating more sales. However, the primary reward for people in this organization is based on the amount they sell, so that selling will always be the primary focus.

The new role for Sales in CRM is still about selling. *Miracle on 34th Street* notwithstanding, we don't expect a salesperson to send customers away to the competition. We do want a sales rep who cares enough about the customer's needs to do what it takes to understand the real business issue or opportunity and to seek to provide a total solution for the customer—even if that salesperson must share the commission. We want sales teams that sell customer solutions, not just products.

KEY IDEA

As a solution seller, Sales will focus on understanding and meeting the customer's real need, even when it means sharing some commission.

Solution selling is one change that CRM brings to the sales force. Another is actually designing the sales experience about what the customer wants it to be. Saturn is a company that was founded on the concept of creating a total customer experience based on what customers have been asking for. Figure 7-1 from the Saturn web site (www.saturnpb.com) speaks for itself. The Sales organization is an integral member of the overall CRM program team.

The truth be told, most of us at Saturn didn't really set out to change the world. We set out to be honest and straightforward with customers and to pioneer a "No-Hassle, No-Haggle" sales policy. Our goals were to work together with people we like and respect, to build quality cars at a fair price and to offer excellent after-sale service.

We figured if we did that, people would want to do business with us.

It worked.

Over the years consumer research has shown repeatedly that our customers rate Saturn top in sales satisfaction.

Figure 7-1   The Saturn experience

Because of the close contacts that the salespeople have with the customers, they are a great source of knowledge about the customer. But, remembering that sales reps are measured and rewarded by how much they sell, it's not reasonable to expect them to spend lots of time entering information. A Sales Force Automation (SFA) project should be aimed at making your sales people more effective in front of the customer. This is how to enable solution selling—giving the sales rep every piece of information available to help him understand his customer's total situation. To reach this end, the project should focus more on giving the reps additional customer information and less on asking them to complete sales forecasts. So many of the SFA implementations fail because they are launched without remembering what the sales force is really there for. Of course, by giving the sales force the benefit of more knowledge about their customers, we improve their ability to sell solutions. In addition, we give them incentive to add their customer knowledge into the overall customer knowledge base.

Many sales organizations think they "own" the customer relationship and that CRM involves only the Sales Department. Sales reps certainly play a significant role in building relationships, but there are just too many points at which a customer interacts with your company for any one function to own it all. Sometimes, this "head-in-the-sand" thinking causes sales reps to think they can stay in control by not sharing any of their customer knowledge. Unfortunately, this ignores the fact that interactions are already happening elsewhere and by not joining the CRM effort, Sales cuts itself off from knowledge gained elsewhere. Also, it costs Sales the opportunity to actually be involved and influence a positive and consistent total experience for the customer.

Sales reps have the most direct and detailed knowledge about the customer's situation, wants, needs, etc. And because sales reps are the individuals who most often interact directly with customers, they have the best opportunity to leverage knowledge from other customer touch points into these interactions. Sales reps have first-hand knowledge of the customer, which can be leveraged to improve the overall customer relationship and loyalty.

7.1.3 The Customer Service Department's Role in CRM

Service organizations are often critical to delivering a customer solution instead of just selling a box. Providing services to customers may be the company's total business, or service may be an add-on to selling products. In many small service organizations, sales and service are one and the same.

As discussed in Chapter 3, Customer Service is often a profit-generating unit that must watch costs and meet financial expectations. The pressure to be profitable may push some service organizations to be extremely cost sensitive. Additional cost pressure results from the fact that service providers, unlike product providers, are almost totally driven by variable costs. The more products that are built and sold, the more you can distribute the fixed costs (such as equipment, buildings, etc.). In a Service organization, there are very few fixed costs. The more you sell, the more human resources you need to deliver the services.

To be successful, Customer Service organizations need to really understand their customer requirements. Redelivering a service costs just as much as delivering it the first time. By integrating all the information the company already has about a customer, your CRM program delivers much needed knowledge so that Service can be prepared to be a true partner with your customers. The Internet has become so pervasive that even small companies need to develop technology capabilities. Many have opted to buy this capability from a third party. Successful service providers build a partnership with their customers and recognize that success is not met because the company meets its own internal metrics, but because the customer's needs are satisfied.

KEY IDEA

As a partner with the customer, Service will measure its results based on the success of the customer's business.

Service benefits from customer information that is gained through other customer interactions, but it also generates significant customer knowledge. The customer service organization must also be fully integrated into your CRM efforts.

7.1.4   The Product Support Department's Role in CRM

The Product Support organization has traditionally been focused on resolving any product problems that occur. In the ideal world, there should be no need for a support organization: everything should be easy to set up and should work perfectly. Unfortunately, we don't live in Camelot, so we need support organizations. Product Support is usually funded as an expense to the product line; so much more attention is paid to controlling costs than to supporting customers.

Endless telephone "trees" that never give you quite the option you need (and never let you get to a live body) are a perfect example. Yes, an automated voice response system is less costly than having a person answer the call, but sometimes the customer's problem really is outside the norm. I recently had problems with my new business telephone lines, but I was traveling, so I needed an appointment outside the window of what the system allowed. After multiple attempts, I finally learned that I had to actually make an appointment (that I wouldn't be able to make) in order to talk to a person so I could change it to a date I could make. My teeth still clench remembering my frustration. I don't have much choice on my local phone service, but believe me; I have moved every feature possible to independent carriers. I'm quite sure that the amount of my business the phone company has lost *far* exceeds the savings gained by making it hard to talk to a human when I needed to.

The new role for Support in our CRM program is to support **customers** (not just products). That doesn't mean we're prevented from using the many automated, cost-saving CRM support tools that are available, but it means that they need to be implemented with the customer's needs and experience in mind. Providing an easy transition from an automated support system to a human being is one of the first steps that should be considered.

KEY IDEA

As a customer support provider, Support focuses on solving customer problems and meeting customer needs.

Support has a tremendous opportunity to influence the customer experience. It has the opportunity to turn frustrated and angry customers into loyal customers. It also has a tremendous opportunity to gain customer trust and gather information about the customer. Information gained in the support process may be the most information you can have to improve your understanding of your customers.

7.1.5   The Information Technology Department's Role in CRM

Information technology plays an absolutely critical role in your CRM program. The IT function will provide the technology and information components without which CRM cannot succeed. Whether Information Technology is part of your company or outsourced, it is critical that the whole CRM team come together to understand what needs to be done for the customer. Information Technology must be included in your CRM program team from the very start, so the IT people are vested in and understand what the business and customers require. They are part of the solution and need to be integrated into the team.

Traditionally, there have been some communication disconnects between the IT function and the business functions based largely on their different training and experience. Sometimes, they really seem to speak a different language. Recently, Information Technology has become much more tightly integrated into the rest of the organization, and IT people understand that their responsibility to support the business and solve business issues. Now we're asking the IT team to take one more step and help us understand and build the enabling infrastructure to go beyond the walls of the company and deliver exceptional customer experiences.

KEY IDEA

As a customer enabler, Information Technology is responsible for implementing the system (technology and information) tools that make it easier for customers to do business with us.

IT people are responsible for understanding the business and customers need (and not to stop asking until they really do understand). Based on their understanding, their job is to present the best solutions so the business can understand what kinds of trade-offs they are making. Table 7-2 shows the benefits to the customer and to the company that a cross-functional, customer-focused CRM effort will deliver.

Table 7-2 Benefits of New CRM Roles

	New CRM Role	**Customer Gets**	**You Get**
Marketing	Customer advocate	An internal champion	The customer's viewpoint
Sales	Sell customer solutions	A problem solved	Happier customers, increased sales
Service	Deliver customer partner-ships	An extension of their company's capabilities	Happier customers, increased sales
Support	Support customers	The help they need	Best mix of cost saving and satisfied customers
IT	Enable customer activities	Tools and processes matched to the way they do business	Technology that helps them meet customer expectations

Within our CRM program, we must do more than just tweak the role of each individual function. These five functions work together to enhance the overall customer experience. Now that we've learned how to get around the three most common barriers, as shown in Figure 7-2, it's time to face the gap created by organizational silos that are so pervasive throughout most companies.

We have a couple of weapons to help us bridge the organizational gap in a multi-functional environment like CRM. The first weapon we learned about was the overall CRM life cycle, which allows us to continuously learn from our previous efforts.

Another weapon that helps us operate across functions is the program encyclopedia we will build. It's a set of key business concepts and what they mean within our company. These will include such things as:

- What does CRM mean within this company?
- What customer segments are important to us, and how we will assign customers to them?
- What are the important elements of the customer's life cycle with our company?
- What data are most important to our business, and how do we agree on what the data mean?
- What are the business rules for managing data? Can an employee change customer data that was created by the customer or by a Sales Rep?

Figure 7-2 The organizational gap

Some of these questions will be addressed during the strategic planning phase, and some will be covered as individual projects are launched.

7.2   Bridging Organizational Gaps

We have described a highly complex organizational structure that requires significant cooperation and coordination across functions because CRM does not fit neatly under one single management structure. We need to learn how to operate efficiently in this cross-functional environment.

7.2.1   Operating across Business Functions

The key weapon for overcoming organization gaps that are the focus here is how to set up an organization and leadership structure for our program that clearly defines roles, responsibilities, and communication paths. This organizational and leadership structure is what will help you operate effectively across all the involved functions; you must build a strong platform that supports the successful interactions between your company and your customers (see Figure 7-3).

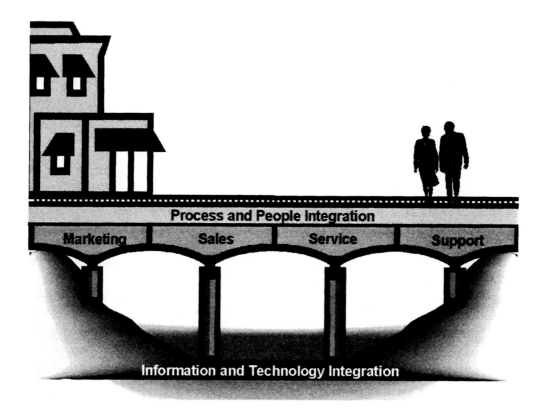

Figure 7-3 The CRM infrastructure bridging organizational silos

The knowledge and perspective of each core function will be contributed through member participation in the steering committee, program council, and project teams. The need for broad perspective and in-depth knowledge is why these teams should be comprised of respected people from within each function. It is also critical that members take ownership for communicating, gathering information, and managing compliance within their respective functional areas.

7.2.2   The Business/Information Technology Relationship

It's all about communication. The communication disconnects between business process owners and technology people are widely experienced. These two groups of people even speak a totally different language. Clear communication is critical, but so is understanding that there are two perspectives and that both are important.

For years, we've encouraged programmers to focus on the business problem and not just the wizardry of the technical solution. Most IT professionals understand this and want to solve real business problems. Otherwise, they would take jobs in labs somewhere. But these IT folks usually don't have actual experience performing the business tasks, so they need guidance from the business professionals. Good communication between business functions and IT functions has never been more important.

In Chapter 5, we introduced the CRM life cycle:

• Develop your company's overall CRM strategy
• Build the infrastructure a piece at a time
• Know (analyze and target) who your customers area
• Deliver the offer to your customers

We also learned about how primary responsibility passes back and forth throughout the CRM life cycle, from heavy business involvement during strategic planning, to almost total Information Technology responsibility during the infrastructure build stage. As we begin to deliver results to our customers outside, the responsibility shifts back to the business team. More IT department involvement occurs during the customer analysis phases, but the responsibility shifts almost totally to the business function as the offer is delivered. In no phase should either constituent group be totally uninvolved.

On the business side, especially with the growth of the Internet, it is no longer appropriate for business people to treat technology as if it were some mysterious black box that they don't want to know anything about. It's not okay to toss a business problem or need to the IT department, and then shrug your shoulders and wait until the system is completed. (This probably won't work, so don't do it.) Marketing managers don't need to learn to write computer code, but they certainly need to understand the basic capabilities of some of the new technologies they depend on. It's important to understand that there is no magic, and that there are some things computers just can't do well (at least not yet).

The first step in assuring good communication is to understand the expectations for each part of the team. It is important to recognize that when the business function and IT department are working together, they have two different responsibilities. The business function is responsible for clearly defining what it needs—the business requirements for information and process automation. Information Technology needs to validate its understanding of the business need and propose the best technological solution to meet the needs. In many cases, there will be alternative solutions available with different pros and cons. These alternatives must be reviewed with the business team for a decision on the appropriate trade-off. Table 7-3 has several examples of business requirements and possible IT solutions.

Table 7-3 Business Function Versus IT Function Responsibility

Business Requirement	IT Solutions
Sales reps spend too much time in the office working on record-keeping. We need to increase the amount of time they can spend in front of customers. (NOT: We need a sales force automation system.)	• Build a system so that sales reps can keep all notes during their normal customer visits. • Buy a sales force automation package.
We have no way of knowing all the interactions our customers have had with the company. (NOT: Build us a marketing database.)	• Link together all the data from existing customer systems. • Buy a customer database package.
We don't have a clue as to who our best customers really are. (NOT: Go buy Package A so we can analyze our customers.)	• Buy SAS. • Buy another package.

Now that we're set to go, we'll begin the real work. In Chapter 8, we will develop our strategic plan.

7.3 Marrying Organization and Governance

So you have all these different functional areas that are integral to your CRM program. Because we know that if everyone is responsible, no one is responsible, how do we avoid the pitfall of having no one in charge? The two most likely alternatives are a formal customer advocate (Chief Customer Officer) or a customer steering committee made up of representatives from each of the core functions.

7.3.1 Organization

In order to bridge all the organizational gaps that exist in most companies, we will set up a tiered CRM organization structure. Different individuals from each of the CRM organizations and Information Technology will be assigned to these groups. Each group has a different role to play and a different set of responsibilities, as shown in Figure 7-4.

Each of these teams is composed of individuals from different levels in the organization. The steering committee generally has the fewest members and requires the smallest amount of time, while the project teams can involve many individuals who are usually assigned 100 percent to the project until it is completed.

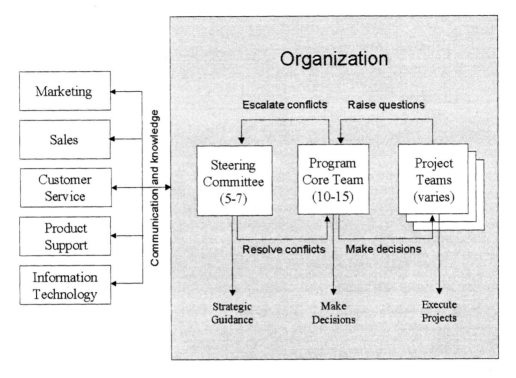

Figure 7-4 The CRM organizational structure

7.3.2   Customer Steering Committee

For most organizations, the steering committee approach is the way to go. It is a little more cumbersome and doesn't have the clout that a CCO would have, but it's much more likely to be accepted in today's environment. At a minimum, the steering committee should be comprised of senior representatives from each of the four core CRM business functions, plus the IT function.

It is absolutely critical that the committee members be senior, well-known and well-respected individuals because one of their most important functions is to communicate decisions and progress within their business area. Too often, the individuals assigned to a steering committee are those who have time to spare – meaning they are not very critical within their functional area. Don't fall into that trap! You'll end up with a lame-duck steering committee, and none of your CRM efforts will be valued or accepted.

You want to establish a steering committee of well-respected leaders whose time commitment is kept small. They are there primarily to resolve cross-functional disputes and to review, approve, and support key decisions. Essentially, they are your board of directors. The steering committee should be comprised of senior leaders from the core functions at a minimum and should be chaired by the Executive Sponsor or his designee. This is a guideline, of course. For a small company, the "committee" may be only one person (and it may be your executive sponsor). For a very large company, the steering committee may be expanded to include other key perspectives such as diverse geographies, different customer segments (B2B and consumer), etc. Whichever leadership model you adopt, two more groups are necessary to ensure the success of your overall program.

7.3.3   Program Core Team

The *CRM core team* includes representatives from each of the key constituencies: CRM functions, IT Department, geographic areas, etc. The core team provides consistent leadership and guidance to the overall CRM program.

Each member of the program core team (chaired by the program manager) should be assigned to this role at a much higher percentage of his or her time than the steering committee members. In very large companies, core team members (or at least the program manager) may be 100 percent dedicated to the success of the CRM program. In addition to making the day-to-day decisions, the core team is responsible for resolving and screening out lower-level decisions and for ensuring that only critical needs are escalated to the steering committee.

7.3.4   Project Teams

Each project will have a team staffed with individuals playing critical IT roles as well as representing the business functions. These teams are assigned to complete the deliverables specified in each project plan. The project team is lead by a project leader. Generally, project team members are assigned 100 percent until the assigned project is completed. Figure 7-5 shows the relationships between the various leaders and groups that make up the staff of a successful CRM program.

Because companies vary so much in size, it's difficult to predict exactly how much time is required of each team member. Steering committee members usually invest 5 percent of their time or less. Program council members may invest anywhere from 40 percent to 100 percent of their time, and project team members are usually fully dedicated. There are no absolutes because companies vary so much in size and in the complexity of their CRM effort. The pie chart in Figure 7-5 gives the approximate percent of the entire program effort that each group is responsible for. If you can estimate the size (in weeks or months) of the entire program, you can use this chart to get a rough idea of how much effort may be required for each member of the CRM program staff.

It is often at this point that companies realize they actually don't have the bandwidth to commit the time of so many people to their CRM program. Few companies have a bunch of people sitting around with spare time on their hands these days. External consultants are one way of filling this gap.

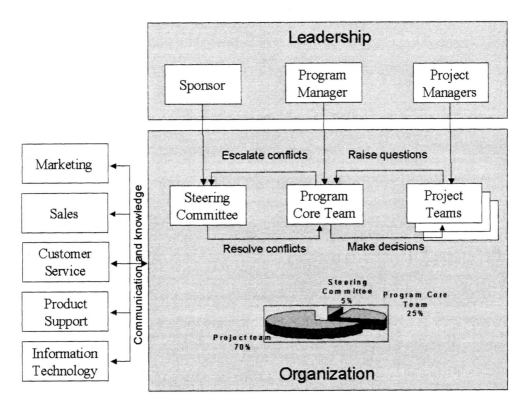

Figure 7-5 Cross-functional CRM program leadership and governance

7.4 Garnering Leadership's Support

Different levels of leadership are needed in order to guarantee success. At the highest level, the executive sponsor provides strategic vision, influence, and (hopefully) money. The program manager and project manager bring continuity and tactical experience and leadership.

7.4.1 Sponsorship

Ah, my favorite topic: the all-important subject of sponsorship. I must confess that I am one of those people who dismissed the value of executive sponsorship. I thought that getting a sponsor interested in what you were doing and keeping his support was just too hard. All you really needed was a good plan and quick, positive progress. I was wrong! A sponsor is not sufficient to guarantee success (you also need a good plan and quick results), but a sponsor is necessary. Having an executive sponsor is critical because nothing in a project ever goes 100 percent right. An executive sponsor who understands this reality and understands the overall benefit the program brings to the organization can smooth over much resistance and remove many barriers. The sponsor should be as close to the top of your organization as you can get. If it's your company head, you're really in luck. In many large organizations, the sponsor won't actually be an active program participant, so his time commitment will be small but essential.

How to Find a Sponsor

The best situations occur when the sponsor finds you. If a senior executive in your company recognizes that if the company doesn't adopt a CRM approach, it's going to be very tough to stay competitive in the new marketplace, then you've got a great opportunity. In many cases, especially in larger companies, the momentum for CRM is identified somewhere in the middle of the organization where the chance of working directly with customers is greater.

If you are faced with finding a sponsor, here's what to look for.

- Someone who knows that no company is successful over the long haul unless it has loyal customers (and who believes that CRM can help)
- Someone who has realistic expectations and wants to know what is really going on, not just the good news
- Someone who is willing to take risks along with the team and is able to the take on the responsibility of removing barriers

Of course, not every executive understands that these are the responsibilities of a sponsor. If you find someone who is really enthusiastic about the opportunity and is "trainable," then you may be fine. Sometimes the sponsor is chosen for you. But if your new sponsor has a reputation for thinking that customers are irrelevant, for wanting only good news, or for having wild dreams about what CRM can do to solve world hunger, then you should look for another sponsor. If that's not possible then perhaps you should walk away. If there's no senior executive who really "gets it," your company may just not be ready for CRM.

How to Keep Your Sponsor Engaged

The most important things that a high-level sponsor can do for you are to keep the CRM program visible at high levels within the organization, keep the visibility positive, and keep executive expectations realistic. The best way to keep a sponsor engaged is to keep him very well informed.

Keeping you sponsor informed doesn't mean that you should come to him daily with problems to solve. But it is important for the sponsor to know the whole truth about what's going on. If he cannot answer questions or concerns that come up, he will quickly lose credibility for himself and for the program. It's also critical that he *wants* to know. If you're working with someone who only wants to hear about what's going well, get a new sponsor—or a new job!

Keeping him informed also doesn't mean loading him down with problems to solve. Use the sponsor as rarely as possible to resolve the most difficult problems or remove the worst roadblocks. The more the team can resolve and accomplish on its own, the more confidence the sponsor will have in your program. Cherish the time you get from your sponsor, and don't bog him down with little details or problems that the team can solve for itself. Briefly keep him aware of what problems and issues the team has been able to resolve so he can become informed about the complexity of a cross-functional program such as CRM.

The other key role that your sponsor can play is team building. Ask your sponsor to present the company's vision/goals/objectives for the future and to address how CRM will help make that happen. Help him to express appreciation for accomplishments at periodic team events. This is great for the team and maybe even more important for the sponsor (so he feels his ability to impact the program).

7.4.2   Chief Customer Officer

Frankly, the concept of establishing a position of Chief Customer Officer who is part of the CEO's staff and is responsible for the total customer experience has not been widely adopted by many companies today. It is very rare for a new senior staff position to be established. Too many factors, mainly tradition and political concerns surrounding power and span of control, stand in the way of enlarging the executive staff. The creation of the position of Chief Information Officer is a good example. Information Technology emerged under the direction of the controller because accounting and finance applications were the first business processes to be automated. As technology spread throughout the organization, there was lots of talk of having the head of the IT Department report directly to the head of the company because technology impacts the entire company. It's true that in the last few years many companies have established a Chief Information Officer (CIO) but in many cases, the CIO still reports into the head of Finance.

Still, the CCO is an idea that's worth discussion. The concept is a great one. Just as the CFO is responsible for seeing that financial considerations are taken into account during executive planning and decision making, the CCO is responsible for ensuring that customer considerations are taken into account. Customer privacy, which we cover in Chapter 22, should be one of the responsibilities of the CCO. Privacy is much more a customer relationship concern than a legal or political one.

7.4.3   Program Manager

The Program Manager brings good business perspective and continuity across all the projects that make up your program. The program manager must have a strong functional background and, in the case of CRM, often reports into the Marketing function, from which the leadership for CRM should spring. In some organizations, the CRM program manager is (temporarily?) assigned to the IT Department. This sometimes reflects that the company considers information technology truly strategic, but usually it means that the business functions have delegated the entire responsibility. Be very wary of this situation.

7.4.4   Project Manager

Each project manager brings a specific perspective and relevant experience to the management of each individual project. There may be several project managers assigned to different

CRM projects at the same time. Each one is responsible for keeping the program manager and the core team apprised of the project status and any issues or risks that need resolution or escalation. The project manager is responsible for seeing that the infrastructure development project stays on schedule and meets expectations. For this reason, project managers often (but not always) report to Information Technology. The project manager is responsible for leading project team checkpoints and status meetings.

7.5   Adding Adjunct Team Members (Consultants and Contractors)

Let's talk about consultants and contractors. These are workers who provide you with specific services but are not employees of your company. The general rule for distinguishing them is that consultants get paid to provide a specific, predefined service. Contractors are hired on an hourly basis to fill in wherever you need them. Many people are confused because companies want to hire a consultant to help them figure out what they need to do—they need expertise and guidance to get a quick start. But no one can tell what it will take to get the company to that point, so consultants are also paid on open-ended contracts. In fact, the real difference is that consultants get paid more, always!

I've been employing consultants for more than 20 years; at this writing, I have been a consultant for less than one year. With that background, I have some pretty strong ideas about what consultants can and can't contribute and how they should be used. There are two reasons to hire a consultant:

- You need the consultant's knowledge and experience to help you identify what your organization needs in a specific area of expertise, and you want the consultant to pass that knowledge and experience on to you so you can learn to take care of things yourself.
- You need the consultant's resources to help you actually do the work that you have already decided you need to do.

Do not hire a consulting firm to tell you what to do, or I guarantee you'll end up feeling like the guys in Figure 7-6. Hire consultants who will ask you the questions that will help *you* refine, articulate, and deliver what *you* know your company needs.

An hourly (daily, weekly) agreement is fine for consultants and contractors who are acting advisors, coaches, facilitators, guides, or additional trained resources. As long as you're making progress and getting what you need, this is a great source of additional expertise and resources. When there's no longer any value, you end the relationship. Beware, though, of consultants who take your money to figure out why you need to hire them to do more work. Look for those who want to help you learn to do it yourself.

Along the same lines, don't hire consultants to deliver an unspecified solution. Unless you have a specific objective (and "Make us CRM-capable" is *not* specific enough), they can't give you a plan with a fixed schedule, estimated cost, and clear penalties. This leaves you with the

"*From the violent nature of the multiple stab wounds,
I'd say the victim was probably a consultant.*"

© New Yorker Magazine, 2001

Figure 7-6 The consultant

hourly time and materials agreement, which means you are taking all the risk. Whether you or the consultant makes a mistake in the requirements, design, or construction, you have to pay for it to get fixed.

One last reason to hire a consultant is that you just want to have them tell your top management exactly what you've been saying for years, but management will listen more closely to the consultant because they're paying the him or her so much more than they're paying you. This is a perfectly valid reason; I've used it often and very successfully!

Questions for Reflection

These questions will help you determine your company's readiness for building new CRM organization and governance structures.

1. Is there an obvious choice for executive sponsor? What position does this person hold in what part of the organization? Can this individual exert influence across all the CRM functions?

2. Are there at least a couple of key executives who get the problem and would be willing to be part of the steering committee?

3. What about the program manager? The individual must have a real passion for CRM because he or she is likely to be eating, drinking, and sleeping it for quite a while. How about you?

4. Who can you get for the program core team? These must be individuals who are good enough at their real jobs that the company can't afford to have them take on anything new. The real test of serious organizational commitment is that the company can't afford to put anyone else on the core team; it has to be the best.

CHAPTER 8

Go! Developing Your CRM Strategy

Okay, we're ready to get to work. As you know, the first step you must take is to determine how your company is going to approach CRM; what is the right strategy for you? To create your CRM strategy, you start by defining where you want to be and decide what kinds of relationships you need to have with your customers in order to stay competitive. You need to understand where your company is now, and you must select the best path to get to your goal.

The questions you have answered at the ends of the chapters are preparing you to think about your organization and begin to formalize and articulate what direction your company's CRM should take. This chapter considers how to bring other important viewpoints into your strategy definition. We will identify all the steps that help us collect the knowledge and perspective of the organization's executives, customer experts, process experts, technical experts, and external experts (our customers). We will see how to organize everything that's been learned so the knowledge you collect leads you to define the right strategy and sets guidelines for the organization to make continuous progress and still get started quickly. Figure 8-1 shows where we are in the overall CRM methodology; we are at the beginning—launching our CRM efforts by developing our strategy.

We know that there is no magic wand, but with your strategy and roadmap in hand, you will be able to build a successful CRM program for your organization. It might even start to look like magic!

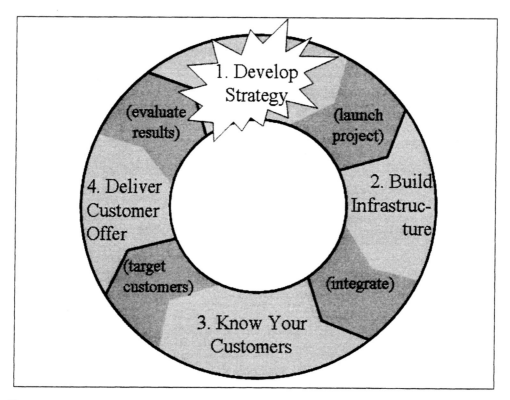

Figure 8-1   Phase 1—The Strategic Plan

8.1   Answering the Three Key Questions

Where do you want to go? Where are you starting? How are you going to get there? These are the three questions that the strategic planning process will help you answer so you can success-fully build your CRM program. Figure 8-2 reminds us of the three vectors that shape the customer experience: what's happening in the *marketplace,* what your company *says,* and what your company *does.* To get the answers, you'll be gathering information from (or about) the marketplace (customers and competitors) and from inside your company (from key executives and employees who have significant customer experience and knowledge).

There are two reasons to take a trip: (1) you want to get somewhere, and (2) you want to see and experience new scenery. If you're just out for a ride, you don't really need to plan a des-tination, take a map, or even choose a direction. But we *are* trying to get somewhere; we want to move to a place where our company is capable of building and managing excellent customer relationships so that we can consistently increase loyalty and revenue. The first thing that we must do is figure out where we want to be at the end of our efforts.

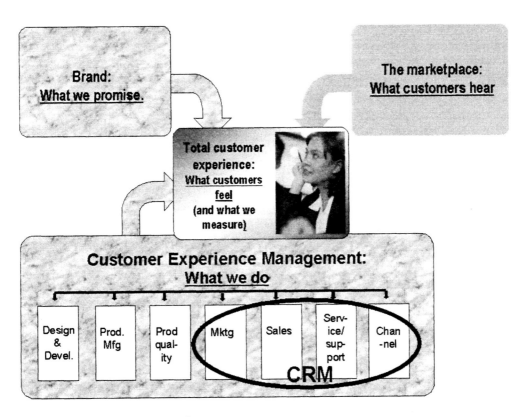

Figure 8-2 The customer experience

8.1.1 Where Do You Want to Go?

The most important deliverable of the strategic planning phase is to define what CRM is going to do for your company; you need to paint a vision of what the future will look like. This goal is what will keep your program on track over the long haul needed to achieve you goals. Remember, there is no CRM nirvana that all companies must strive to reach.

The primary source of input for determining your organization's CRM goal should come from outside the organization. CRM is about your customers. What do your customers want, need, or expect? What is most important to them? You don't want to waste your time and resources on capabilities that your customers don't care about. Of course, no one can afford to give customers everything they ever thought of wanting. A customer survey is a key step, but we must balance it with information about our own value discipline and our position relative to our competition. We also need to understand how our company compares to our competitors: Do we excel, do we have parity, or are we behind? After all, why focus on areas where we're already doing better than the competition? Finally, and obviously, you want to be sure to include the key internal players and CRM constituents. As ideal as it sounds, we can't do everything that customers want. We need to balance customer expectations against the reality of our company's business objectives and plans. The internal interview will allow you to uncover information that will help you put a realistic boundary around your future vision and to answer questions such as these:

- Is your CRM strategy aligned with your overall corporate strategy and business model? If not, you must get it aligned or quit now.
- How internally aligned is the organization around your company's goals? Your chance of success is greatly increased by a strongly aligned organization, but if yours isn't, now is your chance to do the alignment.
- What are your potential program risks? Answering this question allows you to prepare for and eliminate obstructions to successful completion.
- Does your company know who your customers are? What industries, what size, and what other segments are important? You can't build relationships with customers if you don't even know what they are.
- What are the organization's expectations of CRM? If they aren't reasonable or consistent, you can prepare to clarify them.

I want to emphasize the first point: I strongly recommend that you stop your efforts right now if you discover that there is no congruence between what CRM can deliver and your organization's strategic goals. I'm quite serious. Because CRM must cross functions if it is to have any real impact on the customer experience, a lack of company-wide goals means that you cannot be successful. That is not to say that you couldn't decide to implement a call center management system that could be very helpful to customers who use that particular service function. But no matter what the vendor tells you, if the program isn't fully integrated across all the front office functions, it is not Customer Relationship Management.

If you insist on proceeding with a formal, cross-functional program without clear alignment with your organization's business goals, you will end up like Sisyphus in Figure 8-3, forever struggling to push a boulder uphill and never quite reaching your destination. Nothing is more frustrating or painful than having the boulder roll back down over you time and again.

Of course, the internal interviews can actually help you avoid the Sisyphus syndrome. While you are gathering information internally, you have an excellent opportunity to educate the organization about CRM and what to expect. You also have the chance to adapt and align your CRM message with the overall company goals. You will want to gather perspectives from all the CRM functions: marketing, sales, customer services, and product support and from all levels within these organizations. Executives have a great perspective on overall company direction and realities of the marketplace. Individuals such as sales reps and customer service and support reps who work closely with customers often have a greater understanding of your customers and their current company experience.

Although you probably have a pretty good idea of what needs to happen, you will learn much from the internal interviews that will help you set the right strategy and align with com-

Figure 8-3 If there's no link between CRM and your company strategy, you'll find yourself here!

pany goals. But the single most important result of this effort is getting your key constituents involved in the program early.

KEY IDEA

The most valuable result of the internal interview step is that it allows all constituents to get involved, contribute, and influence what CRM will be for their company. As a result, they will feel included, understood, and responsible.

After you've figured out where you are going, it's important to understand where you are now.

8.1.2   Where Are You Starting?

The three data collection tools we used to determine our goals are also helpful for gathering information about where we are today. We will ask both long-term direction and current-state questions of everyone we interview. Senior executives are most likely to provide perspective on long-term direction, while current-state information will most likely come from those individuals who directly interact with and are closest to the customer.

Because of the key role that technology plays in CRM, we also need to get a snapshot of the current information and systems technology state of the company. We need to ask project managers and IT management these questions:

- What customer information and systems do we already have running?
- What customer information/systems projects are underway?
- What customer information/systems projects are being planned?

We will find out who is funding these projects, what they do, what kind of information are already in-house, etc. Project assessments can become political nightmares because many people fear that their pet project will be taken over or canceled. Many disconnected systems result from the widespread belief by IT folks that the only way to get something done is to do it themselves. The result, of course, is fragmentation. Fragmentation costs your company more (small amounts of money invested often enough add up to a large total), and each small project solves the same problem over and over; you never get to some of the bigger and higher impact projects.

In fact, it is likely that you'll uncover some projects that you'll decide to eliminate or combine. But that is not the purpose of the system assessment, and your message introducing the survey must convey that strongly. The message must be about helping the customer, about understanding the ways that we currently touch our customers, and about being able to take advantage of all the knowledge we gain from these interactions to improve the customer's experience and loyalty and our revenue. If the message is about cost-cutting or control, people will feel threatened and become uncooperative. If that's what people think you're doing, you can depend on every project suddenly disappearing underground. This is a common danger and is typified by the agreeable non-complier: "Yes, I agree, it just doesn't apply to me/my function/ my project."

The answers to this second question will give us a complete picture of the company's current situation in the areas that are key to CRM success. We will understand the company's current state: strategic alignment, customer focus, CRM understanding, program risks, and CRM information and systems (current and planned).

The last step in the strategic plan is to understand the best way to move our organization from where it is now to where we want to be. This plan will also be based on the information we've collected so far.

8.1.3   How Are You Going to Get There?

The final question that we will answer is how to get from where we are now to our future state vision. We will develop a set of plans that will describe the path we'll take starting from today and looking out one to two years. After evaluating all the information you have collected from internal and external sources, you will prepare your CRM strategic proposal. The proposal will be comprised of two parts: the recommendations that describe where you want to be and the plan that describes the route you'll take to get there. One section of your proposal will be built around a project roadmap, governed by your business priorities and supplemented by a risk reduction strategy.

The strategic planning process is accomplished through the use of a set of tools that help us collect information from key stakeholders that will answer the three strategic questions.

8.2   Using Strategic Planning Tools

The basic strategic planning process (collecting data, assessing findings, creating a proposal) can be applied to any strategic initiative. Some of the tools we'll be using also are applicable to any strategic planning effort. Others of these tools are specific to a CRM program. And some of the tools are important only for strategic initiatives that include information and technology components. These tools are based on the information systems planning principles outlined by James Martin (and others) more than a decade ago.

The basic strategic planning process that we will follow and the ten tools we'll be using as we follow it are shown in Figure 8-4.

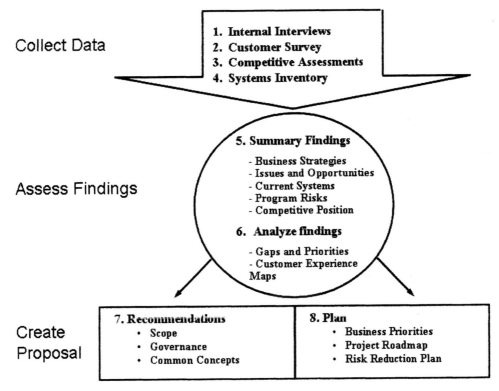

Figure 8-4   Strategic planning process and tools

Now that we've introduced a high-level view of the overall strategic planning process that we'll be using, let's examine how each tool is used each of the process steps.

8.2.1   Tools of the Trade

The tools outlined in Figure 8-4 will help us gather the information needed to answer our three key questions. The data that we collect and the results of our assessment of these data will allow us to create a plan that will form the basis of how we move forward one step at a time. Table 8-1 presents a summary of these tools, explains when they should be used, suggests for what purposes they can be used, and suggests expected results.

Table 8-1 Strategic Planning Tools

Planning Stage	Tool	Questions			Purpose	Result
		Where are we going?	Where are we now?	How do we get there?		
Collect Data	Internal Interviews	X	X		Can we identify the overall current state and future plans?	Know your objectives, goals, opportunities and business issues.
					How can we measure internal alignment around company goals?	The chance of success is greatly enhanced by strong congruence.
					What are the potential project risks?	Be prepared for program risks, and plan how to prevent them.
					How well does the company know who the customer is and their value?	Understand customers.
					What is the company's expectation of CRM, and is it reasonable?	Clarify scope; align and adjust expectations.
	System Inventory		X		Do we understand the current state of CRM information and technology, both current and planned?	Know what you've got; refocus and converge active projects.

Table 8-1 Strategic Planning Tools

Planning Stage	Tool	Questions			Purpose	Result
		Where are we going?	Where are we now?	How do we get there?		
	Customer Survey	X	X		What do customers value? What do they like, and what do they find frustrating?	Customer needs are the key input to priorities.
	Competitive Assessment	X	X		How well do customers think we're doing? How well are we doing compared to the competition?	A competitive position is key input to priorities.
Assess findings	Summarize Findings	X	X	X	Did we present an overview of business strategies, issues and opportunities, current systems, program risks, and our competitive position?	Understand the organization's current and future state; identify areas of congruence and dissonance.
	Analyze Findings	X	X	X	Have we identified gaps and priorities? What does our Customer Touch Point Matrix show?	Understand strengths, weaknesses, and critical customer issues.
Create Proposal	Recommendations			X	Have we defined the scope of the project? Have we included information, processes, technology and people?	Clearly define what is included in and excluded from the CRM program.
					Have we addressed the issue of governance? How will the work be organized and managed?	Organizational change ensures success of the program.

Table 8-1 Strategic Planning Tools

Planning Stage	Tool	Questions			Purpose	Result
		Where are we going?	Where are we now?	How do we get there?		
					What common concepts have we defined and provided a framework for? Did we include "Customer Experience Maps"?	Develop a common language and context for the program.
	Plan			X	Have we identified top priorities based on internal and external information?	Identify the starting project and the next two to three planned projects.
					Did we produce a roadmap of when priorities will happen?	Initial projects have been planned, scoped, and timed.
					Have we uncovered the specific risks that our CRM effort is likely to face?	Be prepared to reduce/ eliminate risks before they actually occur.

For the balance of this chapter, we will take a detailed look at each of the process steps and the tools that are used to accomplish that step.

8.3 Collecting Data

Let's take a closer look at how to use each of the data collection tools that help us find answers to our three strategic questions. Even though the customer must be the central focus of our CRM planning, we will not start by collecting information from customers. Instead, we will begin our assessment effort with the internal interviews. We start here for several reasons:

- **Time:** It's the easiest place to start so we can get going quickly.
- **Cost:** It's important to understand your company's current vision of CRM and how it aligns with the organizational direction before you start spending the money to assess customers and competitors.
- **Scope:** You first need to know what your company identifies as your CRM focus, and then find out what your customers think. A totally blank slate presented to customers (tell us what you want) isn't likely to deliver actionable results.

All projects are affected by the three constraints of time, cost, and scope. *Time* represents how long you are willing to wait for some results; *cost* is obviously how much you're willing to pay; and *scope* defines your expected results such as features, performance, etc. We'll become very familiar with these three constraints as we start to understand the tradeoffs that need to be made during the project planning and infrastructure development phases.

But now we begin with internal data collection, which involves two components: internal interviews (focused on people and processes) and a system inventory (information and technology).

8.3.1 Internal Interviews

As we've discussed, the internal interviews are important because they help educate and shape the organization's expectations for CRM. The interview process also provides some critical insights about the company's current state and future goals. We will construct our interviews so that we get information about both the current state and future plans.

We will develop a standard interview template that will be used consistently throughout your assessments. This allows you to gather information that can be summarized to provide real insights into major concerns of your business. The basic interview questions will be asked of all participants (executives and other employees). Depending on the size and specialization of your company's business functions, you may also have a few questions that are aimed specifically at executive participants or just at a single function (e.g., sales or customer services).

You need to be able to complete each interview in about an hour. You also want to be able to summarize and compare results across all the interviews. Both of these requirements indicate that you need to have a fairly structured interview and avoid lots of sweeping, open-ended questions. This can be accomplished even for the broadest concepts like business opportunities and risks by forming the question to request a specific number of responses (the top three opportunities) and specific time periods (for the coming year, or in the next three to five years). On the other hand, you want to inspire creative perspectives. One of the most effective questions to ask during your internal interviews is "What are the three stupidest things we do to our customers today?" This question interrupts the predictable business train of thought and usually produces an embarrassed laugh as the gears start to engage. Generally, this question elicits some really thoughtful insights about some of those dead elephants that are seldom mentioned.

During the internal interviews, you will also being gathering information about CRM related projects (formal or skunk works) that are underway. You will ask some very specific questions about names of current and planned CRM efforts and who owns them. A summary of the topics to be covered in these interviews is shown in Table 8-2.

Table 8-2 The Internal Interview

Section	Purpose	What to Ask
Company's overall short- and long-term strategic direction	•What do our internal and external environments and current business strategies look like? •What is the brand strategy and primary value for customer? •What are our CRM organizations and locations? •How strong is the alignment across organizations?	1. What are three to five business objectives and opportunities plus business risks and issues for: (1) today and (2) in three to five years? 2. What is the predominant value (brand/discipline) that our company offers to customers?

Functional direction long-term and for the upcoming year	• Picture of the business objectives within each functional area
	• How aligned are we:
	  o With the whole company?
	  o Within the function?
	  o With other functions?
		1. What are three to five goals and objectives for today and future for your function?
		2. How do these objectives align with the overall business objectives?
		3. What current and near-term customer contact efforts do you have? Who is the contact person?

About customers	• How well does the company understand our current/future customers? • Are we ready to segment and what measure is most valuable? • Are we ready to set the stage for having customer needs drive of future CRM efforts?	1. Important customer segments, how are they identified, are they effective, are there different expectations by segment? 2. What are the stupid and inconvenient things we force our customers to do today?
CRM expectations	• Have we assessed CRM understanding and alignment? • Can we identify the value of CRM? • What are the most critical projects and where we should begin? •What are the biggest risks to program success?	1. What does CRM mean? 2. What will it do for your company, your function, and your customers? 3. What is highest CRM priority and why? 4. Are there any other CRM-related projects underway? Who is in charge of those projects?

A sample of an interview survey that was used by a high-tech company in a recent CRM strategy assessment can be found in Appendix C.

8.3.2   Systems Inventory

Information and technology play a critical role in CRM. In order to plan our program roadmap, we need to know what customer information we already have and what customer touch point systems currently exist. We also need to uncover what projects are planned or already underway. Information for the system inventory is gathered initially from the internal interviews. You'll learn about many projects that don't have official status yet by asking about CRM-related programs and touch points.

Armed with this knowledge, the team will again develop a standard form to build a complete inventory of all customer touch systems. Your IT Department will be a major source of this information and may be responsible for completing the inventory. You will learn about some CRM efforts during the internal interviews, so you should follow up with the business project managers to complete the system inventory.

Like the rest of our strategic planning efforts, this system inventory is conducted at a very high level. You want to know exactly what's up and running, what projects are underway, and what is currently being planned. You need to understand what kinds of information are captured in which systems and the complexity of the current and planned technical architecture. Of course, Information Technology may need to gather additional detailed information as part of a specific project, but that is not necessary for the strategic plan. You want to get enough information to understand the general landscape and know where to go if you need more information. Examples of the kinds of information that you need to gather to complete your inventory are shown in Table 8-3.

Table 8-3 Systems Inventory

System	Information	Technology
Name: Purpose: Business Unit: Contact Person: Location: Status: (live, in development, planned)	__Customer ID (name/user ID) __Contact info (address/phone/e-mail/_____) __Company info (name, size, industry) __Owned products (ours/competitors) __Purchased service (ours/competitors) __Suspect/prospect/customer __Deals	Hardware Size (GB) Software/database Closed or open architecture Customer contact (e.g. web, phone)

This high-level inventory will be the basis for understanding what customer information you currently collect, who is responsible for it, and where it's being used.

8.3.3   Customer Survey

The purpose of the customer survey is to understand what is working for your customers and what isn't. You will gather information from customer feedback systems and any current customer surveys that have relevant information. You will want to do a CRM-specific customer survey as well. The customer survey must focus on the *relationship factors* of the customer experience. You shouldn't ask questions that are so open-ended that you receive feedback on anything you're not going to be able to fix as part of your CRM program. Table 8-4 gives one example of how to create an effective but short survey that can used to understand what is important to your customers. This type of survey is usually conducted by phone, but could also be done online.

Table 8-4 Customer Survey

Touch Point	1. Broadcast 2. E-mail 3. Systematic 4. Internet	1. Mail 2. Event 3. Phone/fax 4. Personal
Life Cycle Stage	Consider • Awareness/interest • Investigation	Setup • Install • Learn/customize
	Purchase • Evaluate/choose • Order/purchase	Use • Operate/maintain • Upgrade/retire
Survey (replace the words in *italics* with one of the choices from the appropriate list above)	1. How important is *touch point* **in helping you to accomplish** *life cycle stage*? <u>**Very Somewhat Low**</u> 2. How well does our *touch point* **communication work for you/meet your** *life cycle stage* **needs?** Not at all 1 2 3 4 5 Completely	

This very simple survey is completed by using the two survey questions for each of the life cycle/touch point combinations you want to learn about. The survey is simple enough that you could easily execute it yourself. However, if you hire a research firm to run it for you, you can ask additional questions that will help you gather some competitive information as well.

You should supplement this broad customer survey with some in-depth and open-ended interviews of a few of your most important customers—ones who are representative of each of your important customer segments. You still capture the same basic information, but this is an opportunity to gather some helpful subjective perspectives as well. Both can yield great insights.

The personal interviews can even help build relationships, but it can also backfire if you don't at least follow up (even if you can't act) on the input. Other great sources of information are any customer surveys or customer feedback you had gathered at an earlier time (e.g., a web site satisfaction survey).

8.3.4 Competitive Assessment

The competitive assessment information can be collected through the same customer survey described in Table 8-4. Of course, to be effective in gathering competitive data, you need to commission an independent third party to ask these questions for you. You're not likely to get unbiased answers if you go to your customers directly and ask how you compare to your competitors. This would mean that instead of asking about "our" company's touch points separately, you would just have a list of companies to add to the life cycle/touch point mix. Of course, one of the companies would be yours. The purpose of the competitive assessment is to understand how well you are doing in the various CRM areas in comparison to your competitors. Table 8-5 shows the questions you would probably add to the survey.

Table 8-5 Competitive Assessment

Company list	Create a list of three or four of the key competitors that you're interested in comparing. Of course, you'll add your own company to the list.
Survey	1. What company's *touch point* has given you the best experience? Why was it best?
	2. What company's *touch point* has given you the worst experience? Why was it the worst?
	3. How well does *touch point* communication from *company* work for you/ meet your *life cycle stage* needs? Not at all 1 2 3 4 5 Completely

Secondary research provides another good source of competitive information. There have been numerous studies looking at the relative effectiveness of the various company touch points, especially the effectiveness of a company's Internet presence. You can also do secondary research yourself, but the broad reach and experience of many consulting firms may make a third party a better choice. Of course, like working with any consultant, it's you who must decide what you want to know!

8.4 Assessing Findings

Using all the information you have collected internally and externally, you now want to summarize what you have learned and analyze your findings to produce the strategy. All programs, even those that don't involve technology, follow the same basic assessment steps: consolidate findings and analyze results.

All of the following sets of findings are real, although they are not from a single company. We will be learning from XYZ Corporation's experiences throughout the rest of this book.

XYZ Corporation is a medium-sized company founded in 1992 and headquartered in Chicago. XYZ manufactures and sells environment management equipment (electric fans), as well as environment management consulting and product support to a broad range of customers. They produce very large "systems" (combinations of their large scale 800 and 900 Series fans, plus consulting and support services) to a wide range of customers, including some of the Fortune 50 as well as many mid-sized companies around the world. XYZ also has a few products that are targeted at consumers and very small businesses. These include the very small 100 Series fans as well as portable (100P) and solar-powered (100S) models.

The XYZ examples given have all actually occurred, but for a number of companies of differing sizes, businesses, and geographic locations.

8.4.1   Summarize Findings

The starting point for the plan is the sum of all the information you've collected from customers, competitors, and your company itself. Let's review all the results from XYZ Corporation's data collection efforts.

Internal Interview

The internal interviews give us a picture of where the company is today and where it wants to be. There are two segments of the internal interview findings: interview summary and risk summary.

The **Interview Summary** highlights the key topics that were covered by the interviews. It is very important to clarify each major point with direct quotes you heard. The quotes will make your presentation more alive and will lend credibility to your findings with recognizable language and phrasing. It also another opportunity to let your constituents feel involved and included. Table 8-6 summarizes the key results from XYZ's internal interviews.

Table 8-6 XYZ Corporation's Interview Summary

Topic	Interview Quotes	Congruence
Business objectives	Grow revenue to $100 million Profitable growth	High
Business opportunities	New customer selling model: solutions, installed base, not just boxes Execute on channel strategy. Customers are confused by our multiple channels with different messages. New vertical market product categories	
Business issues	Marketplace consolidation Competitor price gouging We don't know who our most valuable (profitable) customers are. Current infrastructure doesn't support order and revenue growth targets. Improve Sales Force productivity. Too internally/product focused	

Table 8-6 XYZ Corporation's Interview Summary (Continued)

Topic	Interview Quotes	Congruence
Stupid things we do to our customers	Can't recognize customers across all touch points. Don't know who they are. We "sell" CRM solutions, but we don't use them. We make it difficult to do business with us (buying, selling, support). Leave money on the table (installed base upgrade and cross-sell opportunities)	
Customer segmentation and valuation	Industry segments no longer useful; need new approach. Partners	Low
What is CRM?	Customer recognized wherever he interacts Just software: SF automation, call center automation 360° view of customer Loyalty, retention, increased sales Sales sees everything about their customers/territories Scoring/measuring customer value	Low
What will CRM do for XYZ?	Match cost of touch point to value of customer Can't reach financial goals without it	
Where should we start? What are our priorities?	Get a quick win, whatever can be quick Customer database Personalized web sites Total touch point and system integration Sales Force Automation Customer master file ("the bible") Segmentation strategies	Very Low

You notice a column labeled Congruence in Table 8-6. Congruence, the level of company-wide agreement on a subject, is a very important piece of information to know for each of these key points covered by the internal interviews. Any area with a low score is a potential risk to project success. Low congruence indicates that everyone has a different set of expectations in this area. High congruence is an area of strength that can be leveraged to build understanding and support.

KEY IDEA

High Congruence = High Probability of Success

For example, if everyone in the organization knows exactly what your company business goals are, then you can leverage this strong congruence by showing how your CRM program is directly aligned with and supports those goals. If your company's view of business goals varies all over the map, then you have nothing with which to align.

The **Risk Summary** is the other output from the internal interviews. This is a critical, but often ignored, opportunity to prepare for the worst. If the worst happens, you can have your head in the sand and it can wipe you out, or you can be well prepared so that the impact is reduced or even eliminated. Just as people don't want to write a will because it's such a downer, many think it's too negative to focus on potential project risks. But the opposite is true: Rather than being too negative, thinking about potential risks doesn't make them happen; it helps you avoid them. If you have thought about the potential risks and understand their danger, you can identify and implement ways of overcoming or avoiding them. (Okay, the parallel isn't perfect. A will doesn't guarantee you eternal life, but at least you have some control over what happens to your "stuff" when you go.) At the very least, being aware of program risks will make you sensitive to the early signs of problems, and you can stop them before they've really derailed your program.

Each risk should be assigned an owner. This is an individual who will take responsibility for seeing that the risk is resolved by providing any necessary plans and resources. Table 8-7 lists XYZ's key risk areas.

Table 8-7 XYZ Corporation's CRM Program Risks

Risk Area	Quotes	Owner
Sponsorship and leadership	Need passionate executive support. Sponsor must make a financial commitment and **STICK WITH IT** over the long haul. Sponsor must understand that CRM is not a quick fix and needs executive clout. Not enough people understand CRM.	Xavier
Planning	Not having a strategy and plan No means of internal communication Scope creep, project management	Yolanda
Process	Visible benefits (stick and carrot) No culture of consistent processes	Zeke

Table 8-7 XYZ Corporation's CRM Program Risks (Continued)

Risk Area	Quotes	Owner
Organization	Continuing with silos Too inward focused Multiple geographies, but too UK-centric Conflicting functional business priorities	Xavier/ Zeke
Technology	Don't have an overall technology architecture. Do we really perceive Information Technology as a strategic weapon?	Yolanda

By the way, let me introduce you to a few members of the XYZ management team. Xavier is the Vice President of Sales and Marketing. XYZ is lucky that he is a charismatic leader and a very involved executive sponsor for the program. Yolanda is the Chief Information Officer. Yolanda has an MBA and has had extensive experience in business planning, finance, and IT management before taking on the CIO role. Zeke is a senior marketing manager for one of XYZ Corporation's product lines and has been assigned the organization-wide responsibility for CRM.

System Inventory

Through the internal interviews, we learned about the systems that are part of the company's IT infrastructure, as well as those that are being built on or run outside of the IT mainstream. We'll gather this knowledge of projects that don't have official status by asking about CRM-related programs and touch points instead of IT. Armed with this knowledge, the team will contact each of the project owners and complete the system inventory.

The system inventory gives us knowledge of where we collect customer information today. Most companies have hundreds of customer databases, many of which are redundant, inconsistent, or out of date, with more being planned. Large companies are likely to number their customer databases in the thousands. Even small companies often have multiple customer files. Each employee generates his or her own account lists, e-mail directories, and spreadsheets to support his/her business. In Table 8-8, we see XYZ's systems inventory.

Table 8-8 XYZ Corporation's System Inventory

System Name	Status	Purpose	Function	Information	Package
COSMIC	Live	Order admin- istration	Corporate Marketing	Customer Company Product Sales-$ Discount-$	Home grown

Table 8-8 XYZ Corporation's System Inventory (Continued)

System Name	Status	Purpose	Function	Information	Package
OM CENTRAL	Live	Order Customer Master	Corporate Marketing	Customer Company Contact points	Home grown
SFA	In development	SF Automation	Consumer Sales	Customer Account Territory Deals Channel	Package A
CRM	Planned	SF Automation	Business-to-business sales	Customer Company Account Territory Deals	Package B
CRM	Planned	Call center	Support	TBD	Package B

XYZ is actually fairly lucky; many companies have several hundred customer systems distributed throughout the organization.

Customer Assessment

The customer assessment is compiled from your external surveys. After you have defined the life cycle of your customers and identified current (and potential) touch points, you will ask your customers which of these are important supports for each step of their life cycle. Figure 8-5 shows the relative priorities for one of XYZ's customer segments.

This diagram summarizes average responses from all customers on the importance of the touch point for each stage of the customer life cycle. Later, we will use it to help us set our project priorities.

	Consider	Purchase	Install	Use
Person	H	H	H	H
Phone/ Fax	L	M	H	M
Catalog/ mail	M	L	L	L
Internet	M	H	H	H
System	L	H	M	H
Email	L	L	L	L

Low - L   Medium - M   High - H

Figure 8-5   XYZ's customer-prioritized touch points

The Competitive Assessment

The competitive assessment is also created based on feedback from customers and secondary research. Note that there may be cells for which we have no information. Some of these missing cells are not important enough to pursue (such as mail or e-mail during the purchase stage). Others, like mail and e-mail during consideration, we want to continue working on. But what's important for now is that we have enough information to get started in understanding how we're doing compared to the competition. Figure 8-6 shows XYZ's relative position compared to its competitors as judged by customers and the marketplace.

Together with the customer survey information, the competitive assessment helps us understand where we need to start.

	Consider		Purchase		Install		Use	
	Aware	Investi-gate	Choose	Order	Install	Learn	Maintain	Upgrade
Person					●	●	●	●
Phone/ Fax		○		○		◉	●	◉
Catalog / Mail	●							
Internet			○	○		○	○	○
System			●	●				
Email	○	○	○					

Customer Performance Rating

Strong	Average	Weak
●	◉	○

Figure 8-6 Competitive assessment

8.4.2 Analyze Findings

Next, we must analyze all these findings to help us determine what needs to be done, when it needs to be done, and the how it needs to be done.

Priorities

To help identify your priorities, you will look at several factors. The first piece of information comes from combining data collected from the two external assessments. Figure 8-7 illustrates this technique. Start with the Customer Performance Rating, and highlight the cells that the customer indicated were of high importance for that phase of the life cycle.

If you're already doing better than competitors in certain areas, then even if your customers aren't delighted, you may not need to start there. You'll probably want to start your program in an area where you're not doing so well. Sure, the area in which you're outstanding is a competitive advantage, and you want to maintain that advantage. If the competition is catching up, then you may want to widen your lead. The point to remember is that the competitive assessment step will give you the information you need to make objective decisions about where to start and where to go next.

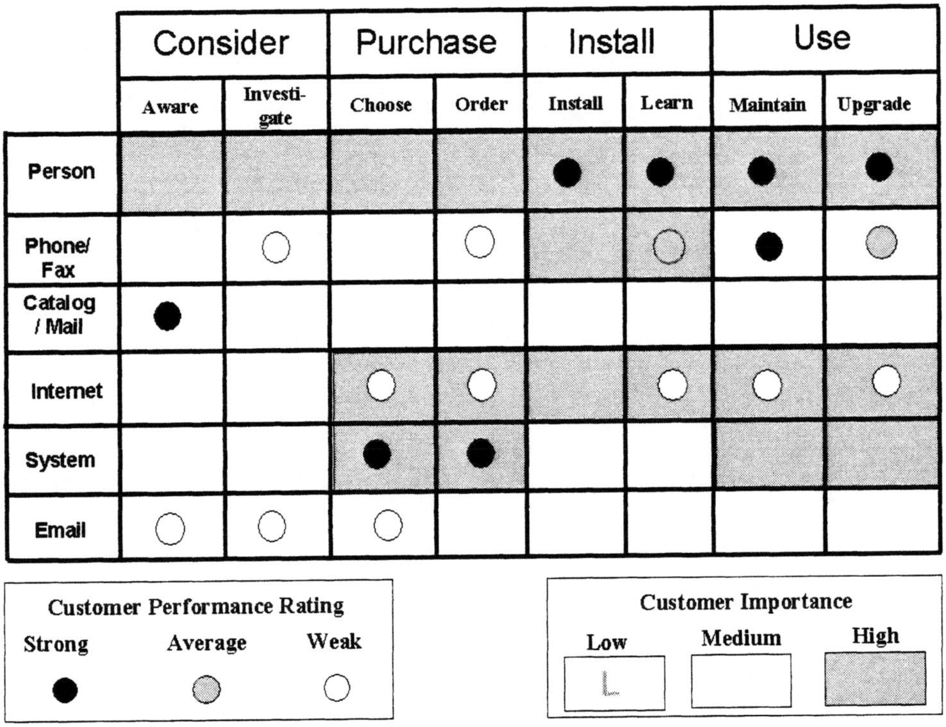

	Consider		Purchase		Install		Use	
	Aware	Investi-gate	Choose	Order	Install	Learn	Maintain	Upgrade
Person					●	●	●	●
Phone/ Fax		○		○		○	●	○
Catalog / Mail	●							
Internet			○	○		○	○	○
System			●	●				
Email	○	○	○					

Customer Performance Rating		
Strong	Average	Weak
●	◐	○

Customer Importance		
Low	Medium	High
L		

Figure 8-7 XYZ customer identified priorities and gaps

Gaps

The customer touch point matrix provides a picture of the various media that your company is currently using to interact with your current customer segments. Figure 8-8 shows XYZ's customer experience matrix for two of its original industry segments and for consumers.

As you can see, XYZ discovered that there was virtually no difference in the way it was delivering industry experiences; that's one of the reasons they decided to rethink their segmentation strategy – they weren't using it anyway!

Using the touch point matrix and the customer priority matrix, we can identify those areas which we are not taking advantage of and which the customer finds to be most important. We also can identify the areas in which we are doing the poorest in comparison to our competitors. These two tools form the basis from which all future CRM projects can be prioritized and measured. Any project that might touch the "large business" segment must be governed and measured by this Customer Experience Map.

	Financial Services				Telecommunications				Consumer			
	Consider	Purchase	Install	Use	Consider	Purchase	Install	Use	Consider	Purchase	Install	Use
Person	X	X	X	X	X	X	X	X				
Phone/ Fax				X				X	X	X	X	
Event	X			X	X		X	X				
Catalog/ Mail								X	X			
Internet	X	X		X	X	X		X	X	X	X	X
System		X			X							
Email	X				X				X			X
Broadcast	X				X				X			

Figure 8-8   XYZ's customer touch point matrix for three segments

8.5   Creating a Strategic Proposal

At the end of the findings assessment, you will have summarized and analyzed everything you have learned through your interviews, surveys, and research. You will have a document summarizing what you learned from each of the four data collection tools. These findings will be used to develop your actual strategic proposal, which includes your recommendations of what should be done and a plan for how to get there.

8.5.1   Strategic Recommendations

The set of strategic recommendations describe where you propose that your company should go. Recommendations are the "what" of your strategy and will cover all of the following:

• Scope (information, process, technology and people)
• Organization and governance (ownership, standards, customer experience maps)
• Common Concepts (definitions, framework)

We will look at each of these recommendations in more detail, but remember that at the strategic planning level, we are still looking down from the 100,000-foot level. The strategic recommendations will be very broad. We will spend time determining the specifics as we work on each individual project.

Scope

Scope sets the boundaries for your efforts. It outlines the information, processes, technology and people that will be included in your CRM program. Of course, there will be impact across the entire company, but the scope (focus, investment) is limited to those people, processes, and so on that directly interact with the customer. At the strategic level, we don't have enough detail to actually build a system, but we can draw a high-level picture of what will be covered by our CRM program. As each project is launched, we will produce a detailed list of actual data elements that we need in each to resolve the current problem or opportunity.

XYZ's strategic results for setting scope are covered in detail when we look at each of the four components in depth in Chapters 11 through 14.

Information at the strategy level is a high-level outline of the stuff that is important for our company to know about. This "stuff" includes:

- People—customers, employees
- Places—countries, cities
- Things—products, equipment, inventory
- Ideas/concepts—targets, plans

Process at the strategic level will usually be a list of those marketing, sales, service, and support processes with which a customer interacts directly: order management, customer support, and direct marketing, for example. CRM does not cover R&D or product quality, although these clearly do have a strong influence on the customer experience.

Technology includes all the systems that currently or are planned to support CRM processes and deliver elements of the customer experience.

People include those who work in sales, marketing, customer services, or product support and who are involved in the CRM processes and/or those who interact directly with customers.

The detailed scope for each of these components will be established for each project as the project definition phase is launched.

Organization and Governance

Organization and governance is a critical element of the strategic recommendations. Because CRM impacts multiple functions, you cannot be successful unless you have widespread understanding of and support for your governance plan. Whether it is a single individual or a steering committee, they must have the POWER to make and enforce decisions that impact the customer. Too many times, Chief Customer Officers (CCO) or Steering Committees are identified but are given no authority to enforce their decisions. This kind of figurehead position doing lip service to CRM principles will never lead to successful implementation of a CRM program. The authority given to the individual or group must be real, and it must be accompanied by the responsibility for delivering success.

Organization for CRM can, as I said, come from an individual, a group, or a combination. Because there is seldom a single individual with responsibility for all the CRM functions, most organizations today choose the committee approach. But there is a real danger to the program if the steering council members are not placed high enough in the organization and don't have enough clout to make change happen.

Another danger is that the CCO or the council members are too high in the organization and don't understand enough of what CRM is and what's needed to make realistic decisions and monitor results. Be wary of the emperor with no clothes! As discussed in Chapter 7, this is the best structure for CRM leadership:

- A senior executive sponsor with visibility who acts as program champion
- A Chief Customer Officer or CRM Council made up of senior functional managers who have authority and responsibility for the program and are highly involved and knowledgeable
- A program team that knows the day-to-day details and can raise cross-functional issues to the steering council or CCO
- Project teams that do the actual work (Project teams include both IT staff and business people. Their relative project involvement shifts from phase to phase of the CRM cycle.)

The size and complexity of this structure varies dramatically by the size of the company and by the CRM program. Just be sure that you have all three functions covered (sponsor, leadership, working team).

Governance includes all the rules, responsibilities, metrics, and so on that ensure the ongoing success of your CRM program:

- Business principles are the bylaws of your CRM program. For each project, you will define specific business rules and company standards that support each principle. At the time you set your strategy, you will have established only high-level principles such those identified by XYZ:
  - We will know who our customers are.
  - We will differentiate our customers and treat our best customers best.
  - We will deliver consistent treatment across all CRM functions.
- Responsibility for delivering customer experience needs to be recognized and widely communicated (up-front communication of who is responsible).
- Measurements need to be established. At the strategic level, this might be reflected as an increase of overall customer loyalty of a certain percentage.

For each project, you will define specific business rules and company standards that support each strategic principle. Individuals throughout the organization must have the appropriate guidance and training. Specific metrics will be established.

Common Concepts

Common concepts are how we develop a common understanding of our current state and future direction. These common concepts provide us with a common vision and language for understanding where we're going, where we are, how we plan to get from here to there, and a consistent way to understand our progress.

Definitions are a critical element of your CRM program because they will make up a common language to describe CRM that everyone in your company understands. We discussed the importance of a common language in Chapter 2 when we created the definition of CRM that we have used throughout this book. Remember, if you don't all agree on what CRM is, you can never be sure that your approach is understood and supported. At the strategy level, you may reach agreement on only a few definitions, such as those shown in Table 8-9.

Table 8-9 Common Vocabulary

Definition	Purpose
CRM	You must define the basis of a common understanding and common expectations for what your company means by CRM if you want your project to succeed.
Customer (prospect/suspect?)	Everyone knows what is included in the term "customer." It's the C in CRM.
Customer segments	You must identify the important groups of customers (a single person, buyers of certain products, a group of customers with similar characteristics, etc.) that your company wants to treat independent of one another.
Customer life cycle	You must determine whether your customer life cycle represents your *internal* perspective (such as market, sell, support) or your *customer's* perspective (e.g., consider, purchase, etc.)
Touch points	You must define what a touch point is and which ones are important to you.

As one example, XYZ decided on a very simple new framework for customer segmentation that it believed was a much better match for how they wanted to manage relationships.

Customer segments had traditionally been defined based on industry. One of the issues raised during strategic planning was that they don't actually do anything differently based on industry segments. There had been an earlier plan to customize solutions as well as sales and marketing campaigns to target a vertical industry. But that plan was never put into practice. As a result of the strategic plan, they have three global customer segments. XYZ assigns its customers to global segments based on the criteria in Table 8-10.

Table 8-10 XYZ's Strategic Customer Segments

Segment	Assignment Criteria
Strategic, large, named companies	People who work at companies that are put on *the list* because they are the most valuable to XYZ
Small/medium companies	People who work at any company not on *the list*
Consumers	People using products at home for personal use

Using these new segments, XYZ was able to define its goal customer experience maps by customer segment. Figure 8-9 shows XYZ's customer experience map for its named customers. It shows both the touch points that will be used for named accounts and the experience standards that will be monitored to ensure that the appropriate level of experience is delivered.

Using the information from the customer and competitive survey, as well as our own internal knowledge, we can define what types of experiences we want to deliver to different customer segments as seen in Figure 8-9. Reviewing and approving the experience standards is one of the responsibilities of the Steering Committee.

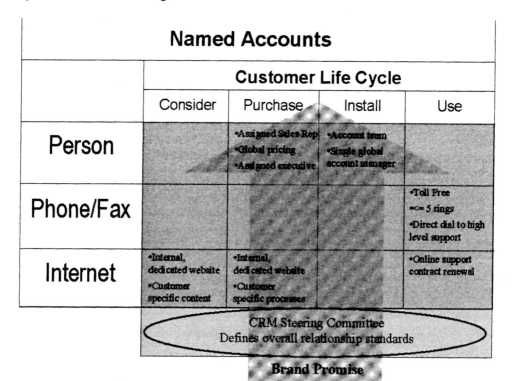

Figure 8-9 The named accounts customer experience map

We create these and other definitions so we have a common way of describing and under-standing what is being worked on. As you begin project work, you will develop common defini-tions of more detailed items such as Revenue, Cost of Sales, etc. You will build a dictionary of CRM terms that mean the same thing across your entire organization. This means that, eventu-ally, when anyone looks at any report, they really understand what each detail means.

Does this mean that all your business people must learn about data modeling? No, it doesn't mean that. But it does mean that the business can't completely delegate decisions to IT; they have to retain ownership of the key data and what they mean because the business is where the knowledge is. Information Technology can help you define the framework and maintain the dictionary, and, of course, they must build any new databases to match.

The CRM framework is the image that brings all these elements together. It shows the relationship between the customer and the life cycle at the center, with touch points and CRM organizations organized around them. It is built to identify which of all these CRM program alternatives are relevant to your business and your customers. Figure 8-10 shows XYZ Corpora-tion's CRM framework.

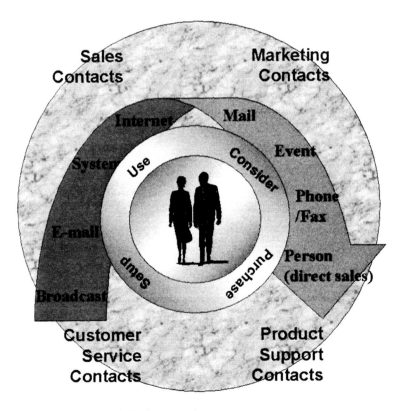

Figure 8-10 XYZ Corporation's CRM framework

Your internal interviews will reveal which concepts have little common understanding across your company. These will be the most important concepts needing clear and well-communicated clarification.

8.5.2   The Plan

The three planning tools (priorities, roadmap, and risk assessment) are built on the results collected during the assessments. Your CRM strategic plan will be built around a project roadmap, governed by your business priorities, and supplemented by a risk reduction strategy. Your plan will include these three elements: project priorities, project roadmap, and project risk plan.

Project Priorities

The Gap and Priorities diagram we saw in Figure 8-7 is the first piece of input we will use to develop our priorities. We want to start with an issue or opportunity in an area that has high customer importance and in which we are in a weak competitive position. Business importance is another key factor.

Generally, we'll uncover four or five areas that meet these criteria. Of course, an actual project must be focused narrowly enough that it can be completed in six to nine months, but we aren't yet at that stage. It is unlikely that we would be able to solve an entire business issue in such a short time frame, so for now we will just prioritize the business areas. If the business priorities aren't immediately obvious (often, they are) a good method for resolving differences of opinion is for the CRM council or other knowledge constituents to vote. Here are a couple of good mechanisms for making these kinds of prioritization:

- **N/3 Test:** Everyone is given the same number of votes. The number is determined by dividing the number of items by three (15 items = 5 votes each; 5 items = 2 votes each). The knowledgeable voters can cast their votes any way they wish: all for one candidate, spread evenly across several, or whatever.
- **100 Dollar Test:** Everyone is given a hundred dollars to spend. They can put all the money on one item or spread the money across several items (the distribution does not have to be in equal amounts).

The candidates are prioritized in the order of votes or dollars received. I have found the N/3 Test to be most successful because the number of votes allowed varies with the number of items to prioritized. In addition, there are fewer voting units to cast, so there is a stronger likelihood of real choices being made. Others prefer the idea that the voters are making a financial investment in their decisions. Either works just fine.

Next, we'll look at the system inventory. What projects are currently underway or planned in the near term? Identify the projects that map to the highlighted cells in the gaps and priorities diagram in Figure 8-7, and corral them into your overall CRM effort. If work has already been started in a key area, try to build on it instead of throwing everything away. It's surprising that so many programs are launched on the basis of reinventing everything. This is a waste of time and money and significantly alienates those involved in the project. After you have identified where you want to be, it is surprising how many current projects can actually be channeled in the right direction with a little analysis and effort. Of course, if there are investments being made in areas that are not important to your customers, you should take a serious look at them. Table 8-11 shows the results of XYZ's program prioritization efforts.

Table 8-11 XYZ's Project Priorities

Project Area	Issue	Priority Votes
A. **MyXYZ:** Personalized customer web sites	We sell CRM solutions, but don't use them. We make it difficult to do business with us.	8
B. Consistent customer identification	Can't recognize customers across all touch points. Don't know who they are.	5
C. **SFA:** Sales Force Automation	Current infrastructure doesn't support growth targets. Need to improve Sales Force productivity.	2
D. Inside Sales Integration	Execute on channel strategy. Customers are confused by our multiple channels with different messages	1
E. Identify most valuable customers	We don't know who our most valuable (profitable) customers are.	0

Now that we've identified our initial priorities, we need build a roadmap that shows what we expect the first few projects to be and when they are likely to be launched.

Project Roadmap

Our first project should be one that is important, given the criteria above, but not strategically critical. Picking a mission critical starting point is too big a risk when you are just getting started. Scope the project to be completed in about six months or less. Six months gives you the ability to deliver a *proof of concept.* A proof of concept delivers real results (unlike a prototype, which is just a mock up) based on real data. It delivers real (if limited) functionality and can be put into use immediately, making a foundation for adding features and functionality. A project of this length is the perfect size for proving that your approach works without the risk that you never get done or that the business or sponsorship has changed before you can finish. If you can select a project that is already underway, that is an additional benefit, but you may need to scope it down to be sure that you can deliver something useful in six months.

Your roadmap lets people know when future elements are planned and the six-month scope allows you to deliver quick wins. This is critical to setting realistic expectations throughout the company. Your strategic direction and the CRM cycle ensure that each project leads you toward your desired goal and checks for changes to the goal before launching the next project. Know where to start, what comes next, and when it will happen. If you've identified projects that are likely to be canceled, you'll have more leverage if you deliver a quick win. Figure 8-11 shows XYZ's tentative project roadmap for the first year of its CRM program.

The project roadmap is especially important for organizations that have low congruence around the direction and priorities of their CRM programs. There is another useful device for improving project cohesiveness. It's important to create an identity for major elements of the new CRM program.

The team decided to name the new customer master for its purpose: electronic customer identification or El Cid (yes, cute acronyms are **very** popular). This internal brand name for the system or project (often with some associated logo) gives the organization a shorthand way of identifying and referring to the project. I'm sure you all have one or two of coffee mugs that are similar to the one in Figure 8-12.

It helps team members come together around the common program goal. And, of course, it's the reason that many of us will never have to buy another T-shirt again.

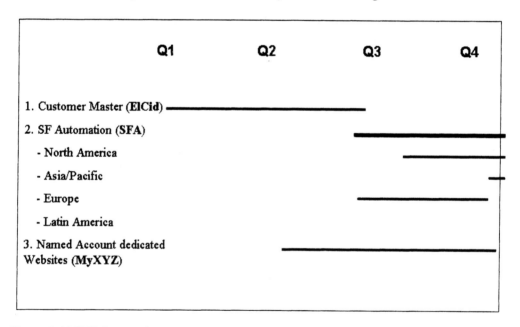

Figure 8-11 XYZ Corporation's project roadmap

Figure 8-12 El Cid Internal Brand Identity

Risk Reduction Plan

The risk reduction plan allows us to be prepared in advance to eliminate or reduce the threat of common as well as company-specific risks to our CRM Program. Table 8-12 lists the key risks identified by XYZ Corporation and the strategies it established to address each of these risks.

We also will have to identify who is responsible for implementing each strategy and when. Are some so critical that we want to take some steps up front? Are there others that can wait until we see signs of the problem arising? You'll answer all these questions as part of your risk prevention plan.

Now that we have completed our CRM strategy, we are ready to start building our infra-structure by launching our first project.

Table 8-12 XYZ Corporation's Risk Reduction Plan

Program Risks	Applicable Strategies	Strategies
Lack of sponsorship, leadership	1, 2, 3, 4, 8	1. Governance model = steering committee and executive sponsor 2. Cross-functional working teams chartered 3. Develop overall plan and roadmap, and keep them up to date 4. Business and technology program managers 5. Well-defined business processes 6. Finalize Information Technology architecture; build key master files 7. Formal change-management plan 8. Formal communication plan
No formal planning method	4, 7, 8	
Lack of consistent processes	5, 7	
Organizational silos	3, 1, 2, 7, 8	
Technology	6, 5	

Questions for Reflection

These questions will start you thinking about where your company is today and where it's headed. First think about where you want to be, then write down your current status for each of the following common concepts:

1. What's the future and current state of your customer segmentation strategy?
2. What's the current state of your customer's life cycle? Should it change in the future? How can you help?
3. What's the future and current state of your customer touch point strategy?

CHAPTER 9

Launching a Project

We've completed the necessary preparations for our CRM program and created our strategy. It's time to start building the supporting infrastructure that will allow us to deliver CRM success. In the second phase of the CRM lifecycle, we will work on projects that will create the components that are necessary for CRM success. As a result of the strategic planning process, we have identified the business goals and opportunities and the customer and competitive priorities that helped us prioritize where we should begin. Figure 9-1 shows that launching the project is the transition step between strategy development and actually building the infrastructure.

Like all the transition steps that will follow, the project launch ends the preceding lifecycle phase and starts the next phase. Typically transitions signal a shift in responsibilities. The project launch is when the IT functions begin to take on more responsibility from the business functions. There are two key steps involved:

- Select the best project
- Determine scope, schedule, resources

These steps do represent the beginning of the transition, but not a complete hand off. Too many companies think the business involvement ends here, but these companies never deliver successful projects.

Figure 9-1 Launch Project

9.1 Choosing the Right Project

First, we will fully define the project focus, objective, and scope. Remember that we will do our best to set the scope of the project so that it can be achieved while we still have the attention of the project participants, leaders, and sponsors, but that it still must deliver meaningful results in the high-priority area we identified.

9.1.1 Project Criteria

In Chapter 5, we introduced the project definition criteria that will help us plan a project we can successfully complete. Such projects will:

- Be completed in a matter of months (before anyone can lose interest)
- Move the organization toward the desired goal (not in the wrong direction)
- Yield a visible and measurable result (which must be communicated widely)
- Build on previous success (show continuous progress and avoid rework)

What is the purpose of this emphasis on taking small, manageable steps? Why not just go straight for the gold?

9.1.2 Why Small Projects?

Bodil Berggren, Chief Information Officer of Wärtsilä Corporation headquartered in Helsinki, Finland, is convinced that small, quick wins are the only way her that program will be successful. Wärtsilä's core business is its three Power Divisions: Marine, Power Plants, and Plant and Marine Services. Wärtsilä is challenged with expanding its e-business presence, and some of the key executives wanted to just "do" e-business and be done with it. Bodil uses an image like Figure 9-2 with the executive team to convey the importance of building success from a series of small projects that each lead in the direction of the company's goal.

At the end of each project, not only has Wärtsilä delivered real results, but also it has the opportunity to check that the program is really on course to the goal and that the goal is still where the executive team thought it was. These checkpoints are critical in keeping a program on course. At the end of an 18-month project, there is likelihood of the program being much further off course. It isn't easy to make major program direction changes, too much rework is likely to be involved, so if the check points are happening every six months or so, there are frequent opportunities to make small corrections.

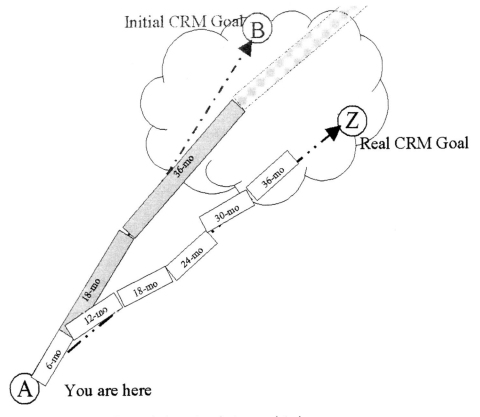

Figure 9-2 Taking small steps helps get projects completed.

If we could be absolutely sure where our ultimate goal is and could clearly see the path from A to Z, then we would follow that path directly to the goal. But even if we were absolutely sure that we wanted to end up at Z and we knew where Z was, we would still be best served by creating small project steps. Large projects are more difficult to plan, more complicated to manage, have a tendency to get further off track before issues are uncovered, and can run into priority and resource conflicts more often than small projects. Perhaps the best piece of coaching I ever received was from my first professional manager who advised me that if a problem seemed too big to solve, I should break it down into smaller pieces until I got to one that I completely understood. That's the place to start.

 KEY IDEA

Divide large problems into pieces that are understandable. Never start a project unless it's small enough that you completely understand it.

Projects with objectives that are too big and broad have virtually no chance of being thoroughly understood and little chance of being successful. A project with a goal of "increasing sales" or "becoming an e-business" are simply not specific enough to allow a clear definition of success, much less be able to tell if you've achieved it. However, a project objective such as "sell upgrades to customers whose product is more than three years old" can be precisely defined, and the results can be measured. We can understand how to identify the specific target customers, we can figure out where to get the necessary information, and we can measure the upgrade sales to that specific segment.

In reality, it's rare indeed to know your precise CRM goal during the early program stages. Even if you spent a year or more creating your strategic plan, it's nearly impossible to know precisely where your organization should be in the future. And we don't intend to spend anything like a year on our strategy. We want to take a quick pulse and get a feel for the general direction in which we want to head. We don't want to spend months invested in analysis that never lets us get started. The development of a strategic goal allows us to identify projects that are headed in the right direction, but give us the flexibility to modify our path for any of these common reasons:

- The real goal isn't exactly where we think it is at first; the future is too cloudy.
- Changes in the marketplace over time will influence the location of the goal.
- Changes in our business strategy over time will influence where we need to be.
- Each project may not take us in exactly the direction we think it does.

This first project is where the rubber meets the road. You've spent time with all the interested parties, including senior management, identifying strategic goals and setting realistic expectations for your CRM program. Now, you've got to start delivering on those expectations. So it's important to pick the right project. We want to begin with a project that has a good chance of being completed successfully, will deliver meaningful results, and is not so critical to the organization's operational success that there will be serious trouble if the project fails to meet all its goals.

9.1.3   Picking Your Project

The success of any project is measured by how well it meets expectations. For your first project, when you are still building support and confidence for your efforts, it is even more important to be able to do what you said you were going to do. The other important project outcome is to deliver results that are meaningful, that deliver a visible business benefit. At the end of the day, you can gauge success by whether or not you continue to have support and funding.

KEY IDEA

A project is successful if you and your team get to do the next one.

We should have two objectives: confidence and contribution. To achieve these objectives, we want to do everything possible to eliminate complexity and risk while ensuring meaningful results. Unfortunately, the two objectives often work against each other. Projects that are highly visible and have lots of user commitment are usually too big! Often, they are also so critical to the company's future that the slightest missed expectation has a very negative impact.

We need to find the right balance between a project that is achievable and important, but not so critical that the risk of failure is catastrophic. We can select the best project by evaluating all the candidates as to how well they meet important scope and impact criteria. In Chapter 8, we saw that XYZ had identified five important project areas and that two of them (MyXYZ and El Cid) were clearly identified as the top two priorities. They used a scoring tool shown in Table 9-1 to select their first project. Although MyXYZ is certainly an important project, the results from XYZ's assessment indicate that El Cid clearly has more characteristics that match what we're looking for, especially in a first project. MyXYZ is just too critical and too risky to tackle at this time. A scoring technique like this helps take the emotion out of setting priorities. A low score on this scorecard is best.

Table 9-1 Project Selection Scorecard for XYZ's First Project

	Project Scoring Characteristics	Target	A) MyXYZ		B) El Cid	
Size	Number of functions impacted	Few	All	3	All	3
	Number of current systems impacted	Few	Many	3	Many	3
	Complexity of business activity	Low	High	3	Low	1
	Number of data subjects	Few	Many	3	Few	1
	Scope or size	Small	Large	3	Small	1
	Number of future systems on which this project depends	Low	1	2	0	1
Impact	Importance—how meaningful the project is to company (zero importance scores 20)	High	High	1	Med	3
	Critical—how critical slippage or failure is to overall business goals	Low	Med	2	Med	2
	User commitment	High	Med	2	Med	2
	Risk—how likely it is to be unsuccessful	Low	Low	1	Low	1
		TOTAL		**23**		**17**

You can use a tool like this for each project selection. Determine the score for the top few projects on your list. Often, the priority-ranking activity discussed in Chapter 8 results in a clear break between the top projects and the rest of the pack. In XYZ's case, MyXYZ and El Cid received 13 out of the total 16 votes cast, so XYZ developed scores for just these two. As you complete an entire CRM project cycle, you will revisit remaining priorities and any new ones that have arisen, and you will go through the same ranking steps with the governance council and then score each of the top priorities. At some point, the lower risk projects will be done, and despite its fairly high risk, a project like MyXYZ will be selected. As time goes by, the important "low-hanging fruit" will be accomplished. And after your program is well established, critical projects will actually be less risky to accomplish.

Don't pick a project that has no importance, no matter how well it scores in other areas. If you start with a project that is selected just because the scope was appropriate, you'll have proved nothing at the end of your efforts. A reaction of "so what" will not gain support for your future efforts.

9.1.4 "Branding" Your Project Internally

Once they'd defined the high-level project scope the team realized they were not going to be able to deliver all of El Cid in six months. They would be able to build only a piece of the whole system. They'd had a painful experience in the past naming a partial implementation of a big system the same thing as the whole system. No one ever understood what they would get out of that first project. *Don't ever do this.* About the only way to recover is to rename the system itself.

Once you've invested in creating a project or system internal brand it's very painful to change. After celebrating the completion of the El Cid *project* it would be difficult to explain why the El Cid *system* still had a long way to go. Since the El Cid system was named after the eleventh century Spanish soldier who conquered the ancient kingdom of Valencia (okay, they probably named it after the Sophia Loren and Charlton Heston movie – but it was the same guy). At any rate, in keeping with the Spanish theme, the team decided to call the first project Valencia (it wouldn't take much thinking to keep on delivering pieces of El Cid with subsequent projects named after other cities in Spain) with the project identity mage shown in Figure 9-3.

Once the team had picked the best project and branded it, they turned their focus on deciding exactly what Valencia will require.

Figure 9-3 Valencia project identity

9.2   Deciding What Needs to Be Done

It's time to determine the requirements of the specific project that we've chosen. We need to specify the focus and direction of the overall project and the project-specific details (scope) of each component. We'll develop these details for each component one at a time in Chapters 11 through 14.

Just as planning your overall strategy is a key first step in your overall CRM program success, so project planning is critical to each individual project success. The best way to begin this transition step is with a *project launch meeting,* a formal meeting with all the proposed team members and sponsors in which you all take a first pass at developing a project overview.

9.2.1   Project Charter

We create a project plan by starting with a meeting that will gather the information needed for the project overview that identifies and builds consensus on a number of key project items:

- Direction: the key opportunity, problem, or issue that we hope to address with the project, including critical success factors and other metrics
- Focus: the project objective or deliverable, target customer, or offer
- Scope: the high-level requirements for information, process, people, and technology

The project overview is completed as a result of a *project launch,* which is a meeting that pulls the whole team together to get agreement and buy-in for the project. A launch sets the stage for a successful project, introduces team members to each other, and takes the first pass at project direction, focus, and scope.

Meeting Attendees

This is the first opportunity to get the whole team together. The project sponsor must at least appear to kick off the meeting and demonstrate strong understanding, commitment, and support. It's important to have an objective facilitator who keeps the meeting on schedule, ensures that everyone participates, and identifies when a discussion or issue is likely to sidetrack progress. These should be logged and addressed at the end of the meeting so that people can be convinced to let go of them and move on. Meeting attendees should include:

- Facilitator (This person should be objective and experienced as a facilitator and preferably not one of the CRM team members. A facilitator can be from a business function, Information Technology, or an outside consultancy.)
- Executive Sponsor (This person provides project support and a welcome, sometimes only at the kickoff.)
- CRM Program Manager
- Valencia Project Manager

- Business team members from each of the impacted functional areas
- Information Technology team members

By the way, if you have 100 people attending your launch meeting, you won't even get through the introductions in eight hours. I suggest postponing the meeting until you get the group down to a reasonable number—no more than 15 participants. Large groups almost never come to any decisions. A successful approach is to assign a spokesperson for each group of five to seven people with similar interests and perspectives. These spokespersons are the meeting attendees, and they are responsible for communicating with the rest of the group.

The facilitator's job is to keep the meeting on track and moving, but you can help by creating and distributing a formal agenda that sets participant expectations appropriately.

Meeting Agenda

The planned agenda totals five hours of real work, but you always need to plan on breaks and allow for interruptions, digressions, extended discussions, etc. Because unexpected things always happen, the attendees should plan to dedicate at least six hours to the launch meeting; a whole day is preferable. If you can provide lunch, you can keep the time limited to a half hour or even make it into a working lunch if you fall behind. Table 9-2 shows a sample agenda for XYZ's project launch meeting for the Valencia project.

Table 9-2 Valencia Project Launch Agenda

Agenda: Project Launch	Project: Valencia	Date:
Time	**Topic**	**Leader/ participants**
20 minutes	Welcome and kickoff	Project Sponsor
10 minutes	Review meeting agenda, expectations, and ground rules	Facilitator
5 minutes per attendee (~ 60 minutes)	Individual introductions: Functional perspective represented, position, why interested in this project	*Facilitator*, all
30 minutes	Set direction: Review driving strategic issue or opportunity; brainstorm issues or opportunities and risks	*Project manager*, all
90 minutes	Define focus: Business functions, customers, customer offer	*Facilitator*, all
60 minutes	Determine scope: Review strategic plan recommendations and identify component scope (information, process, technology, people)	*Facilitator*, all
30 minutes	Review meeting accomplishments; discuss next steps and timing; review action items, owners, and due dates; assign owners to new project issues	Facilitator

Meeting Results: Project Overview

In the Project Overview, we summarize the results and decisions made during the project launch. Generally, a project overview is a single-page document; it is business focused and should be distributed throughout the organization as one of the many forms of communication. This overview should be kept up to date and redistributed whenever changes are made. The project overview shown in Table 9-3 summarizes XYZ's results from the Valencia project launch.

Table 9-3 Valencia Project Overview

Project Title: Valencia		
Direction (issue/opportunity, critical success factors or CSFs)		We don't know who our most valuable customers are, because we identify customers differently in every system. We can't be sure of their total purchases or how much it costs to serve them.
Focus (business functions, target customers, customer offer)		Business functions: Product (S800) Marketing; Business-to-Business Sales • *Target Customers:* Top 50 customers (by last year's purchases) who own a model 815 or 817 fan • *Offer:* Upgrade trade-in to new 825/827 model and get a trade in rebate
Scope (what's in and what's out)		
Component	**Scope Is**	**Scope Is *Not***
Information	Categories	Customer, Installed Base	Product, competitor, etc.
	Sources	Orders, product registrations	Support contracts, etc.
Process		Database Marketing Inbound telesales	Marcom, Channel Sales
Technology		Customer Identification Reference file; client server	Transaction system
People		Product marketing managers for 825 and 827 in North America; North American premier call center reps.	Sales reps, etc. Other products Europe, South America, Asia

Following the launch, we will begin a series of analysis activities including individual interviews, group meetings, and report reviews that will help us identify what needs to be done. We do need to get into some details, but just for the very small project we've selected. We will use several ways of uncovering the business requirements, so we still have to be careful that the detail doesn't overwhelm us. We will use the needs assessment to further refine the scope of the project so we can stay with our six-month plan. With the results of the needs analysis, we will develop a clear project summary including a project time line.

9.2.2   Gather Additional Requirements

To determine the detailed business requirements, we need to find a way of capturing the business knowledge from the affected CRM functions. At this point, virtually no technical decisions need to be made. Your business analysts may report into your IT organization, but the knowledge and decisions need to come from those who are doing the job and who will be directly impacted by the project.

In Figure 9-4, we see the repetitive, drill-down technique used to capture business knowledge and identify needs. We iterate these steps within each project until we have identified the appropriate level of detail, and we repeat the methodology for every project cycle as part of our spiral approach to building CRM.

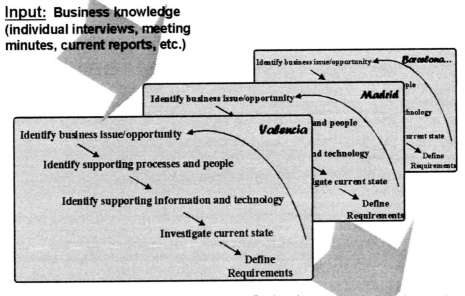

Figure 9-4 Analyzing needs

Each interview with different key individuals, each discussion or planning meeting, each investigation of current reports will be used to improve our understanding of the underlying focus, the objective(s), and the supporting information, processes, people, and technology needed to address the driving issue or opportunity.

9.2.3   Complete the Project Charter

The complete project charter is a very important document that will be the guidebook for tracking and communicating our overall project. The complete project charter will include both the project overview from Table 9-3 and some additional information specifying expected deliverables, timing, and resource requirements that make up the project summary. Because these three variables govern the delivery of a project, it's important to outline expectations in each of these areas so there are no surprises to anyone.

These three variables can be traded off against each other; to meet a deadline, you can add more resources (up to a point) or reduce the scope (up to a point; it must still have some visible value). The fourth section of the project summary is a tradeoff matrix where you can define up front, which of these three project variables is most flexible and which is least flexible. You are *constrained* by the variable that is least flexible, and you will *accept* virtually any outcome in the most flexible variable.

Almost no project exactly meets every element of its plan. Some believe that the average project estimate is off by about 50 percent. (That's another reason to start with a six-month time limit; even if the schedule is off by 50 percent, you can still have results in less than a year.) The tradeoff matrix lets everyone involved in the project know at the very beginning what is most important to control: deliverables, schedule, or resources. This eliminates lots of surprises and guesswork that can come up during the project itself.

The project summary that makes up the second part of the project charter covers these three key project variables and their relative importance. Table 9-4 illustrates some of the key decisions that XYZ made as a result of its further requirements gathering.

Table 9-4 Project Summary

Expected Deliverables
1. Customer reference file for managing consistent identification
2. Key data sources integrated (loaded and linked)
3. Top 50 customer companies audited and managed for high-quality company consistency
4. List of customer contacts at target companies who own 815 or 817 fans

High Level Schedule				
Milestone	**Due**	**Actual**	**Owner**	**Approved**
1. Launch/charter complete				
2. Analysis complete				
3. Design complete				
4. Construction complete				
5. User Test complete				
6. Implementation				

Key Resources			
Role	**Assigned Individual**	**Percentage of time assigned**	**Duration**
Executive Sponsor			
Program Manager			
Project Manager			
82x Series Product Manager			
NA Premier Call Center			
IT analysts, designers, engineers			

Project Tradeoff Matrix			
	Deliverables	**Schedule**	**Resources**
Constrain (least flexible)			X
Optimize		X	
Accept (most flexible)	X		

You can see that the complete project charter is likely to be only a few pages long. In every step along the way, we want to get just enough detail to move on to the next step. I do not believe that 100-page requirements documents serve any purpose (other than perhaps to pay for the salaries of a few consultants). First, it takes too much time to dig into agonizing detail until you're ready to start building. Second, huge requirements documents are seldom (if ever) read or understood. When one of these documents is approved, it is a sign of the user being overwhelmed. They figure that it must be right, because there's so much of it!

The project charter, on the other hand, covers all the key elements needed by the business functions and Information Technology to ensure understanding of business goals and objectives as well as project deliverables and schedule. This document is the blueprint that lets everyone concerned know what they need to know. The blueprint is turned over to the construction team to detail the specific design and construction plan. Our construction team includes anyone responsible for any of the infrastructure components (information, process, people, and technology).

9.3 Determining Component Scope

We know from Chapter 3 that our CRM infrastructure is made up of the four key components: information, process, technology, and people. That means that the project charter must include deliverables, milestones, and resources of these four components. If we define only the technology deliverables for a project, we will not be able to deliver successful results.

9.3.1 The Components

Each of these four components is critically important to CRM success. Let's review the importance of each one.

Information

Information is the raw material of CRM. Without information, there is no way to use automation to build and manage customer relationships. A web site that looks personalized (Welcome, Judy) but contains no information that is relevant to me is worse than visiting an anonymous web site. The information may be collected and stored by the IT organization, but it is the business functions that know what information they need to address the business objective.

Process

Our processes are the means by which we actually deliver experiences to customers. People used to manage the process interactions with customers and protected them from some of the disconnects between processes. Now, we are asking our IT departments to automate many of these processes, but it is still the business team that knows what customers expect, where the breakdowns are, and what doesn't work very well. As we automate more processes, we need to be sure that we heavily involve those who work directly with customers and (heavens!) even the customers themselves. Automating an old, broken process just allows more bad choices to be made faster.

Technology

Technology is the machinery that produces CRM results. All of the best information, process improvements, and change-management programs will be useless if you don't have the right technology in place. This is the reason that it is so critical to keep your IT team and business team working together from the beginning. It's silly to ask Information Technology to make all the business decisions or to wait until all the decisions are made and then throw a project charter over the wall to the IT department and hope they understand it. Build the partnership early, and make it work. The business function is the primary provider of the content of the system and Information Technology is the primary manager of the processing of the system. As we move through the life cycle, IT takes more ownership, but the business function always has some responsibility. Marketing may not do construction, but they must be involved in testing modules as they are developed and in the initial implementation when released.

Somewhere between the project launch (where the project is defined) and the end of analysis (where business requirements are analyzed) is the transition point where business function involvement drops below 50 percent and the IT team's responsibility grows to a significant percentage of the work.

People

Even though people may not be directly delivering some customer experiences any more, it is still people who can really understand and address customer needs. People and organizations can smooth the implementation of the new CRM capabilities and ensure success, or they can, for lack of education, tools, or whatever, guarantee that the new "system" will fail.

Now let's take a look at a concept that will help us understand each of the four CRM components from both the business perspective and the Information Technology perspective: the concept of the enterprise architecture.

9.3.2   Enterprise Architecture

The purpose of the enterprise architecture is to capture all the different knowledge and perspectives held by various key players in the organization about what makes the business work. John Zachman popularized the concept of the enterprise-wide information architecture in an article he published in 1987 in the IBM Systems Journal. Zachman's major contribution was the development of his framework for enterprise architectures.

Why should we care about yet another framework? As we've discussed, tools and methodologies help us understand and organize the work that needs to be done. Any effort that requires the joint participation of business functions and Information Technology needs a formalized model of who is responsible for what and a way that helps improve communication between the two teams. Of course, this is not just a CRM tool; all large programs that include a technology component need a way to bridge the communication gap between the business team and the IT team, which are jointly responsible for delivering the program. It's all about increasing understanding between groups of people who don't exactly share the same view of the situation.

Framework

Zachman introduced his Enterprise Architecture Framework as a way to organize and classify knowledge about the whole business so that this knowledge could be used to design and build an organization's enterprise-wide business infrastructure, including its CRM program.

Building your CRM infrastructure has many parallels with the process of constructing a new house. Let's take a look at what happens when you do decide to build a house. It would be very unusual if you just picked up the phone one day, called a contractor you found in the Yellow Pages, and said, "Hey, can you build a house for me? I've already got the property and some ideas, so I just need you to build it." As silly as it sounds, that is often what we ask the IT department to do when we need them to build our information systems.

 KEY IDEA

You will never get the system of your dreams without a method that helps you formally describe what you want built in terms that the builder can understand.

It is unlikely that any contractor would accept such a job, and if he did, it's unlikely that you would be happy with the result! Instead, you would start by listing and sketching some rough ideas of what you think you want. You give your ideas to an architect who works with you to develop some alternative rough plans or models that might meet your needs. After you pick the alternative you like best, the architect develops an overall picture (blueprint) of what should be built (to the best of everyone's knowledge at that time). Then the architect creates very specific technical specs for every major component (concrete, wood, plastic, finishes, etc.) of the construction. These plans go to the contractor so he can start delivering detailed specs to the individual subcontractors who will work on the various components: concrete, framing, electrical, plumbing, etc.

What we have just described is exactly what Zachman's framework covers, and not surprisingly, the framework is actually based on well-known principles used in the traditional disciplines of architecture and construction. It is made up of columns representing the six different elements of the finished product (for construction, these would be electrical, plumbing, etc.) and rows representing the five different perspectives (levels of detail such as owner, designer, subcontractor). Zachman includes a sixth row representing the end goal: a functioning enterprise.

We already know the critical elements or components of our CRM program: information, process, people, and technology. It should be no surprise that these are also the first four columns of the Zachman framework. The added insight from Zachman, as we've already discussed, is that each of these components must be viewed and defined from the perspective of each of the various stakeholders. These perspectives must be captured in sequence, starting with least level of detail. Each more detailed perspective must be derived from the previous level. (How else will the plumbing actually end up where you want the sink to be?) Each stakeholder, from business owner defining requirements to IT programmer writing computer code, has more detailed knowledge of what it takes to build the infrastructure.

The components of the Zachman framework are data, function, network, people, time, and motivation. Do the first four sound familiar? Just in case they don't, Table 9-5 shows the relationship to our CRM components.

Table 9-5 Components

Zachman's Components	Data	Function	Network	People
CRM Components	Information	Process	Technology	People

Zachman's list of stakeholders and the corresponding homeowner/business owner perspectives are shown in Table 9-6. The highest perspective, the owner's wish list, is the equivalent of the strategic plan that we completed in Chapter 8. As you remember, we developed a high-level outline of our entire CRM program. For each of the subsequent levels, we will drive down to each more detailed perspective for just what is needed for a current project. This is how we achieve quick wins while keeping focused on the overall strategic objective.

Table 9-6 Perspectives

Zachman's Stakeholder Perspectives	Business Scope	Business Model	System Model	Technology Model	Detailed Representations	Functioning Enterprise
Home (or Business) owner's Perspectives	Owner's Wish List	Owner's Needs View	Designer's View	Builder's View	Subcontractor's View	New Home

More information on the Zachman Framework can be found online at the Zachman Institute for Framework Advancement web site: www.zifa.com.

Ideally, companies would use this approach to understand needs and to design and build technology solutions for the entire enterprise. Practically speaking, if your company hasn't already applied this approach for your whole organization, the framework is still incredibly useful for understanding needs within just the front office organizations. Because CRM crosses multiple functions and needs broad business participation and perspective, a framework is a great way to understand what steps to take. If most of your house is okay, you don't need to pay an architect to redesign the whole thing. Just think of it as a remodel; Zachman's framework still works!

Although Zachman's framework is widely used within the IT community (including yours, I hope), we've already suggested the sad truth that Information Technology seldom gets much support or participation from the business owners who think technology is magic and somewhat beyond them. Building IT systems without demanding business owner participation is just like hiring a bunch of subcontractors to do the framing, install doors and windows, and lay electrical conduit without letting anyone know what you want the house to look like.

In Chapter 5, we saw that the relative responsibility for the internal CRM phases (1 and 2) is initially weighted heavily toward the business functions and transitions to heavy involvement of Information Technology. There is an Information Technology project life cycle that continues to be widely used today. The project life cycle steps correspond exactly to the business owner's perspectives as you see in Figure 9-5. As you can also see, the relative business function/IT department responsibilities map consistently to the stakeholder's perspectives and the traditional systems development project steps. The strong parallels between the business and the Information Technology description of the life cycle steps make it easier to understand each other's roles and responsibility. We're starting to develop a common language.

As we know, relative responsibility shifts step by step throughout each project life cycle step. The heaviest business involvement occurs in the early steps where the broadest perspective and least detail are required. Just about the time the project moves from the owner's needs view to the designer's view, much of the responsibility is transferred from primarily business to primarily IT. This transfer of responsibility takes place and can occur at different points for differ-

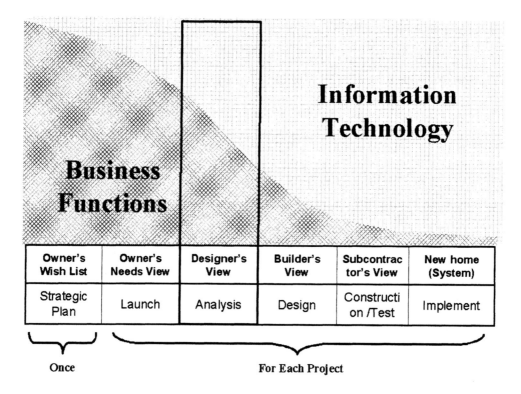

Figure 9-5 The relative responsibilities for CRM lifecycle internal phases

ent projects or even different components of the same project. The business may have most of the responsibility for all levels of the people component, but may be involved only at the highest strategy-setting level for the technology. The transfer is the point at which communication and handoff problems most often occur. For the most part, the transfer takes place sometime during one of the first three levels; this is why we will concentrate most of our efforts there. The handoff is always the most critical point in any technical project.

You will find a very readable and informative introduction to the high-level business view of Zachman's framework in *Building Enterprise Information Architectures* by Melissa Cook (1996). Cook does an excellent job of explaining how to work through the highest information, process, and technology levels. Table 9-7, adapted from Cook's work, shows the framework we will use.

Table 9-7 The CRM View of the Zachman Framework

	Information	Process	Technology	People
Owner's Wish List View	Data class (list of things important to the business)	Business function (list of types of work the business performs	Business location (list of places in which the business operates)	Organizations (list of the organizational units that are important to the business.
Owner's Needs View	Business subjects	Business process model	Business network	Organizational unit
Designer's View	Entity and relationship model	Activity	Distributed system architecture	Job role

This CRM view includes the four CRM core components (information, process, people, and technology) and the highest perspectives (owner's wish list, owner's needs view, and designer's view).

Method: Engineering Each Component

Just as the owner and architect work together to turn the owner's wish list into a sketchy floor plan and then a detailed blueprint, we need to be able to develop ever more detailed requirements and specifications for each of the infrastructure components.

The highest level (the owner's wish list) is actually a deliverable from the strategic plan that we developed in Chapter 8. At that time, we were introduced to the topic of *strategic planning* for the CRM components. However, we postponed the discussion of how to use the methodology until now, because the whole process of going from owner's wish list to designer's view will be easier to follow if discussed in one place for each component. But do remember, the owner's wish list for each of the components was completed as part of your strategic plan. During each project, we'll use the owner's wish list view as the starting point for identifying just enough of the lower levels of detail that we need to complete that project. The strategic plan provides the vision and focus that allow us build a successful CRM program in small steps.

It is imperative that each perspective is based on the preceding level, just with more detail. What would you think of a subcontractor who ignored the specs and just did what he wanted? I can tell you exactly what you'd think, because my family and I had one (or maybe I can't tell you, not in print anyway). We have been living with the shoddy results of the electrical subcontractor (who ignored the plans and did things his own way) for 15 years. Not a single week goes by that we don't have the opportunity to enjoy his creative and independent decisions! Sometimes, you may run into a programmer who has the same brand of creativity. It is great if you get to work with an IT department whose people are creative about how to achieve the predefined goal, but it is **not** okay for them to be creative about the goal itself.

Let's get a quick refresher on the strategic planning process we followed. We used four assessment tools to collect and analyze information from inside our company, from customers, and from sources that gave us information about our position relative to competitors. Then we used other tools to prepare our strategic proposal, which includes the owner's wish list for the information, process, technology, and people components.

9.4 Winning and Keeping Support

Winning and maintaining support for your program may not guarantee success, but the absence of broad-based support will ensure program failure. It's very important to include each of the following as part of your overall project charter.

9.4.1 Involve Key People

Involving key people in the strategic planning process is an important first step. Keeping them involved is also important. Your steering committee members and project team members should be in contact with a network of key players throughout the business (especially in their functional areas). They should be a focal point for bringing together perspectives and input on all key decisions, and they should be responsible for communicating the decisions back to their organizations. Especially in a large organization, you must keep key players engaged.

9.4.2 Leadership

In Chapter 7, we discussed the importance of program leadership. There are three key levels: the executive sponsor who is your strong advocate to the executive team, program governance through a steering committee or chief customer officer, and program management (which actually governs the individual projects).

9.4.3   Communicate, Communicate, Communicate

It just cannot be said often enough. The most important thing you can do to maintain support for your CRM program is to communicate your vision and your progress honestly and often. You can use these tools to support internal communications:

- Bulletin boards
- E-mail
- Your company's intranet
- Company publications
- Coffee talks and other department meetings

If you have an experienced internal communications department, work with these employees early. If you don't have one, I strongly suggest hiring a consultant with an internal communications practice. In either case, these communication experts will work with you to develop a formal communications plan.

This simple step can make the difference between visible and widely heralded success and anonymous failure. Most of us don't really think of the need for communication; after all, if you're doing the right thing everyone should know it, right? Wrong. No one will know it unless you tell him or her. You cannot communicate your key messages too often. To paraphrase an old adage, "Tell them what you're going to do, tell them what you're doing, and tell them what you did."

Honest communication is as important as constant communication. If part of the project changes or even fails, admit it. No revisionism! Sure, it is important to have success; we're doing everything we can to set ourselves up for success. But no human endeavor is ever perfect. Discussing some key learning that has modified a direction midstream lends credibility. Even if you do something really wrong, it's better to admit it and describe what you now know to do differently, rather than pretending you never intended to go there anyway. I hope that you work for a company that believes if you're not making any mistakes, you're not trying hard enough. If you don't work for a company like that, why in the world are you trying to do CRM anyway?

Now that we have our project blueprints, we are ready to turn things over to the project team who will actually develop the infrastructure components. Chapter 10 will introduce the steps for developing infrastructure and how they apply to each of the components.

Questions for Reflection

Pick one burning issue that you know your customers have with your company. Come up with a project approach that leads to a solution, one that can be accomplished in about six months, by answering these questions:

1. How many functions participate in creating the current situation? How many people are normally involved from each of the functions?

2. What processes impact this customer situation? If there is more than one process involved, what are the connections and disconnects between them?

3. What information would you need to access in order to make the customer situation better? Is it currently available somewhere? In how many places?

4. What technology systems are currently involved in creating the situation?

5. If all the numbers are large, the project is way too big. Can you identify a logical chunk of the problem that would make a step toward improving the situation? What kind of "offer" would you want to make to your customers as a result of completing the small chunk?

PART 3

CRM: Building It Right

CHAPTER 10

Building Infrastructure Components

W e've defined the strategic direction for our company's CRM program and identified our company-wide goals and objectives. We chose the project that best matched the characteristics for achieving successful results. We've identified the project team and managed to get everyone (sponsors, business leaders, and Information Technology) to participate in a project kick-off meeting where we focused on identifying the high-level business requirements for the project we've chosen.

We are ready to build each of the components, but we have to be careful. All the components must be developed and completed in parallel for the overall project to yield successful results. We will follow the same basic methodology for managing the development of each of the components so it will be easy to track progress across all four of the pieces. This will help ensure that all are ready to go at the same time because no single piece is much use without the other three.

The predetermined steps of this life cycle phase are not unique to CRM. Even the fact that there are four components is not unique to CRM. What is unique to CRM is what exactly makes up each of the four components. We are about to start the second phase of the CRM life cycle, building infrastructure, as you can see in Figure 10-1.

It's time to roll up our sleeves and get working on building each of the infrastructure components.

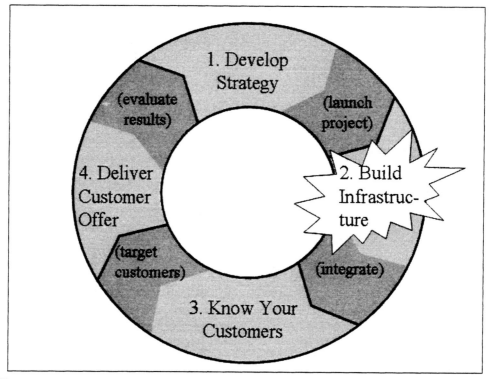

Figure 10-1 Phase 2: Building infrastructure

10.1 Following the Steps to Building Infrastructure

Building anything, from a house to a CRM solution, often involves multiple activities and multiple people. The strategic and project plans keep everyone focused on the end goal. A methodology that governs how the work gets done helps keep everything aligned and on track. I've been asked about how to justify all this effort because it may seem pretty big and very costly. The truth is, after your company has decided to adopt a CRM approach to managing customer relationships, following this kind of process is the quickest, most efficient and least costly way to achieve successful results.

There is a familiar project management method that is used heavily in the Information Technology world, but it also applies to and has been adopted by non-technical project teams. The standard development methodology includes these steps:

1. Launch the project.
2. Gather business requirements.
3. Analyze needs and design component.
4. Construct (and test) the solution.
5. Implement (and support) the solution.

In the CRM life cycle, the project launch occurs during the transition from strategic planning (Phase 1) to building infrastructure (Phase 2), and implementation (integration) occurs during the transition from building infrastructure to understanding customers (Phase 3). As you can see in Figure 10-2, this methodology aligns closely with the first half of our CRM life cycle, which includes the entire project development work that we do to create change inside the company.

The last step, supporting the infrastructure that has been built, is a critical consideration for each of the components. Although strictly speaking, support is not part of the CRM life cycle that focuses on repeated development efforts, it is extremely important to prepare to support each of the components as it becomes part of the organization's operational infrastructure. We will look at some of the considerations for supporting the CRM components in Chapters 20 and 21.

The building infrastructure phase is comprised of the remaining three steps: requirements, analysis and design, and construction. Table 10-1 summarizes these infrastructure-building activities, their deliverables, and who should participate.

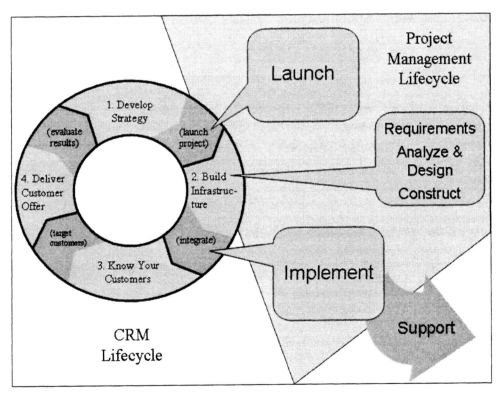

Figure 10-2 Development process methodology

Table 10-1   Steps to Building Infrastructure

Step	CRM Framework
Gather business requirements	Owner's Wants View (project launch)
	Owner's Needs View
Analyze and design component	Designer's View
	Builder's View
Construct and test solution	Subcontractor's View
	New System Implementation (integration)

During project launch we identified the high level scope for the project. Now we'll start with the first development step, which is to gather business requirements for the new infrastructure.

10.2 Gathering Business Requirements

Gathering business requirements is primarily the responsibility of the business function experts. As we know, the highest-level CRM business requirements for each infrastructure component were generated during the strategic planning phase. These inventories of strategic business requirements are focused on the total CRM program and form the starting point for all of the subsequent project-specific and more detailed views.

For every project and every component, we begin from the point of view of the business people who will own and use the new tools and processes. These are the individuals who will make up the business members the project team and provide much of the business perspective. They are responsible for specifying the business requirements (owner's wants and owner's needs) for the project that is now underway, as shown in Figure 10-3.

It's important to have IT team members involved in the process from the very beginning also. The whole point of the work we're doing is to build communication and understanding across the whole team.

The strategic plan forms the overall focus that keeps each project moving toward the final goal. This means that if our goals shift as a result of new information and experience, it's important that the each of the four strategic requirements inventories be adjusted to reflect the change. We will refer to the strategic inventories every time we start and finish a project cycle.

10.2.1 Owner's Wants View

The owner's wants view is the first of the project-specific views. During strategic planning, XYZ identified the very high-level strategic requirements inventory for their overall CRM program. Then, at the project launch, they considered each of the four CRM components and identified which specific elements of the strategic inventory would be the focus for Valencia.

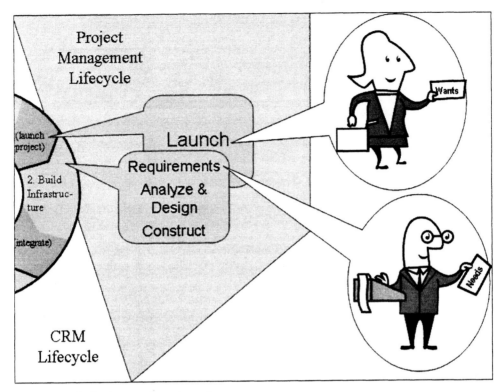

Figure 10-3 Gathering wants and needs

10.2.2 Owner's Needs View

Next, focusing just on the component scope identified during the launch, XYZ began the effort of developing more specific details that would actually help with the design and construction of the project components. The owner's needs view includes a more detailed description of Valencia's business requirements for information, process, technology, and people.

10.3 Analyzing and Designing Components

During the analysis and design step, responsibility generally shifts from primarily business function involvement to primarily Information Technology involvement. Generally, the designer's view (logical design) takes lots of investigation and a little bit of art and is a joint effort. Experts from the IT department do the builder's view (physical design) as you can see in Figure 10-4.

For each of the business views, we will develop the logical and physical design specifications that together make up the overall plan for building each component.

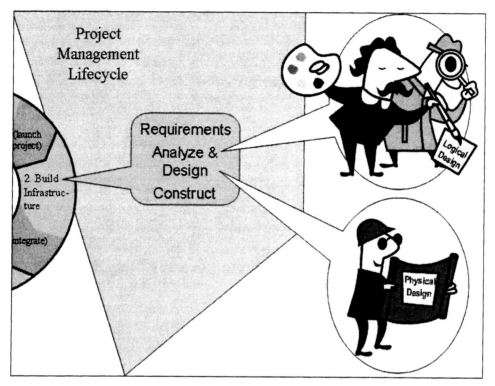

Figure 10-4 The design component

10.3.1 Designer's View

The designer's view is where the responsibility handoff between the business team members and the IT team members usually takes place. In Chapters 11 through 14 you will see that this is not always a fixed transfer point. The handoff happens earlier for the technology component and later for the people component, as might be expected.

In the designer's view, the business experts are asked to be a little more specific in describing their needs than they may normally be used to. The designer's view is a two-way dialog between the IT team members who know what questions they have before they can correctly build the component and the business team members who have the knowledge to answer the questions. This step is successful only if there are strong partnerships and great communication between the business and IT functions. If the business experts are too busy to answer questions, the IT folks won't know what to build. The methodology we will follow facilitates the creation of the designer's view.

10.3.2 Builder's View

Information Technology has virtually full responsibility for creating the builder's view of most of the CRM components. In the builder's view, the physical specifications for construction are specified. The builder's view uses the logical design that was created by business and IT experts working together to outline detailed requirements.

Normally, a system architect or designer in the IT department takes the logical design specifications and translates them into instructions and rules that a programmer can use to actually construct the system. (Of course, for the people component, it is probably someone from the business function, from human resources, or from an outside organization conversant in change management who will create the physical builder's view.)

10.4 Constructing a Solution

The construction step is, of course, when each element of the infrastructure is actually built. Information Technology is responsible for the construction of most of the components. This step includes building the component and testing it, as indicated in Figure 10-5.

And who always does the real work on a construction project? That's right, it's the subcontractors!

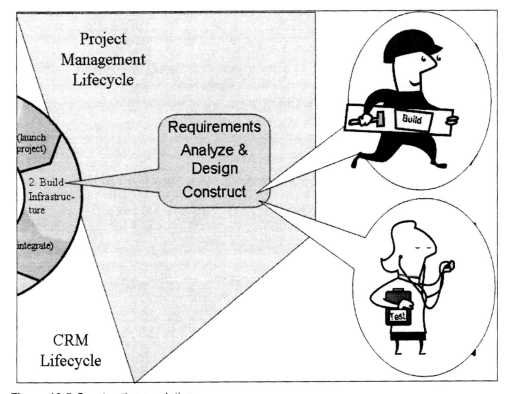

Figure 10-5 Constructing a solution

10.4.1 Subcontractor's View

The subcontractor's view is the actual construction of a working component of your CRM infrastructure. In the hands of experts in Information Technology organization, the component design specifications are turned into physical structures. For the people component, the organizational change infrastructure pieces, such as training, education, performance measures, and rewards, are the responsibility of the business functions in which the behavior changes need to occur, the human resources department with its expertise in education and training, and the IT team who built several of the new components and are familiar with how they work.

Often, as we know, companies will bring in consulting organizations to develop the change management training materials and other elements of the infrastructure. These same organizations have experts trained to facilitate the very complex task of managing change and are often kept on to build and even deliver the people component elements.

A final step in the construction process is to plan and implement thorough tests of each component. The IT team must create a plan to test each piece of data, software, and hardware. A strongly held value by many IT organizations is that the individuals who build the infrastructure should not be the people who test it. Just like proofreading your own work where we often see what we *meant* to write, test results can be misinterpreted by the programmer testing his own code. It's quite normal to test only for situations that were anticipated and that this system has been prepared to handle successfully. The best IT organizations have independent testing groups that do nothing but create and execute test plans.

The business experts must get involved in testing how all the components fit together. Does everything work as expected, and are the results accurate and dependable? For example, was the training class effective in helping future users understand what they can and should do with the new information and software?

10.4.2 Integrate Component

Component integration is the all-important activity of getting the new components up and running smoothly within the existing business environment and developing a support plan. The IT team is responsible for safely installing the new system, and integrating the new tools and data into the existing system infrastructure. Business and IT experts working together will teach the new system users how to operate the tools (which is how we integrate the people component). This is the transition step to the next phase of the CRM lifecycle when we will begin to know our customers. We will discuss this critical step in more detail in Chapter 16.

10.5 Putting It All Together

We are getting ready to start the second of the two internal phases of the CRM life cycle. In preparation, we have reviewed some fundamentals of development project management that will improve our ability to govern the project progress and assist the teamwork and communication between the business and IT functions.

10.5.1   Project Development Framework

The first two phases of the project life cycle focus on what we must do inside the organization to prepare for building better customer relationships. Strategic planning develops a focus for the company's overall CRM program so that infrastructure development can be done in small steps that have a high likelihood of success. The project management methodology is a very familiar framework for managing the administrative flow of a project. The CRM component framework defines the respective responsibilities between the IT and business experts and how and where handoffs will take place. Table 10-2 shows the relationship between the three frameworks and shows who is the primary user of each of them.

Table 10-2 Project Development Framework

CRM Life Cycle (Internal Phases)	Project Management Methodology	CRM Component Framework
Methodology we will follow repeatedly to make sure that each individual project is moving us toward our final goal.	Standard approach to project administration that is used to control project progress and communicate status.	Governs the relationship between business team roles/expertise and the IT team roles/expertise. Clarifies responsibilities.
Used by CRM Program Team.	Used by Project Manager.	Used by working team members, (e.g. programmers).
1. Set Strategy Project launch	Strategic Planning Process	Strategic Component Inventory (scope)
	Launch	Owner's Wants View
2. Build Infrastructure	Requirements	Owner's Needs View
	Analysis and Design	Designer's View Builder's View
	Construct	Subcontractor's View (including Test)
Integrate	Implement (and support)	Working System

As you can see, different members of the team use these frameworks when guiding different parts of the program effort.

10.5.2   Managing the Project

There may be no more critical role in achieving CRM success than the assignment of an effective and competent project manager. Project managers are responsible for controlling the progress of one or more of the infrastructure development efforts and for making sure that all four of the efforts are coordinated and synched. Not surprisingly, the project manager should be identified after the strategy setting is completed and before the full project team is assembled and the project launched, as indicated in Figure 10-6.

Project managers can come from either the IT department or a business function, as long as they have the knowledge, skills, and temperament to keep pushing everything ahead. The best project managers I have known are absolutely dogged in monitoring the plan and the team's progress.

There are some standard tools for helping project managers keep everything on track that will significantly improve their ability to control and manage each of the component projects and to inform and communicate with the whole project team and beyond. These tools are described in Chapter 15.

Figure 10-6 Project management

Questions for Reflection

Consider some recent IT projects with which you're familiar.

1. What kind of methodology does the IT department use to manage projects?
2. Is it standard and consistent, or does each project use something different?
3. Is the process used to enhance understanding or to simply to document disconnects and excuse project slips?
4. Is there clear definition of roles and clear transition of responsibility, or is everyone (and therefore no one) responsible for everything?

CHAPTER 11

Understanding the Information Component

Information is the first of the four CRM infrastructure components that we're going to work on. We'll start with the information component because it is very often an orphan that gets lost somewhere between Information Technology and the business functions. Sales, marketing, customer service, and product support think that information is just the first word in Information Technology; it's somebody else's job. But the IT folks think that their job is the technology, period. Information is used to make daily business decisions but nobody is responsible for it. It's always the other guy's responsibility. That's scary.

There is an historical basis for this; it used to be that information systems were developed within vertical functional silos. The experts who understood the process were trained and focused only on their own responsibilities. Systems were developed for vertical process slices so that only the information needed for that process was considered. For example, a company in Canada might have decided that, for tax and customer reasons, it would ship only to Canadian locations. Its customer file didn't need to include a field for "country" because it was always Canada. Then the company began selling its products to customers headquartered all over North America and now sends bills to locations in the US and Mexico as well as Canada. The billing and shipping databases didn't match: information could not be moved back and forth between them. But that is exactly what we need to do for CRM—share and integrate customer information across the entire set of customer facing systems.

It is imperative that we (business and technology people) put siloed thinking behind us. Information requirements must be defined and documented in exactly the same way that processes and their supporting technologies are designed. It is the responsibility of the business team to determine what information is needed. It is the responsibility of the IT team to recommend and build the best solution for capturing, managing, storing, and sharing that information.

When information is considered a byproduct that just occurs when the system is built it is considered to be disposable. In fact, just the opposite is true.

Information is the raw material from which successful CRM programs are constructed. Throughout this book, we've discussed how important customer information is. Information is the raw material of every CRM effort because, for CRM, electronic knowledge takes the place of human knowledge in building customer relationships. We must get information right!

11.1 Understanding Data and Information: What Does It All Mean?

Webster's Dictionary defines data as "factual information." Does that mean there is no difference between data and information? Are the words simply interchangeable? The answer for our purposes is no; there is a significant difference between data and information.

 DEFINITIONS

Information is data in context.

Let's understand what this means and why the distinction is important. First, we'll take a quick look at what we mean by data.

11.1.1 Data

Data is what we call all the facts that are stored or used anywhere in the organization. It is just like that tin can full of miscellaneous screws that most of us have in the garage or basement. Whenever we need one, we just dump the can out and go through them all until we find the ones we need.

Types of Data

For most of the history of computer usage, the only data we really worried about designing or managing was factual data. Factual data can be described as having specific characteristics. We can talk of a *data fact* as being a certain type (numeric, alphabetic character, date) and having a certain size (bytes). Factual data can be stored in databases, and can be searched for and retrieved to help companies calculate customer value, identify customers owning a specific product, or create a mailing list.

The other type of data is textual data. This could be anything from a comment field that has a defined length to a document of any size or nature that computers stored (although they were pretty inefficient at finding and retrieving them). This is yet another change that the Internet has introduced. We have new search engines and other tools for storing and retrieving textual data that can be a tremendous aid to making decisions. (In fact this book could never have been written without that new capability.)

However, for purposes of the kinds of decisions we need to make at this point in our CRM program (most valuable customers, who owns what), we will consider only factual information. We'll focus on the data facts we need, and on storing and retrieving those data facts for decision-making purposes.

The Problem with Factual Data

There is one difficulty with computer data: unless we are very careful about how we identify, define, and store it, it can lose all meaning. Here's an example of a data fact that I pulled out of a database:

94305

But what in the world does this mean? Even though we understand what the number 9 is, the number 4, etc., this *fact* is of absolutely no use to us unless we know what it means. In the same way, our tin can full of screws is of much less use to us than if the contents were sorted by size and type and placed into labeled jars. Sure, we could sort through the tin can (or database) every time to find what we need for a certain job, but it would certainly be a tedious process if we had to do it very often. This method of finding a screw may be okay at home, but it would be very inefficient for a business purpose at a construction site or a furniture manufacturer, for example. However, after we've sorted and labeled them, they are easier to find and retrieve and become much more useful for repetitive purposes like manufacturing. We've stated that information is the raw material of CRM; just like the can of screws, data becomes useful when it has been sorted and labeled, and after we have defined its context.

11.1.2 Context

What do we mean by context? Context makes it easier to put our hands on what we need and to understand it when we see it. We can create meaning or context for our box of screws by sorting them into like sizes and storing each group in a separate location with a label such as:

#10, ¾", wood screws

We create context for data in the same way, by sorting and labeling it consistently. The same piece of data must be identified the same way everywhere it is used, or we have no context and do not have information. Similarly, we mustn't attach the same label to anything else. What good is it if a box labeled wood screws is full of machine screws instead? They would be useless for your purpose. Whenever we reference the same piece of data, we must label it the same way: whether data elements in a system or columns in spreadsheets and on reports. Ordering wood screws and then storing them under the label Part-123 is dangerous and confusing. Everyone must know what Part-123 is. Without context, data is meaningless at best and seriously misleading at worst. How many reports have you seen that allegedly reflect the same monthly results, except the totals don't match? How does anyone make decisions based on non-information like that? Let's take a look at our sample data in its physical context as shown in Figure 11-1.

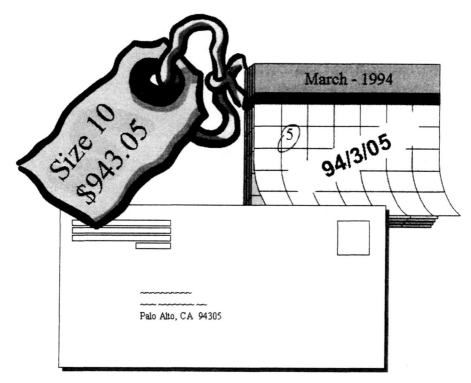

Figure 11-1 Data in context

First, we sort our stuff into closely related piles, and next we label each pile so we don't have to memorize where everything is. Only then do we have useful information.

11.1.3 Information

In designing our CRM information, we want to collect, sort, and label the organization's raw data so it is useful. We do this by sorting data into similar groups and labeling each group. Never do we talk about sorting according to purpose or use; in fact, for data just as for raw material, that's a bad idea. The context defines what the data is, not how it's used. Depending on its context, Table 11-1 shows how we should understand our sample data.

Table 11-1 Understanding Information

Data	Context	Information
	Postal Code	94305
94305	Price	$943.05
	Date	94/3/05

For a parts inventory, we use separate, labeled storage bins to store material and supplies. In a computer system, the sorting and labeling is part of how the database is designed and built. When we retrieve and use the data in reports and computer screens, we use the same labels so we understand the information we are seeing.

A perfect example of non-information occurred a few years ago: a former colleague had been receiving the same report every month for years. Each month, the new report was filed and the old one tossed out. One month, the report stopped coming. That day, the IT support desk got a panicky call asking, "Where's my Numbers Report?" They could find no trace of any report that matched the description. Then someone remembered that some system cleanup had been performed recently. Sure enough, every month since an outdated data file had been eliminated two years earlier, an 80-page computer error report (core dump) had been printed, distributed, and carefully filed away. Was this report full of information? Well, yes (maybe) to a programmer who knows how to interpret core dumps, but the answer is certainly no for anyone else.

Customer information is the raw material of our CRM program. Creating definitions and labeling data consistently is critical to CRM success. This is not an optional activity and must be accomplished with participation of *both* the business and IT functions. You'd be unlikely to ask your facilities department which raw materials you should buy and store or how to organize and label them. But you would definitely ask them to participate in designing and building the warehouse where you store everything. They know about shelf strength, bin configurations, and so on. The same is true for data; the business function knows what's important to successful CRM. Information Technology knows how to capture, store, and present it most efficiently.

Data goes into a computer file, and we hope information is what comes out because it's what we must have in order to deliver superior customer experiences. Only after we have identified the important data and collected, sorted, and labeled it is it useful for planning and building relationships. It is useful when we understand what it means and sharable when everyone understands the same meaning.

11.1.4 Information Is a Company Asset

Information is an asset of your company, just like any other asset. In addition to having a well-defined context, there are three rules about good asset management that apply to information the same as they do to parts inventory.

Standard Parts

It used to be that every product line ordered and stored its own parts, some of them custom-made just for that product. Many years ago, we learned that this was extremely costly for two reasons:

1. If each product line buys and stores its own *#10 Wood Screws*, the company has lost the opportunity to get volume discounts by purchasing in larger quantities at the same time. In addition, if the bin label said *XYZ-part-123* and the product XYZ then becomes

obsolete, the material is frequently tossed out because no one knows what it really is or what else it could be used for.

2. Using custom instead of standard materials in manufacturing is also expensive. Custom parts cannot be reused for other products. Also, to guarantee support into the future, some of these custom parts must be kept on hand (taking up valuable space) so that if a screw comes loose and gets lost, there are spares available without paying to have new ones made.

How do these apply to information?

Manage Value

Just like materials inventory, information value is measured by its ability to meet its intended purpose. Information must be protected against shoddy manufacturing, theft, and deterioration just like raw material. Here are some steps you can take to manage the value of your information:

1. Sources of information must be monitored for poor quality construction at the supplier. Quality should be part of the original data collection process (managed when data is first captured, not as you're trying to fit the wrong screw into a tight corner). There should be an incoming inspection on all data as it enters the CRM system from any source.

2. Information must be kept in a secure location that is not accessible to unauthorized users.

3. Information must be protected from the elements. In the case of customer information, time is the factor that causes the information to deteriorate. Information doesn't get consumed when it is used; over time companies are bought and sold, and people move to new locations. And just like obsolete raw material, we're likely to come across information that is no longer being used. (You want to be sure that the system can track data access at the element level.) Just like obsolete parts, we should get rid of useless data because it costs money to store and maintain it. We can easily identify useless data as long as the system has been set up to track how often different information is accessed.

Most of us aren't used to thinking about information as important in and of itself. It takes time to learn how to define information requirements independent of any use for that information. In order to identify and define the right data, design the right standards, and develop the right metrics and processes for managing quality for OUR customer information, we will use a methodology (surprise!) to design our information requirements. We will look at the critical issue of data quality in Chapter 20. Here, we will focus on identifying the context and standards for our information asset.

Information is a real company asset, and it must be treated like one. For information to be dependable over time and available for use with many applications, it must be:

- In context (sorted and labeled)
- Standard (consistently defined and used)
- Reliable (of high quality)

To be really useful, information must be sharable across the organization; it should be sorted, labeled, and standard. To accomplish this, we will use a methodology that helps us identify, sort, and label our company information. We'll use a methodology called Information Engineering.

11.1.5 Engineering Information

We are going to engineer our requirements for each of the CRM components (information, process, technology, and people) because, just like building a house, we need to be sure that the finished product matches what the owner wants, even if the owner can't describe it in enough detail for a contractor to build it. We use the term *engineering* to mean a process for iterating through increasingly detailed views of each of the project components. In his classic book, *Information Systems Manifesto* (1984), James Martin says:

KEY IDEA

"One of the important realizations that led to information engineering is that data in an organization exist and can be described *independently of how those data are used.*"

Because there is no absolute universal truth about what all information means, what is standard and shared, and what is most important, each company must make these decisions for itself. Of course, common sense tells us that there may be some data that is used in fairly standard ways across all companies. If we can find an external data standard (not a software application standard), we should use it for the time savings and to support open architecture standards. The International Standards Organization (ISO) country codes are a good example of an external standard.

Data models are made up of the "stuff" that helps us answer business questions and make business decisions. Like so many of our other efforts, we will begin designing our data model at a very high level with data *classes*. Next, we'll divide these classes into their component business *subjects,* which will be further subdivided into more specific data *entities and relationships.* Figure 11-2 reminds us that Information Engineering for each project starts with the strategic planning process.

Ultimately, we will have figured out the exact specifications of the physical database structure, and we'll build it! As always, we will follow the principle of getting just the right amount of detailed knowledge to make us successful at each step, and no more.

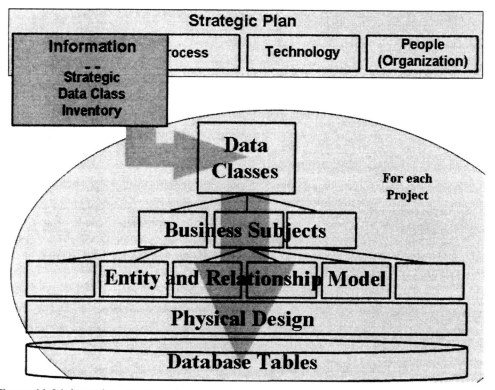

Figure 11-2 Information component

Storage and Retrieval

Most of us keep our paperwork in one or both of two places: file drawers and piles. There is no explaining how you or anyone puts stuff into piles, but information that should be organized so someone can find it easily and quickly is often placed in a filing cabinet. When we organize information for a computer database, we begin in the same way as if we were organizing a paper filing cabinet. This parallel is especially helpful for understanding the business responsibility for defining information context. Computer systems have features that enhance the efficiency of data storage and retrieval activities, but only if they're designed in a way that is meaningful to the system users.

If we were setting up a new filing system to hold our information, we'd probably start by going through all our documents (in drawers and piles) and sorting them into related topics (customer, expenses, employees, invoices, orders). We could then throw each stack into a separate **CUSTOMER** or **ORDER** file drawer and have a slightly better chance of finding something we were looking for. There would be only one drawer to go through instead of the entire office.

Often, of course, we'd take the contents of each file drawer and sort it again into more specific topics like those in Figure 11-3. We often sort these topics into individual piles by the cus-

Figure 11-3 Organizing a file drawer to store customer information

tomer referenced on the document so we can find certain customer's information more easily. We can put these smallest stacks in separate file folders and then group related folders into a single hanging file.

Hey, this looks pretty easy; let's just stick with our filing cabinets. Of course, that's a bad idea for two reasons. Companies have access to much more information than could be stored in a warehouse full of filing cabinets, which means just finding the right filing cabinet, much less the right customer, is much too time-consuming. Also, filing cabinets allow us only one way to organize information, such as alphabetically by customer name. Computers offer much more flexibility, speed, and efficiency in finding the information we have. Can you imagine trying to find all the customers who own a certain product by rummaging through a warehouse full of filing cabinets?

Our goal is to determine exactly what the business functions need to know in order to build successful customer relationships and then to define the context clearly enough that Information Technology knows exactly how to build the storage system. Like our filing cabinet, we want to organize and store the information in such a way that anyone who needs it can retrieve it. We will use Information Engineering to make that happen.

Case Study

Yes, we keep hammering away at following all the steps, and there is a very good reason for it. If you don't follow these steps, you'll end up like one of XYZ's groups did a few years ago. (Remember, this really happened to a real company, just not to XYZ.)

XYZ's Valencia team members had a rough idea of what they wanted and could easily describe it to each other in common business language. After the program manager, who worked for Zeke, tried to build a small system herself, she figured out that it was a bigger deal than could be handled internally, so she contacted several IT consultants and selected the one who delivered the most thorough proposal. The proposal they received (much like the owner's wants view) included a good representation of XYZ's requirements for data, process, and technology with an estimated completion in six to nine months.

Next the members of XYZ received a copy of some design specs (the designer's view) for XYZ's data and processes. These specs were very detailed and complicated, so they were completely meaningless to XYZ. They did see some recognizable terms in the pages and pages of information, so Zeke and his project manager just decided to trust that the IT team knew what they were doing—after all they'd written a good proposal. A few months later, they got to try the first piece of their new system. But it didn't work. They couldn't even get most of the required data loaded into their new system. They were a very long way from being able to generate any reports.

It was never a question of zero communication; the problem so often is the lack of the right kind of communication. For example, the IT consultant suggested building a neat, new capability: automatic transfer of customer information from the e-mail system. It sounded good, so why not? Unfortunately, this feature cost an additional one-third of the original budget, and for just ten new contacts per month! The business didn't know what kinds of questions to ask about the new feature and Information Technology didn't understand the business reality. This project went on for nearly two years. Finally, at well over twice the original estimated cost, they were able to generate their first report – and it was *almost* **correct.**

Was Zeke happy? Absolutely not, he was disappointed and furious and had lost all trust in the IT contractors. Is this the outcome that the IT consulting company wanted? Of course not! They were just as frustrated as XYZ. The problem is that there was no structure to the way that information was exchanged: the business didn't know what to ask for, and the IT consultants couldn't read minds. They all didn't know what they didn't know. This is a sad but common story. XYZ learned its lesson the hard way. Now the project has been integrated into their overall CRM program, and the company has formalized the way it manages communication and knowledge transfer between the business and IT professionals.

11.2 Following Information Engineering Steps

The file cabinet is a good model for information engineering. Would you ask a cabinetmaker to tell you what information is important to you and how you should file it? Of course you wouldn't. You'd decide what and how much you thought you needed to store, and then describe it as clearly as possible. Would you then stand over his shoulder and tell him how to cut the wood or where to put every screw? Not if you ever hoped to hire him again. Don't expect to ask the IT folks to tell you what you want to store in your system. And don't tell them how to build your system. Business experts specify requirements and the IT team delivers solutions. When these roles get reversed (and it does happen), disaster is guaranteed.

For this chapter on information, we will also take a quick look at the IT department's perspectives. For the other CRM components, we will focus only on the two to three highest levels needed to ensure that the guiding information comes from the business functions that will use the system (see Table 11-2).

Table 11-2   The Information Component

Business View	Information View	File Cabinet View
Owner's Wants View	Data classes	File drawer labels
Owner's Needs View	Business subjects	Hanging file labels
Designer's View	Entity and relationship model	Individual folders
Builder's View	Physical data model	Document formats
Detailed Representation	Database: tables, columns, rows	Individual documents
Functioning System	Populated database	Filled filing cabinet

It's important to generally understand both the business function and IT department's roles and especially to see how the early views drive the later views and ensure that what's built matches the business needs.

Of course, XYZ really started their information requirements definition as part of the strategic plan when they identified the program-wide scope for high level information needs (their inventory of strategic data classes).

 DEFINITIONS

Data classes are the high-level categories of stuff that is important to your business.

During strategic planning, XYZ hadn't yet selected a project, so at the strategic highest level, they developed a picture across the whole CRM space. From the strategic internal interviews the team generated a list of business opportunities and business issues that they used to develop the program data classes. To demonstrate the approach, we'll use the summary of issues and opportunities from XYZ's strategic proposal in Chapter 8.

Team meetings and brainstorming sessions with the steering committee and others were some of the other good ways XYZ used to gather strategic perspectives. You may actually start with a list of 100 or more statements on your list, but plenty of these can be eliminated. Consolidate duplicates, and eliminate oddball comments. (Brainstorming sometimes encourages wacky ideas to expand thinking, but that doesn't mean you shouldn't eventually discard the ones that are not reasonable or useful.) Start with the list of issues, opportunities, and stupid things we do to customers that were identified during the internal interviews, and then eliminate/merge duplicate statements. XYZ used these steps to develop the first pass at their strategic data class inventory:

1. Go through the list with a highlighter and mark every **noun.** These are your candidate data classes.
2. Identify and eliminate duplicate data classes as well as any unrealistic or unreasonable data classes.
3. Write a definition of each of the remaining data classes on your list.
4. Organize into global data classes for ease of communication.

XYZ identified twelve data classes (there were really more like 30 at this point), which were organized into the four global data classes, as shown in Figure 11-4. Global data classes are not created for any scientific reason but because a short list is easier to remember. The XYZ strategic planning team said, "We only need to understand four things: who our customers are, the marketplace in which we operate, the investments we are making, and the returns we get from each investment."

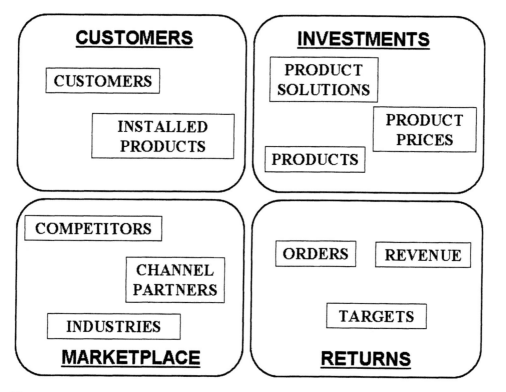

Figure 11-4 XYZ's global data classes

When they began working on each of the project specific levels of detail, efforts would be focused on just what's needed for Valencia, the selected project. Identifying the program-wide component scope during strategic planning, and starting each project there, ensures that individual projects will fit together to create a successful total program. No more information silos!

11.2.1 Owner's Wants View: Data Classes

Now we're ready to start working on the project-specific views for the first piece of XYZ's customer identity system (El Cid). As you know the project team chose Valencia as the name for the first project. The owner's wants view for the information component was defined during the project launch. At that time XYZ reviewed the list of strategic data classes and narrowed the scope to those that they felt were relevant the Valencia project. The team identified the two data classes shown in Table 11-3.

Table 11-3 Valencia Data Classes

Data Class	Definition
Customers	A customer is a person (or a group of persons) who influences or decides on the acquisition of one of our products or services, or who uses one of these products or services.
Installed Products	Products or services owned or used by a customer

They also developed definitions for each of the data classes (and of course leveraged any previous common terms such as the one for **CUSTOMERS** which was given in Chapter 1).

11.2.2 Owner's Needs View: Business Subjects

We always start creating a view with the results from the previous level. Each step builds on the preceding step. If new information is discovered that doesn't logically fit anyplace in the preceding view, we have to go back and add them.

 DEFINITIONS

Business data subjects represent the stuff (people, places, things, or ideas) that is important to your business and about which you need to collect, store, and share certain facts.

After we have defined our data classes (file drawers) we need to identify the major topics that we want to store in each drawer. Business subjects are the hanging files that are used to separate the drawer labeled Customer into its main components so that it's easier to find what is needed. We determine our list of business subjects by deciding what things we want to keep in each drawer. Business subjects represent real things that have different facts that describe them. Like an architect's model, subjects begin to take shape, but there still isn't much detail. These steps can help you develop the list of subjects that will be part of Valencia:

1. Start with the data classes that are were identified as relevant for this project.
2. Identify the major divisions (business subjects) for the data classes.
3. Write a definition for each business subject.

XYZ immediately identified two important subjects within the CUSTOMERS data class, but found none for INSTALLED PRODUCTS, so the subject just carried the same name as the data class as shown in Table 11-4 which lists the subjects that XYZ identified and defined to support Valencia business goals. The subjects were defined **independent of where they were captured or stored.**

Table 11-4

Data Class	Business Subject	Definition
Customers	Customer Companies	An organization that acquires one of our products or services
	Customer Contacts	A person who acquires one of our products or services
Installed Products	Installed Products	A product or service owned or used by a customer company or contact

We never organize data around any of its uses—only on what the thing actually is. Next, we will decide how to organize the facts that we want to collect and store. *Company* is one thing, but what do we want to know about companies?

11.2.3 Designer's View: Entities, Attributes, and Relationships

The designer's view is where the hand-off between business knowledge and IT knowledge takes place. This is the view where the responsibility switches from being primarily business function to primarily Information Technology's responsibility.

Don't think this means that everyone needs to learn how to draw blueprints. This is not required at all. But everyone needs to understand what the blueprints mean, or some very unpleasant surprises may be in store. The blueprint for a database, called an Entity-Relationship Diagram, covers all three elements of the designer's view: entities, attributes, and relationships.

But where do we start? Not surprisingly, we start with the subjects we have just identified. Let's review the steps that XYZ used to identify the entities, attributes, and relationships for Valencia:

1. Assign each fact that is currently used (or desired) by the business teams to the specific business subject that it best describes; these are candidate entities.

2. Identify the KEY attribute (label) for each candidate entity.

3. Apply entity rules to determine the final structure of each entity.

4. Identify entity relationships.

5. Define entities, attributes, and relationships.

We will go through each of these steps in Appendix D, just as XYZ did during its planning for Valencia. Entities represent real stuff; they are concrete enough that we can actually describe them.

DEFINITIONS

Entities are the people, places, things, and ideas that are important to your business. Entities have characteristics (attributes) that the business needs to collect, store, and share, and they have links (relationships) to other entities.

Entities have characteristics we want to capture (what is the customer's name), and they have links to other entities (what customer placed this order). Data classes and subjects are very conceptual, like labels on file drawers and dividers. But an entity with its unique attributes is more like a single folder that contains a number of similar forms. An entity (sometimes called *entity-type*) represents a group of real people, companies, etc. Each real thing (such as a particular consumer), is represented by a single physical form, is called an *entity instance*. The form design describes what we need to capture about each entity.

Attributes

Attributes are all the blanks that need to be filled in or checked on each form. We can generate a list of potential attributes through a number of avenues, such as interviews and brainstorming. The best source of information about attributes is all the documents (forms, reports, computer screens) the company already uses. XYZ has used cardboard product registration cards for years to collect information about its customers. Figure 11-5 shows an example of one of XYZ's product registration cards.

XYZ used this card to generate a list of important facts it needed to store about customers; then the company assigned each attribute to an appropriate entity. For a well-organized computer file, each form type would be designed to hold attributes that describe only one type of data entity, and those attributes would not be repeated anywhere else. Figure 11-6 shows XYZ's *street address* entity (folder).

Every entity must have one attribute that identifies each page in the folder. These are called *key attributes,* and they are the primary way that the computer finds and retrieves a single specific page.

XYZ Product Registration

Product Model _____ Serial # _____ Purchase Date_____

Where purchased (circle one)? <u>XYZ direct</u>   <u>XYZ online</u>   <u>XYZ catalog</u>   <u>Dealer/retailer</u>

           If dealer/retailer: Store name_____ City_____ State_____

| Mr Mrs Ms |
Last name _____ First Name _____ Middle_____ Gender:__

Email address: _____ Title_____

Street address _____ City _____ State ___ Zip_____

Is this your home or company address? | Home   Company | How many employees work here?_____

Company name _____ Total Employees _____ Revenue_____

Industry Code (see reverse): _____ Industry Description _____

This product will be used at | Office   Home   Both | for | Personal Business Travel All |

What competitive products do you own/use? 1._____   2._____   3._____   4._____   5._____

May we contact you from time to time with information you might find interesting (circle one)? <u>Yes</u>   <u>No</u>

Figure 11-5 Sample XYZ product registration card

Figure 11-6 Street address entity

XYZ identified a total of nine entities, two each for the three project subjects and three whose subject area was outside the original project scope. Schedule and resource investments had to be considered when the scope grew. The XYZ team had to take a step back and identify the subjects and data classes for these new entities.

By the way, the naming convention commonly used in information engineering uses plural names for the two highest-level views (class and subject) and a singular form for the rest of the views. This convention is illustrated in Table 11-5, which shows the entities and attributes XYZ identified for Valencia.

Table 11-5 Valencia Entities

Class	Subject	Entity	Attribute
INSTALLED PRODUCTS	Installed Products	XYZ Installed Product	product model
			serial number
			purchase date
			where purchased
			primary use
			where used
		Competitive Installed Product	person identifier
			competitive product
			product quantity
CHANNEL PARTNERS	Stores	Store	store identifier
			store name
			store location city
			store location state
CUSTOMERS	Customer Contacts	Contact Person	person identifier
			person last name
			person first name
			person address title
			person business title
			person gender
			ok to contact?
	Customer Companies	Company Site	company identifier
			address identifier
			employee count here
		Company Organization	company identifier
			company name
			total employees
			revenue

Table 11-5   Valencia Entities (Continued)

Class	Subject	Entity	Attribute
LOCATERS	Locaters	E-mail Address	person identifier
			e-mail address
			e-mail inactive date
		Street Address	address identifier
			street
			city
			state
			postal code
			country
INDUSTRIES	Industries	Industry	industry code
			industry description

Even if XYZ had decided not to expand scope to work on the new data entities, they needed to capture the additional knowledge they had uncovered about the two new business subjects (**Stores** and **Locaters**) and one previously unidentified class (**LOCATERS**).

Relationships

Relationships describe how an entity is related to any other entities: which entities are related to each other, the purpose of the relationship, and how they are related. Relationships allow us to avoid repeating the same information over and over throughout the database. This is where computers really have an advantage over filing cabinets; computers support automatic links between entities so that all the related data looks as if it is physically stored in every linked entity. For paper files, we'd have to search through each of our folders, pull out the related forms, and then tape them all together to get the full picture. That's why we put every piece of information we might need on one single form. (I didn't say the form was only one page.) Because much of the same information is repeated, paper forms get out of date and are usually laden with errors and inconsistencies. But we're used to paper files and very often make the same mistake with computer filing systems.

We know we don't want to clutter our computers with all this redundant and consistent data, but how do we get it organized and linked. In a paper filing system, you might try tying a piece of string between all of the files that have related information about, say, the same customer. Can you imagine? Take a look at Figure 11-7. What a nightmare!

Early computer systems followed the file drawer method: store everything in one big computer file. This approach had the same inherent wasted space, inconsistency, and poor quality as the filing cabinet method. Although computers are faster and bigger than filing cabinets, database software hadn't been designed to take advantage of the computer's potential. The early computer file designs forced programmers to tie figurative strings between related files.

Figure 11-7 Filing cabinet relationships?

But that has changed. The database management systems most prevalent today (relational, object-oriented) are designed to manage relationships between entities such that, after the relationships are defined, the computer does the work of linking everything together so it looks like one big form, with the advantage of eliminating all that redundant data. Software engineers put all this together using a Computer Aided Software Engineering (CASE) tool (trust me, graphics software is NOT the way), and we get the Entity Relationship Diagram for Valencia, which you can find in Appendix D. This is the technical team's blueprint for constructing the new system. As promised, not very many people need to understand how to actually create this model, not even everyone in the IT department. But everyone needs to have some idea of what it represents about the information component.

These first three views are all that the business needs to even think about. But you can see that even getting this far takes a delicate balance of business knowledge and technical knowledge. This is one area in which organizations often need help from outside the company to ensure that all three steps are completed and that business requirements have been clearly articulated, but **not** to make the decisions of course. Now the rest of the steps are up to the IT department.

11.2.4 Following the Rest of the Steps

The two remaining views are the responsibility of the IT organization. Still the business function participation is important to answer detailed questions and review specifications.

Builder's View: Physical Data Model

Just as in each preceding view, the IT designers started with the entity relationship diagram (ERD). It will be reviewed for technical performance issues, and modifications may be suggested to support faster updates, retrievals, and sorting. Each modification recommended should be explained to the business team with pros and cons, and the exception should be documented. System performance is always improving; there may be a reason to go back to the original design sometime in the future. The people who have to make that future change need to know why the database looks the way it does.

The physical data model includes the physical characteristics of the data to be stored, such as type of data (numbers, text) and size (how much space needs to be set aside). These characteristics are generally required for "decision support" data that is used for sorting and searching. There are also many excellent products that support storing formatted and variable-length text for quick retrieval, but this is not a requirement of Valencia.

Subcontractor's View: Individual Tables, Rows, and Columns

Now the Information Technology department can actually build the database. Many CASE tools create code that can be used to generate the physical (empty) database straight from the project design. These reproduce the physical data model in a database management system by creating one table for each entity. The database table is made up of a series of columns, one for each attribute, as shown in Table 11-6.

Table 11-6 Model and Database Terms

Data Model	Physical Database
Entity	Data table
Attribute	Column
Entity instance	Row

The database is empty when it is first built. Just like creating a new computer spreadsheet, you have only the empty spreadsheet and a list of labeled columns.

Finally, the IT department will get the physical database up and running so that data can be loaded, managed and retrieved. Each individual record (set of information about an entity instance) that is added creates a new row in the data table. A specific row is retrieved based on the value of its key. Once accessed, all the data for the entity instance is available, whether it is physically in that table or linked by a foreign key.

11.2.5 The Transition to Information Technology

The Designer's View is where primary responsibility shifts from the business functions to the IT function as shown in Figure 11-8.

There is considerable risk of losing momentum and continuity when a responsibility shift between two separate organizations occurs. The "transition" view is always an extremely critical view and one that must be understood and managed very well.

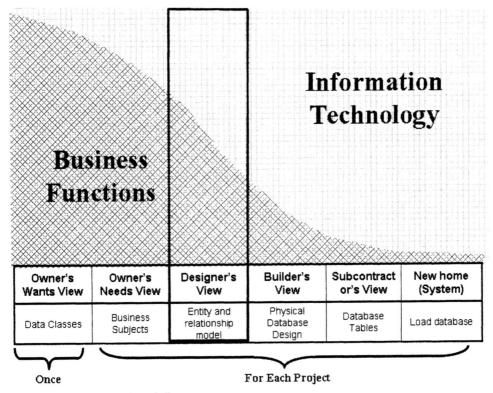

Owner's Wants View	Owner's Needs View	Designer's View	Builder's View	Subcontract or's View	New home (System)
Data Classes	Business Subjects	Entity and relationship model	Physical Database Design	Database Tables	Load database

Once   For Each Project

Figure 11-8 Information Handoff

11.3 Integrating Your Databases (The Information Gold Mine)

Now that we've built the model and dictionary that defines CRM data and have built the system, it's time to look at the match between the source system and our new database design and to think about adding data to our new system. CRM data is available from hundreds of sources. There are many data providers and contact list providers who make their lists available to direct marketers. But there is one source of CRM data that is better than any other – your own in-house systems.

Who knows your customers better than you do? A top consulting firm did a CRM assessment for XYZ not long ago; their conclusion was that what XYZ needed for a successful CRM program was to provide seamless treatment of customers supported by complete and well-maintained databases.

> "The highest priority gaps to close center around data management of customer/prospect information and installed base information, since this data is the backbone of the recommended CRM initiatives. Given the importance of the customer contact list and installed base data to CRM, we believe that building a consolidated customer view should be top priority."

Providing access to all the company's customer information is critical, but there are some significant issues surrounding integrating information from multiple sources. Most legacy customer data sources look nothing like the well-designed model we have planned. To successfully integrate information, we will analyze each source, identifying differences from the new model, and then transform the data to the new format. Information Technology will build a transformation program for each unique data source and run the data through this program on the way into the database.

Also, the web allows customers to look at the data we have about them; this raises significant issues of the quality of our legacy data and how much we want customers to see.

11.3.1 Integrating Data Sources

We can't spend much time discussing physical database content; there are just too many options and no single size fits all. But we must consider how we're going to get information from multiple sources (internal or external) into our new system. Data mapping is a critical tool for converting existing data to a new model and will be discussed in the information integration section of Chapter 16.

11.3.2 Source Data Quality

The Internet throws one very big monkey wrench into our data integration goal: the Internet allows customers to see the data we've collected about them. Our historical data collection processes (which still make up 80 percent or more of most companies' customer knowledge) were generally pretty casual about accuracy. Getting data shoved into the system was more important than getting it in right. (After all, program response rates were measured on number of responses, not the quality or usability of the information.) Remember, you ALWAYS get what you measure. We will learn more about both data mapping and data quality management, but for now our next step is to determine the process component of our project.

Questions for Reflection

This exercise will get help you start thinking about your company's customer information needs.

1. On a piece of paper, jot down a few notes outlining your company's five greatest issues and opportunities for the coming year.
2. Circle all the nouns on your list. At the bottom of the page, write down the circled "data classes."
3. How is your company set to capture, store, and access information about each of the data classes?

Understanding the Process Component

Process is the second of the CRM infrastructure components. All companies use processes, but as with the data component, many companies do not really know what processes exist in their organization. In Chapter 1, we discussed the three value disciplines identified by Treacy and Wiersema: operational excellence, product leadership, and customer intimacy. It is likely that processes are well documented only for operationally excellent companies, for the rest their processes are not formally identified, defined, or managed. Process knowledge is passed on by word of mouth, by example and through on-the-job training. In today's marketplace, employee loyalty has become somewhat of an anachronism for many organizations. Short tenures and rapid turnover have become the norm, and informal management of business processes is no longer an effective way to run many businesses. In addition, we know the Internet has removed people from direct participation in online processes, so formal process definition becomes even more important.

These changes have made it imperative that we really understand all the ways we touch our customers and especially those processes we plan to move to the web. Processes on the Internet must continue to run effectively, even without human intervention. We cannot be concerned with all processes; we will focus just on those that we plan to automate. To make this happen, we must identify each of our customer-facing processes, create documentation of each one, and design plans for ongoing monitoring and managing of these processes. The computer can't sense a customer's frustration with a poor situation. We must design our CRM processes based on human understanding of customers. This is our next step: to determine the process component of our CRM infrastructure.

One word of caution, there is danger in spending so much time on process analysis and over-engineering every detail that we never make progress because there's still more to decide. Process analysis doesn't need to be any bigger than it needs to be. Use common sense!

12.1 Process, Schmocess—What Are We Talking About?

Again, we'll look to a dictionary for a starting definition of a process, which, according to Webster's, is "a series of actions conducing to an end." In their excellent book, *Improving Performance* (1995), Geary Rummler and Alan Brache describe a process as "the way work gets done." For our purposes, a process is the series of actions that deliver a specified outcome.

 DEFINITIONS

A process is a series of work steps that lead to a specific result.

Organizations were initially established to support getting work done. People who had similar jobs all reported into the same organization.

12.1.1 Processes and Organizations

Today the business functions of most companies no longer represent the process classes of the organization. One of the key requirements during strategic planning is to compare the strategic functions to the company organization chart(s) being sure that you have identified all the organizations that directly interact with your customers and noting any dotted-line relationships that currently exist (or should exist) across organizations that have similar responsibilities but report to different functional organizations. XYZ's high-level organization (Executive Team) and the key business units involved with customer interactions are shown in Figure 12-1. (For reference, XYZ's key CRM managers (Yolanda, Xavier, and Zeke) have been identified on the organization chart.)

Many companies are still organized around the traditional boundaries of vertical organizations, like XYZ. As we've seen, the historical basis is that organizations were created according to the way work gets done (organize ~ organization). One of the problems today is that real organizations no longer operate this simply. Many processes that touch the customer actually cross multiple organizational boundaries, but we still operate as if Sales and Marketing don't need to talk with each other.

Much effort has been spent on trying to manage what Rummler and Brache call the "white space" on the organization chart. Organizational matrices have replaced the traditional organization chart. Dotted-line reporting relationships, such as those shown in Figure 12-1, abound. But these organizational methods often fail to actually improve the situation because no one really knows who is responsible for what (or to whom)!

This complexity and confusion has led to a spate of organizational reengineering efforts spawned by Michael Hammer and James Champy's influential book, *Reengineering the Corporation* (1993). Sadly, the results of organizational reengineering have not lived up to the potential, and the concepts have earned themselves a largely undeserved black eye. Too many

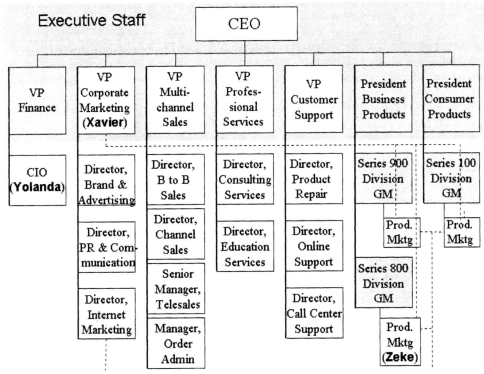

Figure 12-1 XYZ's organization chart

companies were looking for another quick fix and were not willing to do the planning and step-by-step implementation required for any major organizational change. Modern organizations can no longer operate successfully in these kinds of vertical silos, and process engineering is one of the components of making change happen. The people component of our CRM architecture (discussed in Chapter 14) is about engineering change.

12.1.2 Process Engineering

Now that we're ready to "engineer" the process model for our CRM program, the most important goal to keep in mind is that we must be sure that the business processes we define are designed to provide positive customer experiences.

Process models describe the work we do. Like so many of our other efforts, we will begin identifying requirements at the highest level with business *functions* (also called process classes). Next, we'll identify the component business *processes* for each function, which will be further subdivided into more specific *activities*—the real work. Figure 12-2 is a reminder that process classes (functions) are identified during strategic planning. And as we launch each project, we will delve into the details needed to meet the specific project requirements.

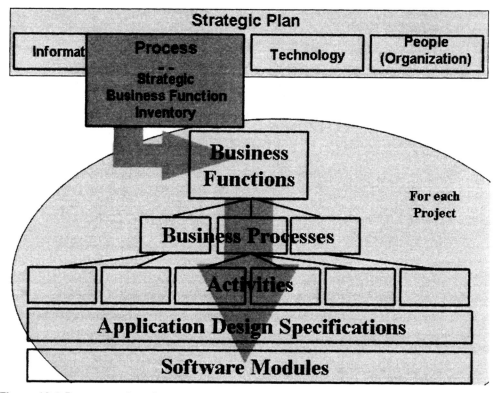

Figure 12-2 Process engineering

As we did for the data component, we will iterate through more detailed views of each of the major process areas we identified when we set our strategy.

12.2 Following Process Engineering Steps

Process engineering is about what we do. The organization chart is important because though organizations were usually been created to represent work areas, the misalignment between processes and organizations (the white space) is the primary cause of process breakdowns. Of course it also reminds us that, at the highest levels, the process model must be developed from the business perspective. Information Technology can definitely help manage and formalize the process definition steps, but the IT team does not do the work that directly impacts customer relationships. Don't expect to ask IT folks to tell you what business processes are important to CRM or how to do them.

As we did for the data component, our goal is to identify, describe, analyze, and improve our CRM business processes based on improved information and technical tools. The three highest levels of the Zachman framework are all that we will cover. These high levels are what Rummler and Brache call the Organization, Process, and Job/Performer levels of performance.

Table 12-1 The Process Component

Business View	Process View
Owner's Wants View	Business functions
Owner's Needs View	Business processes
Designer's View	Activity

For more information on process engineering, see Cook's book on enterprise architectures (1996). For more on the Information Technology views, see Zachman's discussions of his framework (1987).

Just as was done for information, XYZ developed the high level CRM program process scope as part of the strategic plan. They used information from the strategic internal interviews: the consolidated list of business opportunities and business issues that were used to develop the program data classes. The steps that XYZ used to develop process classes were the same as for data, except that since processes are what we do, they highlighted every verb instead of every noun.

1. Go through the list with a highlighter and mark every **verb.** These are your candidate process classes.
2. Identify and eliminate duplicate process classes as well as any unrealistic or unreasonable classes.
3. Write a definition of each of the process classes on your list.
4. Organize into global process classes for ease of communication.

XYZ identified the business functions shown in Figure 12-3 organized into global process classes that match the customer-facing functions that make up the front-office. Notice that many of these business functions do have a strong resemblance to the organization chart at this high level. There are some advantages to using familiar organizational terms for business functions.

It's likely that your company will have some people engaged in marketing, sales, and support, even if they're not fully dedicated to that activity. Many companies, however, do not offer consulting assistance to their customers. A Customer Services Organization doesn't make sense for all products and markets. Virtually all companies operate in the other three functional spaces, and many companies are discovering that service is a highly profitable area with tremendous impact on the customer experience. Of course, like any company, XYZ has since discovered many additional small business units at lower levels in the organization that are also part of the company's CRM efforts. As these were discovered, they were integrated into the overall strategic model.

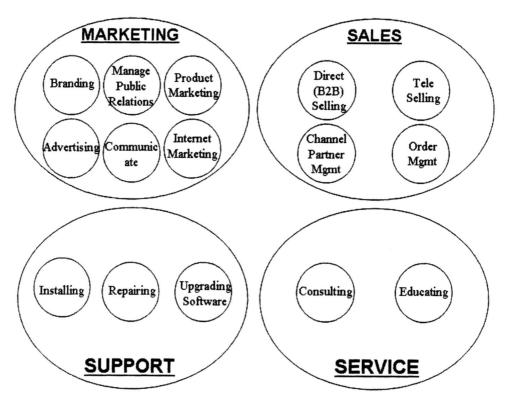

Figure 12-3 Global business functions

12.2.1 Owner's Wants View: Business Functions

During the project launch, XYZ identified the major business functions that will be impacted by this project. This step is critical if for no other reason than that these functions must actively participate, if not provide the sponsorship, in the project. XYZ's process scoping results from the Valencia launch covered in Chapter 9 are shown in Table 12-2.

Table 12-2 Valencia Functional Focus

Project Title: Valencia	
Direction (issue/opportunity, critical success factors)	We don't know who our most valuable customers are because we identify customers differently in every system, so we can't be sure of their total purchases or how much it costs to serve them.
Focus (business functions, target customers, customer offer)	Business Functions: Product (S-800) Marketing, ~~Direct (Business-to-Business Sales~~, *Inbound Telesales*

Notice that since the actual launch the team identified an additional key function, Inbound Telesales, which would be responsible for handling the customer responses. They also discovered that there would actually be little impact on businesses processes for the business to business direct sales team. Of course sales still needed to be included since their customers were being impacted. They updated their project charter to reflect this new information.

Of course, consistently identifying every customer that XYZ has in any system is a huge task. In order to scope the project such that it can be completed in about six months, XYZ started with just its top-tier customers. You'll also remember that XYZ further focused the project by linking with a marketing program being developed for customers who might want to upgrade their current series 800 systems. With these scoping factors in mind, one of the business functions impacted by this first Valencia project is marketing for the Series 800 products. The other, of course, is business-to-business sales. Now we need to identify the relevant processes.

12.2.2 Owner's Needs View: Business Processes

Next the XYZ project team continued working on the project-specific views that support XYZ's first customer identity project (Valencia). Just as they did for data, they always started each new view with the results from the previous level and generated more detail as they went along. These three steps identify the important process steps:

1. Select a team of representatives from the business functions that are relevant for this project.
2. This group will identify the major project-related divisions (processes) within these functions.
3. Write a definition of each process.

There are whole lists of processes used by sales and marketing people to increase revenue, but for now we're focused on finding the right customers, making the offer, and selling upgrades. Initially, the S-800 product marketers wanted to take advantage of the Internet for information delivery and sales – it's the lowest cost means of reaching customers and taking orders. However after considerable discussion, they didn't believe the company was ready; XYZ didn't yet have enough pieces of web infrastructure to support this goal.

The project team members opted to use two well-established processes instead: database marketing (using the postal service to deliver the offer) and the company's mature inbound call centers for presales support and order taking. By making this decision, they avoided the risk of the kind of scope creep that sabotages many new projects. Although the Internet was tempting, they knew that they should minimize the amount of change to only what was needed to make the project successful. XYZ wanted to prove the concept that consistently identifying or recognizing customers across multiple existing systems would deliver successful sales results. They didn't need to change everything at once.

One real concern that the team had was about the quality and accuracy of the data in the source systems. From previous experience with both the order and product registration databases, the team members knew that the quality was poor in both systems, and that the systems differed so much in how they identified customers that combining them would be difficult. A key success factor was to identify all contacts with S815 or S817 products within the top 50 customer accounts. But internally, the company linkages were poorly maintained. The team identified a third key process, customer data quality management, which was critical to Valencia success but was seldom practiced within the company. We will discuss data quality management process more in Chapter 20.

The project team identified three key processes that would become part of the Valencia project, which are shown in Table 12-3.

Table 12-3 Valencia Business Processes

Business Process	Definition
Database Marketing	The process of using knowledge captured in a database to select the customers most likely to respond to an offer.
Data Quality Management	The process of monitoring, evaluating, testing, and correcting data in a database.
Inbound Telesales	The process of answering incoming telephone calls from customers to support, encourage, and accept a product sale.

Of course, if we uncover new processes, we must assign them to a business function. But within which organization will this process be managed? XYZ debated where data quality management should reside; some thought it belonged to the IT department. The final conclusion was that knowledge about customers sufficient to verify accurate data existed only in one of the customer-facing organizations, so the process was assigned to the marketing organization, which was the biggest user of the database and most impacted by poor quality.

It is very helpful to create a diagram like the one shown in Figure 12-4. These diagrams, called process maps, illustrate the relationships between all the current and planned internal processes that are important to Valencia and how they interact with the customer.

Our next task is to focus on each of the processes and determine the actual work steps that make up each of these key processes.

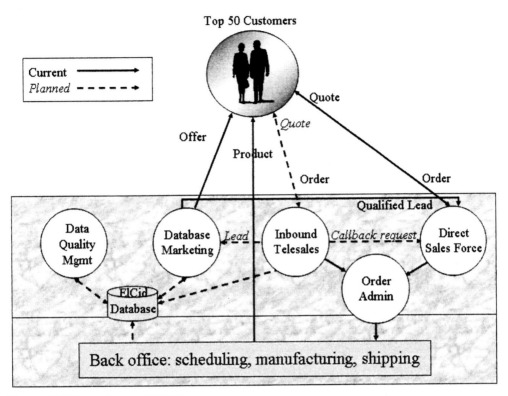

Top 50 Customers

Current ⟶
Planned - - - - - ➔

Quote

Offer

Quote

Product

Order   Order

Qualified Lead

Data Quality Mgmt

Database Marketing   Lead   Inbound Telesales   Callback request   Direct Sales Force

ElCid Database

Order Admin

Back office: scheduling, manufacturing, shipping

Figure 12-4 Valencia process map

12.2.3 Designer's View: Activities and Tasks

Here we are at the Designer's View again, and this is where the handoff between business knowledge of what activities are performed and the skills needed to analyze and create formal documentation for each of the process steps often takes place. As we know, this step is the most critical because so much can be lost during the handoff.

In the designer's view, XYZ identified and documented each of the activities that people do during the process. As they did for the information component they also detailed some of the individual tasks that make up each activity. Only the individuals who manage and perform the business process have the knowledge about what is done. Information Technology often brings in the skill and knowledge necessary to effectively articulate and document each step so that a successful application can be designed and built.

One of the major contributions of the process analysis component is identifying the problems that occur in the "white space" when processes cross business organizations. The process analyst will capture information from all parts of the organization that play any part in the process and put the lists of activities together to identify process redundancy, contradiction, and disconnects.

To understand this step, let's look at the process for Database Marketing. The difference between Direct or Database Marketing (DM) and traditional marketing is that DM aims to generate a desired action from the set of specific customers who have been targeted. Direct Marketing involves creating a relevant offer, selecting the appropriate customers, delivering the offer to these customers, and measuring the results – in other words a match to the third and fourth (external) phases of CRM life cycle. The overall task of drilling into more specific levels of detail is called decomposition and is illustrated for this project in Figure 12-5.

Process decomposition simply means identifying the next lower levels of detail for each of the process views. As a result of the first three phases of process decomposition, XYZ developed the list of activities that are shown in Table 12-4. We use a similar naming convention for the different process levels as we used in Chapter 11 for data.

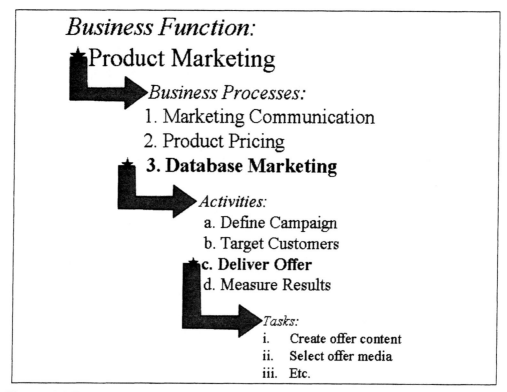

Figure 12-5 Process decomposition for Valencia

Table 12-4 Valencia Process Scope

Business Function	Business Process	Activity	Individual Tasks
PRODUCT MARKETING	Database Marketing	Create product offer	
		Target customers	
		Deliver offer	Define content,
			select media
			etc.
		Measure results	
	Data Quality Management	Sample source data	
		Assess quality level	
		Design integration plan	
		Implement quality improvement	
BUSINESS TO BUSINESS SALES	Telesales	Answer product inquiry	
		Analyze customer requirement	
		Recommend solution	
		Configure order requirement	
		Enter order	
		Manage order status	

Of course, the IT team members will need more detail before they can understand what needs to be built. The IT team develops the remaining levels of detail. They will need both content and review input from the appropriate business experts to make sure they've gotten the right picture.

12.2.4 Following the Rest of the Steps

The two remaining views are primarily the responsibility of the Information Technology members of the project team, and we will not cover them in detail.

Builder's View: Application Design Specification

Application design identifies each step in an activity that is to be automated. Not all activities are appropriate for automation. It's important for the entire project team to understand the cost versus benefit of automating each activity. Often, the costs can't be identified until Information Technology has created the application design.

Detailed View: Software Module

Software modules are made up of computer code that is written to instruct the computer how to accomplish an activity. CRM software uses information about each customer stored in a database to decide what kind of experience to offer each customer. Other CRM software captures customer responses and stores them in a database. This software often allows a computer to perform a process that was formerly done by humans. The computer is much faster and it doesn't get tired, but it has no intuition, which is why the business expertise is so critical in the early stages of process engineering.

An Integrated Application System is the end result of the IT effort on process. Each module will be written, tested, and integrated into the overall working environment of the predetermined system users.

12.2.5 Making the Transition

The designer's view is where the handoff between the business team and the IT team takes place. Some organizations have formal process management organizations that are responsible for documenting, refining, and improving key business processes. If your company has this resource, by all means bring them into the project team at least for this step.

But for many companies, the benefit of such an organization has not been recognized. Most organizations simply don't have time to worry about how work gets done; they are too busy just working! This often results in poor and/or redundant processes that require significant rework. (They have time to do it over, but they don't have time to figure out how to do it right the first time.) In any case, in the absence of a process management team, it often falls to Information Technology to formalize the designer's view, so this is where major responsibility shifts from the business function to Information Technology, as shown in Figure 12-6.

Next, we will look at some of the key decisions involved in process automation.

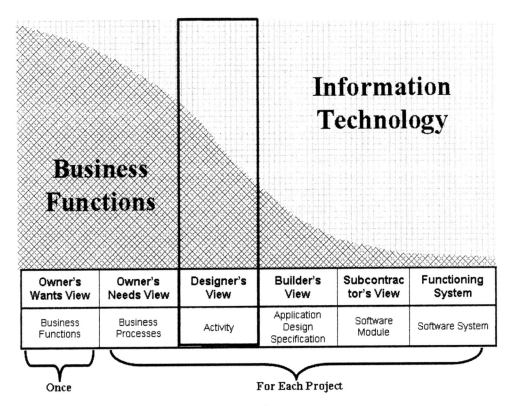

Owner's Wants View	Owner's Needs View	Designer's View	Builder's View	Subcontractor's View	Functioning System
Business Functions	Business Processes	Activity	Application Design Specification	Software Module	Software System

Once   For Each Project

Figure 12-6 The process handoff

12.3 Choosing Process Automation Software

After you've decided to automate a process, the question becomes "build or buy?" This question has been asked more often as more and better software solutions are available for purchase. There is no perfect CRM solution that can possibly meet every company's needs, but custom-built solutions are notoriously difficult to build and extremely expensive to maintain. Educated tradeoffs must be made. We will discuss this dilemma in Chapter 13 when we look at the technology component.

Frequently, company officials hire large consulting organizations to help them understand their processes and pick the best software solution. This can be a good way to jump-start your analysis process and make quick progress. But it's important that your business experts are closely involved in explaining and documenting the key business processes. A consultant can be a good source of recommending process improvements as long as he well understands your business.

12.3.1 Know your own processes first, and then buy a solution that fits

Whether you build or buy, you can never be successful unless you understand exactly what processes your company uses to interact with customers. In the past, companies have tried one or both of these two approaches:

- Automate activities that are not tuned for a technology solution.
- Force-fit a solution onto existing processes without managing the fit.

The biggest problem with the first approach is that automating poor processes doesn't improve the process, nor does it do anything for the customer experience. The problem with the second approach is that people resist change anyway, and when a new technology makes their job harder to do (or they think it will be harder), they won't adopt it, and the project will fail. We need to understand our processes to tune them for how computers work, and then find a solution that best matches what we need to get done. For now, we will just focus on what we need to know about our processes to make the best decision.

Warning: Don't be in love with your own processes. If one of the tools you evaluate supports a better process than the one you're using, be open to change.

12.3.2 Technology doesn't fix broken processes

Let me say it again: "A broken process will not be fixed by technology!" There is no magic. To the contrary, poor processes are usually made worse by automation. You simply have an opportunity to accomplish so much more of the wrong thing faster. As part of the process component of each project, you must understand the process steps in detail, identify and fix process weaknesses, and then map them to potential software solutions.

12.3.3 Managing processes across organizational boundaries

Just as we saw in Figure 12-4, it is rare indeed for processes that impact the customer experience to be completely managed within one organizational unit. For the Valencia project, we can see that both sales and marketing organizations are involved, but the end result to the customer (receiving the product that was ordered) is dependent on the back office functions of manufacturing and logistics. Although we will not cover the back office elements of the customers' experience, the methods we adopt to manage the white space in the front office can be applied to back office white space, too. The most important outcome of the process-engineering step is to understand the following:

- The work goal
- The steps that need to get done (workflow) to reach the goal
- Who is responsible for which steps
- What needs to happen in the handoff (the white space)
- How you measure that you've reached your goal

After we've identified these items, we are ready to start thinking about what the technology component needs to look like.

Questions for Reflection

Look at a copy of your corporate organizational chart.

1. Thinking back to Chapter 1, which value discipline did you identify as being the choice of your company?
2. Look at a copy of your corporate organizational chart. What are the CRM business functions called in your company? Do they map to the four global CRM functions? What are the differences?

CHAPTER 13

Understanding the Technology Component

The third component of our CRM infrastructure is **technology.** In Chapter 11, we learned that data, the lifeblood of CRM, must be stable and dependable over time, but tools can be disposable. Had you heard that before? Probably not: software vendors can't make money selling you your own data. In fact, even selling software isn't all that profitable. It's selling customer services and product support that bring in the real money!

Vendors don't want open systems because they want you to be locked into their solution and to depend on them for consulting, long-term support, and future software purchases. Because new tools are released all the time, in the ideal world, the best option for companies implementing CRM is a sharable customer database surrounded by interchangeable, plug-in tools. This is not to say that this option is available today or even easy to accomplish. But unless there is some incentive for the software providers (like CRM practitioners demand it) the situation is unlikely to change.

After you're locked in with a single software product, you can get stuck there. When you buy a new VCR, do you throw away all your old videocassettes? Well, now you don't, but there was a war between VHS and BetaMax when VCRs were first introduced. Consumers voted with their wallets for a standard, not necessarily the best standard, but the one that was most widely used. As CRM software becomes more pervasive, consumers may also have a decision to make. Will we accept all this proprietary software and be ruled by the software vendor, or will we vote for open standards with our wallets so we can choose the best solution for our companies. Only we can force this situation to change.

But for now, what we'll do is to understand how to pick the best technology to match our business needs.

13.1 Understanding the Technology...That's the IT Department's Job, Right?

Well, right and wrong! Certainly the technology component is primarily the responsibility of Information Technology. However, it was learned long ago that it is *critical* that the technical solution the IT team proposes be based on business perspective and needs. Information Technology must have business input regarding what information needs to be captured, what work needs to be done, and where and by whom this work is to be done.

But let's first develop our working definition for technology so we're all talking the same language. Miriam-Webster's online dictionary defines technology as "a manner of accomplishing a task especially using [specialized] processes, methods, or knowledge." For CRM, the specialized methods are the computer hardware, software, and networks.

DEFINITIONS

CRM Technology is made up of the computer tools (hardware, software, and networks) employed to manage the information and process we use to deliver customer experiences.

In all cases, it is the IT department that will design, implement, and manage the technology solution, but it is the business functions that know where the work is done and who's doing it.

13.1.1 The Business Functions: Setting the Direction

Anyone could probably look at a corporate map or even a company phone book and determine all the places that a company does business. So what's the big deal? The IT team doesn't need any help figuring that out!

But that's not all it takes. The business functions add significantly to the general understanding of how the company operates geographically through their knowledge of what kinds of work are done where and what business connections are required to ensure a positive experience for the customer process. Figure 13-1 shows XYZ's corporate map.

You can see that XYZ is a North American company with manufacturing plants in Canada, Mexico, and the United States. Sales and service organizations exist in all three countries, and the corporate headquarters is located in Chicago, Illinois. The IT department needs to know more than that to implement a successful system.

13.1.2 The IT Function: Engineering the Solution

Like the other components, "engineering" the technology model requires experience and knowledge from both the business members of the team and from the Information Technology members.

Figure 13-1 The XYZ Corporation's location map

Technology models describe the major pieces of the technical infrastructure: hardware, software, and network. We don't start with technology; rather, we begin at the highest-level business perspective by listing our *business locations*. Next, we identify the *business network* for just those locations that will be involved in this project. The business network shows the way work and information must flow to deliver the customer experience. The remaining views are strictly from the Information Technology perspective, and we will not spend a great deal of time on any of them. Figure 13-2 shows the technology engineering process steps; you should remember that the inventory of business locations is actually done during the strategic planning phase. Team members with business functional knowledge will work together to identify the business work and information flow requirements for each specific project and with the technical team to ensure common understanding of the actual business situation.

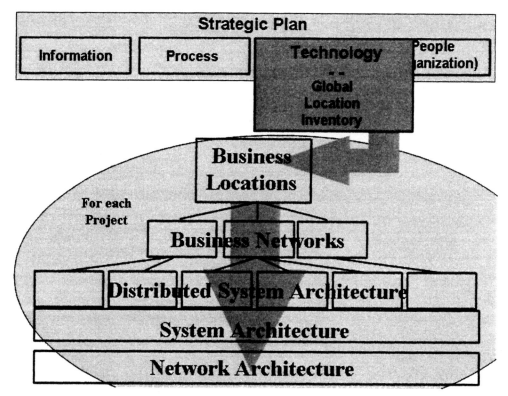

Figure 13-2 Technology engineering

As you can see, just like with the other components we always start with the business per-spective—where the company's various organizations are located.

13.2 Following the Technology Engineering Steps

For the technology component, only the first two views require the combined effort of the busi-ness and IT teams as shown in Table 13-1.

Table 13-1 The Technology Component

Business View	Technology View
Owner's Wants View	Business Locations
Owner's Needs View	Business Networks

For each project, the business team focuses on just those locations that will be impacted by the new CRM functionality. Because this component is primarily the responsibility of Informa-tion Technology, we will look only at the top two business levels.

13.2.1 Owner's Wants View: Business Locations

During strategic planning, we identified a list of locations and high-level process. Many times during strategic planning, we used a matrix as a tool for understanding the relationship between two important topics (e.g., customer life cycle and touch points). Here is another important relationship that was understood and documented during strategic planning, the one between business functions and geographic locations, as shown in Figure 13-3.

For Valencia we know that two major functions were involved, S-800 Marketing and Telesales. Where are these functions located? From the organization map in Figure 13-1, we know that the S-800 Division, including the marketing organization, is located in Vancouver, British Columbia. With the help of the organization/function matrix in Figure 13-3, we see that telesales call centers are located in Tampa, Vancouver, and Guadalajara. The database itself was to be physically located in Chicago, so the key company physical locations that are important to the success of Valencia are Chicago, Guadalajara, Tampa and Vancouver. Of course, there are always options for reducing project scope by implementing in only one location. XYZ wanted to roll out all regions because most of these top 50 customers were located in multiple countries.

	Corporate	Marketing				Sales				Service		Support	
	Executive Team	Internet	Brand & Advertising	PR/Communications	Product Mktg	Direct	Channel	Telesales	Order Admin	Consulting	Education	Repair	Phone
Chicago	X	X	X	X		X	X		X			X	
New York						X					X	X	
Los Angeles						X		X	X			X	
Dallas					X							X	X
Tampa						X		X				X	
Toronto						X	X	X	X	X	X		
Vancouver					X			X				X	X
Mexico City	X					X	X		X			X	X
Guadalajara					X			X				X	X

Figure 13-3 XYZ's function/location matrix

The function/location matrix acts as a roadmap for where different business organizations are located. At a very high level, Information Technology uses this matrix to understand the system access and network links that need to be in place to support information and work flow requirements of the business.

13.2.2 Owner's Needs View: Business Networks

Now we'll look at the business network for XYZ's first customer identity project (Valencia). The key business connection requirements for the project were also identified in Chapter 12: Database marketing sends an offer to the customer who dials the telesales call center to place an order. Telesales takes the order and sends it on to the factory that will build and ship the product to the customer.

The network connection requirements for Valencia are from the S-800 database marketing team to customers (not shown), from customers to one of the call centers, from the call center to the S800 factory, and from the factory to the customer to complete the transaction, as shown in Figure 13-4.

Figure 13-4 The Valencia business network

Although there are important project communications between the executive team, the corporate IT team and project team, these network links are not part of the *project* work. They have been indicated by a dashed line in Figure 13-4.

13.2.3 The Remaining Views

As we know, most of the responsibility for technology engineering rests with the IT department, which is responsible for developing each of the remaining views and for the final implementation and support of the functioning technology network. The three remaining views are based on the information, process, and physical location requirements that were identified in Chapters 11 and 12.

Designer's View: Distributed System Architecture

Using knowledge about what work needs to get done, where, and by whom (how many), the IT team can plan where to locate computer servers that will optimize business and application performance.

Builder's View: System Architecture

Current application software and connections (interfaces) between them result from the system inventory. The future system architecture will show the integration of new software (additions or replacements) and what new interfaces will be required. The system architecture is often shown in stages or phases such as the following:

- Where we are today (created once during strategic planning)
- What we will have after this project is completed
- Where we plan to be when we're finished (created once during strategic planning, but updated as plans change)

Here's an example of XYZ's current system architecture, as well as what is planned to be in place when this project is finished. You can see the current and future states in Figure 13-5.

This system architecture shows that as a result of the Valencia project, a new system (El Cid) will be built or purchased and data from the order processing system and the S-800 product registration database will be loaded. The database marketers will select target customers from the El Cid database and send the offer. These are the new elements of the architecture. The rest of the applications and connections already exist (although some connections, as indicated by broken arrows, are manual or are only semi-automated). It is quite common to organize a System Architecture diagram by the organization that owns/operates each element. For each project, it will be important for the IT department to create a map of what the architecture will look like when the project is finished. This is just one more way of showing the progress that has been and will be made, and it's just as important for the IT team to show visible progress to their management as it is for the business functional members of the team.

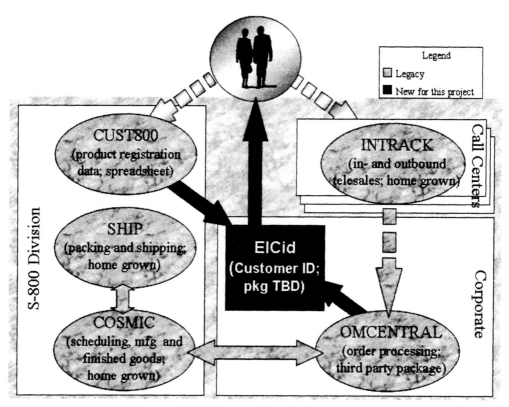

Figure 13-5 Valencia System Architecture

Subcontractor's View: Network Architecture

Using all that has been planned about where work is to be done, where computers are located, and what people and systems need to talk with each other, Information Technology defines a network architecture showing all the network connections (including backup redundancy) that are required to support the system. The important thing is that the IT team has an overall plan and architecture that is guiding the development of your company's CRM solution.

By the way, there is another good way of describing the system architecture. The view in Figure 13-5 is organized around the company's organizational structure. The view in Figure 13-6 is from the perspective of what kind of work needs to get done, operational or decision-making activities.

The benefit of this architectural perspective is that it emphasizes the difference between transaction processing applications and decisions support applications. The IT analysts need to design the two very differently, because transaction systems are tuned to capture and modify data about events that take place (orders, shipments, etc.) and decisions support applications are turned for searching, selecting, sorting, and summarizing the transaction data. Most of the ele-

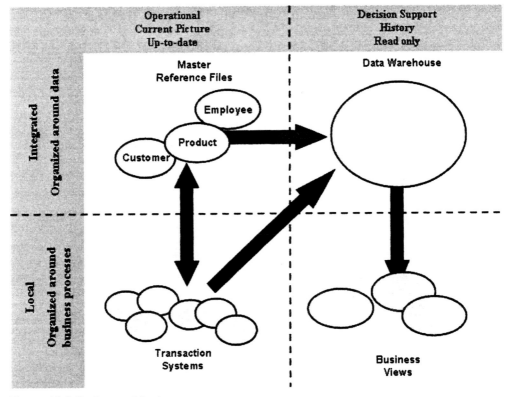

Figure 13-6 System architecture

ments of the traditional system architecture are located on the left side of this architecture. Having only the data needed to support a specific interaction optimizes transaction systems. There is a strong link between the transaction systems and the master reference files that capture and consolidate information that is to be shared across the various transaction systems (such as the customer information in the El Cid database). The CUST800 system would be located on the right because its main purpose is reporting, analysis, and market research. Many companies have created a central data warehouse that collects all the details of the transactions and master file changes over time so that trend analysis and reporting can occur. But this is too much data for almost any reporting tool to handle efficiently, so this architecture includes the creation of local copies of portions of the warehouse that are relevant to a specific function (e.g., marketing) or a specific decision (who are our most valuable customers).

At the end of all this work, for which the IT team is largely responsible, is the functioning network that connects all the system pieces together and supports sharing of information and work flows across the whole company.

13.2.4 The Transition to Information Technology

As we've learned, most of the responsibility for the technology component lies with the IT department. The handoff between business and Information Technology happens very early, during the development of the owner's view, as shown in Figure 13-7.

Now we'll look at some of the considerations we have to make when we are ready to select a specific technology approach.

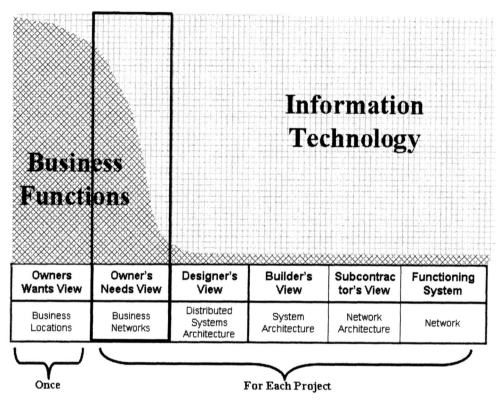

Owners Wants View	Owner's Needs View	Designer's View	Builder's View	Subcontrac tor's View	Functioning System
Business Locations	Business Networks	Distributed Systems Architecture	System Architecture	Network Architecture	Network

Once   For Each Project

Figure 13-7 Technology handoff

13.3 Making Technology Decisions

We have often discussed the dangers of creating a CRM infrastructure component without heavy involvement of the business functions that are already working closely with customers and delivering customer experiences. But few people outside the IT profession have any confidence in their ability to make technology decisions. The truth is that some elements of the IT solution require little, if any, perspective of the business, and others require a great deal. With a good understanding of the business organization and where work gets done, the IT team has a lot of the information they need to design the overall network architecture and select the appropriate hardware components that will best satisfy the business requirements.

13.3.1 Application Software—It's Always a Tradeoff

Application software tells the computer what information is needed to make decisions and how to perform activities based on that information. Picking the right software to automate processes and capture and store business information requires functional knowledge and expertise from the people who know the work that needs to get done. How do we get and keep the business engaged during the critical step of making software application decisions? The bottom line is this: the functional team needs the information about the business impact of the different options available for some of the key decisions. There are many decision-making tools in general use, and one of the simplest is the decision matrix.

As we discussed in Chapter 12, many companies hire expensive consulting firms to help them select the best software solution, but it can't be totally done for you by a consultant any more than your own IT team can do it alone. The business experts must be involved comparing the business requirements to the software capabilities and make any necessary tradeoff decision. Consultants and Information Technology can help a lot, but they can only help.

The decision matrix is a useful tool for comparing two or more alternatives across multiple factors. The simplest version looks like Table 13-2. Here's how you create a decision matrix. First, list all the alternatives across the top, and then list the important decisions factors down the side. For each cell, indicate how well that alternative meets that factor (0 for "not good at all," 1 for "adequate," 2 for "good to great fit"). The highest score *wins*.

Table 13-2 A Decision Matrix

	Alternative 1		Alternative 2	
Factor 1		2		0
Factor 2		1		2
Factor 3		2		1
Factor 4		2		1
Total		**7**		**4**

A good way of getting started on a decision is to put a brief comment in each cell that describes the characteristics or impact of the alternative. Give this to all team members, and have them input a score. This can be done via e-mail, interview, or in a team meeting in which each alternative or factor is discussed in detail. More sophistication can be introduced by adding a weight to each factor. Sometimes, these are called simply "Musts" and "Wants." If an alternative can't meet a must-have factor, it is eliminated. Alternatively, the factors can be grouped into importance ranks from high (5) to low (1). The final score is determined by multiplying the score by weight. All of these decision making variations work well, depending on the complexity of the decision and the time available. One of the most important results is the discussion that is generated through the weighting and scoring process.

Making sure that a package has adequate functionality is not the same as insisting that it accomplishes the function exactly the same way you do today. It was important that XYZ's call center had the tools and information necessary to create a customer quote and take an order. It was not important that the quote and order be created using exactly the way it's always been done. And finally, don't get stuck in terminal consensus building. Sometimes somebody just has to be responsible and make the decision. Be sure your sponsor and steering committee are up to this.

Build or Buy?

One of the first decisions that must be made is whether to buy a product off the shelf or build a customized solution. In the early days of computer automation, little software was available on the open market; everything was custom-built. This turned out to be a very expensive proposition, and many companies today prefer to buy solutions whenever possible. As more options become available for business activities, your choices continue to grow. Let's look at a simplified version of XYZ's decision-making process for Valencia, as shown in Table 13-3.

Table 13-3 XYZ's Build or Buy Decision

	Build		**Buy**	
What's the time to market?	Always slower than estimated	0	In spite of claims, often very slow	1
What is the cost to build and support?	Cost to recreate functionality that is available on the open market	0	Should be less costly to implement and support as long as we minimize customization	2
What is the software core competency?	We are not a software company	0	Great to depend on software that is being developed and supported by a company focused on this single problem	2
Does the functionality match our needs?	Can be made perfect, at least in theory	2	So far, no solution found	?
Is the software developer a reliable vendor?	If it's not, software is the least of our worries.	2	To be determined	?
Total		**4**		**5**

From the decision matrix, it appeared that buying is a better choice for XYZ, but there was one problem. Because of all the work that had been done, XYZ knew what it needed to consistently identify customers, but they had not yet found a product on the market that met their needs. Because buying software was so advantageous, the company decided to wait and do a more in-depth analysis of alternatives available, including a benchmark of what companies with successful customer relationship programs were doing.

Single Solution or Component Best in Class

This is another tough decision, and it's related to the "build or buy" choice. If you get a single, totally integrated solution, you should be able to minimize the amount of customization that needs to be done. This should be (and is) much cheaper than having to build and maintain all the connections between bunches of different tools. But there's a catch; it is not possible for any total solution to be best at everything that needs to get done for a successful CRM program. Most are outstanding in one or two areas, but often barely adequate in the rest. Even if acceptable for the majority, it's tough to remain in the lead position for everything. Remember that we want to keep the information and replace the tools as better ones become available.

The big problem is that most integrated software solutions are proprietary. Their database structure is built into the application and is not easily made available to other vendors' products. Nonetheless, XYZ's basic system strategy was built around integrating the best-in-class modules. XYZ took the approach of minimizing the number of connections that were required by connecting systems through hubs, rather than linking every application to every other application.

There's another problem, too. If you decide that you will only select a product that provides a total solution for everything you need, then you are forced to evaluate/compare all the functions at once, instead of being able to take small steps. It is difficult, if not impossible, to make such a big decision in a reasonable amount of time. Even if you plan to implement in chunks, how do you compare across all the activities you will need. Sometimes, companies will select a vendor who promises that its solution can be tuned to fit all requirements. Be forewarned; in most cases, one size fits none.

And finally don't forget your current (legacy) environment. You can't replace everything at once, so it will be a long time before you are actually running on one single total solution. If you are a small company that's just starting up, you may be able to buy a solution off the shelf and just operate your business the way the product works. The first time most of us learned to use an electronic spreadsheet, we just learned that typing "\c" allowed us to copy data from one place to another. Changing that familiar task was difficult because we didn't even think about what we were doing. Even if a new product was better, at first it was frustrating and made us much less productive. This is the same situation. Of course people can learn to change, but it takes planning, resources, and effort to make change successful. So despite all the hype and promises, forget it! There is no silver bullet. This leads us finally to the question, what happens if we decide to integrate components?

Component Integration

There are several integration issues that must be faced if the organization opts for integrating best-in-class components. Of course, unless you can replace everything at one time, you will be faced with these issues anyway if you are fitting new tools into your existing environment.

1. First, we must be concerned about integrating information. Both the form of the data and the quality of the content can differ. We will take a closer look at these issues in Chapter 16.
2. New processes must be integrated into the existing process environment. This involves all of the change management activities that we will discuss in Chapter 14.
3. The new technology must be integrated into the existing technical environment. This is largely the responsibility of the IT organization, but we will take a quick look at some of the issues in Chapter 16.

The decision you make will be based on the cost of the integration efforts versus the value of being more independent of technology single solutions. You also have to ask whether your IT department has the knowledge and experience to manage complex integrations.

Evaluate and Select Your Tools

This is what you've been waiting for, right? This is where you find out exactly which CRM software products you should buy. Sorry, it just doesn't work that way. Even listing names of applications and vendors is so time-sensitive that, in a year or two, it becomes be meaningless, and forget keeping up with all the changes in what they do or how well they do it. Look at the example in Table 13-4, which presents the results of a survey done about two years apart. Each survey identified the CRM product leaders at the time. Look at all the changes.

Table 13-4 CRM Application Products

	Marketing/Sales		Service/Support	
	Survey #1	Survey #2	Survey #1	Survey #2
Baan			X	X
Blue Martini	X			
Broadvision	X		X	
Clarify		X		X
Edify EWF				X
Epicor Clientele			X	X

Table 13-4 CRM Application Products (Continued)

	Marketing/Sales		Service/Support	
	Survey #1	Survey #2	Survey #1	Survey #2
E.piphany			X	X
Frontoffice	X		X	
Goldmine			X	X
Great Plains			X	
Oracle E-Business			X	
PeopleSoft			X	(Vantive)
Remedy Sales Continuum	X		(Perigrine)	
SalesLogix			X	
SAP	X			
Saratoga Systems			X	
SAS	X			
Siebel			X	X
Vantive		X	(Peoplesoft)	

By the time you can buy this book, some of these applications will have disappeared, others will have expanded functionality, and new ones will have emerged. What we can do is help you learn how to make your own decision as to what's right for your company and the time you need to make a decision.

Remember that different people learn in different ways and need different types of information to make a good decision. Some people learn by reading; these people want scads of product documentation. Others learn by hearing and want a visit from a sales team with product expertise. And some learn by doing; they want to get their hands on the product and try it out. Be sure you can meet the needs of all three types of learners.

There are several places you can go to help your company make the decision that is best for your business:

- **The Internet:** This is probably the best source of information because it is easy to find current information. From the Internet, you can find lists of products to consider, decision methodologies to apply, consultants to hire, and tools to use. Use your favorite Internet search engine, and enter your criteria (e.g., "CRM software selection"). One of the best sources of information that I found was a very practical and information-rich source at www.softresources.com.

- **Consultant:** Consultants bring a wide range of knowledge about different applications and experience about how different companies are using them.
- **Books:** The ones that tell you what to buy are not my favorite because of the aging issue. But if you're in a hurry and don't have time to do lots of investigation (and you can find some recent results), the $900 price tag on some of the customer satisfaction survey books (i.e., Consumer Reports for CRM) may be worth it to you. They do a very decent job comparing features and reporting results. However, my preference is for the books that tell you how to make your decisions such as Dick Lee's straightforward (read that "blunt") and highly readable book about surviving CRM. Lee's Survival Guide presents a ton of common sense and practical guidance. He says, "NEVER, NEVER, NEVER let CRM software dictate how you do stuff," and I wholeheartedly agree.

So, what we really have to do to make the decision that is best for our organization is to again create a plan and follow a process. This is how you will be able to make the best choice based on the information you have already generated as part of the project. Every step builds on previous steps; there is no starting over. These are the application selection process steps:

1. Identify important technology architecture and business requirements.
2. List the activities that you identified as being part of your project.
3. Generate a list of the software applications you will evaluate. (SoftResources suggests generating a long list from multiple sources such as the Internet, industry publications, etc. Then use a list of high-level criteria, such as hardware platform, stability of vendor, etc., to reduce the list to the three or four that you will evaluate in depth).
4. Deliver a Request for Proposal (RFP) to vendors listing all your business functionality requirements.
5. Evaluate vendor responses, evaluate functionality, and talk with current users of the software.
6. Score each application for the appropriateness of fit to every business activity.

Table 13-5 shows the high-level summary of XYZ's RFP results for the database marketing process. Of course, the RFP itself divided activities into lower-level work tasks such as the various campaign management steps like the contact plan, execution, and results tracking. The complete summary for the project also included the data management and sales functionality.

Table 13-5 XYZ's Database Marketing RFP Summary

Function	Process	Activity	Application			
			E.piphany	Oracle	SAS	Siebel
Marketing	Database Marketing	Create Offer	Not appropriate for automation			
		Customer Database (Consistent ID)	?	?	?	?
		Analysis and Segment	X	X	X	X
		Deliver Offer	Not appropriate for automation			
		Campaign Management	X	X		X
		Report Results	?	X	X	?

Based on these results, XYZ decided to eliminate SAS as an alternative because (at that time) SAS didn't offer campaign management capabilities. Even though it had the strongest analysis and reporting capabilities, the team needed campaign management capability integrated into its database marketing solution.

Notice that although all four products had databases, none had clearly met the customer database (ID) requirement. Even though all four vendors had indicated that they had database and customer identification capabilities, it wasn't clear what "yes" meant. SoftResources has determined that, on average, vendors answer yes to 85 percent of RFP questions. They claim that "Yes" can mean anything along a whole continuum from having exceptionally robust features in that area to having the ability to modify the product to meet the requirement (as long as you're willing pay us lots and lots of money). Sometimes it even means "I don't know what you're talking about and I don't think you do either, so I'm just going to answer, 'Yes'." That's why the next step is so critical; XYZ set out to do due diligence by actually testing the applications in-house and walking through the company's operation. Even more valuable is talking with companies who are currently using each of the products.

13.3.2 Where to Start—On or Off the Web

The reason there's a dilemma about where to start is that most companies even today get very little of their data from web sources. Although that's where everyone hopes to be, the web sources provide only about 15 percent of new data captured. Considering that many companies have been collecting customer information for years, the web probably accounts for less than 5 percent of a company's total customer information. Although we expect and hope that this will change over time, it will be quite a while before web sources overtake non-web sources as data generators.

So why is this imbalance such a problem? Web-captured data is likely to be pretty high quality because presumably the customer himself or herself has supplied the information directly to our web site. But few companies have enough web data to really answer the important questions they have about their customer relationships. To get more information, we are forced to supplement web data with older (legacy) data. Now, if we integrate all this old stuff into our Internet application, we are giving customers online access. They will be able to see all that horrible old data we have about them. It's just plain embarrassing!

The way to get around this problem is to begin your integration efforts offline, using either web or non-web data as appropriate to your project. Make data cleanup and quality a large part of the project effort. (We'll discuss this more in Chapter 20.) After you have sufficient customer information at an acceptable level of quality, you can begin to integrate your online access capabilities. Whenever possible pick the alternative with the lowest risk.

13.3.3 Putting the "I" Back in Information Technology

Remember that customer information is a company asset and must be treated as such. The IT department is responsible for more than just doing technology right. The business functions are responsible for identifying what information is important to them. Information Technology has an equally important role: They must capture the information the way the business users describe it—not because it's easier to implement something else. If the system doesn't capture the context of the information, we don't have any. Then it's just data.

Now we're ready to look at the fourth component of CRM – the people component. Without a doubt, this is the most difficult component to manage, and it will make or break your CRM program.

Questions for Reflection

Consider your answers to the following questions. Your answers will give you an early insight as to how your organization might go about making its technology selection.

1. Do you have a large legacy environment, or are you starting with a relatively clean slate?
2. Do you have a highly competent IT department that is always looking for the best tools to meet business needs, or do your IT people largely just keep the ship running?
3. What is the basic system architecture: large central systems or smaller, distributed systems?

CHAPTER 14

Understanding the People Component

People are the fourth component of our CRM infrastructure, which is by far the most difficult of the four to manage. This is also the most critical of the components, but one that is often overlooked in the rush to begin a CRM program quickly. (After all, technology will fix everything anyway, right?) The people component is about changing the behavior of the people who interact with customers either directly or indirectly. We're not going to try to engineer people; instead, the people component is about engineering change. And for that, we are going to develop and follow a plan.

14.1 Engineering People?

We're not going to even think about engineering people. We won't be using any clipboards or stop watches to manage the people component. In fact, this component isn't about work at all; we already looked at what needs to be done in Chapter 12 when we discussed the process component. Rather, when we talk about the people component, we are talking about helping people to change their behavior. The dictionary defines change to mean "to make different," and behavior is defined as "the way in which some[one] functions or operates."

 DEFINITIONS

The people component refers to people changing the way they function or operate.

As we discussed earlier, organizations were originally created to improve the way work gets done. People doing similar jobs all reported into the same organization.

14.1.1 Understanding Why Change Is So Difficult

People don't like change; often, we are afraid of the unknown. Even very positive changes like getting a promotion or buying a new house are stressful because there is still something lost— the old team and all the stuff you know how to do, or the old neighborhood, schools and shops.

For our purposes, there are four stages that people must work through whenever they are faced with change. These behavioral stages are actually a learning process and not all that different from what happens when people learn anything new. Consider, for example, learning to ride a two-wheel bicycle. People often start by believing that the change isn't really going to happen or won't have much impact – sort of like putting training wheels on your bike; it's not all that different from riding a tricycle. When we finally take the training wheels off, we often get angry, sad, or frustrated because it's just so hard to stay upright. Anyway, it's not our fault because we can't practice without help from Mom or Dad and they're always too busy. Then there is a break-through when we start to understand what's different, and, at least for a moment or two, we start to figure out this thing called balance. Finally, we get it! It seems like a miracle; not only have we mastered the balance thing, but we've also found out how much faster and farther we can go on two wheels with much less work. It did just take practice after all.

Change represents the end of something and the start of something new. Getting from one state to the other requires going through a transition that includes the four stages shown in Figure 14-1.

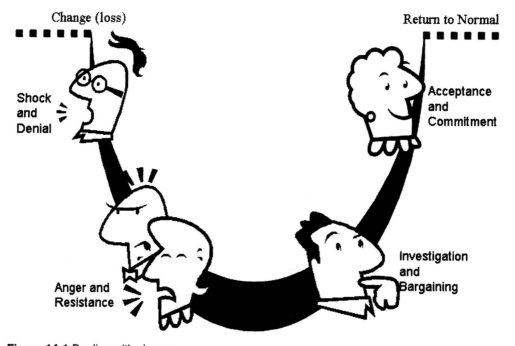

Figure 14-1 Dealing with change

The transition takes time. Change, even for the better, still represents a loss of some kind. The purpose of the people component is to make the transition as short as possible, returning people to a level of productivity that is at least as good as it was before we started the transition. The first and most important thing we can do is to understand that individuals go through a process to accept change. With this knowledge, we can be prepared to provide as much support as possible.

14.1.2 Supporting Change

If our CRM program is to be successful, we want to see two big changes in the behavior of those individuals who interact directly with customers and help form the total customer experience. These individuals are certainly employees, but also include contract workers and third party service providers. All of the same basic behavior requirements apply, though of course the methods for governing change are not the same for individuals not directly employed by your company. We will use the term "employee" to include all individuals who work on your company's behalf, no matter who pays their salary.

- Employees will change **what** gets done and ensure that they understand our customer interactions from the customer's point of view
- Employees will change **how** things get done, and we will make sure that everyone understands how to use all the new tools, information, and process

We know it's unrealistic to expect people to flock instantly to the adoption of these kinds of changes, but how can we support and encourage the transition? Table 14-1 lists the tools that are available to assist employees through the change ahead.

Table 14-1 Change Transition Stages

	Denial	Resistance	Investigation	Acceptance
Communication	X	X	X	X
Training and Education		X	X	X
Metrics and Rewards			X	X

All three of the tools listed in Table 14-1 are critical to successful implementation, but it is not surprising that the first of these is **communication!**

14.1.3 Engineering Change

By now, we can't be surprised that engineering the kind of change required by a CRM program requires input and perspective from both business experts and technology experts. For this component, the responsibility for the engineering process resides primarily within the business function, but Information Technology has lots to contribute, too.

Behavioral change requires a clear understanding of the company's strategy and direction. This must be the motivational driver behind the change that is taking place. So where do we start? Just like always: We begin with a high-level understanding of the *organization* and its business goals. Next, we focus on the Valencia project and identify the *business units* that will be impacted, and particularly the *job roles* of individuals who will be making any required changes in their behavior. Then, we will define a *change management plan* that we will use to manage the communication, training, and rewards that support and encourage transition. The remaining view, the security architecture, is primarily the responsibility of the IT team, although business management must identify specific individuals and what they are authorized to access. Figure 14-2 illustrates the change engineering process steps.

We will work down through each of these views as we have for all the other components. Each view depends on the previous, and each adds lower levels of detail about what's required.

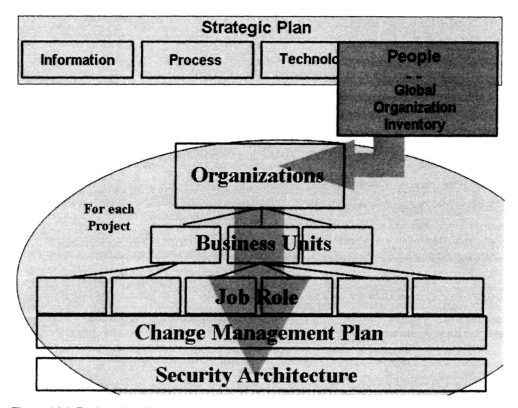

Figure 14-2 Engineering change

14.2 Following Change Engineering Steps

For the people component, almost the entire engineering process is the responsibility of the business team. The component steps are shown in Table 14-2.

Table 14-2 The People Component

Business View	People View
Owner's Wants View	Organizations (goals)
Owner's Needs View	Business Units (objectives)
Designer's View	Job Role
Builder's View	Change Management Plan

During strategic planning, XYZ identified the major company organizations and strategic organizational goals. Their high-level organization chart is shown in Figure 14-3.

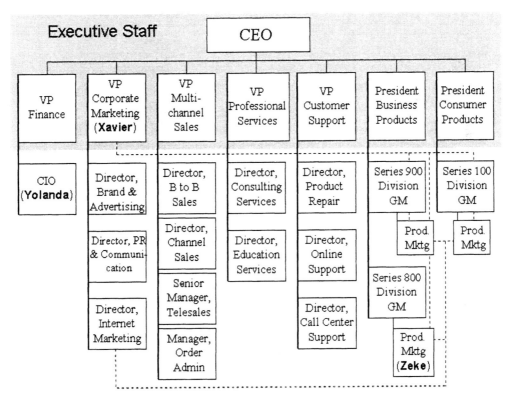

Figure 14-3 XYZ's organization chart

We used XYZ's corporate organization chart as a check for understanding the process component. We already know that there is a very close relationship between processes and organizations of people. The same organization chart provides the strategic organizational inventory as the starting point for the people component. Starting with an element that is high level, familiar and broadly understood makes the component engineering processes much easier to do.

14.2.1 Owner's Wants View: Organizations

The highest level strategic organizations from the strategic plan include the whole company, or the entire front office as a minimum. You'll remember that XYZ also collected organizational goals and objectives during the strategic planning phase. Focusing on the front office organizations, they created the strategic organizational goal matrix for the CRM program that is shown in Table 14-3.

Table 14-3

	Corporate Marketing	Multichannel Sales	Professional Service	Customer Support
Grow Revenue to $100 Million	X	X	X	X
Grow Profitably	X	X	X	X
Solution Selling		X	X	
Execute Channel Strategy	X	X		
Vertical Market Product Categories	X	X	X	X
Relationship Sales and Marketing	X	X		

The first two are XYZ's company-wide goals. The entire organization is responsible for these two goals, but they are so broad that it can be hard for individuals to feel they can have any impact. The other three are more specific to the CRM organizations and are likely to be more relevant for motivating change. During the project selection and launch (even before), the team identified two of the strategic goals that would be impacted by the Valencia project. These were

• Execute balanced channel strategy
• Increase relationship based sales and marketing

From the organizational/goals matrix XYZ could see that the organizations involved in these impacting these two strategies were Corporate Marketing and Multichannel Sales. The responsibility for the people component sits primarily in the lap of the business functions involved, and that is who will identify what's required in four of the five levels. Only the final subcontractor's view (Security Architecture) is the primary responsibility of Information Technology.

14.2.2 Owner's Needs View: Business Units

Next XYZ identified the specific organizational units that will be directly impacted by the first customer identity project (Valencia). XYZ got a head start on this step when they worked on the process component. They already knew what organizations should be involved and what processes were important to the project, so the next step was to identify the organizational units responsible for these processes. These three steps help identify the important organization units:

1. Map relevant project processes (from Chapter 12) to the organization chart.
2. Identify the departments (organizational units) within each major organization that are responsible for each of the processes.
3. Define department-specific objectives for project.

People can be motivated by corporate-wide goals, but they are much more affected by the objectives of the organization in which they work because there is a much better chance that they can understand how what they do impacts these objectives. Figure 14-4 shows how the Valencia project business processes map to the company organization and business units.

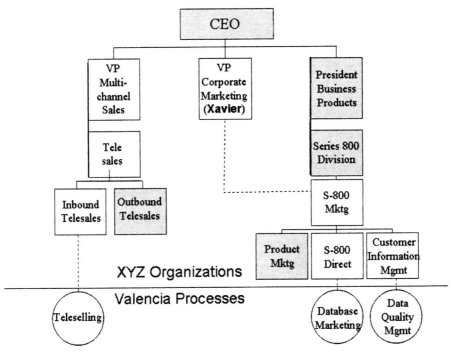

Figure 14-4 Valencia processes in the organization

Working with telesales and the S-800 marketing department, the CRM team identified the three departments that were the targets of the Valencia project. Notice that it's the dotted relationship from Corporate Marketing that links to the S-800 Marketing department. To ensure consistent communication, XYZ added the solid business reporting organization to the organization list. The business units are listed in Table 14-4.

Table 14-4 Departmental Project Objectives

Organization		Business Unit	Project Objectives
CORPORATE MARKETING	BUSINESS PRODUCTS	S-800 Direct	Identify target customers and measure results; upgrade sales compared to satisfaction
		Data Quality Management	Improve linkage accuracy by 30% to increase customer reach
MULTICHANNEL SALES		Inbound Telesales	Measure customer satisfaction with sales process

Now we are ready to identify the positions and people who will actually take part in the project.

14.2.3 Designer's View: Job Role

The Designer's View is where we identify those individuals whose work will change and what they do today. Some companies have an excellent set of well-defined and well-organized position descriptions that can serve as the documentation you need for this step. But many companies have simplified the human resources function by eliminating work-specific positions and creating a generic template with general responsibilities and "other duties as required."

If your company has good job descriptions, by all means pull out the project-relevant position plans for the organization units that have been selected and identify the individuals who hold these positions. This is the pool of people from which you'll select the users for the initial implementation. These people are the targets of the change management process.

14.2.4 Builder's View: Change Management Plan

The change management plan will include a section on communication, training, and rewards. We need to have a plan for each of these, and we need to know how we will use them to support the transition. This isn't easy. Many companies feel that don't have change management experts anywhere in-house (you know who you are), so they hire external experts to assist in planning and managing change. This is a perfectly good approach as long as your expert is telling you **how** to support change, not **what** to change.

Communication

Without a doubt, the most important thing you can do for the success of your CRM program is to let everyone know early and often what is planned and how the project is progressing. Tell them what is going to change, tell them what is changing, and tell them what has changed! It's been estimated that organizations communicate only 10 percent of the information that's really needed to help their employees understand and accept a major change. You cannot communicate too much. Even when there is nothing new to report, you need to communicate that everything is going well!

Different people need to hear different information. It is just as important to communicate why, when, and how change will happen as it is to communicate what the change is. Your communications plan needs to pay equal attention to each of the four types of messages.

Start the communication early. The more time people have to learn about what's going to happen, the sooner they can move through the denial and resistance stages and on to the positive steps of investigation and finally acceptance. Make sure that the message is being clearly communicated and supported from the top to the bottom of the organization. It's great to have a really enthusiastic project team full of eager early adopters. But if the rest of the organization is getting bad vibes from management, you'll never get past the first proof of concept implementation.

Be sure that communication is two-way. You must be listening to concerns and questions that are being asked. Hey, somebody might even have a good idea! Getting your people involved in the decision making and planning for the new direction is a very powerful way to encourage adoption of the change.

Training and Education

The next major tool at our disposal, training and education, consists of the materials needed to help the new users of CRM understand how to ride that new bicycle. One key factor in influencing people's behavior is that people learn differently. Our training plan must take that fact into consideration. Some of us learn by reading, some by listening, and others by practicing. Which learning style is yours?

Metrics and Rewards

The third important tool that we will employ is a set of measurements and rewards. If one of your key objectives is increasing sales of S-800 upgrades, how will you measure success? If it's just straight sales volume, how do you know the new way is any better than the old way? In the new process, XYZ wanted the telesales reps to spend more time with customers up front explaining the advantages and value of the new products and trade-in package, showing how the cost of ownership overall would be decreased.

There are so many variables that can impact straight order volume changes that it can be extremely difficult to identify exactly what was responsible for any growth. But what if you measured customer satisfaction on the sales process, information and support received, etc., and matched that to order volume within the same customer segments. Then you have an opportunity for really understanding differences. If you continue to measure and reward your telesales reps on how many calls they can process in an hour, guess what kind of behavior you'll get.

When the "employee" is actually paid by someone else, it is obviously more difficult to impact the individual's metrics and rewards directly. Measures and incentives should be included in the terms of the contract with the employee or service provider. Contract workers who sit at your site can receive similar communication and training material as employees. For third party employees located at the service provider's site provisions must be made to ensure that new requirements are coming and what's expected. The means for achieving this should also be included in the contract.

14.2.5 The Remaining Views

Okay, there's only one view left. The governance and implementation of the security architecture is the responsibility of the IT team. Still, the IT folks can be successful only if they have the correct information about **who** is going to be using the new system and what **authority** they have to access and update the system. For every reason, between avoiding the potential scandal if your customer list falls into the hands of a spammer to protecting your valuable customer information against vandalism by a disgruntled employee, the security architecture must be well-thought-out and planned.

Subcontractor's View: Security Architecture

The IT department will design the security architecture based on the company's technical approach to risk management. This architecture covers everything from password setup, change, and recovery approaches to firewalls that protect the internal network from hackers.

At the end of all this work (which is largely the business function responsibility) is the fully functional CRM project, with all the appropriate people having knowledge and access to the tools they need to deliver and track the customer offer.

14.2.6 The Transition to Information Technology

For the people component, the handoff between the business functions and the IT function occurs during the creation of the change management plan. Both sets of expertise are necessary for the creation of a successful plan. The business team members bring their knowledge of current and desired process and objectives. The IT team has the knowledge of how the tools work, how they should be used, and what the system can't do. This transition is shown in Figure 14-5.

Just as for the other three components, this step is most difficult because any handoff between organizations creates such a high risk of misunderstanding.

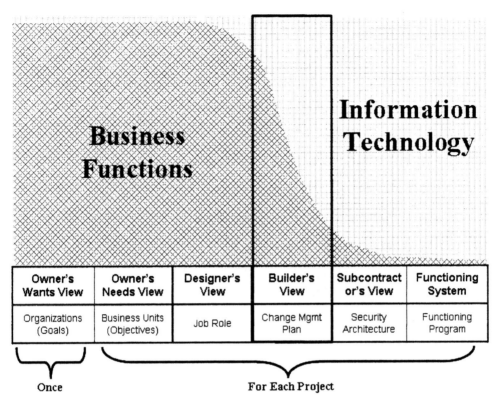

Owner's Wants View	Owner's Needs View	Designer's View	Builder's View	Subcontract or's View	Functioning System
Organizations (Goals)	Business Units (Objectives)	Job Role	Change Mgmt Plan	Security Architecture	Functioning Program

Once   For Each Project

Figure 14-5 People transition

14.3 Moving Forward: Beware of Black Holes

The biggest threat to success for the people component comes from organizational black holes. These black holes occur when the targets of change are not hearing the same thing from their local management as they are from project management and executives, as illustrated in Figure 14-6.

This phenomenon, like its astronomical namesake, is an organizational structure that continually consumes resources. In this case, the project communication disappears into the black hole, and no one knows what she's really supposed to do. This is a pervasive danger, particularly for large companies, because change does not actually become imbedded overnight. Learning and practicing new behavior is easier than internalizing and living the change. If there is no plan for ongoing support of the new behavior, the long term success of your project will be significantly undermined. You must prepare for this situation.

Black holes are another reason why two-way communication is so important; keep checking to find out what the target audience is hearing. If you find a black hole, address it right away. In this situation, the executive sponsor and/or steering committee can be brought in to address the problem with more communication and training for middle management.

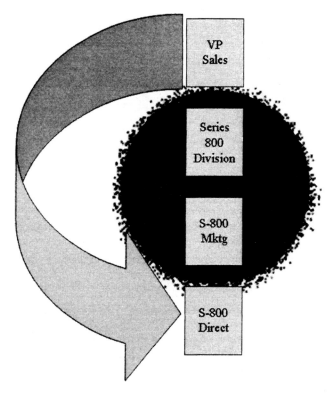

Figure 14-6 The black hole of CRM

We've looked at all four of the important CRM components; now it's time to take a quick look at managing all the pieces as a single project.

Questions for Reflection

When thinking about the following questions, keep in mind that the fundamental success of your CRM program will be based on whether you can get the organization to adopt the new program.

1. How far down the organization do you have to go before work actually gets done? This is the level from which the project team and other business experts will be found.
2. Is the organization fairly hierarchical or highly matrixed? Dual reporting relationships found in matrixed organizations add risk to project focus and success, especially if the project relationship is the less formal of the two. People will always set priorities based on the organization that manages and pays them. What can you do to reduce the risk?
3. How do you think most people in your organization generally learn? Do people generally prefer reading material in advance, listening to presentations, or trying something out before making a decision?

CHAPTER 15

Managing the Project

Project management is a topic that has been the subject of many books. Many successful models exist in the area of information systems project management, but the basic principles apply to the successful management of any project. Eric Verzuh, in his book *The Fast Forward MBA in Project Management,* says that a project is any work that we do only once. Projects have a beginning and an end, and they produce unique results. Designing and developing a piece of your CRM infrastructure is a project; using your web site to answer hundreds of customer support questions is not.

Why do we worry about managing projects? A CRM project involves so many organizations, processes, and people that it cannot succeed without a strong project management process that keeps everything moving along together. We've discussed that work must be done on all four components at the same time. Figure 15-1 summarizes the close interaction and frequent handoffs that we learned about in Chapters 11 through 14.

The work may be about 50-50 overall, but there is no clear demarcation. The line is fuzzy, and it moves. With so many people working together on so many different aspects of the CRM infrastructure all at the same time, how in the world can we possibly keep track of what's going on?

We will introduce several tools that will help your organization manage the IT development project. Of course, these tools also apply to any project in the CRM project cycle (or elsewhere—some day I'll show you the four inch project notebook I created for my daughter's wedding). But if you already have project management tools that are well understood within your company, you should use those. In addition to Verzuh's general overview of project management, Richard Murch has written a very informative book called *Project Management: Best Practices for IT Professionals,* which focuses on some of the aspects that are particular to technology projects. You can also find lots of help by searching the Internet using "project management" as your search term.

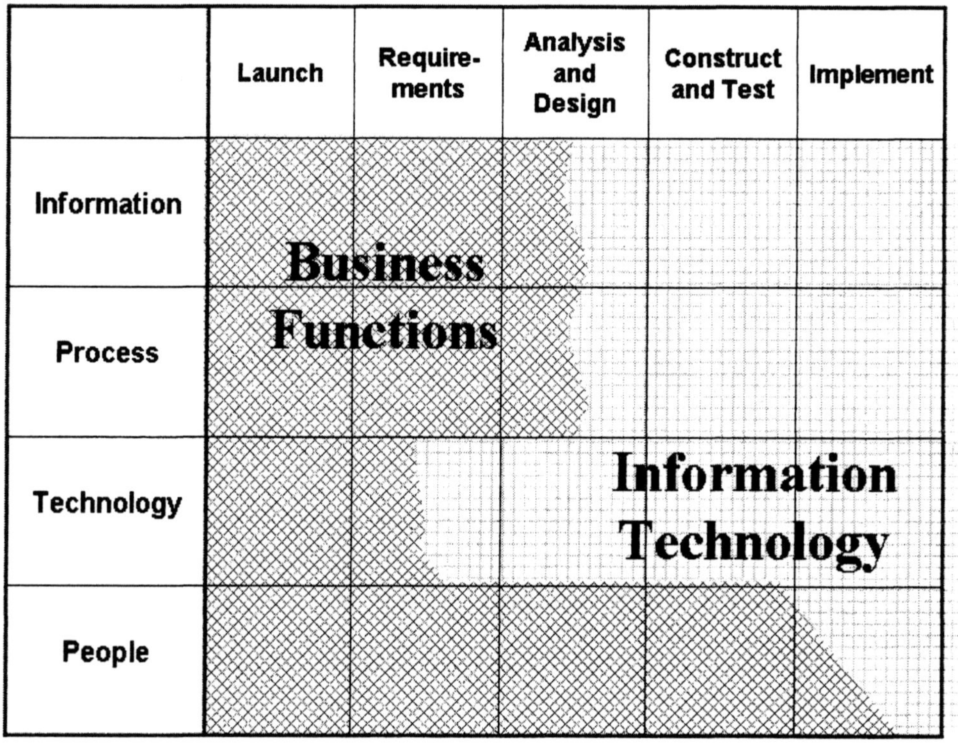

	Launch	Require-ments	Analysis and Design	Construct and Test	Implement
Information					
Process		Business Functions			
Technology				Information Technology	
People					

Figure 15-1 Shared responsibility for CRM

15.1 Beginning the Development Project

In Chapter 9, we saw the importance of picking the right project and learned how to rank alternatives to ensure that you have chosen the project with the best chance of success.

15.1.1 Selecting the Team

After the project is selected, it is time to select the project team, including representatives from the impacted business functions (as identified by the people component analysis) and from Information Technology. By this time, we've already identified the steering committee and program core team members, so now we need to assign specific individuals to the project team for Valencia (see Figure 15-2).

The program core team is lead by the business program manager who will provide continuity across multiple projects. For each project, we will select a project manager, often, but not always, from the IT department. The role of the project manager is to lead the work and ensure that the project remains on track from beginning to end.

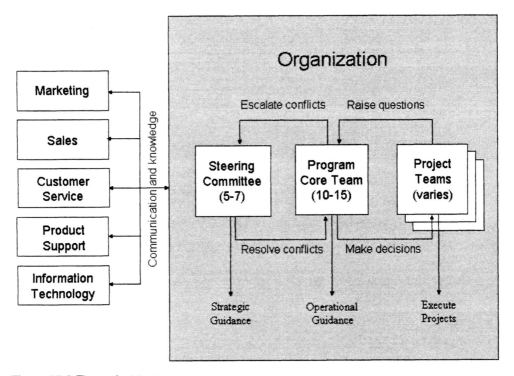

Figure 15-2 The project team

15.1.2 Chartering the Team

The next step is to charter the team. This involves the whole team in an exercise (project launch meeting) to identify high-level scope, resources, and timing requirements for this project. We identified the individuals who must attend the project launch in Chapter 9 when we developed the project overview document and the project summary document (shown together here as the project charter) for Valencia (see Table 15-1).

Table 15-1   Project Charter

PROJECT CHARTER		
Project Title: Valencia		
Direction (issue/opportunity, critical success factors)	We don't know who our most valuable customers are because we identify customers differently in every system. We can't be sure of their total purchases or how much it costs to serve them.	
Focus (business functions, target customers, customer offer)	Business functions: Product (S800) Marketing; Business-to-business Sales •*Target Customers:* Top 50 customers (by last year's purchases) who own a model 815 or 817 fan •*Offer:* Upgrade to new 825/827 model and get a trade-in rebate	

Scope (what's in and what's out)

Component		Scope Is	Scope Is *Not*
Information	Categories	Customers, Installed Products	Product, competitor, etc.
	Sources	Orders, product registrations	Support contracts, etc.
Process		Database Marketing Inbound telesales	Marcom, Channel Sales
Technology		Customer Identification Reference file; client server	Transaction system
People		Product marketing managers for 825 and 827 in North America; North American premier call center reps.	Sales reps, etc. Other products Europe, South America, Asia

Expected Deliverables
1. Customer reference file for managing consistent identification
2. Key data sources integrated (loaded and linked)
3. Top 50 customer companies audited and managed for high-quality company consistency
4. List of customer contacts at target companies who own 815 or 817 fans

High Level Schedule				
Milestone	Due	Actual	Owner	Approved
1. Launch/Plan completed				
2. Analysis complete				
3. Design complete				
4. Construction complete				
5. User Test complete				
6. Implementation				
Key Resources				
Role	**Assigned Individual**		**Percentage of time assigned**	**Duration**
Executive Sponsor				
Program Manager				
Project Manager				
82x Series Product Manager				
North America Premier Call Centers				
IT analysts, designers, engineers				
Project Tradeoff Matrix				
	Deliverables		**Schedule**	**Resources**
Constrain (least flexible)				X
Optimize			X	
Accept (most flexible)	X			

The project charter serves as the high-level direction. It develops a clear sense of scope and an understanding of the relative weight of the tradeoffs that will drive future project decisions.

15.2 Controlling the Project

The purpose of project management is to ensure that the project stays on track and delivers the intended result. The project manager plays the key role in this activity. This individual will be responsible for tracking, overseeing, and communicating each step in the infrastructure development phase. As always, communication is a key responsibility of the project manager: communicating actual status, and identifying and escalating issues or changes that occur during any of the four development steps.

15.2.1 The Steps of an IT Development Project

The steps of every IT development project include gathering requirements, analysis and design, and construction (build and test). As we saw in Chapters 11 through 14, most of the work on developing each component falls to the IT team. But the level of responsibility varies by both component and project stage. This necessitates clear communication and understanding on the part of the whole team, especially during the handoff steps we identified for each component.

- **Requirements:** Generally, an IT analyst works closely with the business team members to develop a clear understanding of what is needed from the business point of view.
- **Analysis and Design:** The analyst compiles and translates these specifications for the IT designer. Next the IT designer works with the analysis document to create documents (design specs) that specify exactly what needs to be constructed during the development step. During design, the business members of the team generally clarify requirements and resolve contradictions.
- **Construction:** An IT programmer works with the design document to build the data structures, code, and technical platform. The critical involvement of the business team comes at the end of this step when the system and its components need to be tested to ensure that they really do what the business team needs.

Every infrastructure development project must include these steps. It is not a requirement that different individuals from IT perform different steps. Small organizations are unlikely to staff all these specialized resources. However, the skill sets required are very different from step to step. Many projects fail when a programmer tries to do business analysis (and vice versa, of course). Be sure you have access to all the different skills you need for the project.

15.2.2 Project Management Tools

In addition to the project charter document that is created during project launch, the project manager will use four more documents to track the project and communicate the current situation to the project team, program team, and sponsor.

Project Plan

The project plan is an actual schedule for what needs to be done and when it is expected to be finished. There are some very sophisticated tools available that automate time-line development and resource management. These tools, such as Microsoft Project, are detailed and very complete. They can also track task dependencies (a task that cannot start until another is finished) and resource constraints that have significant impact on the project schedule. For very complex projects with lots of resources and lots of dependencies, an automated tool can be a tremendous timesaver. For smaller, less-complicated projects, it is perfectly fine to use a spreadsheet like the one shown in Table 15-2.

Table 15-2 Project Plan

<table>
<tr><td colspan="9" align="center">Project Plan</td></tr>
<tr><td colspan="6">Project Name:</td><td colspan="3">Revision #</td></tr>
<tr><td colspan="6">Planned Start:</td><td colspan="3">Actual Start:</td></tr>
<tr><td>Task#</td><td>Priority</td><td>Milestone Task</td><td>Assigned to</td><td>Est. hours</td><td>Due</td><td>Done</td><td colspan="2">Comments</td></tr>
<tr><td>1</td><td></td><td>Analysis</td><td></td><td></td><td></td><td></td><td colspan="2"></td></tr>
<tr><td>2</td><td></td><td>Design</td><td></td><td></td><td></td><td></td><td colspan="2"></td></tr>
<tr><td>3</td><td></td><td>Construction</td><td></td><td></td><td></td><td></td><td colspan="2"></td></tr>
<tr><td>3.1</td><td></td><td>Build</td><td></td><td></td><td></td><td></td><td colspan="2"></td></tr>
<tr><td>3.2</td><td></td><td>Unit Test</td><td></td><td></td><td></td><td></td><td colspan="2"></td></tr>
<tr><td>3.3</td><td></td><td>System Test</td><td></td><td></td><td></td><td></td><td colspan="2"></td></tr>
<tr><td>3.4</td><td></td><td>User Test</td><td></td><td></td><td></td><td></td><td colspan="2"></td></tr>
<tr><td>4</td><td></td><td>Implement</td><td></td><td></td><td></td><td></td><td colspan="2"></td></tr>
<tr><td colspan="9" align="center">Assumed Resource Availability</td></tr>
<tr><td colspan="2">Team Member</td><td>Role</td><td colspan="2">Percentage of Time</td><td colspan="4">Comments</td></tr>
<tr><td colspan="2">Joe</td><td>Project Manager</td><td colspan="2">100</td><td colspan="4"></td></tr>
<tr><td colspan="2">Susan</td><td>Analyst</td><td colspan="2">60</td><td colspan="4"></td></tr>
</table>

The project plan helps set realistic objectives about when the project can be completed given current resources. It is also valuable for tracking the addition of new requirements and testing how they will impact the overall schedule. An actual project plan will contain a much lower level of detail about the work that needs to be done. Each major task should be broken down into steps that take only a few days. Otherwise, it is impossible to estimate resource requirements with any accuracy.

Weekly Status Report

The weekly status report is a critical document, and I do recommend that you complete it **weekly**! Remember, we are doing small projects; a weekly report keeps the team focused on progress being made and highlights issues so they can be addressed quickly. A monthly status report for a six-month project leaves too much time for things to get off-course between checkpoints. Table 15-3 shows a sample template for the weekly status report.

Table 15-3 Status Report

Weekly Status Report					
Project Name:				**Week Ending:**	
Status Key: Green = On-track *Yellow = Caution* <u>**Red = Critical**</u>					
Status: (use color) **Green**/*Yellow*/<u>**Red**</u>	**Explanation:**				
Task	**Milestone**	**Respon sible**	**Sched- uled**	**Com- pleted**	**Comments**
(1)	(match project milestones)				
(2)					
(3)					
(4)					
(5)					
(6)					
Unplanned Activities		**Respon sible**	**Sched- uled**	**Com- pleted**	**Comments**

Table 15-3 Status Report

Accomplishment(s) This Week		Responsible	Scheduled	Completed	Comments

Objective(s) Next Week	Owner	Due	Comments

New This Week

Issue/ chng	Item	Reported by	Description	Comments
Iss				
chg				

Open Issues List

Issue Item	Description	Status/Resolution	Date Resolved

Communication is the key purpose of the status report; that means they must be **read.** Keeping the document to a length of no more than one page should ensure that everyone has time to at least glance over it. Put a colored Status Flag and brief summary at the top of the report so that with a quick glance everyone should at least know how the project is doing. (This works best if the "flag" is the name of the color for those who print in black and white.)

Issues (or project changes) that are identified over the course of the week are listed under "New This Week" and are added to the Issue Log or Change Log as well. A running list is kept of all *open* issues. Unresolved issues have significant potential for derailing the project, so it's best to keep open issues in front of everyone at all times.

Issue Log

The issue log is where the project manager tracks problems that arise. These are problems that if not addressed will threaten the success of the overall project. An example of the format for an Issue Log is shown in Table 15-4.

Table 15-4 Issue Log

<table>
<tr><td colspan="10" align="center">ISSUE LOG</td></tr>
<tr><td colspan="8">Project Name:</td><td colspan="2">Date:</td></tr>
<tr>
<td>Issue ID</td>
<td>Category
Information
Process
Technology,
People</td>
<td>Severity
Critical,
Serious,
Medium,
Low</td>
<td>Descrip-
tion</td>
<td>Reported
by</td>
<td>Report
Date</td>
<td>Owner</td>
<td>Resolution/
Plan for
Resolution</td>
<td>Close
Date</td>
</tr>
<tr><td>1</td><td></td><td></td><td></td><td></td><td></td><td></td><td></td><td></td></tr>
<tr><td>2</td><td></td><td></td><td></td><td></td><td></td><td></td><td></td><td></td></tr>
</table>

The issue log is another important document for the project manager. It makes clear how many potential roadblocks have been encountered and information that might prove useful if the issues cause the project schedule to slip. In addition, the project log can be used as part of the overall development project review. If too many unexpected issues arise, there may be some basic problem with the company's readiness for, or basic approach to, CRM. In addition to keeping track of what the problems are, the project manager tracks information about assignment and resolution.

Change Log

The change log is the third important tool for managing the project. It is where any changes to the original scope are tracked. Obviously, this document is critical: It is just like a construction change order. If the change request is approved and will impact schedule, cost, or scope, the project will take more time, cost more, or change in scope. It's important that changes are well understood and widely communicated so expectations are kept in synch with plans. A sample change request log is shown in Table 15-5.

Table 15-5 Change Request Log

CHANGE REQUEST LOG									
Project Name:								**Date:**	
Change ID	**Priority Critical, Serious, Medium, Low**	**Request By**	**Request Date**	**Description**	**Assign to**	**Assign Date**	**Status (open, in progress, closed)**	**Close Date**	
1									
2									

The change request log tracks requests for additions or deletions to the project. Once approved, a change will be assigned to a project resource (and the project schedule and other project documents will be modified to reflect that the change has been approved). The estimated completion time is added to (or subtracted from) the schedule. When a change is completed or cancelled, it is marked closed.

Beyond the Project Team

The preceding project management documents are primarily aimed at those who are closely connected to the project on a daily basis – the project team. But we know there are lots of other individuals who have a strong need to know what's going on with the project. These include but aren't limited to the company's executive staff, project sponsor, steering committee members, and future users and their management.

When should these reports go out? They should go out as often as necessary. That's correct; there is no one right answer. How frequently they should be distributed depends on who the audience is (very hands-on or largely arms-length) and how the project is doing, as explained in Table 15-6.

Table 15-6 WHEN Guidelines

Management Style	Status		
	Green	**Yellow**	**Red**
Hands-on style	Biweekly	Weekly	Daily
Arms-length style	Monthly	Biweekly	Weekly

What should be said? The content depends largely on how often the information is being distributed (which, of course, depends on management style and status). The minimum content is the project status and status summary (first four lines of Table 15-3); the maximum content is to send everything to the extended team that is sent to the project team (at least in a summary form), as shown in Table 15-7.

Table 15-7 WHAT Guidelines

Management Style	Frequency			
	Monthly	**Biweekly**	**Weekly**	**Daily**
All management styles	Everything (with a summary)	Full status report	Status, status summary	Status update and brief summary

Frequency is important to this decision because the bare minimum information may not be enough if it's distributed only monthly and the full detail is way too much for a daily distribution.

How should the message be communicated? Again, know your audience. Who learns by reading, by hearing, by doing? Many companies have a fairly consistent culture around communication and learning, everything in writing or always by voice mail. If your company has just one preferred style, then you are probably safe picking just that one. But if your company has no such learning culture, or you want to be extra sure of communicating with certain critical extended team members, you might want to have a version for all the learning styles. The guidelines for how to choose the communication method that best supports each learning style are given in Table 15-8.

Table 15-8 HOW Guidelines

Management Style	Learning Style		
	Reading	**Hearing**	**Doing**
All management styles	E-mail, hard-copy report	Voice mail, face to face, status meetings	Demos, requests for barrier removal

A word of caution: Some media are appropriate only for short messages. Ten-minute voice-mail messages are not a good thing.

Finally, you can never get it perfect. Always make it easy for people to get additional information and detail. The best way is to keep everything on an internal project web site that is well organized and well publicized. This is the backstop for all your communication plans.

15.3 Finishing the Development Project

We know that a CRM project is not really complete until the offer has been made to the customer and the results have been analyzed and reported. However, the end of the infrastructure development phase marks a major milestone in that the remainder of the CRM life cycle does not require as much interaction between business functions and the IT department. Because this is a cycle that will be repeated over and over until you have done as much CRM as you need, it's important to examine the partnership and how well it worked, as well as how the overall project went. This is how we can learn from the experience and results before launching the next cycle.

15.3.1 Project Retrospective

The project retrospective has two parts. First, the project manager will develop and distribute a questionnaire to all team members as well as to other key contributors to the overall CRM effort. The questions should be focused on how satisfactory the team members found different aspects of the project process, such as the following:

- Scheduling
- Resource availability
- Project definition
- Consistency
- Communication
- Overall satisfaction
- Organizational learning
- Repeatability

Then the project manager will schedule a retrospective meeting in which the outcome of the questionnaire can be discussed, and improvements and key learning identified.

15.3.2 Formal Signoff

Always get a formal signoff on each major milestone of every project. This should be accomplished in a fairly informal, discussion group setting, where it's clear that the relevant executives (program manager and sponsor at the very least) actually understand what has been achieved and where the project stands. Then communicate the heck out of both the milestone completion and project status. The formal signoff is another way to ensure communication and involvement of key stakeholders throughout the organization. Some combination of the business project manager and IT project manager should submit a recommendation for signoff to the steering committee and the executive sponsor. This gives the project team "face time" with these key supporters to discuss progress and issues, as well as reasoning behind the plan.

Remember that formal signoff is for the purpose of communication; it's not for covering your @##. Make the process simple, clear, and painless. Never ask anyone to approve the whole program or even the whole project at one time.

15.3.3 Celebrate

Again, our six-month CRM projects must be repeated for us to achieve the program results we're aiming for. Now that you've learned what could have gone better by getting team and management feedback during the retrospective and signoff, it's time to celebrate the hard work and success that has been achieved. The team will be much more willing to begin a new project if the work they've done so far is recognized and rewarded. Even if the project manager is not an individual who enjoys this kind of celebration, many of the team members are. Find someone on the team who really knows the benefit of recognition and celebration, and let him or her organize a suitable event. It is critical to take notice that a major event has occurred and to thank those responsible, particularly if you expect them to continue delivering successful projects for you.

Now that we've completed the development project, it's time to move to the next transition: integrating our new components.

Questions for Reflection

It's likely that most operationally excellent companies already have strong processes developed for successfully managing and delivering projects, but so do many other companies. Successful IT organizations always use formal and consistent project management processes. These questions will help you determine how ready your company is.

1. Does your company have a formal process management methodology? Is it used only for IT projects, or is some form of it used for all projects?
2. If you have such a process, is it strictly applied or is it just wallpaper? How widely is it understood and followed?
3. What incentives are there for following a project management methodology? Are there consequences for projects that miss deadlines?

PART 4

CRM: Using It Right

CHAPTER 16

Integrating Components

Thu project team (both business and IT experts) has finished the construction of the pieces of the infrastructure that we need for this CRM project. Now we're ready to turn on each of the four components that we've built. This is the transition step from the work we've done inside the company to the work we will do to actually deliver the project outside – to our customers.

16.1 Transitioning From Inside to Outside Work

Transition steps are always difficult because they represent a change in gear and often a shift of responsibility from one part of the team to another. The component integration transition step may be the most difficult of the four. In addition to normal difficulties, we have the added complication that virtually no company has the luxury of installing their new CRM components into a totally empty environment. In fact, this is the reason we call this transition step "integration" instead of implementation. Implementation is like building a brand new house – starting with an empty lot and building. Integration is more like a remodel. The builder has to work with all of the existing elements of the house—at least those that will remain standing when the remodel is complete. Just ask any building contractor which kind of job is easier to do.

This may seem to make the notion of buying a total solution even more appealing: Just get rid of everything and start over. No integration, right? But it's virtually impossible to replace everything at once, so some integration always has to be done. You might be able to purchase a pre-fabricated family room to add to your house, but you still have to worry about aligning doorways and rooflines and about linking up to the power and water supplies. In some cases, those things are still easier than building from scratch, and in other cases, the existing infrastructure is so poor that starting from scratch is easier.

As you can see in Figure 16-1, we are taking the second transition step in the CRM development life cycle, integrating the infrastructure we have just completed.

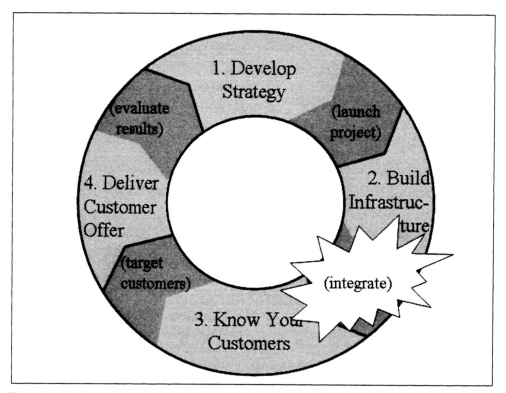

Figure 16-1 Integrating infrastructure components

We're going to cover a fair amount of detail in this chapter. It is complicated because all four components must be integrated at once, and different parts of the organization are responsible for the integration of different components.

16.1.1 Integrating Is a Partnership

Coordination and cooperation are absolutely required between the business team members and technology team members for integration to be successful. Table 16-1 shows the basic purpose and primary responsibility for each of the components.

Component integration is about fitting the new pieces of CRM infrastructure into the existing environment. It's like adding a new pipe to your kitchen plumbing so you can get water to the icemaker in the fridge you just bought. The plumber will compare the connection requirements of the icemaker to the plumbing that's already there, note any differences, and figure out what it will take to get the icemaker connected. You're probably thinking that it's easier to just hire somebody to come in and do the work, and then you can come back when everything's working. That's ridiculous, of course. Even a small plumbing job needs to have coordination

Table 16-1 Component Integration

Step	Primary Responsibility	Integration Result
Information Integration	Information Technology	Data consistency: Data flows reliably across the organization and has stable and consistent meaning.
Process Integration	Business Function	Process continuity: The process works reliably and is completely connected into any existing related processes.
Technology Integration	Information Technology	Technical compatibility: All hardware/network pieces physically operate together.
People Integration	Business Function	Compatible behavior: People know what to do and how to do it.

between the technical expert and the homeowner. The plumber must have access to the kitchen and must know where the existing pipes are.

If there are any special requirements, like a water filter on the icemaker line, it's much cheaper to have the plumber do it now than to come out again to do it later. It's a partnership! Integrating the new appliance into the kitchen requires knowledge and experience from both the homeowner and the plumbing expert. Communication and coordination are always needed, but that doesn't mean the homeowner has to stand around watching or hand the plumber the tools! The plumber in Figure 16-2 knows what it takes to connect an icemaker, but he doesn't know anything about your existing plumbing or your special requirements.

Component integration is similar, but it's much more complicated because not only are there the four components that all must be integrated at the same time, but different people will often be responsible for each one.

16.1.2 Integrating the Components

We are going to spend time understanding exactly how integration works because, as always for CRM, everyone on the team is involved and everyone needs to understand the basic process so that the right questions are asked (and answered) at the right time. Information Technology should make sure that their business partners understand the steps, what needs to get done, and when they should make a contribution. Business experts need to make sure that their IT partners are following a standard methodology that guarantees a good fit without lots of expensive rework.

Integration may be difficult to do, but anyone can understand the basic method we'll use – and that's always the place to start. Executing these steps for each of the different components may require different skills, but the steps are always the same:

Figure 16-2 Plumbing integration

- Detail the characteristics of the future state.
- Detail the characteristics of the current state.
- Identify the differences between them.
- Design the connection tool.
- Build and use the tool.

In most cases, we should have already documented the current and future states as part of the analysis and design of the new component. This should have been completed during the building infrastructure phase. We will follow these steps for each of the four components, as listed in Table 16-2.

We will work through, in detail, the steps of information integration as an example because this is the least understood of the four components. Okay, so information is my passion, so sue me.

Table 16-2 Component Integration Steps

	Information	Process	Technology	People
Future State	New data model	New process map	New system	New behavior
Current State	Legacy data files	Current process map	Current systems	Current behavior
Differences	Data map			
Design	Data transformation table	Process design (white space mgmt plan)	System map (system obsolescence plan)	Change management plan
Build/Use	Data translator	Connect processes (no disconnects)	Interface or eliminate	Execute plan

16.2 Integrating the Information Component

Information may be the trickiest of the four components to integrate because it is so poorly understood and so seldom practiced. The myth that information just happens when a system is built has caused much expensive rework (or total failure) of so many projects. It takes work and attention to detail to get it right, but don't give up. It's easier than it looks.

"The data is all wrong," is one of the most common statements made by users after a new system is implemented. Unfortunately, this is the reaction even if only a few of the hundreds of fields are incorrect. The problem arises because the users of the data think the *content* of the system belongs to the IT department just the same way as the hardware and software aspects of the system do. Functional experts must understand that if they are careless in the way they describe their current and future data requirements, or the data was entered incorrectly in the first place, the IT team can't do anything about it. The tools built to integrate information won't be successful if the business experts forget to mention, for example, that, "Well, that field is called 'product option,' but if there's an 'M' in the field it means it's a special marketing program discount instead." The fact is, that in spite of everyone's best efforts, glitches will be discovered during the integration phase and rework will be needed. Rework isn't different from the original project work, we just go back and clarify the misunderstanding about the source and target data and tune the transformation tool. However, rework isn't fun and it's not very productive which is why we use formal methods to help us to communicate clearly in the first place.

16.2.1 Documenting the Future State: El Cid Database

We identified the future state data as part of our information analysis and design activities described in Chapter 11. Table 16-3 shows some of the Installed Product attributes that XYZ identified for Valencia (see Appendix D for more information).

Now we're talking about physical data, and the IT department prepares this document, so we will switch to using the technical field name, as it will appear in the physical database. Fortunately, XYZ's IT department has some excellent data naming standards that make it easy to name a field directly based on the business logical name. This is a great opportunity to reinforce the partnership between the business and IT functions, it confirms that the IT team is listening, and it generally makes it easier for users to understand what they're looking at if they accidentally find themselves in the database. These naming rules are outlined in Appendix D.

Table 16-3 Installed Product Definitions

Attribute	Field Name	Definition	Size	Type	Required	Validation Rules
product model	prod-id	Name/ID of the specific hardware or software product installed	18	Text	Y	Must be on product file
serial number	prod-ser-nr	Identifies the specific physical hardware or software product	16	Integer	Y	Greater than zero
purchase date	purch-dt	Date of purchase	8	Date	N	Valid date: ccyymmdd
where purchased	purch-chan-cd	Sales channel of purchase	2	Text	N	1) Direct 2) Catalog 3) Channel 4) Telesales
primary use	prim-use-cd	Purpose for which product is used	2	Text	N	1) Personal 2) Business 3) Both
where used	use-loc-cd	Primary place where product is used	2	Text	N	1) Home 2) Office 3) Both

In Chapter 11, we looked at existing sources of data, such as the Series 800 product registration cards. These cards formed the basis on which the CUST800 database was built, but now we need to understand exactly how the data is physically stored. You can't connect a half-inch copper tube to one-inch galvanized pipe without the appropriate fittings, and you can't choose the fittings until you know the exact dimensions of the old and new plumbing.

16.2.2 Documenting the Current State: CUST800 Database

For each of the source systems that have been included in the Valencia project, the IT team will create the same kind of inventory about the data actually stored as was done for the new (target) data in Chapter 11. As always, we focus just on the legacy sources that have been included in the project. We never take on more work than we need to be successful. There are many software tools available for capturing this information (data about data has a special name: metadata) about current and planned data resources. Obviously, Information Technology could just use tables or spreadsheets as shown in Table 16-4, but then it's very difficult to keep the metadata up to date. Many of these tools, called data dictionaries, require data to be entered into the system, but some can be run against the physical database (schema) and load lots of the information automatically.

Table 16-4 Cust800 Installed Product Data

Attribute	Definition	Size	Type	Required	Validation Rules
prodnr	Name/ID of the specific hardware or software product purchased	18	Text	Y	Must be on product file
prodsn	Identifies the specific physical hardware or software product	16	Integer	N	Zero or greater
purchdate	Date of purchase	8	Date	N	Valid date: mm/dd/yy
purchloc	Sales channel of purchase	1	Text	N	XYZ direct Catalog Retail Wholesale
produse	Primary use of product	2	Text	N	1) Personal 2) Business 3) Both
prodloc	Primary place where product is used	2	Text	N	1) Home, 2) Office 3) Travel 4) All

The next step is to compare the source and target data to each other and identify what needs to be changed so the information integrates correctly.

16.2.3 Identifying Differences: Data Mapping

The IT team will do the rest of the information component transition. So why in the world should anyone else even read this section? If the business experts don't know what Information Technology is going to do with the information they've been given, it might not seem very important to be careful with the documentation. If your company falls into that trap, you will indeed end up with a system full of garbage because the careful translation will just produce a garbled mess.

The data mapping exercise may seem overwhelming, but it is critical to the success of your project—and it's not as hard as it looks. The only time that the IT team needs to do anything special with data is when there is a difference between the source (legacy) and the target (new model) in their respective definitions (meaning, size, type, required, validity). In Table 16-5, you will find the data map between the source (CUST800 database) and the target (the new data model for the El Cid database).

Table 16-5 Data Map from CUST800 Database to El Cid Database

Attribute		Size		Type		Required		Validation Rules	
Source	Target	S	T	Source	Target	S	T	Source	Target
prodnr	prod-id	15	18						
prodsn	prod-ser-nr	10	16	Text	Integer	N	Y	Zero or greater	Greater than zero
purch-date	purch-dt			Text	Date			Valid date: mm/dd/yy	Valid date: ccyymmdd
purchloc	purch-chan-cd	1	2					XYZ direct Catalog Retail Wholesale	1. Direct 2. Catalog 3. Channel 4. Telesales
produse	prim-use-cd								
prodloc	use-loc-cd								

Notice that only differences between the source and the target need to be identified. This makes the map a little easier to read. Similarly, we left out the "definition" column because the portion of El Cid's data model designed for Valencia was based on the same registration card used for CUST800. The data definitions for the source and target were identical.

16.2.4 Designing the Connection

The next step for the IT team is to define exactly what must happen to the data so it can successfully be moved from the source to the target. These transformation rules tell the programmers what instructions they must write for the computer so it knows how to handle every piece of data coming from the source, as shown in Table 16-6.

Table 16-6 Data Transformation Table

Attribute			Transformation Rules		
Source	Target	Size	Type	Required	Validation Rules
prodnr	prod-id	Increase field size to 18			
prodsn	prod-ser-nr	Increase field size to 16	Convert text to number Failure = 0	Make required	0 is a valid value. Don't add duplicates (i.e., only one with SN = 0)
purch-date	purch-dt		Convert from text to date Failure = blank		Validate mm <13 and dd < 32 If yy = 90-99 then cc=19 else cc=20
purchloc	purch-chan-cd	Increase field size to 2			X = 1 C = 2 R = 3 W = 3

These rules are usually written in a simple programming pseudo-code familiar to most IT professionals. (After all, that's who'll create the rules and then use them to generate the translation tools.) It may look overly complicated to see all this written down. But if your IT team follows the methodology, it's pretty much common sense getting from one step to the next. For example, XYZ wasn't founded until the early 1990s, so only years (yy) that start with a '9' can be in the century labeled 19. And once the IT folks have figured out how to convert one date, it's just a matter of repeating the same rules for the rest. The problems arise when there is no methodology and the IT department puts all the business information in a file drawer and starts over from scratch for each project. And, of course, data integration will only be successful if the business team has described the source (current state) and target (future state) accurately.

16.2.5 Building and Using a New Tool: Data Translator

A programmer uses the transformation rules to create the actual data translation engine that will convert the old data to the new format before loading data into the new database. Some products currently on the market allow you to enter the source and target data characteristics and then automatically change the appearance of the old source data to the new target data.

After the translation is built, the source data is fed into the translation tool, and the output is formatted and loaded into the new database. Sometimes, if the source system is to be eliminated after its data is moved, this data translation happens only once. Other times, the tool will be run periodically on an ongoing basis whenever new data needs to be loaded from that same source.

Another data integration complexity is that data sometimes must be exchanged in both directions, requiring a two-way translation. Resolving the difficulties that arise for two-way interfaces is the topic of my next book (that's a joke!). Table 16-7 shows the results expected from the CUST800 to El Cid database translation tool.

Table 16-7 Test Cases

Field Name	Source Data	Target Data
prod-id	12345	12345
prod-ser-nr	232111	232111
	89A	0
purch-dt	06/26/98	19980626
purch-chan-cd	R	2
prim-use-cd	2	2
use-loc-cd	2	2

Documenting test cases showing some sample source data and how it should look after it has been translated needs both Information Technology and business input. Using the test cases to validate the accuracy of the new tool should be a mandatory practice for all IT departments. Make sure yours is one of them.

16.3 Combining Process, Technology, and People

This transition step is about the same for all the other three components. Identify what's going to be different: creating (build or buy) whatever it takes to make the new component successful. New processes are successful if there is a smooth flow between steps and nothing falls into a black hole along the way. Technology is successful if there is enough equipment, storage, and network to support the new project and it all can work together. The people are successful if they have the information and training they need to do their jobs differently.

16.3.1 Process

We identify process integration requirements by combining current and future process maps on one piece of process map, like the one in Figure 16-3.

Any dashed arrow indicates a process that didn't exist before or one that has changed and, therefore, needs to have a new connection designed and built. Of course, telesales has always taken orders, but never for products with such complex configurations that a quote needed to be prepared and submitted to the customer for review.

There are six new or changed processes on the map in Figure 16-3. Four of these relate to new processes for updating the new Customer Master, El Cid. Eventually, these will be direct system connections to the new database. For the first project, the connections are going to be made by paper messages (like a copy of the shipping document sent from Shipping to a data administrator in the Data Quality Management team who will enter the information). That leaves two processes for which an integration plan must be defined:

- Telesales sends quote to customer
- Telesales sends lead to Database Marketing

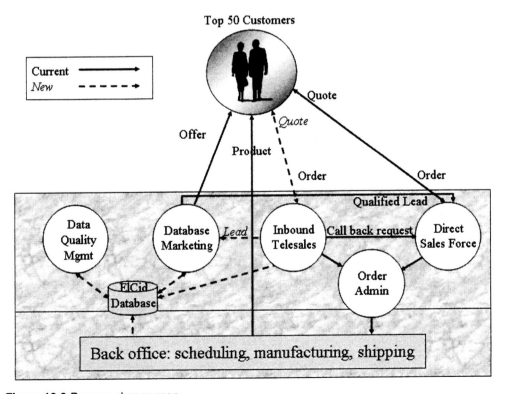

Figure 16-3 Process change map

Process connections include the infrastructure that enables each step in the process to flow easily and properly into the next step. These connections may be made up of software interfaces, or they may be as simple as designing a paper form and some well-practiced behavior. The capability specifies what needs to happen, and the design indicates how, as you can see in Table 16-8.

Table 16-8   Valencia Integration Table

New Process			Capability	Design
From	**To**	**What**		
Telesales	Customer	Quote	Capability of preparing a quote and sending it to the customer.	Electronic quote form e-mail
Telesales	Database Marketing	Lead	Capability of capturing lead information (formerly could only capture orders) and sending to marketing	System access to El Cid for ID assignment Electronic lead form email

The integration tools that are built to support these new process capabilities may be anything from sophisticated computer system interfaces, electronic forms and e-mail, or paper notes made into paper airplanes and thrown to the receiving group. The design decision determines who is responsible for building the integration tool.

There are of course other required capabilities. For example in a customer centered CRM environment we would *never* set up a new lead system without some means of tracking follow up, qualification and results. This is a critical capability that in practice can't be forgotten. For simplification and expedience this and other critical examples have been omitted.

16.3.2 Technology

The technology integration requirements apply to the physical wires and boxes needed to run the new system. The IT department will define technology requirements considering important technology compatibility factors, such as operating system compatibility and network requirements. XYZ's IT department used a structure like the one shown in Table 16-9 to identify the technology integration requirements for the Valencia project.

The business wants a direct link between telesales and the El Cid database (which will be located at Corporate Headquarters in Chicago). This piece of the network infrastructure will be purchased and installed by the IT team, as would any other requirements identified to support the project such as new computers, additional disk space, or even revamped backup and support schedules based on business requirements. Not surprisingly, Information Technology has total ownership for building the technology integration component.

Table 16-9 Valencia System Map

	Operating System		Disk Requirements		Network Requirements	
	Have	**Need**	**Have**	**Need**	**Have**	**Need**
El Cid database	Unix	Unix	50 gig	1 gig		Network link from telesales to corporate

16.3.3 People

During the building infrastructure phase, we identified all of the behavior change requirements for project success. The Change Management Plan is the design for integration of the people component. What's left to do during integration are the logistics and execution of the plan to connect people's behavior to the new environment, as shown in Table 16-10.

Table 16-10 Process Change Plan

New Behavior	Logistics
Create quote for customer	Create electronic quote form Create product configuration instructions Prepare training material Deliver training classes Test understanding Monitor number of incorrect quotes and orders taken Relax measurement of number of calls handled
Capture customer lead and log customer into El Cid database	Create product configuration instructions Prepare training material Deliver training classes Test understanding Monitor number of incorrect quotes and orders taken

Do you see why all the components have to be so well coordinated for your CRM program to be a success? Information is what makes it possible to use computers instead of people to manage relationships. Software automates many of the processes that form relationships and transfer information to where it's needed. Technology is the physical mechanism where information is collected, processed, and shared. People can evaluate and define the relationship so it's a positive experience. Thus, people can ensure success or guarantee failure.

We've finished the transition step from internal construction and are ready to begin the work to deliver the results outside, to our customers. The next phase is to use the information we've collected to better understand our customers so we can pick the right ones for the offer.

Questions for Reflection

Think about the relationship between your own business and IT teams and what it would take to fix the situation if the answers to these questions are "yes."

1. Does the company think that Information Technology has a critical strategic role to play or is it a necessary evil, just there to keep the computers running?
2. Do business team managers completely ignore what IT people have to do to be successful? Do they think it's just another necessary specialty, like a company nurse, that they don't need to think about?
3. Does the IT department think the business users haven't got a clue about what they want, much less what they need?
4. Does Information Technology like to maintain its aura of mystery; the experts who have the answers can do magic?

CHAPTER 17

Finding the "Right" Customers

We've defined our strategy and built a piece of our CRM infrastructure; now we're ready to turn our focus outside and identify the specific characteristics and customers who are most likely to respond to the offer we plan to make. We use information about our customers to make predictions about how they will respond to our offers. We also use information to measure the results of our efforts (see Chapter 19). Information is the raw material of CRM.

For now, we will focus on using information to identify the right customers to receive our offer. To be effective, an offer must generate a response. To get a response, understand what our customers are like, what they value and how they are likely to behave (respond). Like most of the other life cycle phases, we started thinking about key customers early in the methodology at a high-level perspective. (Actually I hope we all have been thinking about our customers even before CRM.) But now it's time to work our way through to finding the specific customers who will be targeted for the current project. First, we will get to know our customers well enough that we can identify groups or segments likely to respond to the same offer the same way. Then we'll pick (target) exactly which customers to include.

Segmentation and targeting are iterative. Every company is likely to pick some high-level strategic *segments* very early, even before a CRM program is launched. Often, these segments are based on broad customer characteristics, such as whether this is a consumer or business customer, or large versus small businesses. Intuitively and experientially, we believe these groups are different. (By the way, one benefit of CRM is that we can use information we've gathered to validate and refine these early assumptions.)

Next, for each project, we identify a *target* profile (set of characteristics) during the project launch. These are the customers to whom we plan to send the offer because we believe they will return the most value. Next, we are likely to segment our customer information according to the characteristics of the target profile. Then we refine our early criteria and target the specific set of

287

customers to whom we'll actually deliver the offer. Again, we may segment this targeted group into smaller groups who are likely to behave differently based on other characteristics. Of course, we're all aware of the dangers of analysis paralysis by this time, so we'll definitely apply common sense about the number of repetitions.

During the strategic planning efforts discussed in Chapter 8, XYZ identified its strategic customer segments. (Remember they asked about customer segmentation during the internal interviews.) Strategic segmentation takes a very gross cut at profile similarities and differences among customer groups and is used to help your company make global decisions as to how the company organizes or sets strategy. As the business changes, strategies may change and so can strategic segments. We will also build segments that are much more precise and detailed. These "project" segments are identified as we identify the specific audience for a particular project offer. XYZ's strategic segments are shown in Figure 17-1.

XYZ's first segmentation cut was to separate consumers from business contacts as having quite different needs and potential value. Then it chose to create two business segments: the top-valued customers and the rest. They found no strategically different groups within the consumer segment.

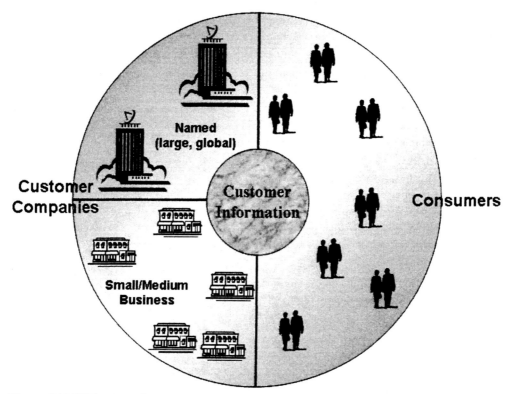

Figure 17-1 XYZ's strategic segments

There are many tools that help us use information to make the best possible decisions about which customers we want to include in the current offer. CRM in theory is about relating to customers personally and individually. But in practice, most of us have to find groups of customers who are enough alike that we can relate to all members in about the same way. We apply the various decision support tools to the information we have collected to help us understand our customers and recognize similar groups. Then we can use the same or similar methods to pick the segments that we believe are the most likely to respond. We're starting the third phase of our CRM life cycle and will cover both Phase 3 and the transition to Phase 4, as shown in Figure 17-2.

Get to know your customers! That doesn't mean you should have each one over for dinner. This life cycle phase is about creating customer segments or groups that respond about the same way. Segments, according to Webster's, are sections defined by "natural" boundaries. An orange can easily be separated into pieces because it has naturally defined segments. Customer segments also have natural boundaries that are defined by having similar sets of characteristics, which we call profiles. We want members of the segment to react the same way as long as we treat them all about the same. And we want to treat them differently from how we treat all the other customer segments.

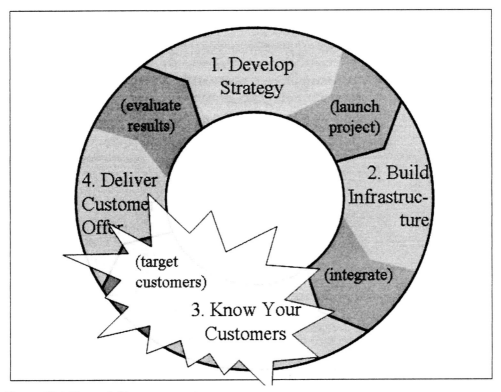

Figure 17-2 Phase 3: Know your customers

Before we get started putting customers into similar groups, we need to understand the different types of characteristics that make up a customer's profile and where the data comes from. We'll look at the three different sources of customer profile data: marketplace facts that describe customers as they exist in the world, relationship facts that describe your company's interactions with customers, and calculated facts that come from finding patterns and relationships between the other two types.

17.1 Creating a Customer Profile

When we select customers to receive the project offer, we are hoping to effectively predict what the customer's response will be to that offer. We define a profile based on characteristics we know about the customer. Frankly, we could segment and target by any characteristic, but not all are useful. Customers' first names, for example, are almost universally available. But a customer's first name is extremely unlikely to predict anything about behavior. Using customers' first names would not produce actionable segments.

Of course, no one would really choose "first name" as one of their segmentation criteria, but many companies (especially those that are product-centered) do something similar. They try to segment their customers based on what product the customer purchased. It's not that the purchased product isn't extremely valuable information; it's just that it doesn't really tell us much about who the customer is. For example, XYZ's consumer customers didn't buy large-scale products, but those darn business guys were always buying products designed for consumers. "Purchased product" isn't great for segmentation, but it can be very useful for targeting (such as for an upgrade offer sent to all those who own a certain product). We need to look at the characteristics that do help us understand customers.

17.1.1 Using Marketplace Information

Marketplace information about the customer is easily obtainable, often from third-party sources such as list compilers and brokers. This demographic data is available for both business and consumer customers. The data is generally leased or purchased for a one-time use as a contact list or to add/validate profile characteristics to your own file(s). Remember that using a brokered list as a source of contact names, though certainly a widely used direct marketing tactic, is not CRM. Of course prospects can become leads who can then become customers and then you can begin building and managing their relationships.

The work to append additional profile data to your customer information can be accomplished by either your internal database team or by the data providers themselves, who are often well equipped to provide you with this kind of service. Table 17-1 gives examples of some of the demographic data that is available for purchase.

The advantage of using marketplace facts about customers is that they are fairly easy to obtain because these facts are generally observable. This data is available for purchase, so why would any company bother to collect this data directly from customers? Just buy it, and save your company and your customers much valuable time. The major disadvantage to marketplace

Table 17-1 Marketplace Information

Type	Consumer Customer	Customer Company
Individual	Age Sex	Function Title
Financial	Household income Years of education Own/rent	Revenue Fortune rank Capitalization
Size	Number in household	Number of employees
Demographics	Average cost of homes in area Median income in area	Industry Region
Psychographics	Interests Preferences	A "best place to work" company Company style (top down, consensus)

data is that the same information is available to all your competitors, so how can it be any kind of advantage to your company?

17.1.2 Using Relationship Information

On the other hand, only you can know anything about your company's interactions and relationship with customers. This is where your company's real competitive advantage can be found. This information can be either objective (numbers of support calls, size of orders) or subjective (vendor preferences, opinions, feedback). It is usually related to behavioral and attitudinal facts based on the interactions that have taken place between the customer and your company. Because relationship data most often describe events that occur directly with customer contacts (business or consumer interactions), there isn't a significant difference between the types of characteristics captured. The big difference is in the way we aggregate some of these facts. For B2B customers, the individuals we market to are often not the same people who place the order. Instead, we have to assume a link if the company is the same. Because of that, the link between contact and company is a major data quality focus for all B2B marketers. Business contacts inherit many of the characteristics of the companies they work for (as indicated in Table 17-2).

As you can see, business-to-business marketers have different criteria (information, aggregation) for segmentation and targeting. Other differences exist as well. Many companies that sell to consumers don't sell to them directly. The valuable purchase data (point of sale) may be available through third parties. Of course, most B2B companies also have partners that sell at least some of their products. It's important to work with the channel to make sure they understand that you have not abdicated your relationship with your end customers to them. This is a very important source of customer information which too many companies have ignored in the name of

Table 17-2 Relationship Information

	Relationship Information	Aggregate by	
		Consumer	**Company**
Response Behavior	Order, point of sale (from partner or other third party)	Individual	Company
	E-mail offer responses	Individual	Individual
Interests	Product inquiries	Individual	Individual
	Product ownership	Individual	Company and individual
	Hobbies, sports, etc.	Individual	Individual
Product Uses (Applications)	Reason for purchase or use of product	Individual	Company or individual
	Number of users	Household	Company
	Where used	Individual	Company

avoiding channel conflict. It takes work to turn the channel relationship into a partnership, but for most companies it must be done.

Another significant difference between B2B and consumer data is in the numbers of individuals and amount of data available. The vast amount of consumer data available always requires the use of automated analysis tools. There are differences between consumer and B2B types, and sources and aggregations of information, but we will see that the methods and tools are the same.

Relationship information gives you knowledge that only you have access to, and because it is behavioral, it's generally *much* more appropriate for defining and targeting customer segments. Past behavior predicts future behavior better than any other information we can get. The disadvantage is that it takes lots of time and resources to collect enough of this information in your database to do much good.

17.1.3 Using Calculated Information

If relationship data is so much more effective, why do we even bother with marketplace data? The answer is that we don't always have enough relationship data available to determine customer segments. Often, we can get more complete results by using both market and relationship data together. We can combine information in different ways.

Derived Information: One way to improve the accuracy of our segmenting and targeting efforts is to use relationship or marketplace facts in combination with other facts or to summarize them over a period of time.

Inferred Information: The fact is we often use market and relationship information in combination whenever we can. We use relationship facts to determine value, and then use market facts to find other customers who look just like our target customers and (we hope) behave the same. We can infer behavior even for potential customers who have never bought from us before and who have no relationship with us. These new customers can be from internal (e.g., leads) or external customer information sources.

There is a progression of scenarios from simple to sophisticated that most companies adopt as they are building up their CRM capabilities. The three scenarios described here show that progression. It takes a while to build the level of database content required for Scenario 3.

1. Use marketplace data plus common sense and experience to identify customer segments that will identify actionable groups of customers with similar value.
2. As relationship data becomes available, use this interaction information to verify segment value and to test and refine your segment decisions.
3. Look for marketplace characteristic similarities that predict well which members belong in which segments (data mining). Then look for other customers and prospects that match these market facts but don't have relationship facts to include in the same segments.

All three types of information can be used at different times and in combination, depending on the specific project goal. There are definite tradeoffs. Demographic information is readily available and fairly easy to use, but not very predictive. Relationship data is a much better predictor, but it only helps with customers for whom we have captured the required relationship attributes. Calculated information is extremely powerful because it is the best predictor, but it depends on tools and expertise that are often not available. Calculated data also has the advantage that it can be used for "new" customers (prospects or customers for whom you don't have much relationship data).

A number of tools and algorithms can be used to calculate new information from existing information. They are covered in more detail at the end of this chapter. These tools are used for both segmentation and targeting.

17.2 Knowing Your Customers

Remember that, for CRM, we get to know customers because of what we know *about* them. CRM success is measured by how well we have been able to use information to predict and influence future customer behavior. We want to make our offer only to the customers who will provide the highest return (greatest response rates, highest profit margins, or lowest cost to serve). Table 17-3 lists the steps needed to get to know your customers.

Table 17-3   Steps to Knowing Your Customer

Steps	Purpose (Actions)	Participants
Getting Down and Dirty with the Data	Customer profile Enhance profile coverage	Product team Database marketing team Data quality management team
Segmenting Customers	Define segmentation strategy Group customers by similar profile characteristics	Product team Database marketing team

The first thing we have to do is get our hands dirty in the customer database.

17.3 Getting Down and Dirty with the Data

Now the database marketing team members need to actually get their hands on customer data so they can eventually pick exactly the right customers to receive the offer.

17.3.1 Determining a Customer Profile

We often start a project with a target customer profile in mind. The description of that target profile indicates what we believe to be the important characteristics of customers who will respond to the offer. For Valencia, the target customers were:

- Top 50 customers (based on sales)
- Owns one or more target (815 or 817) products

These were characteristics they used to divide the database into groups. Sometimes, there are no criteria this specific. The target audience might be customers who spent the most in the past six months or customers who live in Canada. Whatever the criteria, they are used by the database team to put customers into groups. For Valencia, there were really only two segments, the top 50 customers who own an 815 or 817 and all the rest—which was where they started. It's a common practice to use the target characteristics to divide the database into multiple groups, more than just "in" or "out." For example, sales were used to pick members of the top 50 list, and owners of 815 or 817 products made the final chosen group. XYZ might well decide to extend the offer beyond the top 50, so they might divide the whole database of 815/817 owners into even segments based on total sales the previous year. Remember, we're trying to keep our examples simple.

17.3.2 Enhancing Profile Coverage

One of the first things that XYZ's database marketing discovered is that there was simply not enough good data in the database. The database had problems ranging from invalid product numbers to missing customer relationships.

Appending Missing Data

It was critical for XYZ to be able to identify all the top 50 customers with 815 and 817 installations. Unfortunately, there were lots of B2B customers in the database who weren't linked to the appropriate company. The database team purchased a third-party service to append company and site information on all the unlinked database records.

Managing Quality

Another problem that XYZ found was poor quality. There were records without valid product numbers that needed to be researched and corrected. They also found that company names were often misspelled, which frequently resulted in broken links to the parent company. XYZ asked the data quality management team to review the database and correct any record that looked as if it should be part of a top 50 company. We will talk more about data quality management in Chapter 20.

17.4 Segmenting Customers

Don Peppers and Martha Rogers introduced the concept of marketing to each customer one at a time in *The One to One Future* (1993). Their book paints an exciting vision—a future in which information about our customers allows us to interact with each customer individually, just as if we were standing behind the counter of the corner grocery store and able to deliver a friendly greeting to each customer as he or she walked through the door. In the "old" days, storeowners knew their best and most loyal customers by name, and they often saved them the special cuts of beef or personally delivered the grocery order to their homes because they had been such valuable customers over the years. This is a wonderful picture that brings back visions of a much friendlier and more personal time; and it is the vision for CRM as well.

17.4.1 Information Based Relationships

But few companies today have the luxury of having so few customers (and still being in business anyway) that they can afford to customize experiences to one individual at a time. In today's marketplace, businesses may have thousands of customers, and they may be located all over the world. It's very likely that no one in the company has ever met most of them. But in this new marketplace, customers still expect personal treatment. CRM, the alternative that is practical for managing relationships in today's marketplace, uses information to identify groups of similar customers and to support personalization.

Segments Like One

CRM creates the feeling of personal experiences by using information to identify group of customers who are enough alike that we can treat all members of the group in the same way. This way we reduce our thousands of individuals to a few segments that we learn about and understand. Peppers and Rogers introduced us to *segments of one;* CRM introduces us to *segments like one.*

 DEFINITIONS

Customer segments are groups of customers who *look like one*. We want to treat all group members the same—and all groups differently from other groups.

We create segments because it's the only way possible to build relationships with thousands of customers. Assigning customers to *segments like one* means putting them into natural groupings based on having similar characteristics so that they meet these criteria:

- They are likely to react to an offer in about the same way.
- They have the same value, so we want to treat them the same.

Customer segments have natural boundaries that are defined by similar characteristics. We believe that if we treat each of them the same, they will respond the same.

Personalization

Personalization uses electronic customer data to address mail (or e-mail) to specific individuals and has been used to create direct marketing for years. Not only were marketers able to send mail to specific named individuals, they were able to 'merge' the customer names into the body of the document. Some even tried creating newsletters or catalogs aimed at the buying patterns of specific groups of customers. In Chapter 20 you'll find one example of a personalized direct mail piece.

The Internet has taken the potential of personalization to new levels. The computer uses customer data to create a web site that not only recognizes a returning customer, but suggests new products and accessories to enhance products the customer has already purchased. Or perhaps the website provides service options tuned to exactly the level of sophistication and needs of the customer. Sounds perfect; it's almost like having a personal conversation. What's the catch? It's the completeness and quality of the data. There is nothing worse than logging on to a website and being welcomed with the wrong name or being inundated with suggestions and pop-ups that are completely inappropriate.

Achieving the full potential for personalization is still a long way off for most companies. We will focus on using information for segmentation strategies since that was what XYZ needed for Valencia.

17.4.2 Defining Segmentation Strategy

To segment customers into natural groups, we use information about the customer (company or person) himself and the relationship we have with that customer.

Customer Profile

We develop the customer demographics from marketplace data (which we can usually purchase from a third party). The starting assumption is that there are facts about customers that will influence behavior so we can predict outcomes. We just have to find which facts are important. Of course, we know that past behavior is the best predictor of future behavior. But relationship data often is not readily available early in the CRM program. Of course you can purchase consumer buying behavior data, but it is often huge, unwieldy, and difficult to match to individual customers.

For customer companies, commonly used segmentation criteria are size (revenue, employees) as a surrogate for value and industry for companies that have different offerings for different vertical markets. For consumers, income is often used to indicate potential value. For Valencia, the profile is the top 50 customers owning 815/817 products.

Customer Value

As we've discussed, the purpose of CRM is to be able to know who our best customers are so we can treat them best and so that they remain valuable or become even more valuable. What does "best customer" mean anyway? We mean, of course, the customers who deliver increased profit to the company because they display the wonderful behaviors we learned from Reichheld (see Chapter 2). For many reasons, loyal customers provide more value to our company than other customers. Remember, we don't manage customer relationships just because we want customers to like us; we do it so they will prefer us to other vendors and buy more of our stuff. But just buying more isn't enough. Look at these three different value scenarios:

- If one customer bought 1,000 products with a profit margin of only $1 each, and another customer bought only 500 products, but the profit was $5 each, which customer is the most valuable?
- If two customers choose exactly the same support coverage, but one calls for help weekly and the other calls only twice a year, which is most valuable?
- If the profit from one customer's purchase this year is $10,000, but they never buy again, and profit from another was only $1,000, but this customer has continued purchasing at the same rate for 15 years, who is the most valuable?

Our most valuable customers are those who add the most to the company's wealth over the long term. The fact of the matter is that that ideally we would use *only* value to segment our database. Unfortunately we don't usually have enough of the information we need about a customer's total orders and the cost to serve them.

Interestingly, we don't always want to target our best customers; sometimes the most appropriate segment is not the most valuable segment. Table 17-4 shows the method that XYZ used to select the _right_ segment for any project.

Table 17-4   The Right Segment for Different Offers

Cost of Offer	Relationship Impact	
	Plus	Minus
High	High-value segments	No segments
Low	All segments	Low-value segments

The next step is to used electronic data to assign each customer to the correct segment.

17.4.3 Grouping Customers by Profile Characteristics

When just getting started with CRM, most companies must use a less predictive marketplace metric because that is the only information available. Third-party data is an excellent way to get started quickly. Table 17-5 shows how XYZ used marketplace data to develop its strategic segments and it shows the plans XYZ has to use relationship information in the future.

Table 17-5   XYZ's Strategic Segmentation

XYZ's Segments	Definition	Marketplace Criteria (Current)	Relationship Criteria (Planned)
Named	People who work at companies that are put on the list because they are the most valuable to XYZ	Revenue > $1 billion Employees > 10,000	Average annual purchases > $150 million; top valued customers making up 80% of total customer value (80/20 rules)
Small/ Medium Companies	People who work at any company not on the list	The rest of the business marketplace	The rest of the customer companies in the base; the remaining 80% of business customers
Consumer	People using products at home for personal use	No business relationship identified	Exhibits consumer behavior (e.g., selects consumer newsletter, uses for consumer purposes)

One of XYZ's early goals was to improve its ability to segment and target customers based on relationship data. But like most companies just getting started, they had only marketplace data available. They must wait until they have a much more integrated customer view.

XYZ considered a fourth segment during strategic planning: the channel. Channel partners buy products from your company, but they are not customers. They don't make final buying decisions, and they don't necessarily use your products. The kinds of offers made to partners and how a successful relationship is measured are so different for partners that companies eventually learn they must treat them as a separate case altogether. Programs to build partner value, known as partner relationship management, are very important, and they follow the same type of planning and implementation methodology we have been using. However, you would have to collect very different information to complete your strategy, planning and implementation efforts.

Even though this example used XYZ's strategic segments which don't help us understand customers as *segments like one;* the method for using data to segment customers is the same for all segmentation levels. But now let's look at how XYZ identified its target segments for Valencia. After we've divided the database into groups, we will choose (target) the segments we plan to include in the project offer. Targeting customers is the transition to Phase 4 of the CRM life cycle. The alternative to targeted offers is mass marketing—but that's not CRM. CRM is about sending the right offers to the right customers, and customer information is what we use to decide.

17.5 Targeting Customers

Targeting customers is the transition step between getting to know our customers and delivering the offer. This is where we pick exactly the customers we plan to contact with our offer. Targeting decisions are based on predicting responses based on past behavior and expected returns. We want to provide each customer with the most appropriate experience possible. "Appropriate" does not necessarily mean the best experience. We cannot treat all customers the same. For each project, we need to target the segment(s) that are the best match to the offer because of the expected behavior of that segment. If you're planning to provide an expensive new capability, you might limit the offer to those who are highest value, highest potential value, or highly visible and influential in the marketplace.

 DEFINITIONS

Targeting is choosing the segments most likely to deliver the highest project return.

Targeted project segments must be much more specific than strategic segments. They are narrower because campaign (offer) resources are usually limited. To target customers for an offer, we want to pick those customers whom we believe will respond best and be in the right value segment (remember, not always the highest value). Target segments need to be precise and actionable, or we're back to mass mailing.

The El Cid system eventually will be used for all customers, of course. But to get started, XYZ chose to focus the Valencia project on the top 50 customers who owned at least one 815 or 817 product. They wanted the top 50 best customers because El Cid would greatly improve XYZ's ability to recognize customers and build relationships. Target customers were determined based on the selection steps and criteria in Table 17-6.

Table 17-6 Targeting for the Valencia Project

Tasks	Valencia Decision Criteria
Select candidate strategic segments	Eliminate small/medium businesses and consumers
Eliminate unlikely members of remaining segment(s)	Eliminate companies that don't have at least one product A installed
Score each customer based on selection criteria	Total order dollars for the previous four quarters; sort from high dollar total to low
Select members	Count off the top 50 companies
Segment targeted customers	Identify small groups for special treatment

XYZ wanted to start where the expected returns were greatest. Also, these top customers *expected* to be recognized. And the company chose customers owning an 815 or 817 because there was a big upgrade release and campaign planned for these models in the second half of the fiscal year and they wanted to be prepared. Remember that we want to tie any infrastructure project to a specific customer offer, so the project team needed a real marketing campaign to help "prove the concept." We always must be able to deliver some tangible business results.

Very often, the team will want to again segment the targeted customers into smaller groups because even the top 50 customers are not all alike. They also may decide that they want to do some test offers to see if there would be different messages that would appeal to different types of customers. As we discussed earlier, targeting and segmentation are used iteratively, as shown in Figure 17-3.

In general, XYZ has learned that product application (the kind of environment/purpose for which the product is used) is a very good predictor of their customers' behavior. The overall parent company industry code was not considered very valuable because different parts of the company are often in different lines of business. But they didn't always have application data available, so they decided to use the US Government's Standard Industry Code (SIC) for the customer site as an approximation of application. As part of the company's data management effort, it purchased and enhanced its database with the site SIC code (for sites with Series 800 installed), as shown in Table 17-7.

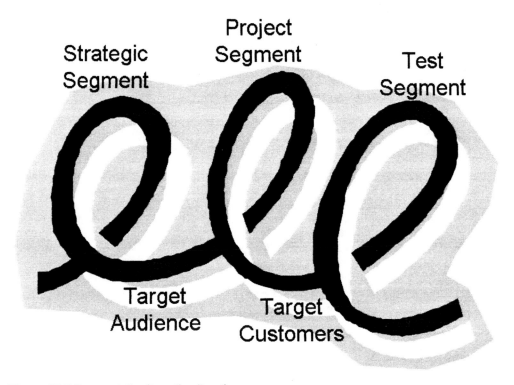

Figure 17-3 Segmentation/targeting iteration

Table 17-7 Valencia Target Segments

Segments of Top 50	Laboratory	Small shop floor	Theaters, auditoriums	Exercise rooms	Miscellaneous
SIC Code	8731	21xx-39xx	7832, 799935	79xx except 799935	(everything else)
Number of Companies in Segment	8	12	7	15	8

Actually as you can see, XYZ was using the newer North American Industry Coding System (NAICS) 6-digit codes. The first four digits of NAICS are the same as the old SIC, but XYZ needed the additional specificity—they just never got around to learning the new name. Let's look a little closer at some of the best-known tools used to assign similar customers into actionable segments and prioritize the segments for matching to specific offers.

17.6 Understanding the Tools

Often, we want to use calculations, statistics, and modeling tools to define and target the most actionable customer segments. We've discussed some of these tools already; now let's look at how and when they are used. Table 17-8 lists some of the most commonly used calculation tools.

Table 17-8   Segmentation and Targeting Tools

Tool	Description		When to Use
Scoring	Rank customer's likelihood of response based on specific characteristics	Target	Develop a ranking for customers based on some other attribute(s)
RFM (Recency, Frequency, and Monetary Value of Customers)	Customers who have bought recently, who buy more often, and who spend more have been shown to be the most likely to buy again	Target	Previous behavior predicts future response
Value	Company income from orders less cost to acquire and serve customer	Segment	Measure actual value of customers (net profit from customer); the best customers
LTV (Lifetime Value)	Projects profit over the number of years customer remains loyal	Segment	Justify larger investment because of payback over life time
Data Mining	Discover data patterns that predict response	Target	Identify new customers who look like the target segment
ROI (Return on Investment)	Cost of project divided by Revenue from project	Evaluation (offer or project)	Measure fiscal results of each project

Now let's spend a little more time understanding more about how each of these tools can be used.

17.6.1 Scoring

Marketers have used scoring techniques for a long time. Scoring is simply assigning a rank to each customer depending on specific characteristics (such as total annual purchases) that have been identified as being important. The algorithm to assign scores can be very simple or extremely complex. For Valencia, XYZ scored each customer based on the company's total orders for the previous year. We use scores to rank various segments from most valuable or most likely to buy to those that are least likely.

17.6.2 Recency, Frequency, Monetary (RFM)

RFM has been a staple for database marketers for years. The principle is that customers who have bought most recently and most often and the most stuff have been shown to be the most likely to buy again. In *The Complete Database Marketer*, the bible for database marketing, Arthur Hughes gives a complete overview of RFM that includes both instructions and case-study examples. If all customers were ranked by these three factors, then the most likely customers to buy again would be those represented by the cube shown in Figure 17-4.

Another excellent resource for RFM is *Drilling Down*, Jim Novo's easy-to-read book about turning customer data into profits. In fact, Novo's book is a great resource for all these tools because he presents lots of common-sense approaches to analyzing data and gives examples using simple spreadsheets. Here is a wonderful quote from the book describing the early days of marketing data analysis simply using the index card files the sample company kept on its customers:

> It happens that while going through these cards by hand, and writing down orders, the catalog folks began to see patterns emerge. ...

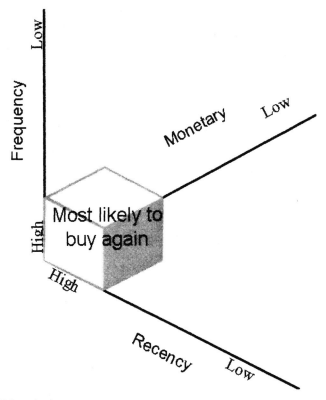

Figure 17-4 RFM analysis

The group who ranked "best" in the three categories above [recency, frequency, monetary] always had higher response rates than the group who ranked "worst." It worked so well they cut back on mailing to people who ranked worst, and spent the money saved on mailing more often to the group who ranked best. And their sales exploded, while their costs remained the same or went down. They were increasing their marketing efficiency and effectiveness by targeting to the most responsive, highest future value customers.

Now we have computers to store the information for hundreds of thousands of customers and can do the analysis in a very short amount of time. RFM tells us lots about buying behavior and Novo correctly points out that customers who buy frequently and spend the most ought to be some of the most valuable customers. But RFM doesn't always predict customer value.

17.6.3 Value

As we have discussed, *value* measures how much a customer adds to your company's bottom line. This is an extremely powerful tool and fairly straightforward to calculate: customer-generated revenue less cost to produce purchase(s) less cost to acquire and serve customer.

The difficulty in determining customer value stems from the fact that it is usually very hard to link together all the various internal sources of data (order, support, call center, cost of sales) for each customer. XYZ has been using a simple model for determine value based on calculating an average cost to serve (e.g., how much did product support cost last year divided by the total number of customers). The problem is that XYZ was concerned that for their very large customers (the target audience for Valencia) an average cost to serve was not meaningful. They wanted to know the real cost to serve, at least for some of their biggest customers. This is just one more reminder that all customers are not the same and we are likely to invest more in understanding some customers than others. This is one of the benefits that XYZ hopes to get from the El Cid database when fully operational.

17.6.4 Lifetime Value (LTV)

After we've determined customer value, we can take the next step, which is to determine the lifetime value for customers and segments. LTV is the expected net profit a customer will contribute to your business over the entire time the customer remains a customer. It takes into account factors such as customer defection rates and discounted cash flow, which is the current worth of revenue received in the future (net present value calculation, see Chapter 2). This is a very accurate but complex calculation, which is based on the number of years an "average" customer remains a customer (lifetime) and a standard discount rate based on inflation. Novo says that one of the biggest difficulties companies have is determining the right length of the customer "lifetime". When does a customer stop being a customer? Most customers just stop calling, they don't file divorce papers. (I guess it's more like dating than marriage.) Once again we must not agonize over the exact figure. As long as we use a consistent lifetime calculation then the relative customer LTV will tell us a lot even if the absolute LTV is not perfect.

LTV is an effective analysis tool because it recognizes that customer value is not a static single snapshot, but the sum of previous behavior that can then be used to predict future results. LTV can be used to justify investment in campaigns that have a high cost of acquiring new customers and wouldn't normally be recouped by a single purchase. LTV can be very useful, but it's difficult to get all the necessary data that depends on knowing when customers have *stopped* buying. Few organizations have enjoyed lots of success using LTV. Figure 17-5 shows an example of one company's analysis of its customer value by industry.

A simple way to estimate LTV was suggested by Tony Vavra in *Aftermarketing*. The average value of a particular set of customers is determined by dividing the total purchases of the all customers by the number of customers in the set. The set can be a predefined segment, the respondents to a particular offer, or anything else. The importance of estimated LTV is not the actual value of the customer. The importance comes from being able to compare two sets to each other.

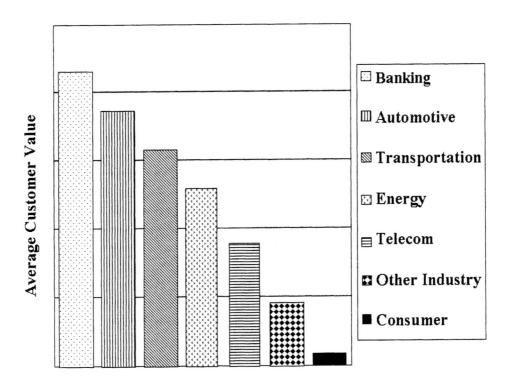

Figure 17-5 Customer average value by industry

17.6.5 Data Mining

Data mining techniques depend on the development of models that predict behavior based on patterns and associations the computer finds in the (often vast amounts of) customer data. Of course all the tools use customer information, even the exact same fields such as recency of purchase. Data mining is the only one that is dependent on machine analysis to look for unexpected patterns. Data mining starts with a reasoned hypothesis about how we think a certain set of customers (with the same "pattern" of attributes) will behave. We analyze the information on a test set of customers whose behavior is already known (e.g., some very good customers and some not so good ones) and look for both similar and different characteristics between the two groups (e.g., household income, company size). We use any patterns we discover to build a model, and then test that model against another set of test customers. After reviewing these results (and discovering whether the model predicted actual behavior accurately), we will refine it and then apply it to customers or prospects whose behavior we don't know.

If this high-level explanation is intriguing, get a copy of *Data Mining Techniques* by Berry and Linoff. It's a good resource for this topic and related analysis tools such as cluster analysis, decision trees, neural networks, etc. Their book is both readable and very comprehensive, presenting clear explanations and good practical examples of all the analysis tools described.

17.6.6 Return on Investment (ROI)

We hope that every investment we make in CRM will improve company performance; we want to send offers to those customers who are likely to deliver the highest return on the investment we have made. Return on Investment measures the relationship between the money that was spent and the money that was received as a result of that investment. ROI is commonly used for measuring the results of any business investment. We can use ROI to measure the results of the offer, as well as the results of the overall project—but that takes some special treatment, as we will see in Chapter 19. When we evaluate the overall CRM project results, we may find that the cost of the infrastructure development may not be recovered during just one offer cycle. Because infrastructure investments are large and the return is expected over time, the absolute ROI of a project may be discouraging. We need to project payback over a period of time rather than at the end of a single project.

Now that we know whom we plan to include in our offer, we need to work on developing the details of the offer itself. In Chapter 18, we learn a method for preparing and delivering the offer to the selected customers.

Questions for Reflection

What strategic segments has your company identified? Think about these segments, and answer the following questions to see whether the segmentation scheme is providing any value to the company.

1. Are the segments used consistently, or does every group have a different set and different definition?
2. Are there any real differences in the way you treat customers in each segment, or do you need to pick new ones?

CHAPTER 18

Delivering the Customer Offer

Now that we've chosen the set of customers most appropriate to the offer we plan to make, it's time to design and deliver the offer to these customers. The "offer" is what all our project efforts so far have prepared us to do. The offer can be anything from a marketing campaign to an opportunity to take advantage of a new online capability, as long as we want the customer to perform an action in response. For CRM projects, all decisions should be based on customer information. We are going to work on defining the right goal and the right offers for each customer segment.

The actual creation (content and design) is important enough to be at least a course topic, if not a full degree program, in most universities and MBA programs. You may very well want to hire professional experts either on staff or as consultants to help you with these communication tasks. But it's important to understand the basics so you can tell whether you've hired the right consultant! As you can see in Figure 18-1, we are starting the last phase of our CRM methodology.

We have identified the customer set that we believe will return the most value (greatest response rates, highest profit margins, or lowest cost to serve). Now it's time to deliver the offer.

18.1 Delivering the Offer

Remember that for a CRM program, the customer offer is always aimed at generating some kind of response from the targeted customers. We hope to persuade customers to act in a certain way. Persuasion, according to Jay Conger in his book on the topic, is

"Quite simply ... to present a message in a way that leads others to support it."

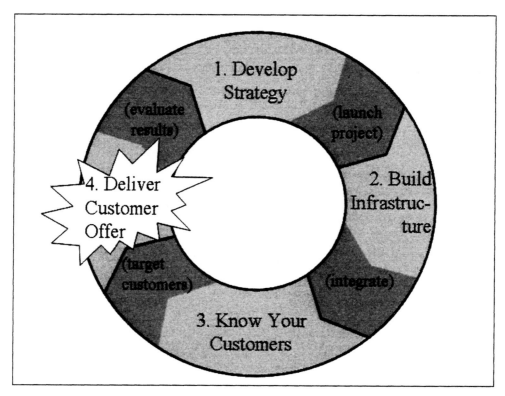

Figure 18-1 Phase 4: Deliver the customer offer

This response may be anything from buying a product to adopting a new service offering. Naturally, whatever the offer, we want the experience to be positive, improve the relationship, and increase loyalty. The steps to build the offer and get it out the door and into the arms of your targeted customers are outlined in Table 18-1.

Table 18-1   Deliver Customer Offer: Steps

Step	Purpose	Participants
Design the offer	Describe customer segments Define segment value proposition	Business offer sponsor and/or manager
Prepare the offer message(s)	Define offer details Goals and measures Offer value Call to action	Depends on offer: Project team Business offer sponsor IT department

Table 18-1 Deliver Customer Offer: Steps (Continued)

Step	Purpose	Participants
Present the offer	Select communication media Test offer Transmit offer Receive and capture response Fulfill	Depends on offer: Project team Business offer sponsor IT department

Be aware that the fulfillment activity usually involves much more than the front office functions, and it is absolutely critical to delivering a positive experience. Communication must be established and nurtured with the people in the back office who complete the fulfillment of your offer. Don't expect that they'll be able to ship 1,000 new S-800 products next week if they don't learn about it until the orders start to come in. We'll talk about fulfillment more when we discuss offer preparation. For now, let's tackle the first step, which is to design an offer that will provide value to the target customers and encourage the right behavior to occur.

18.2 Designing the Offer

Not surprisingly, before we actually define our customer offers, we want to understand more about the different characteristics of each of the segments we've identified. We know that XYZ has targeted the top 50 customers who owned at least one 815 or 817 series product. They recognize that, within this "best customer" group, there are very different needs and uses for the products. These product uses (applications) were believed to be an important way to personalize messages.

18.2.1 Describing Customer Segments

How the product is used (product application) varies significantly from customer to customer, as does the product configuration they choose to install. In her excellent book, *The DMA Lead Generation Handbook (2002)*, Ruth Stevens emphasizes the importance of customer research to campaign design. Stevens tells us that "Consumer direct marketing research ... takes the form of in-market testing [while] B-to-B marketing makes considerable use of primary research such as surveys and focus groups." In either case the goal of research and analysis at this stage is to better understand the customer's product needs.

As we saw in Chapter 17, XYZ identified five different target segments for the top 50 customers. The actual segments were created based on the site industry code because XYZ didn't have consistent or reliable application data for even its top customers. Table 18-2 presents the customer segments and the usual product use (application) for each segment.

Further analysis of the installed base revealed that the product configurations differed significantly based on the amount of cooling required and the need for air purity. These differences were important in designing a message that had the appropriate value for each segment.

Table 18-2 S-800 Segment Configurations

Segments of Top 50	Laboratory	Small mfg shop	Theaters, auditoriums	Exercise rooms	Miscellaneous
Division SIC Code	8731	21xx-39xx	7832, 799935	79xx except 799935	—
Product Purpose	Temperature control for delicate, heat-sensitive equipment in small environments	Temperature control; small or few heat generating tools, machines	Air Circulation; temperature control for large groups of people	Air Circulation; temperature control of sweaty bodies	None specified
Typical Product Configuration	Cooling=H Air qty=L Air pure=H	Cooling=M Air qty=M Air pure=M	Cooling=H Air qty=H Air pure=M	Cooling=H Air qty=L Air pure=M	Cooling= Air qty= Air pure=

18.2.2 Defining Segment Value Propositions

XYZ was about to release its new series 82x products. The main advantage of products in the new product line was that the 82x products could be integrated into a 900 Series system, thus eliminating the need for an independent cooling system and significantly reducing power and maintenance expense. However, the air purification capabilities of the 900 series are not as precise as the 800 models, so an extra filter unit was developed that matches the original 800 series air purification standards. The additional filter unit at high air quantity volumes consumes enough power to essentially offset the savings from eliminating the cooling unit, but it is quite reliable and support costs are low. The customer value (benefits) differs fairly significantly based on the segment, as shown in Table 18-3.

Table 18-3 Valencia Customer Value

Segment	Configuration	Customer Value Propositions
Laboratory	Cooling=H Air qty=L Air pure=H	Lower support contract costs Increased cooling capacity Equal energy cost due to extra filter step More dependable
Small shop	Cooling=M Air qty=M Air pure=M	Lower support contract costs Lower energy cost More dependable

Table 18-3 Valencia Customer Value (Continued)

Segment	Configuration	Customer Value Propositions
Theaters, audi-toriums	Cooling=H Air qty=H Air pure=M	Lower support contract costs Increased cooling capacity Lower energy cost Increased air quantity capacity More dependable
Exercise rooms	Cooling=H Air qty=M Air pure=H	Lower support contract costs Increased cooling capacity Equal energy cost due to extra filter step More dependable
Miscellaneous	Cooling= Air qty= Air pure=	Depending on customer needs, modular choices that: Can lower support contract costs Can increase cooling capacity Are equal to or lower than energy costs Can increase air quantity capacity Are more dependable

With this information in mind, the product team was ready to create the various offers.

18.3 Preparing the Offer Message(s)

The major purpose of the offer is to persuade customers to accept the call to action. This is best accomplished by matching the offer to the value proposition for each segment. We will look now at the mechanics of preparing an offer. There are four elements of the offer message: offer details, goals and measures, offer value, and call to action. All may be varied by customer segment, although the offer details, goals, and call to action may be the same for all segments. If the value is the same for all segments, then you have not identified any that are meaningful and actionable. This may be your intention, but make sure that it is a conscious decision or go back to the drawing board. In any case, don't waste your time trying to measure differences between segments when all the message elements are the same.

18.3.1 Creating the Offer Details

We must be very clear that everyone involved with the project understands exactly what is being offered, the desired result, and how we will be able to tell whether the project has been successful. We need first to be sure that we completely understand what the specific offer actually is. The entire project team (from finance to manufacturing to product marketers) will participate in this step. Valencia's offer is shown in Table 18-4.

Table 18-4 Valencia Offer

Offer	Offer Details
1. Trade-in discount	15 percent off 825 or
	20 percent off 827 or
	25 percent off extra filter
2. New service contract with reduced rates	35 to 50 percent rate reduction, depending on configuration

The details describe the specific offer elements that must be clearly represented in the offer message.

18.3.2 Creating the Offer Objectives and Measures

Next, we have to determine the objective of the offer to be made. What is it exactly that we hope will happen? The goals need to be measurable (and the measurements decided up front) so that we know when we have achieved them.

Objectives

Like any company, XYZ's goal, frankly stated, was to increase company profit – period. Generally, increasing revenue or reducing cost can accomplish that; these are the guidelines we use to determine our goals. The offer objective(s) must deliver one of these two company benefits, and we have to understand how it will happen so we can measure results.

XYZ's main goals for Valencia were to sell a specified number of new 82x series systems and to reduce the number of 815 and 817 installed products under support contract. Table 18-5 outlines the stated objective for the Valencia project.

Table 18-5 Valencia Offer Objectives

Objective	How Impacted	
Sell 150 Series 825 or 827 systems to the targeted customers within six months	Increase revenue	High margin from new 82x products
Reduce number of support contracts on 815 and 817 systems owned by targeted customers by 35 percent	Reduce cost	Reduce 81x machines on support contract because cost to deliver has gone through the roof.

We're hoping customers will take us up on our offer because we have been able to persuade them of its value. (Remember that customer loyalty means loyalty in the absence of contradictory information. That's right, only customer *disloyalty* is truly emotional and can't be overcome, no matter how convincing your argument). How do we measure success?

Metrics

Obviously, one way to measure success is to count the number of orders for these products that come into the call center from the targeted customers. But what about calls that came from the target audience but instead of placing an immediate order they asked for more information? Surely, that is a better response than ignoring the whole thing. For any type of offer there is a continuum of possible responses, as shown in Figure 18-2.

So how *should* we measure success? Obviously, some of these actions are hard to measure. How do you know that a customer has put the offer into a folder to talk about with her sales rep instead of tossing it into the garbage? You won't know unless you can spend the money to call every customer and ask – and that's simply not feasible. We can measure results only when the customer takes one of the actions that involve actually contacting the company. All of the "below the line" actions count as initial failures, even though some will actually produce results down the line.

Hmmm, this is a dilemma; we have some customers who just called for information and others who didn't even call. But it's very likely that some of them will eventually make a purchase.

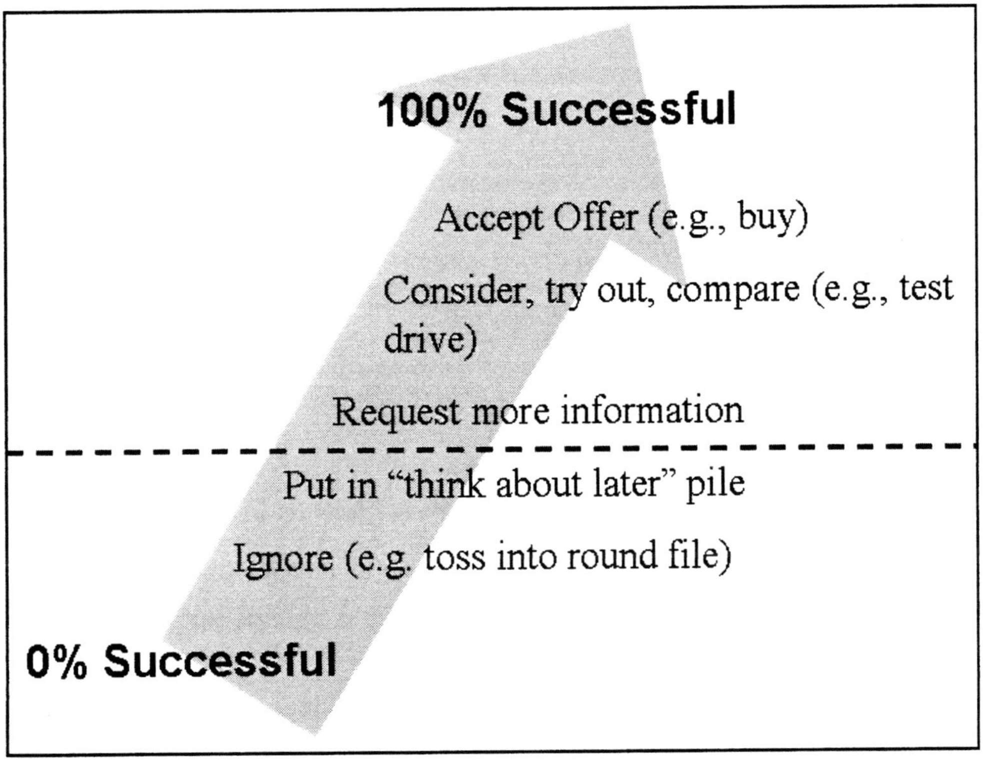

100% Successful

Accept Offer (e.g., buy)

Consider, try out, compare (e.g., test drive)

Request more information

- -

Put in "think about later" pile

Ignore (e.g. toss into round file)

0% Successful

Figure 18-2 Customer action continuum

So how do we measure the full impact of the project? We apply common sense and experience. We also need to count project response calls that don't produce an order and project initiated purchases that come through the sales force. To track project calls, we need a way of knowing what precipitated the customer's response. Measuring direct sales rep orders means, well, do we have to get the sales rep to tell us? No. Sales reps should spend their time in front of customers, not sitting in front of a computer entering data that doesn't help them manage their accounts. Let's get real; no sales rep really believes that anything beside his own sales technique influenced any of his customers to place an order anyway. We're not making much progress so far, but there are some good approaches that do work.

One such approach that works very well is the lead management funnel. Put all inquiries into your lead management system. Once there, it's marketing's responsibility to contact the lead and ask questions agreed on with the sales force about what constitutes a qualified lead that should be passed to the sales force (see Figure 18-3).

Once qualified, the lead should be passed to the direct sales force or to the outbound telesales team depending on the project and the desires of the customer. Steven's *Lead Generation Handbook* provides some excellent information on lead qualification and conversion.

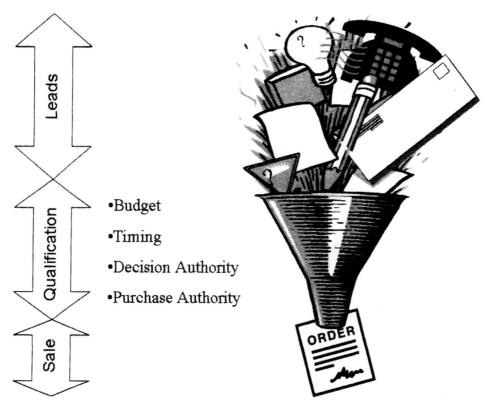

•Budget

•Timing

•Decision Authority

•Purchase Authority

Figure 18-3 The lead management funnel

Of course, this still leaves us with the question of how to recognize that a project related purchase has been made if the customer didn't take the exact action called for (e.g., place an order using the toll-free number provided).

1. One of the most effective means, and one used often by catalog direct marketers, is to slightly change the product number for each project. For example, a two-digit suffix appended to the end of the product number can track up to 100 different projects for the same product, and if you combine letters and numbers you can track even more. When the order is placed, we get the information that identifies the source of the order. The problem: Many companies have legacy systems that don't know how to handle a product suffix and can't process the order.

2. Another mechanism is to ask the customer for the media code printed on the offer. Variations include a dedicated post office box or toll-free number used only for that project. Sometimes, companies can set up their phone system so the customer is asked to enter a "telephone extension" after they've reached the call center. This is another familiar direct marketing method, but unfortunately it doesn't work very well when sales reps take the order. Variations of this method include special e-mail accounts, fax telephone numbers and so on.

3. A final method is to use the information you can collect to determine an approximate result. Match the site (household or business location) of any order placed during the project timeframe to the target list. This may slightly overstate results (some target companies may have already been ready to buy the new product). In most cases, the overstatement is minimal. And remember that we don't need perfect measures. We just need to look at the relative differences across projects.

Okay, let's get down to it. What did XYZ decide to measure? The metrics for the Valencia project are shown in Table 18-6.

Table 18-6   Valencia Measures

Performance of	Metric
Orders	Toll-free number orders for 825 and 827 products
	Number of total 82x purchases by target customers
Leads	Number of inquiries
Overall project	Number of calls

The project team wanted to know how many calls were received, how many inquiries were received (and later turned into qualified leads and finally sales), and how many customers did exactly what the offer asked them to do (buy via the toll-free number). Maybe most importantly,

XYZ measured all the orders for 82x products placed by targeted customers during the six-month project period.

18.3.3 Creating the Offer Value

The value statement should be customized for each customer segment. Customized does not necessarily mean personalized, but it does mean that we use knowledge we have about the customers to make the offer appropriate and appealing to the customer's particular value proposition. Of course, personalization does make messages more appealing to customers. Whenever possible and appropriate, we should use customer information to actually address individuals.

The caveat for business-to-business marketers is that job churn can make it very difficult to know that the person you're contacting is who you think he is, or that he is the appropriate person for the message. B2B marketers are often interested in reaching the person holding a certain position (President, Manufacturing Manager, and Chief Information Officer), so they address the message to an individual and his title. Nothing gives a message lower value than inaccurate personal information.

XYZ's offer values for each of the Valencia target customer segments are shown in Table 18-7.

Table 18-7 Valencia Offer Value

Segment	Customer Value Proposition	Offer Value
Laboratory	• More dependable • Lower support contract costs • Increased cooling capacity • Equal energy cost due to extra filter step	Reliable, high quality, protect your expensive equipment investment, safeguard health. <u>Proof</u>:
Small mfg shop	• More dependable • Lower support contract costs	Efficient, reliable, green, economic. <u>Proof</u>:
Theaters, auditoriums	• More dependable • Lower support contract costs • Increased cooling capacity • Lower energy cost • Increased air qty capacity	Reliable, air quality: high comfort of patrons, economical. <u>Proof</u>
Exercise rooms	• More dependable • Lower support contract costs • Increased cooling capacity • Equal energy cost due to extra filter step • More dependable	Reliable, economic, health. <u>Proof</u>:

Table 18-7 Valencia Offer Value (Continued)

Segment	Customer Value Proposition	Offer Value
Miscellaneous	Depending on needs, modular choices that • Are more dependable • Can lower support contract costs • Can increase cooling capacity • Are equal to or lower than energy costs • Can increase air quantity capacity	Modules that can work together as your needs grow; Reliable, economical. <u>Proof</u>:

Here is my sole piece of "creative" advice: All of the message components must be appealing, must be clearly stated and easy to understand, and must include some tangible proof points. Proof points include hard data and examples from real installations or live benchmarks that give evidence that the product really is more dependable, costs less to support, etc. As an example, XYZ had extensive test results from their alpha and beta test installations showing that the number of failures was nearly 60% lower and the meantime between failures more than doubled for the 82x products. Making a value claim without proof points is too reminiscent of our proverbial emperor's new clothes. Did anyone say "Vaporware?"

Now we will determine which media we will use for both the communication and response.

18.3.4 Creating the Call to Action

The call to action is just what it sounds like. What specifically do you want the customer to do? This includes specifics about both how to get in contact your company and what the customer should do after they reach you. For Valencia, the call to action is shown in Table 18-8.

Table 18-8 Valencia Call to Action

How to Do It	What to do
Call 1-800-CALLXYZ, and ask for extension 19.	1. Place an order.
	2. Request more info or sales rep visit.

The message must contain an easy-to-find and highly visible request for action if you really want anyone to do anything about it. Never make it hard for customers to give you the response you're hoping for!

18.4 Presenting the Offer

Presenting the offer includes all the steps we take to select the details of sending out the offer and preparing to handle the responses.

18.4.1 Selecting Communication and Response Media

Now we decide how we will deliver the message. This delivery decision is based on a number of different factors that must be prioritized for each project. These factors influence the anticipated return on investment from the project because they affect either the cost of delivering the offer or the likelihood that the offer will generate a positive response, or both. For example:

- Cost per contact
- Volume of contacts
- Appropriateness to message
- Appropriateness to customer
- Availability of medium

Media selection can be based on matching these factors to the customer and the offer; purely on cost considerations and, for consumers at least, by creating some trial offers to see which ones actually generate the best response. Stevens presents a very helpful model (Chart 5.3) that calculates expected cost per response (lead) for different media.

In addition to the outbound media, we need to select the media for the inbound responses too. After all, a call to action is useless if there is no way for the customer to respond! We also need to prepare that channel to receive the responses (e.g., telesales reps trained on new products, support options, etc.) and we need to set up the mechanics for measuring results. Not all media can be measured in the same way; preparation must be made. The media selection decision matrix for Valencia is shown in Table 18-9.

Table 18-9 Media Selection for Valencia

Message Medium (Touch-point)	Outbound Criteria			Inbound Criteria		
	Simple	Reliable	Convenience for customer	Currently operational	Get configuration requirements	Cost
System						
Internet		X	X			X
Mail	X	X	X	X		X
Event						
Phone/fax	X			X	X	X
Direct Sales		X	X	X	X	

You probably remember that the Valencia team had decided to use the postal service to deliver the message and the Telesales Call Center to receive responses. This matrix shows the criteria they identified as important for making each of their decisions.

18.4.2 Testing the Offer

As we mentioned earlier, it is often a good idea to test the offer on small samples from various customer segments. You need to pick just a few important variables, or the number of possible combinations becomes astronomical. Just test what past experience suggests might actually make a difference in response rates. You can test different combinations of offers, media, and segments, and track the response rates (percentage of number mailed) in a matrix like the one in Table 18-10.

Table 18-10 Test Offer

Segment	Media Response %		Offer Response %		Response Media Response %		Message Response %	
Lab	mail		discount		phone		cooling	
Lab	mail		discount		phone			
Lab	mail		no discount		phone		cooling	
Lab	mail		no discount		phone		air purity	

We all know that the standard response rate to direct mail offers is generally around three percent or lower. Sending out ten messages per test cell wouldn't be enough to deliver accurate results. XYZ decided not to use testing for Valencia because they couldn't afford to waste the fairly limited number of target customers on test offers. They decided that if they wanted to expand the offer to a broader audience, they would run some tests then.

18.4.3 Transmitting the Offer

For Valencia, this involved the logistics of printing and mailing. Decisions made about the packaging of the offer and even the postage rate chosen impact both the cost of the project and, even more important, how the customer perceives the offer, which in turn impacts the response rates. And all of these things affect ROI.

18.4.4 Receiving and Capturing Responses

CRM success is about measuring the response to a customer call to action. The organization needed preparation to be sure that it could do something with any responses it received. Again, we'll use the Valencia project as an example. XYZ decided to use a specific telephone extension with its standard inbound toll-free number. The first task was to make sure that the automated phone routing system was set up to know what to do when the customer selected this extension.

XYZ also needed to be sure that it had enough telesales reps to handle the anticipated volume. There is almost no worse experience that you can give a customer than a busy signal or a long wait on hold. The Valencia project was not anticipated to produce a large number of calls, so no special staffing was required.

The telesales reps had to be prepared to take calls. They needed education on the products and their advantages, alternative configurations, how each product satisfies different customer requirements, and also pricing and delivery. Even more important, the expectations of the telesales reps needed to be reset to understand the new behavior requirements. In this case, the new measures were meeting the customer's product information needs and closing a sale – not taking the most calls. Telesales needed to know that there would be a follow up survey to measure customer satisfaction with the way the call was handled.

Finally, the system needed to be capable of handling any project-specific information such as a project identifier (media codes, product extensions) and any other project-specific metrics. The Valencia metrics required that calls could be classified as orders or inquiries. Remember that it's wise to also have a miscellaneous or "other" category for the person who got the phone number from the offer but called to complain about a service problem. (Hey, at least the customer picked up the offer and looked at it!)

18.4.5 Fulfilling Requests

The last step was to fulfill requests. The XYZ Valencia team needed to be sure that there was sufficient production capacity to meet anticipated order demand, product literature or other types of product data for those who want more information before they decided, and the logistical system to satisfy the request in a reasonable amount of time.

Being prepared to meet customer requests in a reasonable amount of time is absolutely critical. Nothing hurts your credibility (and customer relationships) like disappointing a customer who has gone out of the way to contact you with a request. But sadly, recent surveys show that 65 percent of all inquiries are never answered at all, and that is NOT reasonable! You spent the money on the project, so why would you toss away the opportunity to contact a customer who was interested enough to respond in any way?

Wait a minute! I thought CRM was just about the customer-facing organizations. What's all this production capacity and logistics stuff? Well, CRM *is* about the front office, but we know that the customer experience is impacted by the full set of interactions with XYZ. A wise project team will realize that communicating with manufacturing early in the project and often is a really good idea.

18.5 "Doing" CRM On and Off the Web

The basic method is the same whether the offer is made (and responses accepted) on or off the web. The differences are in the capabilities of the different media and how they can be used most effectively. Patricia Seybold lists these eight critical success factors for electronic commerce in her widely read book, *customers.com* (1998):

1. Target the right customers
2. Own the customer's total experience
3. Streamline business processes that impact the customer
4. Provide a 360-degree view of the customer relationship
5. Let customers help themselves
6. Help customers do their jobs
7. Deliver personalized service
8. Foster community

Seybold developed her list based on extensive research she completed with the sixteen companies whose informative case studies are included in the book. Where does it say Internet or World Wide Web or dot.com? Customer Relationship Management, whether implemented on the Internet or not, is about managing relationships with customers. My favorite Seybold quote is, "It's the customer, stupid." And she's right, it is!

We're almost finished with one complete project cycle, but there's one last transition that we must take before beginning the next project. In Chapter 19, we will evaluate the results of this project.

Questions for Reflection

Certainly your company has a marketing history. Think about various marketing campaigns that you're familiar with or other CRM-related projects (such as your web site navigation).

1. How does your company create marketing offers? Are they based on product features or customer value?
2. How must a customer navigate through your web site? Is your site based on internal organizations and product lines or designed from the customer's perspective?
3. What might it take to shift the focus to the customer when designing an offer?

Evaluating Project Results

We've completed building a piece of the infrastructure and reviewed the effectiveness of the development phase. Then we delivered the offer to the targeted customers and measured those results. Now it's time to evaluate the impact of the overall project. This is the transition step to beginning the next project. This is when we evaluate not only the results of the last project, but gather and analyze the information we need to decide what, if any, strategy corrections need to be made for the next project cycle. As you can see in Figure 19-1, we are taking the final transition step before we're ready to start the cycle all over again.

It's important to keep in mind that in any real world CRM environment multiple CRM projects are likely to be underway simultaneously. Many of these "steps" are going on at once and, of course a single CRM project will be the basis for multiple and simultaneous offers. This can get complex very quickly which is another reason for following a standard process and tracking results.

In Chapter 18, we looked at offer performance measures, but now it's time to evaluate the results of the entire project cycle we've just completed. We will evaluate the project from the standpoint of company results and impact on the customer by using two sets of tools:

- Performance Metrics
- Value Metrics

Performance metrics measure the results of a particular campaign; it's a one-time snapshot. Value metrics measure and project results over a period of time for the investments made during a particular project cycle.

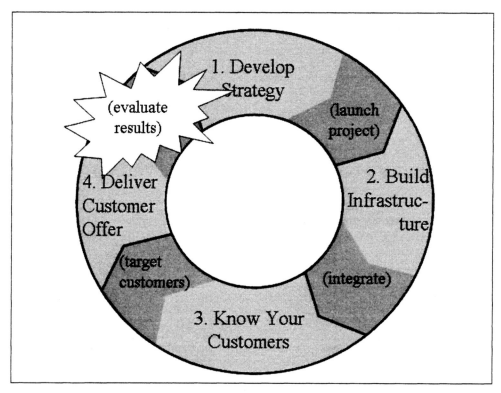

Figure 19-1 Evaluate Results

19.1 Evaluating Performance Metrics

In Chapter 18, we set some very specific and measurable goals for the project offer as shown in Table 19-1 (specific, measurable, and time bound).

Table 19-1   Valencia Offer Objectives and Measures

Objective: Increase Profit	Performance of	Metric
Sell 150 total units of either Series 825 or 827 systems to the targeted customers within four months	Orders	Toll-free number orders for 825 and 827 products
Reduce by 35% the number of 815 and 817 systems owned by targeted customers and under support contract.		Number of total 82x purchases by target customers
	Leads	Number of inquiries
	Overall	Number of calls

The project team wanted to know how many calls were received, how many inquiries were received (and later turned into qualified leads and finally sales), and how many customers did exactly what the offer asked them to do (buy via the toll-free telephone number). Maybe most importantly, XYZ measured all the orders for 82x products placed by targeted customers during the six-month project period. Of course, it can be valuable to look at new results periodically. The period should be based on the average buying-decision time for the product, but a good rule of thumb is to check twice more over a period equal to the original project period (e.g., for Valencia two more checks at three-month intervals is a good plan).

The purpose of performance metrics is to measure the impact of the specific campaign in two areas: the overall company performance, and customer satisfaction and loyalty.

19.1.1 Company Results

As we know, the end goal of CRM is to increase profit by either increasing revenue or reducing costs.

Increase Revenue

We counted the number of orders that were received during the project period, so now we can easily calculate the increased revenue, and by subtracting the cost of sales, we know the impact on profit. But this ignores the reality that many campaigns don't deliver immediate results. We also need to measure sales that might be gained through the influence of the project on future product purchases:

- Leads that were converted to buyers who purchased after the four-month project window
- Orders resulting from referrals and offer information that was passed along to customers not in the target segments
- Orders resulting from success with the original offer (test purchase)

And the influences go on, depending on your project situation. For example, there is the "top of mind" result from receiving a recent (and appealing) offer. In fact when surveyed, 65 percent of HP's customers complained that they didn't receive enough information! It is difficult to measure indirect influences, but there are ways to identify the *source* of the order that we discussed in Chapter 18.

Reduce Cost

For the Valencia project, there was a major cost savings that contributed to company profit. Product support contracts on the old 815 and 817 models were no longer moneymakers. Over time, the equipment had become prone to failure, and some of the replacement parts were not standard and needed to be special ordered, so they were very expensive.

Not all projects will have this particular cost savings feature, but there are other ways of reducing company costs. The Valencia call to action encouraged the use of the call center to place the order. On average, it took about two hours to identify the proper product configuration, prepare the quote, and enter the order. A very conservative rate for a sales rep (fully loaded) is $500 per hour. For a telesales rep, it's about $150 per hour. It is safe to subtract about $700 from the average cost of sales for orders taken by phone. Here are some other examples:

- A new system for configuration is easier and more efficient to use.
- The telesales team has an automated knowledge base, so configuration and quote generation takes less time.
- Targeting the *right* customers means fewer wasted offers.

Remember to look at all the cost saving opportunities that impact profit, not just the increase in revenue. Even though increased revenue is the true benefit to be derived from CRM, it can be difficult to show adequate short term profit results.

Return on Investment (ROI)—Reality or Myth

ROI is another performance metric that is often used to compare the cost of delivering a project to the financial results achieved. Financial return on investment is calculated by dividing the total cost of completing the project by the total cost savings and sales (minus the cost of sales). It's a very sound measure of the worth of the value of a project, and it has long been favored by Finance. But it's not completely clear that a CRM project can recover in the short term the cost of building the new infrastructure. Certainly, we can measure the ROI on the offer (cost to produce and deliver message divided by profit that resulted from the offer), but to justify all the computer and network costs, programmer salaries, and training and education of the project team and the new end users is another story. To fairly evaluate the whole CRM project cycle, we need to consider returns over a period of years. Of course, no one wants to wait five years to see whether an investment was worthwhile. Generally, we measure the results of the initial offer(s) and project what we'll expect to gain by using the same infrastructure to repeat the offer over a period of years. The time to recoup all the expense is called the payback period and depending on the company's financial situation, about three years is generally considered reasonable.

Arthur Hughes prefers Lifetime Value (LTV) measures to ROI for just this reason. Time framed measurement approaches like simple ROI have, according to Hughes, the problem that although

> ROI is clearly the way to measure the immediate result of any direct marketing effort...LTV [Lifetime Value] calculations include such factors as the retention rate, the referral rate, and the (long-term) spending rate, rather than just the response to an immediate promotion.

Calculating the payback period is much like LTV in that both look at the contribution over a number of years.

19.1.2 Customer Results (Loyalty and Satisfaction)

Another area, in our customer-centered organization, that is important to measure and understand is the impact on the customer relationship. At the very least, check a sample of customers for satisfaction and/or loyalty changes after every project. Remember, as long as you perform these tests on a fairly regular basis, the trend in what you find is more important than whether or not you have the perfect survey and perfect tools to product an absolutely reliable score. We know that satisfaction is a necessary but insufficient condition for customer loyalty, but it is a good place to start.

Satisfaction

Satisfaction can fairly easily be measured simply by asking your customers how they feel about the contact they just received from you. Of course, we don't want to have the *survey* cause dissatisfaction; too many interactions can be a bad thing. Satisfaction surveys should be used judiciously in the context of an overall plan for customer contact.

I recently bought a new car. As I was leaving the dealership, my salesman and his manager both told me that I would be receiving a survey regarding my satisfaction with the buying experience. Unless I could answer that I was satisfied with the experience, I was told, my salesman would be in trouble. Hmmm, I got the point—but did the auto company? What did they think they were measuring anyway? Did they know what was happening in the dealerships? If they did, were they serious about really understanding customer satisfaction or just serious about being able to publish high satisfaction scores? Unless I absolutely despised every moment of the car purchase (in which case I probably wouldn't have purchased anyway), I was going to indicate that I was at least very satisfied if not delighted with the experience. I didn't mind helping out the sales guy, because he seemed to need the support. But doesn't the auto company really want to know if their dealerships are satisfying customers? Frankly, the whole experience turned me off – but of course, I didn't tell them that! Now I just share the experience with clients as an example of what not to do.

There are so many better alternatives if you really want to know what your customers think. Why didn't the car company just send me the survey without any coaching? Better yet, they could have contracted for a telephone survey from an independent telemarketing company. If you want to avoid bothering too many customers, remember that you don't have to sample everyone. You can gain significant information from a small, random sample of customers

In all our relationship management efforts (from interaction to follow up to satisfaction surveys), we should always remember the meaning of the Hippocratic oath: **First, do no harm.** The oath not only makes good *moral* sense, it makes good *practical* sense too. Campaigns that damage customer relationships (for example, unsolicited e-mail, which is always perceived as spam) should be halted immediately and never, ever repeated. At least you've shown your customers that you listened to their concerns even if the original practice was unpopular. Remember that we discussed that fixing a customer problem can actually increase satisfaction. Never making any mistakes is about like never borrowing any money; it doesn't hurt your "credit" rating, but it doesn't do it any good either.

As we've discussed, satisfaction is most valuable when you also ask the customer how important each characteristic is. Don't spend time improving areas that customers don't care about. An example of such a two-pronged question is shown in Table 19-2.

Table 19-2 Satisfaction and Importance

What is your impression of your salesperson's knowledge of the product?
Poor 1 2 3 4 5 Extensive
How important is it that you have a knowledgeable salesperson when making a purchase?
Not Important 1 2 3 4 5 Very Important

Finally, satisfaction is more important as a customer relationship trend than as an absolute score. Compare current satisfaction scores to the results from previous surveys to identify the current experience as a relative measure, rather than an absolute one.

Loyalty

In many cases, loyalty is a blind emotion, but customer loyalty is based on the customer's value perception and is measured by behavior. Satisfaction is an indicator, but true loyalty is evidenced only over time. For some products (like refrigerators or, in my case, cars), the buying cycle is very long; it may be years before the dealer knows whether I will be a loyal, repeat buyer. One good measure, though, is where I get the car serviced, which also can impact overall loyalty. Loyalty must be measured over time, but satisfaction is often used as a loyalty indicator.

Share of Wallet

Market share measures the percent of purchases from your company compared to all purchases made in your market. In the customer relationship world, Peppers and Rogers popularized the concept of "share of wallet." Share of wallet represents the percentage of what a customer spends in total in your market compared to how much of that money comes to your company.

Share of wallet is another good indicator of loyalty. Of course, the calculation is made based on a budget estimate (size and type of company, income and address of consumers). Few customers will tell you how much they have to spend on computer technology or on dining out over the next year.

19.2 Understanding Value Metrics

Value is a two-way street. The customer value proposition is comprised of the advantages that our product has over other products. Customer Lifetime Value (LTV) is the concept of using a customer's purchase history to predict how much she will spend over the entire time she remains a customer.

The lifetime of a customer is an expected retention rate based on historical averages. Value represents all the revenue from a single customer over a period of years less the cost to acquire and serve that customer. Besides retention rate, other factors such as referral rates and spending rates are used. As discussed in Chapter 17, LTV is the expected profit from a customer over the number of years the customer remains a customer.

The formula can become very complicated, and there can be concerns about accurately capturing all the possible variables. For this reason, it's often recommended that you worry about trends in LTV rather than the absolute score. If you always calculate your LTV in the same way, then you can tell whether you're making progress (or losing ground), even if the precise LTV value isn't perfect.

Okay, we've finished a complete project and measured and learned from our results. The next step is to start all over again.

19.3 Reviewing and Tuning Your Strategy

We are ready to begin the next project cycle by taking everything we've learned during the project (about business priorities, customer expectations, and technology—all the elements of the original strategic plan) and testing that all our assumptions are the same as we get ready to launch the next project. As indicated in Figure 19-2, we will repeat the same process that we've done before, but hopefully we'll be a little better at it each time.

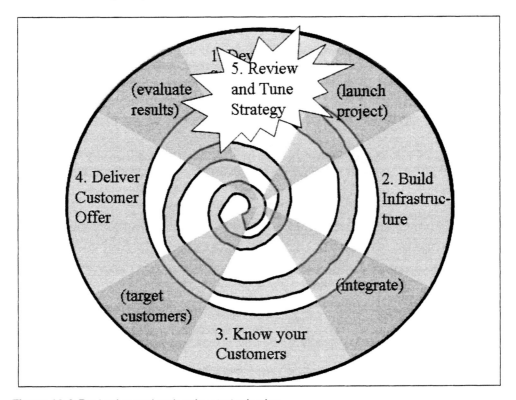

Figure 19-2 Reviewing and tuning the strategic plan

I want to make one more point: You don't *have* to wait until one project is completely finished before starting the next one, in fact that is rarely the case. You just need to be sure that use whatever you have learned from one to tune the next. Still, it's best to finish the first project completely.

We've finished one complete cycle and are starting the next. The process will remain the same except for any improvements we've identified and adopted. Now let's take a look at how we keep all this great new stuff humming along. Even more important, in Chapter 20 we'll look at another good way to improve project ROI business results: managing data quality.

Questions for Reflection

Think about how your company goes about making investment decisions. This will tell you how prepared you must be to justify the value of any project before you start and how to carefully measure results. With this understanding, you know how much work you'll have to do defining metrics and capturing information.

1. Does your company require a detailed cost justification for every project, or does it generally give out small budgets to test ideas?
2. Does anyone actually look at the financial results? Is anything different done if the results are good versus when they are bad?
3. Is the "fox guarding the chicken house," or is someone who is not part of the project team calculating (or at least reviewing) metrics calculated ?

PART 5

CRM: Keeping It Right

CHAPTER 20

Managing Quality Information As a Company Asset

F or information to be useful in building relationships and making good business decisions, it must be accurate. Otherwise, CRM just helps us make bad decisions faster. These bad decisions often have a very negative impact on our relationships with our customers; they make our company look inept, if not plain stupid. In Chapter 11, we learned that information is data in context and focused on creating the context for our CRM information needs. At the time, we defined the containers where we could store our information so we could get at it easily and use it effectively. Now we are going to take a look at another aspect of information that impacts its usability: the content of the database and its level of quality.

Why bother with information quality? A senior marketing manager I once worked with said, "It cost (hundreds of) thousands of dollars to build this database, and now you want me to keep paying to maintain quality? That's ridiculous! It's just names and addresses after all. How hard can that be?"

20.1 Understanding Information Quality—Why Bother?

However much you and everyone else may want to believe that information quality management doesn't really matter, the fact is that securing and protecting the quality of your customer information is as important as safeguarding any other company asset. Do you leave stacks of money lying around on top of desks? Hardly!

Let's start with why we bother to manage any asset. What is an asset anyway? Well, according to Webster's, assets are like resources; they represent "computable wealth" that is "applicable or subject to the payment of debts." (You may have guessed that I had a mother who always sent me to the dictionary whenever I had trouble with a word.) In other words,

DEFINITIONS

> An asset is anything a company owns that has significant value and can be sold to pay off debts.

Well, information doesn't really seem like an asset, does it? After all, you can't hold it in your hand like cash and raw material inventory.

20.1.1 Identifying Assets

Though it may seem strange at first, assets are not limited to tangible objects. Many balance sheets include a line for intangible assets like "brand value" and "goodwill." The two key words in the asset definition are ownership and value.

Ownership

Ownership means that no one else has the right to possess or use your stuff. Table 20-1 shows some tests we can apply to various potential assets to determine that they are assets.

Table 20-1 Ownership Tests

Ownership	Tangible		Intangible	
	Cash	**Raw Material**	**Identity**	**Information**
Legally acquired and owned	Borrowed, earned	Purchased, manufactured	Birth (certification, registration)	Purchased, collected, or calculated
Exclusive right to use	Misappropriation is called theft or embezzlement.	Misappropriation is called burglary.	Misappropriation is called identity theft.	Misappropriation is called hacking.

Currently, many consumers, legislators, and privacy advocates question whether a company really owns the data it collects about its customers. We will look at this again in Chapter 22 when we look in depth at the issue of customer privacy. For now, we will stick with the currently accepted practice that the company owns its customer database. (European companies or companies selling to European customers must be particularly aware of customer privacy because governments consider customer privacy to be an extremely important value. European customers have much more control over what can be done with their data.)

Value

So, at least for now, customer information does meet the ownership test, but what about determining its value? The value of intangible property is more difficult to calculate, but intrinsically it is obvious that there is value to intangibles like reputation and identity. There is even stronger evidence that customer data has value. You certainly have to pay money to the owner of a customer list in order to add those names to your campaign. With so many dotcoms failing, there have been many efforts to sell customer data as part of liquidating assets. Of course, we know there is ongoing debate about whether this is legal, but for now it appears that customer data does have a price tag. Table 20-2 lists some tests for determining the value of different types of assets.

Table 20-2 Value Tests

Value	Tangible		Intangible	
	Cash	Inventory	Identity	Information
Acquisition/ Replacement Cost	Whatever the going interest rate is	Purchase price	The time and cost to recreate an identity that has been stolen	Cost of acquiring customer data from vendors
Selling Price	Unless one of you is nuts, you can sell it for exactly its face value (collectors excepted, of course).	Something less than the original purchase price based on age, condition, etc.	Spies and crooks buy identities. I have no idea of the price. But just ask someone whose identity has been stolen how much it cost him.	Efforts to sell customer information are becoming more common.

As you can see, although it is more difficult to calculate a specific price tag for intangible assets, it is possible. And just any old value isn't enough. Merely having some value is not enough to classify something as an asset though; a significant value must be attached (i.e., meaningful in relieving debts). Lots of things have actual values, but those values aren't big enough to be worth protecting. Paper clips, for example, cost money to buy and would cost money to replace, but I know of no companies (other than paper clip manufacturers, of course) who include paper clips in their asset management inventories. But information doesn't fit into that category. It is valuable enough to be considered an asset; we just need to find a way to calculate that value.

Determining Information Value

If something can be sold, it must first be owned, and thus it has a value. Value is actually what someone is willing to pay for something—eBay is the perfect example of this phenomenon. There are a few bargains to be had, but many instances where competition and bidding go wild. But there are some ways to estimate a value for customer data even when most of us don't have any experience selling it. You can determine the value of your customer data based on the factors shown in Table 20-3.

Table 20-3 The Value of Information

Test	Factors
Cost to acquire or replace	• Purchase price of data or software • Cost of campaigns to generate information • Cost of building infrastructure (all four components)
Selling price	• Benchmarking against list brokers • Benchmarking against purchase price of customer data sold as part of liquidation (plus cost to confirm permission)
Cost if not available or of poor quality	• Wasted marketing dollars (offer preparation and transmission expenses) yielding poor response rates • Bad decisions and negative customer impact

Frankly, computing the value of customer information is not all that different from computing the value of your raw material inventory. It hasn't been done only because companies are just not familiar with thinking about data this way.

Because we can compute a value for our customer data and we do *own* it, we should treat it just as we do any other asset. Like raw materials, we store information in facilities (computer files and databases) where it is protected, secured, and easily accessible to the business processes that need it. We store raw material in protected warehouses because parts and materials cost money to buy and replace. Inventory can get lost, broken, rusty, or made unusable in any number of ways. Worse, similar parts can be mislabeled and then misused in manufacturing. This can cause damage to expensive manufacturing equipment or worse, defective products with disastrous results. We manage and protect raw material inventory because it makes good business sense. The downside risk has the potential of being much more expensive than the cost of the maintenance. The same is true for customer information. This is not so much an issue of managing the return on an asset management investment, as it is an investment to reduce risk. No company can afford to squander its assets, and many companies are now learning that intangible assets are just as important to protect as tangible ones.

20.1.2 Getting Unbeatable Competitive Advantage

Why would anyone be willing to pay money for your customer information? Only your company has the unique customer relationship information that you have been able to accumulate over the years. This information gives you knowledge of customers' behaviors, preferences, and dislikes that no one but you are aware of. It's almost like having (sometimes it even *is* having) your customer's direct, unlisted phone number. Only you can develop and deliver an offer based on this special knowledge, and that should be a tremendous advantage.

But Only If It's Correct

The trouble is that bad data leads to bad decisions that waste money and irritate customers. Lawrence Hefler, Vice President of E-business and Strategic Alliances for Hilton Grand Vacations Co., was quoted in *B to B Magazine* as saying that quality data is the foundation of CRM, and "only quality data will lead you to the right customer." Data quality problems often cause all of these issues and probably more:

- Your offer won't reach the customer (because of a wrong/undeliverable address).
- Your offer reaches the wrong customer (because you no longer have the right contact: job change, lost interest).
- Your offer is irrelevant and annoying, not anything the customer is interested in.
- Your offer actually conflicts with some other message the customer is hearing from your sales team or sales partners.
- Your offer medium conflicts with a specific request from the customer (no e-mail, no phone calls); we ask, then we don't care.

Each of these examples has a negative impact on the customer's perception of and relationship with your company.

20.1.3 Implications of Being a Valuable Asset

Now that we've decided that information is a valuable asset, what are the implications? The bottom line is that companies have a vested interest in taking care of assets. If we don't protect our assets, they lose their value. We are just throwing good money away. Invariably I tell clients right up front that if they're not interested in paying to maintain the quality of the data they capture, they shouldn't invest one cent in collecting it.

KEY IDEA

Never invest a single dollar to build a customer information database that you are not willing to spend money to maintain.

I guarantee that unless you plan to invest in the care of your information assets for as long as you use it, you will have wasted every penny you spent. This is the first law of Customer Information Management.

We're all convinced now, right? We will invest in the maintenance of our information asset. But who should actually be responsible for the care of our information assets? Well, who takes care of raw material inventory? Do we just leave it up to manufacturing, or to the finance department? No, they have different responsibilities. Manufacturing should focus on making the best possible products as efficiently as possible, not checking up on spare parts. Finance is concerned with tracking the total value of the asset, but they have no experience in caring for it.

Do we give it to the facilities department? After all, they're responsible for the physical storage facilities. Of course not, that's ridiculous. The fact is most companies have a materials management organization responsible for stocking, protecting, and securing the companies' raw material assets. This organization is usually aligned with or part of the manufacturing function because that is where the pain will be felt if problems arise with material quality. In exactly the same way, many companies have established organizations responsible for managing the customer information assets.

20.1.4 Types of Data

As we discussed in Chapter 13, data comes in four basic flavors: reference data, transaction data, warehouse data, and business view data. These four types of data are represented in Figure 20-1.

The operational data on the left of Figure 20-1 changes to reflect current reality. Reference and master data represent a list of things of the same type, such as the list of products on your product master file. Transaction data represents repeating occurrences of the same type of event, such as an order file.

Decision support data on the right side of this figure must remain stable. Warehouses are where data that was captured elsewhere is stored for analysis purposes. Business views are subsets and summaries of data in the data warehouse aimed at answering a particular business question.

Reference and Master Data

Generally, master data is not terribly volatile, but it does need to be kept up to date to reflect the most up-to-date information we have. Master data contains one record for each individual product (or industry or country) for which there are unique characteristics that are known in advance. All or most decisions about what the product is, how it's made, what it should sell for, etc., are made long before the product is added to the product master file. A very straightforward example of a master file is the International Standards Organization country code List (ISO 3166-1) that we will discuss later.

Reference data differs from master data in that it does not need to be set up in advance before a valid entry can be created. Reference data reflects reality, while master data creates

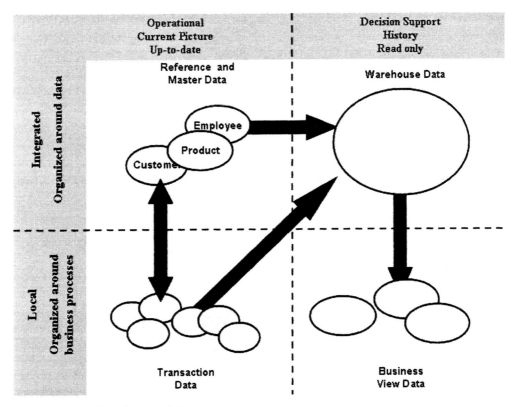

Figure 20-1 The four flavors of data

reality. For example, most companies cannot take an order for a product that hasn't been set up in the product file, but they can take orders from customers who are first-time buyers. The reference record can be created at the same time the order is being taken. Once created, reference files prevent duplicate information from being entered for the same customer. Customer information is stored in a reference file. Reference data tends to be more volatile than master data. For example, a recent study by the Sales and Marketing Institute shows that more than 70 percent of business people change at least one element on their business cards each year. The information on a business card is, of course, reference data.

Transaction Data

Transaction data is extremely volatile and time sensitive as well. Transaction data should be changed to reflect reality. As an example, every single order (hundreds or thousands per day) creates a new transaction record (usually a set of records) in the order file. If the customer changes his mind on the quantity or product before it has been shipped, we need to change the record to reflect the new quantity so the customer receives what he wants. But it's also important to know what the original quantity was. Quantity changes can affect other transactions down the line, such as sales rep quota. If a sales rep is concerned that his quota doesn't match what he thinks it should be, the original and current purchase quantities can explain the discrepancy. The data warehouse is where this issue is resolved.

When an order has been completely shipped and is no longer active, transactions are usually removed from the open order database (for system performance, if for no other reasons) and archived in a data warehouse, file cabinet, or other offline storage.

Transaction systems are notorious for collecting low-quality data because total accuracy isn't necessary to complete the transaction successfully. Transaction system performance measures are based on factors other than quality, so little attention is paid to quality of data collection. Unfortunately, it is much more costly to correct bad data than to capture it correctly in the first place, but that issue is seldom being tackled. Today, most organizations focus initial efforts on ensuring that transaction data is clean as it moves into the data warehouse (incoming inspection). Redesigning the standards and process for data capture within each source system may be addressed later, but only as justified.

Warehouse Data

Data warehouses are built from the information captured in transaction systems and reference or master files. After data warehouse records have been loaded, they should not be changed even if the source transaction changes. Rather than update the first warehouse record we create a new record that reflects whatever change occurred.

The data warehouse tracks all transactions and changes over time so that companies can analyze history patterns and trends. We know one of the best predictors of the future is what's happened in the past, so the past must not change! I learned a very hard lesson during my tenure as a database marketing manager at HP. One year, the manufacturing responsibility for a large number of products switched from one product line to another. Because it was a very tiny change to the data warehouse, we just went through and updated the product line for all the affected products. The trouble was the next time we went to pull a mailing list for one of our newsletters, the subscription list size dropped by two thirds! That's right; we had inherited a list pulling process that depended on the product line of a group of products, not the products themselves. After the warehouse was updated, we no longer knew which product line the products used to be in. It took lots of time and effort to recover the earlier information so that we could pull the right list. The launch of the newsletter was seriously delayed.

This is why, even when transaction or master data changes, we never directly update warehouse data, but create a new record reflecting the current state instead. If we had tracked the start and end dates for the assignment of a product to a certain product line, we could have easily recovered from our newsletter subscription disaster. Data warehouse development considerations are covered in detail in Bill Inmon's work on the subject (*Building the Data Warehouse*, 1992) which is still one of the most widely read books on this topic.

Because transaction data is of notoriously poor quality AND we don't want to update data after it's in the warehouse, we usually manage and clean transaction data before it gets into the warehouse. In a recent white paper, Larry English (a well-known expert in information quality management) said that one of ten mistakes to avoid when building a quality warehouse is "Assuming the source data is 'OK' because the operational [transaction] system seems to work just fine." The data warehouse has a different purpose and different quality requirements.

Business View Data

Business view data is generated from the data warehouse. Business views are calculations or summaries of historical information that often compare trends over time. Business views focus on a particular business area, such as answering a business question like "How many customers in North America increased purchases by more than 10 percent per year for the past three years?" Reporting and analysis tools run much more efficiently against a consolidated business view than they do against the entire data warehouse. Business view data is never updated; the views are just recreated from the data warehouse periodically.

In Figure 20-2, you can see that our data scrubbing efforts are focused on the operational data on the left side of the picture. This is where data is captured and managed.

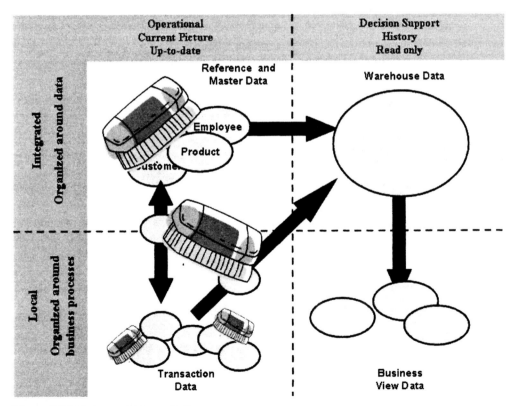

Figure 20-2 Data scrubbing activities

We will develop and apply our data management plans to these two areas. As you have undoubtedly understood, El Cid is a customer reference file that needs to be constantly managed for quality. This is where we will focus our attention, because the basic maintenance processes are the same no matter where they are applied.

20.2 Identifying Data Quality Issues

We understand why we have to manage the quality of raw material inventory, but why is data quality a problem? Just like manufacturing material, data can be bad when it comes from the source; it can become damaged during handling (shipping and stocking), damaged while in storage, or misused in the manufacturing process (wrong part). Here are the most common sources of data quality problems:

1. Customer data deterioration (customers move and change jobs)
2. Source data quality (database design, lack of standards)
3. Lack of trust (sales rep resistance and customer resistance)

The last of these is specific to the information asset; few vendors will purposely send you the wrong parts because they don't trust you to treat their products with care. Sadly, many customers do have little trust in what companies do with their data. Sadder still, many companies deserve this mistrust, and we all end up tarnished by the same brush.

Now let's look at how each of these factors impacts data quality so we can be ready to do something about it.

20.2.1 Customer Data Deterioration

The *minute* you start to put information into any customer database, the quality starts to deteriorate. Some seven to ten percent of consumers and businesses physically relocate every year, and their old contact information becomes useless. Add to that the large number of business people who change jobs (even if the business itself doesn't move), and the rate of deterioration for B2B names can be more like 30 to 35 percent a year (or more than 70 percent if we add in all the business card changes). This means that in less than two years more than 50 percent of your B2B database names will be incorrect if you do not invest in data maintenance.

20.2.2 Source Data Quality

Transaction data sources have highly variable levels of quality—and it's often poor. No one who is responsible for the source transaction data was ever measured on the quality of that data. For example, as long as there was enough good order information to get the product shipped and the bill successfully mailed, that was all that mattered. No one cared if there were three or four (or twenty) different addresses for the same customer—at least not until businesses began to want to understand their customers and who they were. It was much more important to get the order entered than to have it accurate.

Quality concerns have increased because companies now recognize the gold mine of customer knowledge they capture in all these transaction systems. They want to consolidate all the data to achieve the highly sought-after *360° view* of the customer for analysis and planning purposes. But because of nonexistent standards and a database designed to support operational activities, much of the data can't be simply fit together. The shipping address on an order is used to print the mailing label; that's four or five lines of information that gets the product delivered. The first line may hold the customer's name, or it may hold an "attention" line or special shipping instructions to the carrier. The transaction system worked fine anyway, but your customer reference file or data warehouse would be full of garbage because the source was not consistent. Translators cost money to build (or buy), but they do work. That is, they work except when the source data isn't what the translator was designed to expect.

Lack of Standards and Edits

An eloquent example of what can happen when there are no standards governing data entry and no edits applied when data is being captured in the source system is provided by the situation that XYZ encountered with one of its customers.

XYZ had a sales rep on the East Coast of the United States who was responsible for the General Dynamics account. One month the rep got very upset because a huge sale didn't show up in his monthly quota. *Many* hours of investigation revealed that this large order was booked to a customer named GD/EBD that the computer didn't recognize as a General Dynamics order. How did the order get entered that way? Simple, for expedience the sales rep always referred to this particular account (Electric Boat Division of General Dynamics Corp.) as GD/EBD – wouldn't you? Of course he counted on the order administrator who handled his orders to recognize and correctly enter General Dynamics on the order. But that week the experienced administrator was out sick. Because it was month end, the order entry couldn't wait. The temporary worker filling in had no idea that "GD/EBD" was shorthand for General Dynamics. So the order was never credited to the GD sales rep. Imagine the outrage if this incident had impacted the customer's volume discount contract!

The same principle needs to apply to the reference file. For the most part, data that does not pass the edit screen should be rejected and returned to the source system for review and correction before it is accepted into the reference file. The cleaner you can keep the data in the reference file, the more credibility it will have and the more the company can be converted to using it for making better customer decisions.

Use *external* data standards whenever possible. There are standards for the domain of certain fields (such as Standard Industrial Code, SIC) and for the format of certain transaction fields (like the Electronic Data Interchange, or EDI, standards that allow standard transactions, such as purchase orders, to be exchanged electronically between companies). External standards are available from a variety of different sources, such as:

- Governments (e.g., SIC, NAICS, NACE (Europe))

- International standards organizations (e.g., ISO)
- Technical groups and consortia (e.g., XML/XNAL)
- Business interaction standards (e.g., EDI)

It's advantageous to use external standards for a couple of reasons. First, it's easier to adopt something that someone else has already created rather than doing all the analysis yourself. Some of these standards change rapidly (e.g., country codes, since countries are pretty volatile) and keeping up to date is probably not a core competence of your organization. Second, using external standards allows you to compare internal statistics to external statistics, such as matching company sales by industry to total national industry sales to estimate market share.

If not available, build your own *internal* standards. For example, XYZ developed its own standard for identifying product applications (uses). Before the company defined its standard, there was virtually no consistency in how any product application data was collected, and it was useless for most analysis and decision-making purposes.

Poor Database Design

As we've discussed, most databases were designed to optimize one particular operation. It never occurred to anyone that the data might have any other use. It was expensive and took a long time to build new systems, and changing them was even harder. When business needs changed, people got into the habit of using rarely used fields (or freeform "comments" fields) to store new facts.

As we saw in XYZ's OMCENTRAL system, an "M" in the product option field indicated a marketing discount that affected the product price. This type of abuse leads to nothing but trouble as possible interpretations of the content multiply over time. Who can remember all the rules? The *context* is lost. All databases should be built and used in a way that ensures that each data element means only thing and stores only that one kind of data.

 KEY IDEA

Remember this rule: One field, one fact.

This is the second law of Customer Information Management. The older the system, the more misappropriations you'll find. Sometimes, there is absolutely no knowledge anywhere in the organization as to what the content of certain a field means. It was a total waste of effort to collect this information in the first place.

20.2.3 Trust

We've talked about how important it is to develop strong relationships so that customers trust us enough to share their information with us. There's another situation where trust can impact the quality of our database.

Sales Rep Willingness to Share (The Politics of Data)

The politics of data arises from the fact that information really is power, and like political power, most people don't willingly share it. Many employees have special relationships with certain customers that make them uniquely able to serve (sell to and support) that customer well. In particular, sales reps know that their income is based on their ability to build relationships and influence customers to purchase. Where is the possible benefit for a sales rep (or anyone else with special knowledge of the customer) to share the information they have? Believe me when I tell you that sales reps don't see a single one. They believe that giving away customer data is like giving away their bread and butter.

The problem is that one of the most complete sources of information about customers is the sales rep or anyone else in the company who frequently interacts directly with the customer. The broadly held notion that no one else will have any information about a sales rep's customers unless he or she gives it away is a pure fantasy.

KEY IDEA

Customers contact the company through different means, and many of these interactions are automatically captured in electronic form.

Like the ostrich in Figure 20-3, the only thing the sales rep can ensure by locking all his data away in a file cabinet is that he doesn't know that anyone else already has information about these customers. Campaigns may already be planned that will compete with the sales rep's communications, but no one has any way of knowing it.

Okay, you know I'm right, but have I convinced sales reps of this obvious fact – frankly, not very often. Historically, most companies have done a poor job of integrating and making available all the customer information it actually possesses. Why would a sales rep ever be concerned that her customers were at risk unless she submitted the names herself? How do we get sales reps to participate in our overall CRM program?

One quick fix to this problem is to require that sales reps (support engineers, etc.) participate. As an incentive, these "requests" are usually connected to a specific campaign, and reps are required to submit a specific number or percentage of their customer names. But guess which ones they send in? Yep, you'll get those names that have been in the old account book for a couple of years but never responded to a single call. I have seen this approach work only when the incentive is something that the sales rep's *customers* are asking for.

Figure 20-3 Do you recognize anyone?

No, the real answer is that although we can rebuild trust, but it will take time and results that demonstrate benefit to the sales rep! It is a rare CRM project that starts with field data and is ever successful. Successful CRM programs start building the customer reference file (and data warehouse) with information they *can* get without pulling teeth (marketing sources and central transaction systems for orders, customer service, etc.). After collecting and cleaning a meaningful amount of customer information then go out to the field with some results. After reps see that most of their customers are already in the database, or better yet, that you know more about their customers than they do, they will finally get it.

Customer Trust (Or Lack Thereof)

It's been suggested that Mickey Mouse (among others) is one of the most frequently entered customer names in many online databases. Given the unlikely situation that this has actually become a name that parents commonly give their children, we're faced with a problem: a bunch of bad data and no way to fix it. This situation occurs when you require (or even request) information that you don't really need or the customer doesn't understand why you need it. This practice makes people suspicious!

Asking for just what you need to complete the transaction starts to build the relationship with a sense of trust. As the relationship continues and you have more opportunities to interact, you can ask for more information about the customer. As customers start to see value in trusting you with their data, they'll be willing to reveal more. If the customer feels overwhelmed or invaded by your lengthy registration forms, they are turned off and will give you only what they think you should need.

20.3 Planning Information Quality

Managing the quality of our customer data asset, like managing raw material, requires good planning and elbow grease. Like all our efforts so far, we will depend on having a methodology, including an action plan, for our data quality efforts. We will examine five steps in the data quality methodology:

- Detail the characteristics of the future quality state (target).
- Detail the characteristics of the current quality state (baseline).
- Identify the differences between them.
- Design the data quality action plan with responsibilities and dates.
- Execute the action plan.

Sound a little familiar? Indeed, we used these same basic steps to manage the integration for each CRM component. That was a transition to a new way of managing customer relationships and in the same way, the same method can be used to transition to higher levels of data quality.

There are different approaches that we can take to ensure that *appropriate* data quality can be achieved. Ad hoc quality programs are usually linked to a specific project. Scheduled maintenance, not surprisingly, occurs on an ongoing basis. All the same tools and processes are used no matter the approach, and almost all companies must use both.

20.3.1 Detail the Future Quality State (Goal)

We know that data maintenance costs money and that all customers are not the same. It makes sense to spend more money and have higher quality goals for the most valuable customers than for the least valuable. You may want the accuracy of the best customers to be 95 percent or higher. You may not be able to afford to keep the lowest value customers any more accurate than about 60 or 70 percent, maybe even less. Of course, if the data quality gets too low and you really have no idea who your customers are, you are not doing relationship marketing. This is mass mailing, which may be appropriate, but it's not CRM!

XYZ identified three global customer segments: named, small-medium business, and consumer. These were chosen because XYZ believed that they should be treated as separate groups and different from each other based on actual or potential value. Most companies have different quality goals for each segment because the impact of making a mistake is much greater for the higher value segments. XYZ developed different data quality goals and different maintenance tasks for each of the segments. Of course, the Valencia project targeted a specific customer segment (the top 50 customers), and XYZ planned to invest quality maintenance resources only in that group of customers.

20.3.2 Detail the Current Quality State (Baseline)

As for all other measures, the trends in data quality are usually more important than absolute scores. You can measure the change in data quality only if you know the baseline quality for each segment. Quality can be measured using data quality assessment tools and analysis software. After you know the changes in quality levels, you can compare these to changes in campaign success.

20.3.3 Identify the Differences (What Needs to Change)

As usual, we want to focus on where we can make the biggest improvement, so we start by identifying the biggest gaps. But there is more to it. Just as we can't afford to treat all customers the same, not all data has the same importance or value. Some data is readily available and some isn't. The absence of some data makes a record worthless: What is a customer record worth if it has no customer name or no way to contact the customer. Some data is very important but not essential, and other data is just nice to know or is planned for future use but is not necessary today. Remember, we get through this by taking small steps and doing only what's necessary for now.

Using some of the Valencia data as an example, XYZ segmented the list of attributes into three tiers. The results of the decision process are shown in Table 20-4.

Table 20-4   Valencia Data Value Tiers

Attribute	Tier	Attribute	Tier
person prefix title	2	company name	2
person last name	1	total employees	3
person first name	1	Revenue	3
person business title	3	Street	1
person gender	3	City	1
ok to contact?	1	State	1
product model	2	postal code	1
serial number	2		

Tier 1 data was required, tier 2 data was important but not mandatory, and tier 3 data was nice to have. But this wasn't the end. Some of this data has more (or less) importance for the different customer segments, so XYZ matched the data tiers to each of the segments and made changes where appropriate. This step was taken because XYZ will create a different data quality action plan for maintaining the appropriate quality level for each segment.

The Valencia project targeted a specific group of customers and had specific data quality needs. The target segment (top 50) was a subset of XYZ's named customers, but there was an additional critical requirement. For Valencia to be successful in reaching the right customers, it required very high quality (accurate, complete) data linking people to the correct company.

It was reasonable for XYZ to use the named account tier assignments as a starting point for Valencia. Then XYZ addressed the additional need for very accurate company linkages by making "company name" a required field. In Table 20-5, you can see the results of XYZ's data goals for Valencia and for El Cid overall.

Table 20-5 XYZ's Data Management Goals

	Valencia	XYZ's Global Customer Segment		
		Named	**Small/Medium Business**	**Consumer**
1. Required	person last name	person last name	person last name	person last name
	person first name	person first name	person first name	person first name
	street	street	street	street
	city	city	city	city
	state	state	state	state
	postal code	postal code	postal code	postal code
	company name			
2. Important	person prefix title	person prefix title	person prefix title	person prefix title
	product model	product model	product model	product model
	serial number	serial number	serial number	serial number
		company name	company name	
3. Nice to Have	person business title	person business title	person business title	person business title
	person gender	person gender	person gender	person gender
	total employees	total employees	total employees	
	revenue	revenue	revenue	

The next step is to match the target quality goals for each tier and each segment. We do the same thing at the project level. For example, for Valencia's top 50 customers, the goal was to reduce the number of unlinked customers and sites to zero.

20.3.4 Design the Data Quality Action Plan

You may have noticed that there are slight differences in the approach we take to project quality management versus overall project management. There is a baseline (by segment) below which we should never allow quality to sink. We'll design a regular quality maintenance plan that will be run on a scheduled basis as long as the customer file is in use. In addition, specific projects often have special quality requirements. Ad hoc maintenance is usually related to a specific project and focuses on just the customers targeted for the project. Fortunately, all database hygiene efforts are cumulative and improve the overall database quality. For any type of plan, we will include a before (and after) snapshot of the database quality, identify which tools are to be used, assign responsibility, and determine what results are expected and when.

Whether the maintenance effort is ad hoc or scheduled, the action plan has the same basic elements as shown in Table 20-6.

Table 20-6 Data Quality Action Plan

Project or Segment Name: Valencia		Project Manager:		
	Data Elements	**Baseline**	**Goal**	**Focus**
Tier 1/Required	person last name	99%	100%	
	person first name	95%	100%	
	street	80%	100%	X
	city		100%	X
	state		100%	X
	country		100%	X
	postal code		100%	X
	company name		100%	X
Tier 2/Important	person prefix title	85%	95%	
	product model	80%	95%	X
	serial number	80%	95%	
Tier 3/Nice	person business title person gender total employees revenue	60%	80%	

Table 20-6 Data Quality Action Plan (Continued)

Action Steps			
Data	**Plan**	**Tools**	**Notes/Issues**
street city state country postal code	Standardize address elements	Address Standardization Software	Treat all address elements as one
	Audit against third party company list	Leased data	
company name	Use third party company organization data to identify links Develop alias file	Leased data	
product model	Identify all invalid product models, phone customer to verify product	Manual update	
Key Resources			
Role	**Assigned Individual**	**Percentage of Time Assigned**	**Duration**
Data Analyst			
Data Administrator			
Project Tradeoff Matrix			
	Deliverables	**Schedule**	**Resources**
Constrain (least flexible)		X	
Optimize			X
Accept (most flexible)	X		

For a quality project, the tradeoff matrix is part of the data quality action plan (but not for scheduled maintenance). Note that the data quality matrix may not have the same priority tradeoffs as the major project. For Valencia's quality efforts, meeting the schedule was the most critical requirement so that the overall project would not be delayed.

20.3.5 Execute the Action Plan

Now that we've designed the plan, we are ready to put it into practice, and then to measure results and track progress. We will take advantage of the appropriate combination of the following tools to execute the plan.

20.4 Getting Information Quality

Information quality requires measuring the quality of the information stored in company databases, identifying quality issues, and having processes in place to fix them.

20.4.1 Building In Quality

The best way to achieve high-quality customer information is to capture it correctly in the first place. However, those responsible for data capture often are managed by siloed organizations with no data quality performance measures. This can be changed over time, but it's seldom an effective place to start. Start showing the value of the data, illuminate the cost of hygiene and the poorest quality sources, and go after these.

Usually, companies only become concerned with quality of data when it flows into a reference file or a consolidated data warehouse.

20.4.2 Managing Quality for the Life of the Data

We know that there are many factors that impact the accuracy and completeness of our customer information. We use some tools proactively to prevent and/or fix reoccurring problems. We can also use many of the same tools to repair unexpected problems that occur.

Proactive (Preventive) Maintenance

There are several standard data hygiene activities that all companies should use as a matter of course, such as processing return mail. It costs just a little more to have the undelivered post returned to you, and you can save much more than that by not mailing to the same address again and again.

Scheduled database audits that test for quality levels by segment and data tier are also very helpful. Some scheduled data quality efforts are costly and time consuming, so we want to do them only when they are needed. Sometimes, the results of one of these audits will drive the launch of an ad hoc data quality action plan to address the specific issues that were identified. Of course, we can also use any of the ad hoc maintenance plans we've created as part of scheduled maintenance if they turn out to be useful.

Some, but not all, of these data hygiene activities can be done by computer using special hardware and software. Examples are the several software products that are available for address standardization and matching. Also, many data services firms have proprietary processes that accomplish the same thing and that can insert additional information into each of the company's customer records. Of course, some of the work may be done directly on the database itself. But don't give everyone access to directly update your customer reference file, only qualified and trained data administrators should be given this responsibility.

Ad Hoc Maintenance

Ad hoc maintenance is used to meet the criteria of a specific project effort or when a data quality problem is discovered unexpectedly. If the problem appears to recur, these ad hoc cleaning projects should be made part of regularly scheduled maintenance.

20.5 Using Tools to Manage Data

We've already mentioned several of the external sources for improving data quality, but there are many more ways of verifying and validating the customer information we have captured in our files.

20.5.1 Measuring Data Quality

The basic method of measuring data quality for both the baseline and final result involves selecting a random sample of target customers from the target database and examining each of the elements (or sets of elements) as to whether it passes the criteria shown in Table 20-7.

Table 20-7 Information Quality Elements

Component	Definition	How to Measure
Completeness	Non-blank	Can also apply to groups of attributes (e.g., the postal code must match the city plus state)
Accuracy	Represents reality	
Consistency	Logical coherence between sets of data	If gender is "Female," then prefix title should not be "Mr."
Validity	Conformance to accepted standard	A member of a specified list of values

Each selected field of every sample record will receive a pass/fail for each of the four elements. A field passes if all four elements are correct. Next, calculate the percentage of correct records for each of the fields and for the overall sample.

20.5.2 Sources of Standardized Data

The best source of data against which you can audit your database is from a third party that specializes in just this type of information. You could never do as good a job as can an organization that is completely focused on the data. Choosing an external source allows you to focus your internal knowledge and expertise to develop the quality tools that aren't available on the marketplace. Here are some examples of some of the services for data hygiene that are available for purchase.

Undeliverable Contacts

Whenever you learn that an address or phone number you have on file is not reaching that customer, get rid of it. These undeliverable records, known as "nixies" in database marketing, only diminish the perceived value of your database. I don't mean physically delete the record, but flag it as undeliverable. Why in the world would you want to keep calling the same wrong number? You not only have to pay for the call, you also have to pay the telemarketers for making the call. Would you ever want to do that more than once? Of course, the same is true of the postal service; you're paying for the contents of the envelope and the postage.

Why flag the record as deleted instead of just deleting it? Every time you integrate a new data source (or rent an external list) you are likely to find customers that you already know about, and some of them will have undeliverable addresses. Keeping track of these bad records prevents you from reinserting the name in your database as active or wasting more mail on an address you already know is bad. And of course, if you keep the customer and her information on file, if you ever do get an updated address, you won't have lost all her history.

E-mail almost seems free, so why bother to correct e-mail addresses? Some day you may really need to send this customer an e-mail (for a recall or other legal purpose). Use the information about bad e-mail addresses to run period e-mail verification campaigns—at least for those customers who are really important to you. It is insane to throw undelivered mail in the trash; use it to improve the quality of your database.

Postal Service Address Change Files

The postal services of some countries store information about people (usually consumers) who have moved from one residence to another. Periodically schedule a checkup of your database for people who have moved.

Customer Mailroom Changes

The alternative for the B2B world to post office change files is changes that come from the company's mailroom. Frankly, most mail clerks would prefer not to have to process and sort mail for employees who have left the company. Build a relationship with the folks in the mail distribution room. (It's called MRRM. Oh, I'm only kidding!) In more cases than not, they will be glad to periodically review your mailing list for their company and let you know about address changes and terminations so they don't have to sort through undeliverable mail.

Global Changes

Global information changes reflect changes in the marketplace. When the USSR broke up, millions of customer records worldwide had to be changed to reflect all the new countries. In the United States at least, the proliferation of cell phones and other telephone devices has caused tremendous upheaval in telephone area code assignments. Sometimes, this information can be purchased; sometimes, you may have to enter the changes by hand.

Quality Assessment Tools

Some tools on the market capture quality statistics and allow statistical and trend analysis. An example of this type of tool is Quality Manager from Ascential Software, which was used by XYZ's data quality team for the Valencia project.

Consultants and Service Providers

There are a large number of service providers capable of applying the data hygiene tools and processes as mentioned earlier. Many of these service providers also provide compiled data and list enhancement services (e.g., appending county data or SIC codes). Other experts bring their years of experience working to improve data quality for business clients to help organizations set up their own programs. Here is another appropriate use for consulting – to provide experience and direction in a specific area of your overall CRM program.

20.5.3 Asking an Expert

Honestly, who knows more about the customer than the customer himself? And it is amazing the results that be achieved by just asking customers to review what you have. Of course, you wouldn't want to show them too much suspect data, so use this approach sparingly for your most critical information.

With a Mailer

I have seen astounding response rates to programs that sent a personalized printout of known customer data to that customer, asking for correction and return of the form. One such campaign is illustrated in Figure 20-4.

This project was focused primarily on data quality and got an astounding response rate of more than 17 percent! Not as effective as a telemarketing campaign, but much cheaper to run. Customers even wrote little notes saying they appreciated being asked. You can use such a campaign for more than just data quality, but also to gather/verify contact permission and for improving relationships.

On the Web: Let the Customer Do It for You

The Internet throws one very big monkey wrench into our data integration goal: It allows customers to see the data we've collected about them. Our historical data collection processes (which still make up 80 percent or more of most companies' customer knowledge) were generally pretty casual about accuracy. Getting data shoved into the system was more important than getting it in correctly. (After all, program response rates were measured on number of responses, not quality or usability of information.) Remember, you ALWAYS get what you measure. Sales reps were reimbursed based on the orders they booked, not on data accuracy. It just had to be

Verify and authorize your customer biography.

Allan XXXXXXXX
XXXXXX Corporation
16 XXXXXXX Street
XXXXXX, NJ 07999
Phone: (201) 555-9999

__Yes, keep me on your subscription mailing list

__No, please remove my name from your subscription list

1 **Allan, please indicate your occupation and then go to question 2.**

1 __ Engineer	11 __ Engineering Technician	4 __ Medical field
21 __ Scientist	5 __ Business/Admin	71 __ Educator
31 __ Programmer	54 __ Purchasing Agent	__ Other
33 __ IT equipment operator	56 __ Marketer	_____

2 **If your department is information technology, please go to question 3. If not, check the most appropriate choice below.**

35 __ Engineering	62 __ Computer Operations	21 __ General Management
31 __ Manufacturing	63 __ Telecom/Networks	22 __ Accounting/Finance
32 __ Research & Development	26 __ Purchasing	4 __ Sales/Marketing/Support
61 __ Software development/ support	53 __ Education/Training	__ Other_____

Figure 20-4 Example of a data quality mailer

good enough to get the product delivered and the invoice submitted and paid – who cares about the overall customer picture?

20.6 Owning Data Versus Responsibility for Data

Always ask yourself these questions: Who cares about the result? Who is measured on the result? Whose career will be impacted if the results are lower than expected? If the answer to any of these questions is "no one," then you will never achieve the data quality level you need for a successful CRM program. Just as we have a materials manager, we should have an information manager responsible for all the quality programs, training, metrics, and processes that are needed to protect the information asset.

20.6.1 Who Owns the Data?

Who "owns" the database content? If customer information is a company asset, then someone should own it. But who should that be? Is it Sales, Information Technology, Support, the VP of Marketing, the CEO?

One issue is the difference between owning the information and owning the customer. If knowledge is power, then owning the customer information implies having control over that information. But frankly, that's not true. If anyone owns customer information, it's the customer. All privacy advocates (and many citizens) are moving in this direction. And privacy legislation is moving in that direction as well. In fact, ownership isn't even the right question. If no one owns the information, is anyone responsible? Responsibility is the real question.

20.6.2 Who Is Responsible for the Data?

The materials manager is responsible for maintaining the value of the raw material inventory, but he doesn't own it. The company as a whole owns this asset and uses it appropriately; the materials manager is the custodian of this material. Similarly, customer information is an asset of the whole company, but there must be someone responsible for ensuring that its value is maintained and that it is used for the best interests of the company.

A better question to ask is this: Who should be responsible for the data? The custodial role is as important for information management as it is for materials management. In many companies (such as XYZ), a new job has been created to manage information quality. XYZ calls this organization data quality management, but many organizations that focus just on the customer asset are lead by a customer information manager. The customer information manager, like the materials manager, needs to be very familiar with the asset he is responsible for, as well as the environment in which the asset is stored. Table 20-8 gives a list of potential data custodians and rates each one along several important qualifications for the position.

Table 20-8 Who Is Responsible for the Data?

Potential Custodian/Qualification	Information Technology	Marketing, Sales, Service, Support	Customer Information Management
Familiar with customers	1	3	2
Knows what data is important	1	3	3
Experienced/trained to manage data	2	1	3
Familiar with database	3	1	2
Existing function/resource	2	3	1
Measured on quality results	2	1	3
Total	**11**	**12**	**14**

The trouble is that people in the business functions are "afraid" of data because it just smacks too much of that technical stuff. Why isn't it the job of the IT department? On the other hand, Information Technology just doesn't have the experience to know what data is important and how it needs to be maintained. They don't have to use this information to get their jobs done. Many successful CRM organizations have invested in dedicated staff focused on maintaining the quality of the data. Customer Information Management (CIM) organizations are most successful when they are organized as part of one of the customer-facing business functions where lots of customer expertise and knowledge are available.

20.6.3 Customer Information Management

The customer information management organization is usually aligned closely with sales (providing support for the quality of the reps' customer lists) or marketing, especially database marketing. There should be a single CIM organization for the entire customer database, not separate data managers for each product group or even each customer segment. Consolidating resources and expertise is the way to build the most successful team.

There are generally three different roles that make up the CIM organization: strategic planning and management, data analysis, and data administration.

Management/Strategic Planning

An individual who has extensive experience working with customer information can best fill the strategic/management role. Only someone who has worked with customer information can fully understand its potential and how poor quality prevents the potential from being met.

Analysis

Data analysts are generally responsible for sampling and analyzing data for a number of purposes. They will certainly be involved in determining the baseline for any quality improvement project and for extracting sample data. They often are asked to generate database lists for marketing campaigns. And some analysts have very sophisticated skills and can run very complex data mining projects. Generally, database analysts come from backgrounds in statistics and modeling or from information technology. They must be very comfortable with the system and especially the data.

Administration

Data administrators are the individual involved in actually making the database changes. Running standard audit reports, reviewing results, and entering data are normal responsibilities. Data administrators usually come from clerical and administrative support backgrounds with strong process orientations and considerable patience and determination.

Think Global, Act Local

How then should we organization such a team? There has been lots of debate over the question, and it's not over yet. We've just discussed that the more you consolidate these special skills into one organization, the more effective are the training, metrics, and sharing of expertise at a lower cost. For companies whose customers are primarily located in one or two countries, this approach probably works very well. On the other hand, CIM organizations need to be close to where the customer knowledge exists. In large global companies, how does someone sitting in Dallas know what customers are important in Hong Kong or Prague?

The best alternative is to create a central CIM organization in which the basic goals, methods, and metrics are defined and which manages distributed branches in various key locations around the world where local knowledge is readily available. It is a little harder to manage a distributed organization than a central one. It takes special effort and planning to ensure proper alignment, education, and communication. It may also be a slightly more expensive approach, but the improved results will more than make up the difference in cost. Figure 20-5 illustrates the careful balance that CIM organizations need to make between the advantages of local customer knowledge and extra cost to manage a distributed team.

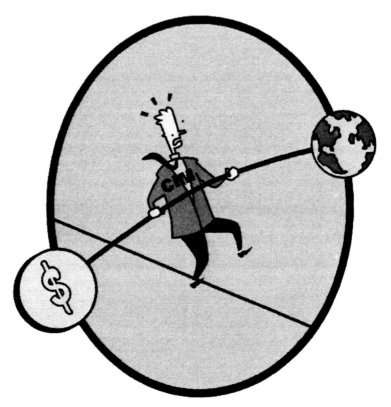

Figure 20-5 A balancing act

A last caution, you want to be sure that the ONLY reason your company creates small, local CIM teams is to be closer to the customer, not for political or control reasons! Now that we've discussed the value, protection, and management of the information asset, we'll look at managing the other big investment that the company has made, the new system.

Questions for Reflection

Thinking about your company's customer information, does anyone in the organization recognize and value it as an asset?

1. Has anyone in your company taken responsibility for the company's customer information asset? Who? Where do these folks report?
2. Are there standards and processes applied to managing the information asset? Is anyone measured on the results?
3. Does your company have data standards that are universal and consistently applied?
4. Does the company have a large, global customer base, or is it primarily made up of local domestic customers? How local can your company afford to act?

CHAPTER 21

Designing Quality Systems for a Competitive Advantage

I t should go without saying that the rest of the CRM infrastructure components (process, technology, and people) also comprise assets of the company, although some are more tangible than others. The technology component is the most obvious asset among the remaining three. Most organizations today have a good handle on the computers and networking equipment used to manage their company's operations. Of course, this wasn't always the case. At one time, computer hardware was purchased and managed everywhere throughout the organization, with no overall coordination. Connectivity, scalability, and usefulness were severely reduced by this fragmentation. The problem wasn't resolved until the total responsibility for all systems was given to the Chief Information Officer.

The process and people components are certainly less tangible assets than computer hardware. Still, most companies understand at least that the software that embodies business processes costs enough to be treated as an assets. The value of the people component is certainly the most difficult determine, but it's certainly clear that employees are still the key to customer satisfaction and loyalty. No matter how much we can (and should) automate, people are heavily involved in defining what the computers are taught to do for customers. and that basically it's employees who can build.

The CRM "system" is comprised of all the hardware, software and people that make CRM a reality for your customers. CRM success depends on system quality plus information quality, as illustrated in Figure 21-1.

This success model for CRM is very consistent with the care we've taken to understand and manage information as an independent component, not just part of the system. (Of course the model is really an information technology success model which applies to any IT system). CRM program success will be measured through increased company profit (revenue minus cost). The CRM approach is to improve customer experiences and increase loyalty (how often

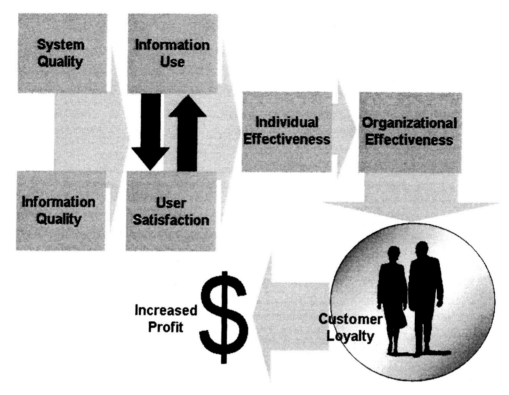

Figure 21-1 The CRM Success Model (adapted from the ISWORLDNET IT Success Model)

and how much the customer buys from our company) through better customer knowledge and improved systems which will result in increased efficiency and organizational consistency. These improvements will enable companies to deliver better customer service because employees and systems have the information and tools necessary to recognize and respond appropriately to customer interactions.

The customer-facing individuals and systems must be able to use the information and system(s) based on appropriate design and sufficient training. All of this depends on the ongoing quality of the information and the system. We examined information quality methods in Chapter 20 because it is the one component for which quality responsibility is shared between the business teams and the IT team. Now we will look at the quality management of the remaining components that make up the system.

Most of system quality management falls exclusively to Information Technology, although the people/organization certainly does not. Managing the quality of software and hardware has been a topic for much research and investigation by IT professionals (academics and practitioners) over the past 20 years. The technical details of system management are well beyond the scope of this book, but we will look at the basic principles of system quality management, which takes planning and work, just like managing any other asset. If your organization needs more information in the area, there are some excellent web-based references on this subject. An example is ISWORLDNET, which is supported by the College of Business Administration at the University of South Carolina. The web site is located at dmsweb.badm.sc.edu/grover/isworld/isoehom3.htm. You will find some very good and widely shared information about the topic of system quality and how to manage it.

21.1 Understanding System Quality

First, we must understand what system quality is, and how we get it and keep it! The ISWORLDNET web site defines system quality as measuring the information processing system itself:

> Measures of System Quality typically focus on performance characteristics of the system under study. Some research has looked at resource utilization and investment utilization, hardware utilization efficiency, reliability, response time, ease of terminal use, content of the database, aggregation of details, human factors, and system accuracy.

Hmmmm, I don't know about you, but to me that's about as clear as mud. One thing's for sure, there is a difference between the way we determine information quality and what we measure to determine system quality. In Chapter 20 we calculated data quality by checking individual database fields (i.e., a single spreadsheet cell) for factors like completeness, accuracy, consistency and validity, Quality was measured as the percent of data that was correct.

For systems, based on experience and the definition supplied by ISWORLDNET, quality is determined by how well the entire system (people, process, technology) is performing as a whole. Sometimes called "total cost of ownership," system quality is determined by measuring the total cost to build, run, support and use the system. High quality systems have a low cost of ownership – system functions are understandable and easy to use, the system is up and running and it's available when it's needed, and performance is satisfactory. We'll focus on the quality issues and process, but first let's learn more about system assets.

21.1.1 Identifying System Assets

Few organizations question whether the hardware or application software that they own has value. The big systems that run the business generally cost so much to buy (or build) that there is no question about the financial side of the equation. The "system" is made up of these plus the people who operate it. Though it's still a stretch for many to consider people as assets, it is clear for our purposes that enough of the components that comprise systems are indeed assets. We will agree that our CRM system should be treated like a valuable asset that should be managed and protected. Of course an important factor in protecting the value of an asset is to manage and improve quality so it can be used effectively.

21.1.2 Getting Unbeatable Competitive Advantage

The problem with CRM is that the fundamental measure of success, increased profitability for your company, is based on increasing revenue from loyal customer while holding or reducing costs. Frankly, one of the easiest ways to increase loyalty would be to assign one of your employees to baby-sit each customer, learn everything about the customer, and make sure that every customer need and desire is met. Naturally another way would be to just give your products away for free. (Of course sometimes you *can't* even give products away -- but that's a whole other book!) Neither of these easy solutions does anything to increase company profits, much the opposite.

Loyalty is based on positive experiences. Selling stuff for more than it cost you to build, produce, and deliver it increases profit. Adding lots of employees to "care" for customers just adds cost, but system managed customer experiences yield a tremendous opportunity for providing service that is better than your competitors, especially on the Internet, and at a reduced cost. This is the CRM promise: better experiences to more customers for less cost!

But Only If It's Correct

If the system is delivering highly satisfying and reliable interactions with customers, you will be able to make many more customers happy with much less human effort and cost. But, if the systems deliver poor or unreliable experiences, then the situation for your customers is worse, not better. Computers are notorious for not being able to apply common sense or evaluate exceptions. Customers won't take being annoyed and frustrated for very long before they decide to go somewhere else.

Systemization is *necessary* for CRM success, but not *sufficient*. If you want to keep customers loyal, don't ever think that fast, available, computer-automated service can replace good, efficient, and reliable service. The real quality of a system is measured by understanding its impact on the people who interact with it.

21.2 Identifying System Quality Issues

System quality is measured by the total cost to the customer of building, running, supporting and using of its components, then system quality issues occur when any single component fails to be cost effective for the primary system owner: the customer. There must be a balance among all the cost sources. Throwing a quick and dirty solution together may be have a small build cost, but the supportability costs and failure rates may be astronomical.

21.2.1 Determining Cost Of Ownership

System "ownership" costs can show up in many different ways, from websites that are so difficult to navigate that they confuse and frustrate customers to call centers with long wait queues to system support problems that bring the system down so call center reps can't provide customer service. Table 21-1 illustrates some of the system quality issues that XYZ was concerned might arise for Valencia and deliver poor customer experiences (and related increase in the customer cost of "ownership").

Table 21-1   System Quality Issues

Component	Customer Cost
People and organization	• Customer needs to know company organization to navigate the website. • Poor internal communication leaves customer questions unanswered • No one able to make a decision that would help the customer
Process	• Processes break down because of white space, customer left hanging • Online processes confusing and very difficult to perform • Processes have much wasted activity and wait time.
Technology	• System not reliable, frequent hardware and software failures • Scheduled backups prevent customer access • System doesn't "do" what it says it will.

There are many potential causes for poor system quality that causes customer frustration, bad experiences and decreased loyalty. Understanding the cost to the customer of some these issues is a really good way to get the organization thinking from the customer's viewpoint. Of course we could easily add the information component to this table as well, but we looked at data quality issues in Chapter 20.

21.2.2   Using a System Quality Checklist

Another commonly used and well understood tool for measuring system quality is known as **FURPS** (Functionality, Usability, Reliability, Performance, and Supportability). One example of a FURPS checklist is shown in Table 21-2, although you can find a number of variations on the Internet. Use the FURPS framework to develop a quality template for your own systems and project efforts.

The FURPS checklist should be used to plan and build in system quality up front, as well as for deciding among a number of different software products. FURPS is an excellent tool for evaluating system quality issues during the selection and implementation process as well as after the system is running.

Table 21-2 Software Quality Elements Adapted from Ulrika Wiss

Element	What It Means	What to Look For
Functionality	What can the system do?	• What functions are there? • How general are they? • How's the security?
Usability	"User friendly" is the term most often used. Usability means simple, obvious, easy to understand, and familiar.	• Human Factors • Aesthetics • Consistency • Documentation • Localizability (language, character sets) • Openness (standardized, integratable)
Reliability	Referring to both the hardware and the software elements, how dependable is the whole system?	• Failure frequency and severity • Output accuracy • Mean Time Between Failures (MTBF) • Failure recovery • Program predictability
Performance	How does the system (hardware and software) actually operate? How available for use is it?	• Speed • Response time • Resource consumption • Efficiency • Access and up-time
Supportability	How well does the system run over time?	• Maintainability: extensibility, adaptability, serviceability • Testability • Compatibility • Configurability • Ease of installation • Flexibility and portability

21.3 Planning System Quality

Systems are company assets. We already know that asset management doesn't just happen; it's a result of planning and hard work. The absolutely most effective way to ensure high-quality systems that perform as they are expected is to build quality in up front. Using tools like the FURPS checklist and understanding the basic sources of system failure are tools that can be used to check for quality problems before the system is selected or built.

System maintenance is the second most effective quality tool that we have. System maintenance schedules should include the following:

- All the commonly understood maintenance checks that are known (like taking your car in for an oil change on a regular basis)
- Checks for particular known trouble spots (my car's tires tends to lose pressure)

After the oil change, we build in checks for a few common situations that might occur (oil gets changed whether or not it "looks bad"). These tests start by testing whether the particular part is working as expected. If it is, we go on to the next test. If not, we follow a plan we've previously determined will solve the problem.

Ad hoc maintenance is the kind we all dread – when the darn thing just stops running. When the system (car) just quits, the IT organization (or your mechanic) investigates the situation to determine what's not working right. In other words, each system component is checked against its normal or expected state. Then, just as we did for information quality, the IT folks will follow the same basic steps:

- Detail the characteristics of the desired quality state (target).
- Detail the characteristics of the current quality state (test).
- Identify the differences between these two states.
- Design the data quality action plan with responsibilities and dates.
- Execute the action plan.

In fact, even the scheduled tests follow about the same methodology, except that if the test state and the target state are the same, nothing is done. If a difference is found, we don't need to create a new action plan; we just execute the one that has already been defined.

21.4 Getting System Quality

CRM system quality means measuring and managing the quality of the hardware, software and people/organizational performance that supports your company's CRM program. The system must meet the expectation of the customer – whether that customer is interacting directly with the system or is working with a company employee using the system to provide support and service. Hardware and software are so inextricably intertwined that, for example, hardware failures are indistinguishable from software failures to the end user. "The system crashed" can mean that a failure occurred anywhere in the system, including human error. This is why we manage all three components as part of the overall system. Customers experience the system as a single thing.

21.4.1 Building in Quality

All of the efforts during the building infrastructure phase of the life cycle are aimed at accurately understanding the business requirements for the new system. Meeting user expectations is the minimum quality goal for the construction (build or buy) process. Of course, exceeding expectation is even better, but it's harder to define and measure.

We used a standard project management methodology during the development and implementation of hardware and software components to ensure that we have matched the solution to the user expectations as described in Chapters 11 through 14. Some of the system requirements that must be considered are shown in the FURPS checklist (Table 21-2).

21.4.2 Managing Quality for the Life of the System

Unfortunately, system quality is not static. Quality can deteriorate over time, just like any other asset. Maintaining system quality is equally important as up-front quality. Ask yourself "How is this system working for me today?" Quality can deteriorate because business requirements change (new customer expectations, new competitive threats, business growth) and because any of the system components can wear out or fail.

Long-term system quality efforts (i.e., system maintenance) come in two forms. Proactive maintenance is everything we do to guard against potential future failure. Reactive maintenance is what we do to recover from a failure that occurred in spite of all our best efforts.

Proactive (Preventive) Maintenance

Using the standard system quality checklist in Table 21-2, a preventive maintenance schedule is designed and executed on a periodic basis. Preventive maintenance includes system software and data backup and recovery, as well as periodic testing for potential hardware problems such as running out of disk storage space or corrupted jobs that no longer run. Preventive maintenance can be planned and scheduled in advance. Designing the plan is a one-time event; executing the plan is based on the schedule and the results of any sampling that has been performed during the schedule. The problems tackled by preventive maintenance are anticipated and understood.

Reactive (Ad Hoc) Maintenance

The only difference between ad hoc and scheduled maintenance is that ad hoc maintenance occurs when a problem is encountered for the first time. In this case, a process will be established to track the source and solution to the problem. It is an excellent business practice to add any check to the maintenance schedule for each new error situation encountered. The biggest investment required to solve system problems is identifying the source and solution. After your IT department has figured these out, your company should never spend time and money again to investigate and resolve the same problem.

21.5 Understanding Why Web-Based Systems Are the Most Demanding

Web-based CRM systems support customers directly. The good news is that the cost of human (employee) interaction has been eliminated. The bad news is that brain of the human employee has also been eliminated. Web-based systems must be very carefully designed and operated to ensure that the experience for the end customer is smooth and easy.

In the past, we've relied on employees to connect any broken links. After all, employees know lots about the company, its products, and how each process should work. We pay employees to connect the dots. We should never expect the same of customers. Customers are not familiar with our company's organization and products. They don't (and shouldn't be expected to) give a fig about any of it. Customer experiences must be integrated and consistent, whether or not there is a person involved.

21.5.1 Integrating Customer Experience across Channels

One of our CRM expectations is that customers will have a dependable and consistent interaction with our company no matter where they choose to interact with us. There are two approaches to integrating the customer experience across various channels. The first is simply to connect the systems to each other so that information and knowledge available in one is available in the other. The second is to allow an easy way for the customer to access another touch point if the current interaction isn't meeting his needs.

System Integration

Connecting systems to each other, like connecting plumbing, was discussed in Chapter 16 as part of component integration. After systems are connected to each other, the information should flow, just like water through pipes, and should be available everywhere. This is how we've been able to get information to where it was needed to improve the customer experience. It is the means by which web sites can be customized based on what products the customer has actually purchased, for example.

The trouble that we run into is that every single system connection (or interface) requires more software that must be built and then maintained. This can get quite costly as more and more interfaces are built between more and more of the system components, as illustrated in Figure 21-2. You can count the lines or use the calculation shown to see how quickly the number of software interfaces can grow.

If you had only 15 systems running your business, the potential number of interfaces required is already over 100! This is the reason that the most efficient operational system architecture, as we saw in Chapter 20, shares commonly used information through a master or reference file (hub), rather than passing it back and forth.

Interaction Integration

We know that there are still many customers who are not very comfortable going to the Internet for support and purchasing assistance. The web interface is too confusing and hard to use, or the customer just plain doesn't trust the Internet at all. On the other hand, companies want to encourage customers to use this more cost-effective channel.

An excellent approach, characterized by the Land's End web site shown in Chapter 4, allows customers to "escape" from the web page to a live conversation with a service representa-

How many Interfaces if the number of customer systems is 6:

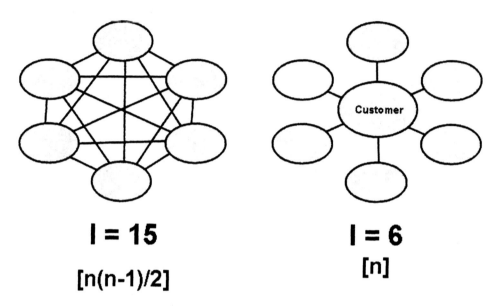

Figure 21-2 Number of required connections for two different architectures

tive with just the click of a mouse. Customers are willing to try the web self-service alternative because, if it's not working for them, they have an easy way to talk to a real person.

21.5.2 Humanizing Your Web Site with Virtual Reality

An emerging web technology is the use of virtual reality tools to really humanize the online computer experience. This technology can be used to control a screen figure based on mimicking actions of a human being. Using sensors and sophisticated software, the screen figure (called an avatar, which is the embodiment of a human form) can be made to move around and mouth words just as if spoken by a human being. Avatar technology is extremely useful in helping customers become familiar and comfortable with Internet technology.

Now that we understand what we need to do to protect the value of our CRM assets, we will look at another significant aspect that ensures a successful CRM program. Customer privacy is a fantastic opportunity to build customer trust and loyalty by treating your customers' information the same way you would like to have yours treated.

Questions for Reflection

The trouble with system maintenance is that, like any utility, there are few rewards for doing it right. When was the last time you called your telephone company just to thank them for keeping your phone working for the past month? Do you treat your company the same?

1. System maintenance should be a business fundamental, but is it?
2. Does the IT organization plan and manage preventive maintenance schedules, or is everything done as an emergency fix after something breaks?

Customer Privacy: Seize Your Opportunity

Customer privacy, once upon a time a topic of great interest and ever increasing importance is still around. California's state legislature came very close to passing a law to establish a no-phone zone, a "do not phone" list that anyone telemarketing to California residents would be required to use. It didn't quite pass—this time.

Privacy is still a huge political issue and a huge legal issue, but most important, it is a *huge* opportunity for you to build trust and loyalty with your customers and enhance your brand image! Like many of the things we've already discussed, the Internet hasn't created the privacy issue, but it has significantly raised its visibility and importance. Nothing illustrates how pervasive a topic has become better than when it becomes the subject of humor in a publication like *The New Yorker* (see Figure 22-1).

The political and legal implications of an individual's right to privacy (to be left alone) are far from understood, much less well defined. Globally as well as in North America, the political climate regarding privacy is inconsistent, and the legal situation continues to evolve. Europe enacted its Directive on Data Privacy in October 1998, which prohibits the transfer of personal data to non-European Union nations that do not meet the European "adequacy" standard for privacy protection. The United States government initially favored industry self-regulation based on industry shouldering responsibility for adopting sound privacy practices, hoping to limit the amount of restrictive legislation hampering the fledgling industry. Little industry movement coupled with strong consumer concern resulted in the creation of some industry-specific legislation in the United States, with the possibility of more to come.[1] Much of the rest of the world seems

---

1. Medical and educational information has been legally protected for years. Just in the past year, we have seen new legislation in areas such as financial services and children's privacy.

   The Direct Marketing Association (DMA) has an informative web site that answers common business questions regarding the new Gramm-Leach-Bliley Act passed early in 2002. You'll find it at www.the-dma.org/government/grammleachbileyact.shtml#top.

   For more information on the Children's Online Privacy Protection Act (COPPA) which went into effect in April, 2000, see the Federal Trade Commission's excellent KIDZPRIVACY web site at www.ftc.gov/bcp/conline/edcams/kidzprivacy/index.html

"We don't want just anyone coming in here and
making toast. Type in your password."

Figure 22-1 A little privacy humor

to favor limiting legislation, thus encouraging the growth of the Internet. There is a strong case for a consistent global approach to privacy because the Internet knows nothing about country borders, but it may take a long time to get there.

Because so many customers are adopting the web to transact business, e-commerce has been exploding. Electronic sales to consumers passed $20 billion in 1999, and consumer online revenue is projected at $184 billion in 2004. Internet sales in the business-to-business market are growing at an even faster rate and will eclipse the consumer e-market. Still, there are many customers who remain reluctant to move to the web, with privacy and security concerns identified as the biggest barriers. The Gartner Group reported that of those customers who bought online in Q3 1999, 38 percent agreed that privacy concerns prevented them from placing further orders. And Jupiter Communication tells us that 58 percent of customers they surveyed were worried about a company selling their information to a third party.

This is where your opportunity presents itself. The *opportunity* is the difference between doing right and not doing it wrong. You must stop thinking about privacy as a political issue or legal threat that is about to be imposed. Privacy is a tremendous opportunity to improve your customer relationships, increase trust, and build loyalty. Bob Dorf, President of the Peppers and Rogers Group, put it this way:

Privacy is the single greatest threat to the successful implementation of one-to-one [relationship management]. Any company that is going to do [one-to-one] and not totally respect the privacy of the customer's information is just waiting for disaster…begging for a disaster.

I could not agree more!

22.1 Why Should You Care?

As we've already discussed, there is general agreement that customer loyalty and satisfaction will be *the* differentiators between successful companies and unsuccessful ones. You may be one of the many businesses hoping to move customers to the web. After all, it's clearly the most cost-effective way to enable many sales, marketing, and support activities. Speaking at an Internet conference in New York on the topic of whether privacy laws would crush many promising Internet businesses, IBM CEO Lou Gerstner said:

Trust is the most fundamental element of branding, and if we do not act responsibly on this matter, then we run the risk of choking off this entire industry.

You may also be using information you have collected from your customers to help you manage and improve your customer interactions. After all, information is the key ingredient when building excellent customer experiences on and off the web. In lieu of direct interactions, this critical data will help you understand your customers' needs, target and personalize interactions, and customize product and service offerings. With that said, customers currently are pretty reluctant to give you their data. They're especially worried about giving you data online because of the perception that it is just so easy for anyone to access large amounts of data at warp speeds. Customers are especially concerned about fraud, harm to their financial and/or credit standing, identity theft, and invasive marketing. All of these are based on misuse of personal information and, although the web increases perceived risk, none of these is limited to web-collected data. (My credit rating was temporarily ruined by someone who used my name, address, and phone number from the telephone book to get a new phone account, and then never paid. It took months, hundreds of phone calls, and intervention by the police to finally straighten it out and stop the threatening phone calls from collection agencies.)

So why have consumers been so hyper-aware and so nervous? First, much more information is collected and seemingly available to more people at a much faster rate. It just seems logical that if someone is storing lots of information about me in a database and the databases are all connected to the Internet, then there is little to stop thieves and hackers from getting their hands on it. Second, thank the media. Internet abuse is a much more exciting story to write about than telephone book abuse.

If you're serious about doing some (or all) of your business transactions on the web, you now have a golden opportunity to make privacy part of your brand image and your strategy for building customer trust and loyalty. In fact we've all bought a little more time right now. Issues of security are outweighing issues of privacy for many customers. But this hiatus will never last, we can do privacy ourselves or it will eventually be done to us!

The privacy opportunity is twofold. First, you can use your company's position on privacy to enhance and strengthen your brand image. (Note that, as always, image/message alignment matters. If you have a poor reputation for doing the right thing for customers, then positioning yourself as a privacy leader will appear hypocritical and will actually backfire.) Second, because information is the lifeblood of relationship management and e-commerce, the most successful companies will be those that earn customer trust, because only then will customers share their information. I strongly disagree with the well-known Silicon Valley executive who told customers that they should "Get over it," because they *have* no privacy rights. Privacy is *not* going away, so get over that! All this privacy frenzy makes governments nervous and that should make *us* nervous. We have a small window of opportunity to take some steps that show we understand the importance of privacy. We must take responsibility for our own actions so we can slow down the legislation that could significantly restrict our ability to conduct business – but we must do the right things. So how do we know what the right things are? Let's look at what privacy really is so we know what we're dealing with.

22.2 What Is Privacy?

First, let's try to demystify the whole topic. Privacy is about an individual's right to have his/her personally identifiable data protected, at home and at work. Personally identifiable information includes all the data that helps us to identify or contact an individual, plus all of the additional facts that we store about these individuals. It does not cover anonymous behavior that is not linked to an identified individual or trend data that is just a summary of what lots of individuals have done. Privacy applies to all the data you collect (or have collected) about your customers, whether online or off. But in spite of all the legal and political rhetoric, creating an effective privacy policy and protecting your customers' data is really not rocket science.

22.3 What Do the Five Elements of Privacy Mean to You?

There are just a few basic principles that you need to understand: notice, choice, access and accuracy, security, and oversight. Then you need to know what they mean to you in building your company's CRM program.

22.3.1 Notice

Awareness is telling the truth about what data you collect, where you get it, why you need it, how you use it, and whom you let see it. Start with developing an internal privacy policy that will be the basis for defining your company's practices and the foundation from which you'll make customers aware of your intent. Keep your policy simple and accurate. Because your internal practices *must* match your stated policy, begin by documenting what you already do. This way, you don't need to worry about getting massive approvals or making lots of changes happen immediately.

Next, you should create an online Privacy Statement. This is where the rubber meets the road for your customers – where you disclose what you're doing. Create a very short statement that briefly summarizes your company's policies. You should begin placing this on all hardcopy response documents such as product registration cards. It can also be used on the phone when customer service reps are collecting customer information that would be extremely valuable for understanding your customer's experience.

Make sure your partners (with whom you must share customer information in order to do business) have a privacy policy that is at least as stringent as yours is. Include this requirement in your contract with them. As in all other aspects of the total customer experience, the customer perceives that he is doing business with you, not the retailer or dealer.

Get involved with educating your customers about what they should expect regarding the privacy of their personally identifiable information. Use common language. You need to build confidence and not hide behind confusing language that no one understands. It would tremendously help customers to understand what to look for if we all organized our privacy statements around these same five elements. Make it part of your brand strategy. If you're doing better at this privacy thing than your competitors, let your customers know. But don't do it by slamming your competition; tell customers what to look for and how effectively you are protecting them!

22.3.2 Choice

Choice involves giving the customer the ability to decide whether or not he agrees to let you use his data in the ways you've described. After you've made the customer aware of what you intend to do with his information (besides the basic transaction he is performing), give him a chance to refuse giving permission for these additional uses. But no matter what he chooses, he can still complete the current transaction. Note that this is much better than losing an order because the customer didn't like your policy and didn't have any other way to let you know! Choice requires that you provide a way to let the customer answer "yes" or "no" to whether you can use his data after the transaction is completed. How would you use this data? Typical uses would include unsolicited sales and marketing contacts from you and/or selling or leasing his information to a third party. Choice requires that you have a way to store the answer somewhere safe so that you can continue to honor the customer's decision over time and across the organization. If you do what you promised and continue to develop the relationship, customers will often relent over time, recognizing that you are a company with integrity that they can trust with even more of their information.

Important concepts that relate to giving your customers control over how you use their data include what you do if they have not told you what they want (opt-in versus opt-out) and your policy on sending unsolicited e-mail (spam).

Opt-in/Opt-out

The question of opt-in/opt-out is one element of choice, and it is less confusing than it has been made to appear. It involves only one thing: What do *you* do with customer data when the customer has not answered the choice question? Obviously, it is perfectly fine to contact a person who has said "yes," and it is absolutely not okay to contact a person who says "no." But what should you do with those people who did not answer either way?

- Opt-in means that if a customer did not answer the question, you must treat him as if he answered "no" (do not contact). This is the *law* in Europe, and many companies are making it their policy. For example, HP has changed its contact policy to opt-in.
- Opt-out means that if a customer did not answer the question, you may treat him as if he answered "yes" (okay to contact). This is standard for most of the world outside Europe.

The most important thing to understand about this opt-in/opt-out question is that it does not change what you ask the customer, but how you behave after he has made his decision. An opt-in policy *includes* only those who answered *yes*, while an opt-out policy *excludes* only those who said *no*. Therefore, you must know what the customer actually said. It is critical that you *never* infer (default) the customer's choice. You must store the actual response, whether it is "yes," "no," or nothing (didn't choose either).

Spam

I'm including spam within the "choice" section, although technically it offers customers no choice at all. Spam is narrowly defined as sending thousands of completely untargeted email messages by calculating common name variations (e.g., jdoe@ibm.com; john-doe@ibm.com; john_doe; john.doe; doejohn; and so on). In the broader meaning that has come into popular use, it is any @!*!*# e-mail that you didn't want to receive! Spam is unacceptable. If it's not yet against the law where you are, it will be soon. Worse, it has a horrible impact on your customers' ability to trust you. You should e-mail only if a customer has given permission (opt-in is becoming the universal standard for e-mail) and always make it easy for her to say no to future email by providing an easy to use "choice" option in every e-mail you send.

In addition to addressing the basic questions of unsolicited contact and third-party access, you may also want to track customer preferences in terms of how they wish to be contacted. Which touch points would they prefer you to use? Their choices could include phone, e-mail, and direct mail. Strictly speaking, asking the two basic questions covers you, but it's a good business practice and good relationship management to get customers preferences. Some people feel that the telephone (or e-mail, or whatever) is more invasive than other touch points, so if you allow them to choose the ways you can contact them, you get a "relationship" advantage. You can continue to communicate with them while acknowledging and respecting their preferences. Why give up all opportunity to contact a customer just because he doesn't want to be telephoned? By capturing and saving contact preferences, you will keep access open to more of your customers (just not through all touch points).

After you have gained permission, you must not substantially change your policy (at least you must not relax it) without regaining the customer's permission. In other words, before changing or relaxing your policy, you must ask for permission to continue using the customer's information! This requires that you not only save what the customer said, but when he said it (date) so you know which version of your policy was agreed to. For example, should you decide to change current policy and start to link your anonymous web behavior data to your customer list, you must get customer permission first.

Throughout this book, you have been encouraged to think of your customer data as a company asset and to treat it as such. It might logically follow that if your customer database is an asset, it should be available for use as you wish or even for sale if a company must liquidate all its other assets. No final decision has been made as to what will be illegal, but most courts have taken a conservative stand supporting consumer privacy protection.

The difference between a customer information asset and data warehouse is that there hasn't been agreement that you actually *own* your customer information asset. It still belongs to your customers, even though they have given it to you to use. It parallels the situation in which you lease equipment or stock inventory that you haven't purchased yet. There is great benefit to having access to these assets, but if you go out of business, you don't get to sell those assets; they go back to the owner.

22.3.3 Access and Accuracy

Accuracy and access refers to letting a customer review and correct his own data. This is often the most difficult item for a company to accomplish, especially because, in theory, it should apply to all offline data as well as online. By the way, "access and accuracy" has been the law in many countries in Europe for a long time, long before most of us ever heard of the web. So what can you do? The minimum – but acceptable – solution is to have tools and processes in place (such as an inventory of all your major customer databases) that will allow you to easily retrieve and print all stored customer information. (Credit bureaus have done this for years). Send it to the customer with an offer to correct information that he marks up and sends back to you. (Obviously, you should actually make the requested corrections to his data.) It's even okay to charge the customer a reasonable fee to cover your costs for creating this type of report. (Again, the credit bureaus are an example.)

Clearly, you need to build a capability for customers to review and correct as soon as possible any data that they have given online. This is a big step in building customer confidence. Customers are much more nervous about the thought of turning their information over to a big black box where it will remain forever invisible and inaccessible. Also, consider that this can be a great opportunity to have your customers maintain your database for you (yielding a more accurate database for much less money). Make this part of your data quality management strategy. Customers are certainly in the best position to keep their profiles accurate and up to date. If you have built a strong relationship with your customers, they will see a benefit in keeping you posted about changes in their lives. (I *never* change my e-mail address without letting United Airlines know right away.) And, you'll get an additional indicator of your most loyal customers. Someone who's maintaining his data at your site is investing his time in your relationship!

22.3.4 Security

Security is keeping customer information safe from anyone with whom you have not planned to share it. You should protect your customers' personally identifiable data from the moment it leaves their PC until you no longer keep it. While it travels over the Internet, data should be encrypted. After it's stored in one of your company's databases, it should be protected with a combination of a firewall, encryption, and passwords. Don't forget that this requirement extends to any database that is part of your business environment but hosted on a third party's computer. I know companies who've been very proud of their internal system security only to have one of their databases hacked while it sat outside the company's walls. Security involves finding the right products and technology and *using* them. For example, don't turn off your network firewall because you know you plan to log on remotely while on vacation. This could open the way to a computer break in.

22.3.5 Oversight

Oversight refers to giving your customers the option to contact an independent party if they feel their privacy rights have been abused. Providing access to a third party is an excellent way to build customer trust, and it's a responsible way to combine self-regulation with deflating the argument that self-regulation leaves the fox guarding the chicken house. Third-party privacy seal programs, such as the BBBOnline (subsidiary of the Better Business Bureau) Privacy Seal, offer policy review and dispute resolution, but in an impartial way. The first step is to give the company a chance to show that the complaint is unfounded or to fix an issue they weren't aware of. Only if the company refuses to correct a reported violation will BBBOnline refer the issue to the FTC for final resolution under the false advertising statutes that have existed for years. I am a strong supporter of BBBOnline because they have all the bases covered, including these:

- A strong brand image in the consumer advocacy arena
- A robust assessment process
- Existing infrastructure for dealing with consumer complaints and for working with the Federal Trade Commission to resolve disputes
- Global visibility and global connections

BBBOnline has worked with government groups and consumer organizations around the world to develop a global network of privacy seals. Much like the Better Business Bureaus fair advertising seal, these privacy seals indicate that the company that displays the seal has been reviewed, has met a set of privacy standards, and is authorized to display the seal. The seal also guarantees the customer an avenue through which any concerns he may have can be addressed. The first international partnership of its kind was established with the Japanese Privacy Seal authority (JIPD). BBBOnline has also been actively engaged with the Department of Commerce on another initiative known as Safe Harbor. In an effort to resolve the differences in privacy approaches, the United States government and the European Union jointly launched the Safe

Harbor initiative that the European Union approved in July 2000. Safe harbor is currently in use with Hewlett-Packard being one of the first large companies to be certified. The BBBOnline Privacy Seal includes all requirements for the United States/ European Union Safe Harbor Agreement. Companies who receive Safe Harbor certification from the Department of Commerce are compliant with the European Union Data Protection Directive and may, therefore, transfer European customer data across borders. Having the seal means that customer information can be transferred across country borders. This is a huge advantage for the many companies whose business crosses borders and almost mandatory for online businesses that can't control who accesses their web site.

22.4 Writing Your Online Statement

While each company has its own culture, practices, and economic situations, little is to be gained by providing customers with a lengthy discussion of developing the details of your internal policy. But the external statements we make to our customers are a different story. We will focus on developing your online privacy statement because the more we can use a standard framework for communicating our policies, the easier it will be for customers to understand what they need to understand. The online statement is critical because so many customers are particularly concerned about releasing their personal data over the Internet. If you have uncovered some areas where you are particularly vulnerable since you first created your internal policy, you can include information in the online statement about which areas you are working to improve. The goal is to write a true statement that is clear and complete, so you earn your customers' trust and get them to trust you with more of their online business and personal information.

The online statement should be created with the following points in mind:

- Outline your company's commitment to respecting the privacy rights of your customers. Follow through on your promise with your actions. Make your privacy statement easy to find. Providing a direct link from your home page (and preferably from every page on your standard navigation banner) is a strong statement.
- Organize your statement around the five key elements. Including these elements will ensure that you have thought about all the issues you need to cover, and it will help educate your customers as to what they should look for in a privacy statement.
- Use simple, clear language. If your privacy statement reads like your Terms and Conditions document, then you have missed the boat (that is, unless your Terms and Conditions are also very easy to understand, and then you're way ahead of the game).
- Provide an easy way to contact your company if a customer has concerns or questions about the privacy statement. Don't forget that you have to respond! This is a very sensitive issue with some customers. If they took the time to raise an issue or concern, you better follow up – or you've lost that customer plus everyone else he can influence.
- Speak the truth. If you can't do it, don't say that you do. Nothing reduces trust quicker than a broken promise.

• Include a date. This lets the customer know that privacy continues to be of current importance to you (at least as long as the date isn't two years old). It also lets customers know that your policies are active and will evolve over time.

There are some "privacy statement generators" available on the web that can also help you develop an online statement. I haven't found one that really creates a simple, readable, and understandable document that is organized around these five principles. However, these tools offer another good way to get started. Generator programs ask a series of questions about your information collection and management practices, and then produce a document that summarizes your responses. You can find a good example of a generator at the Direct Marketing Association web site:

> www.thedma.org/library/privacy/creating.shtml

You can also use existing privacy statements to help you create your own. You can easily find examples on your own, but I've listed a few here that cover a wide range of formats and content (from May 2001). I recently checked and some have been improved, but many are just the same.

• **Sony Corporation of America:** Sony has imbedded its statement in its Terms and Conditions. Up until recently Sony's privacy statement included a single paragraph on children's privacy in addition to the paragraph quoted below.

Privacy Policy

This web site, including any subsite accessible through the homepage, (the "Site") is published and maintained by subsidiaries, affiliates and/or related entities of Sony Corporation of America ("Sony"). You can e-mail us at *webmaster@www.sony.com*. When you enter any subsite accessible through this homepage, such subsite may have its own privacy policy, which is specific to such subsite. When you access, browse or use this Site you accept, without limitation or qualification, the terms and conditions of any privacy policies set forth in any subsite.

> www.sony.com

While the intent was clear, would this statement inspire your confidence? Happily, Sony has significantly updated its online privacy statement to cover the basic principles though it is still imbedded in the Terms and Conditions section.

• **Sun Microsystems:** Sun has done a good job keeping its statement simple and organizing it around most of the basic principles (excluding oversight). This is a sound effort to get started and to honestly describe what they do and what they're working on. They also include a date on their statement. Unfortunately, this date is almost three years old! Does this feel like an up-to-date policy?

- **Amazon.com and Visa:** Both of these companies have easily understandable statements organized around the basic elements, again excluding oversight. Visa in particular has done a good job of making the key elements very visible while still allowing the customer to drill down and get more detailed information. Visa has also added a section on "Customer Service and Recourse," which is a step toward third-party oversight. When you are already doing the right things, there is no restrictive burden added by displaying a third-party "seal of approval." Instead, it will build your customers' confidence and loyalty.

> www.amazon.com
> www.visa.com

- **Intel, Kodak, and HP:** These three companies have created fairly simple, understandable, online privacy statements that cover the five elements, including oversight. All carry a privacy seal. All directly link from the home page, and all have an obvious e-mail button for feedback. Intel's feedback request clearly tells the customer that if he is not satisfied with Intel's response, he should contact the seal provider via the supplied link. This is an excellent practice.

> www.intel.com
> www.kodak.com
> www.hp.com

Table 22-1 contains a sample framework for a privacy statement that will help you ask yourself all the key questions. Your statement should address each of these elements and should reflect your own company's position on each point.

After you've created your initial policy and customer communication documents, you have at least made your customers aware of what you are doing. They can vote with their mouse or trash basket if they're not comfortable with the way you do business. But, because that's not really the outcome you're looking for, over time you will want to enhance your policy to improve your privacy practices and image. Because policy and internal practices must remain in perfect alignment, you will have to provide training to all individuals who interact with (capture, manage, use) customer data about your new policies. As in all other "people behavior" change management projects, you must have a way of measuring and enforcing results. Everyone in your company must understand and abide by your privacy policy.

Table 22-1 Privacy Statement Framework

Privacy Commitment (Brief statement of your overall position)

• Your privacy and the safety of the data you give us are very important.

• We want you to understand what we do with your data.

• We want you to be comfortable with these practices. If you are not comfortable, you have the right to withhold permission to use your data. We may modify this statement from time to time. It was last updated on dd mmm yyyy.

Notice (What information we collect and use)

• What data we collect (directly and from third parties)

• How we use it

• With whom we share it

• Do we target children, and if so, how do we deal with COPPA?

• Do we use cookies, and if so, how can you turn them off?

Choice (How we determine what you will allow us to do with your data)

• What we do when we first collect your data

• What we do when you change your mind

Access/Accuracy (How we plan to let you review and correct the accuracy of your data)

• How we give you access to review your data

• How we make the changes you request

Security (How we physically protect your data)

• What we do while your information is traveling to our site

• What we do once your information is inside (electronic and physical storage)

• What processes we have set up to ensure physical safety and protection

---

Oversight (What options you have if we haven't lived up to our promises)

• How to contact us

• Where to go if you're not satisfied with our response

22.5 Managing the Balance between Self-regulation and Legislation

One of the most negative outcomes from all the rhetoric around privacy is that companies are actually discouraged from posting their privacy policies. Because only U.S. companies that actually display a privacy policy can get into trouble for not living up to it, companies think they're safer not having a policy. Unfortunately, this is head-in-the-sand thinking. The real result of ignoring privacy will be complicated laws created by legislators who don't understand business realities. These are likely to be much more restrictive and difficult to work with than anything we would enact ourselves or that our customers would demand. Unfortunately, hard-liners on both sides of the privacy questions make things worse. Self-regulation advocates reject all proposed legislation rather than working to make sure the laws are reasonable. Hard-line privacy advocates reject solutions that aren't perfect. An example of a great initiative that many privacy hard-liners criticize because it doesn't solve every bit of the problem is the Platform for Privacy Preferences (for additional information on P3P, see www.w3.org/P3P/) developed by the World Wide Web Consortium. P3P is a software tool that allows a customer to define his privacy preferences so that his computer can check a company's policy and decide whether it's an acceptable place to do business.

On the other hand, direct marketers and database marketing advocates reject any attempts at legislation, no matter how benign. This includes the attempts by the Federal Trade Commission to require that all companies doing business on the web have a basic privacy policy. Having such a policy would, at a minimum, eliminate the problem we just discussed: Some companies avoid displaying a policy because only then might they be vulnerable to privacy complaints. Although this head-in-the-sand thinking might be technically correct, it only makes customers less trusting and more leery of sharing their information with all companies. It's a vicious cycle. We want to be self-regulated, but we're reluctant to take the first step and make any privacy promises. So customers' trust of our sense of intentions goes down, as does the government's opinion of how responsible we're being. Government then raises the prospect of legislation as the only viable alternative because industry isn't taking responsibility. This causes more fear that one small legal step will lead to a totally restrictive environment, so we scream self-regulation even louder. We have to break this cycle. We all *must* create and post online privacy statements on our web sites now. Because it's a reasonable requirement, we should also get behind the efforts to adopt legislation to that effect, making the playing field level for all of us and taking a step toward building credibility with our customers and the government.

22.6 Getting Started Now

If you are serious about doing business in the 21st century, then you need to realize that privacy is a real issue and one that's here to stay. You can use it to your advantage to build strong relationships by taking steps to ensure that customers are comfortable. Your company should act now or privacy will be done *to* you. Take these first steps:

- Understand what privacy is all about.
- Develop a company privacy policy that reflects what you do. It can evolve over time as your capabilities improve. It's better to be accurate than to have an ideal policy. Post an online version of your policy.
- Get a Privacy Seal. Use simple and consistent language to describe what you do.
- Take responsibility and demonstrate leadership. Let your customers know that you accept the responsibility of protecting their personally identifiable information as carefully as you would the credit cards in your wallet.
- Help lead the charge in building awareness and educating the marketplace. Make your efforts visible.

As you have probably guessed by now, I am a strong advocate of taking a common-sense approach to things and not overcomplicating matters. If you overanalyze an issue, you just get paralyzed. Use common sense, and use yourself as an example. How do you feel about how your personal data should be used and protected? Understand what your company is doing today, fix the things that are obvious and/or easy to fix, and involve your staff in order to start the ball rolling. JUST DO IT!

Questions for Reflection

Think about what kinds of privacy commitments your company makes to your customers

1. Is there a privacy notice on your website? Do you have a separate privacy policy?
2. If there are any, are they widely known and understood inside the company? Are they widely followed?
3. Do your policies cover all five elements?

CRM: You Got It, Right?

Managing customer relationships today really means turning the management of the relationship over to your customers. It's a scary thought, isn't it? How *do* you let customers manage their own relationships without giving up total control of your business? And even if you did give up control, it wouldn't really do your customers much good if you lose money and have to go out of business because you "delighted." them. The dot.com debacle taught many people that important lesson.

Customers require that companies give them what they want, the way they want it, and when they want it. The trick is giving customers choices about how they interact with your company without giving the company away. Balancing priorities is what customer relationship management is about.

23.1 Knowing Your Company's CRM Goals

Surely, any company could "buy" customer loyalty with great free products and services. Many of the now defunct dot.coms did exactly that! And where are their customers today? I can't tell you exactly, but they're certainly no longer the loyal customers they once were to companies that no longer exist. Happy customers and loyal eyeballs are not the only measure of success; profit is still important. The secret to CRM success is finding the right balance between customer experience and company profit, as illustrated in Figure 23-1.

Almost every CRM business decision involves finding the right balance between internal and external investments, between actions and results.

Figure 23-1 Balancing profit and customers

23.1.1 Profit

Okay, we know the Internet didn't change the basic fact that a company that isn't profit-able cannot stay in business forever. Company profit is not an evil motive. It doesn't mean that we have to sacrifice everything in its name. Dave Packard and Bill Hewlett created one of the best discussions of why profit is important when they articulated the corporate objectives for their new company.

> *Profit.* To recognize that profit is the best single measure of our contribution to society and the ultimate source of our corporate strength. We should attempt to achieve the maximum possible profit consistent with our other objectives.

Bill and Dave made profit the first corporate objective because, without profit, the com-pany wouldn't be around to innovate for customers, create jobs for employees, or be an active citizen in the community. If your CRM program is not well aligned with your company's profit and other business goals, you cannot be successful.

23.1.2 Customer

It is clear that customer-centered organizations aren't required to keep all customers happy at all costs. CRM involves two parallel concepts:

1. All customers are *not* created equal.
2. Customer focus really means focusing from the customer's viewpoint—always.

The first principle tells you to look for your company's best customers and worry most about them. The second principle teaches that when implementing any CRM capability, whether it's for process improvement, cost reduction, or customer loyalty, think about it from the perspective of how it will look (feel, sound, etc.) to your customers.

Customers Are Not Created Equal

Too many organizations think that CRM means treating all customers the same. In fact, that was what caused so many dot.coms to end up as non-profit organizations. The neighborhood grocer once knew which customers were the best, and they were treated in a special way. Today, we use information about our customers to identify different customer value segments. Using this information we can customize appropriate experiences for different segments. This allows us to optimize the balance between what we invest in various customer relationships against the return we expect to receive.

Walk in Your Customer's Shoes

This is really the easiest principle to follow. After all, we are all customers from time to time. We really *do* know what it's like to be a customer. It is so simple that it's mind boggling to think that there are so many organizations that go about implementing CRM programs without any consideration of what these changes will do for (or to) their customers. As we first discussed in Chapter 3, we need to know how our organization looks from the customers' view (see Figure 23-2).

Customers are operating in a certain stage of their product life cycle (not our sales cycle), using a combination of many different company touch points. They are not aware and should not be forced to be aware of how our company is organized.

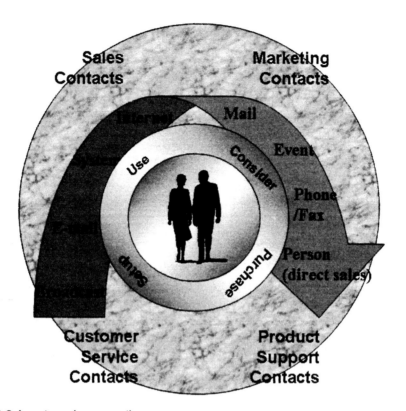

Figure 23-2 A customer's perspective

23.2 Knowing What a Successful CRM Program Looks Like

Customer Relationship Management is not a piece of software; it's an entire discipline. Hence, a successful CRM program must involve all aspects of how your company interacts with its customers. This frightens many, but the size is easily scalable as long as you understand all the steps that are necessary to deliver success for each of the four CRM components.

23.2.1 CRM Program Life Cycle

The CRM program life cycle that was introduced in Chapter 5 breaks down every CRM program into a series of projects having four major steps. Figure 23-3 will remind you of these four phases of the life cycle and the four transition points that help move the project from one phase to the next.

Here, too, we need to achieve a careful balance between how much we focus on the internal change and infrastructure and how much we focus on the customer.

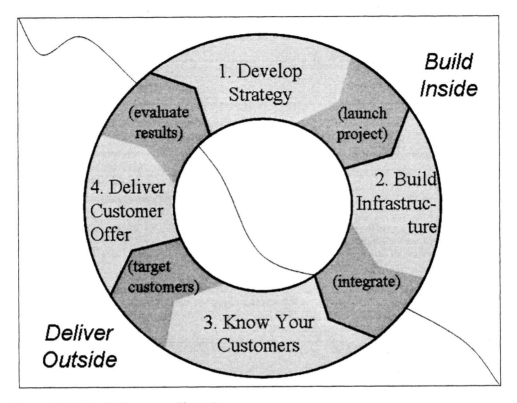

Figure 23-3 The CRM program life cycle

23.2.2 CRM Components

If a CRM program seems too big, we have the life cycle to help us manage the process. The other danger is that we treat CRM as too small—just a piece of software, just a database, or just a new online support function. CRM is comprised of all four of the components described in Table 23-1.

The product of the CRM manufacturing process is your company's ability to deliver excellent customer experiences that are appropriate to each customer. But how do we get all these pieces working together at the same time to achieve this CRM goal?

Table 23-1 The CRM Components

Component	Description
Information is the raw material of CRM.	Identification Data—Name/address/phone data collected from customers to complete a business transaction
	Marketing data—Descriptors/traits/preferences collected from customers during a transaction (either by asking questions or tracking behavior)
	List data—Names/addresses collected by a third party that can be bought or leased
	Overlay data—Customer profile data collected by a third party that can be leased and appended to existing customer records
Processes are the methods employed (human or computer) to deliver the customer "product" of CRM.	All current/future processes that directly touch the customer
	Touch points—means by which we interact with customers, such as phone, e-mail, etc.
	Integrating and rationalizing processes from the customer's point of view
Technology is the machinery that enables the CRM processes to operate.	Software products (process automation tools, analysis tools, web site development and management tools)
	Networking and integrating applications and databases
	Databases—Purchased solutions and home grown, central and distributed
	Security, such as encryption tools and firewalls
People are the power supply of CRM. The energy source has to be set to the right voltage for the system to work. People are "reset" through various change management tools and support mechanisms.	Training and education
	New tools
	Measurements and rewards
	Identifying and eliminating process disconnects and white space

23.3 Knowing How You're Going to Get There

Customer Relationship Manage is actually very simple; but it's not easy. First, there is no magic wand. Successful CRM programs occur when your organization is ready to invest the time and energy required to successfully manage communications and work across all the front office business functions and Information Technology. You need to be able to successfully balance your dream of what the future can look like and the time and sweat needed to make it all happen (see Figure 23-4).

Figure 23-4 Balancing dreams and sweat

It's critical to know where you plan to take your CRM program and what path will get you there while addressing the company's most important business priorities. Setting realistic expectations within the organization—and repeating them—is critical, because there are no shortcuts for doing the work. There is no magic.

23.3.1 There Is No Magic

CRM programs take real work and involvement from key people within your organization. But there is a piece of "magic" that all companies have available to them, although they don't often use it. Common sense goes out the window with the promise of all the wonders that CRM will bring.

Of course, common sense isn't really magic. It just looks that way sometimes when the occasional program team decides to take charge of the program and use their business knowledge and experience to set priorities, identify requirements, and decide on scope.

23.3.2 Use Strategic *Vision* and Take Small *Steps*

Dreams are about painting a vision of where you want to be. Dreams should not be limited by common sense. Instead, reach for the sky. Dreams should always stretch the imagination. They are too big to be done overnight (since there's no magic involved). As you work to achieve your vision, you must identify small, high-priority projects that have specific, limited, clear objectives that you can measure.

CRM projects are the small steps we take to achieve our vision. In addition to being clear and measurable, the objectives must be linked to a well-defined customer offer with a measurable response (e.g., a product launch, upgrade campaign, new CRM customer functionality). In Chapter 19, we introduced the CRM continuum shown in Figure 23-5. The continuum illustrates that you should repeat these small projects until you've achieved the level of CRM functionality that is right for your company. The projects are always guided by your strategy and vision, and the vision and strategy are evolved based on project results and changes in the environment.

Each project cycle starts from the strategic plan, focusing on just the elements that are relevant to the current project. Each project cycle ends by comparing the results to the current strategy and vision and incorporating into the strategic plan anything that was learned or that has changed. The updated strategy is then used to launch the project having the next highest priority.

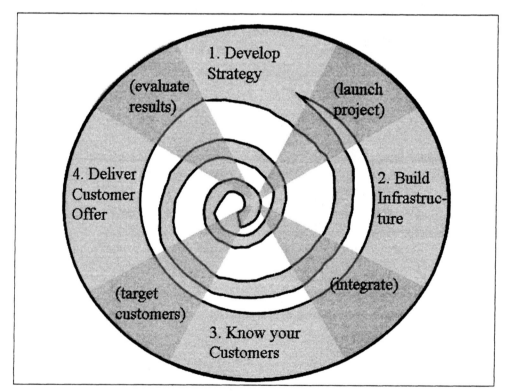

Figure 23-5 CRM continuum = baby steps

23.3.3 Bridging Organizational Disconnects with Organizational Support and Communication

It's been said that our ability to communication is what separates man from beast. Don't you wonder sometimes whether the animal kingdom has taken control of your company? The most important result of effective communication is to achieve understanding. All CRM programs fail if there is no common understanding between the business functions and the IT team, yet these two sets of people generally have little in common—not even a common language at times. (Of course, the same could be said for some sales and marketing organizations, and even more so for product support and customer services.)

We use formal organizational structures and project management methodologies introduced in Chapter 10 to clarify roles, responsibilities, and expectations between the various important organizations. Different experts with different skills must work *together* to make sure that technical results meet business expectations, as illustrated in Figure 23-6.

Of course, the project manager plays a key role in keeping the work on schedule and eliminating misunderstandings within the project team. The project manager and the program manager together are responsible for communication with the extended program management organization.

Figure 23-6 The project team

23.4 Knowing What It Takes to Achieve Success

What does success look like? If you don't know that up front, how will you know when you get there? If you don't get agreement to the goals before you start (and keep reminding everyone of what you're doing), how will anyone else know you're successful? Communication is one key to success, but there are others.

23.4.1 Measure—Everything—Twice

Always measure the current state before you start changing things so that you can show the progress that has been made when you take another measurement after the project is finished. Some CRM results are highly intangible and difficult to measure, but those that can be measured should be. You can illustrate results from even small projects by demonstrating progress you have made relative to your original position (as illustrated in Figure 23-7).

Changes in response rates, changes in web site hits, and changes in data quality levels and undelivered mail are all evidence of the impact of your CRM program. It's the change that's most important, not the absolute measurement.

Figure 23-7 Measuring everything twice

23.4.2 Keep It Simple

CRM is not rocket science; keep your efforts practical and simple. Objectives must be achievable in a reasonable amount of time (six months or less) so you don't lose the attention and support of key sponsors and experts in the middle of the project. Getting a new sponsor on board at the start of a new cycle is easier than trying to swap sponsors mid-project.

The other advantage of simple projects is that everyone can understand what you're trying to do. Masking the project objectives in complex, obscure, or technical terms does not protect you from failure; it ensures failure. If people don't understand the objectives or what they are supposed to do, they will decide for themselves. The chances are slim that what they decide matches what you want.

And for heaven's sake, if the problem is so complex that even you don't understand it, *stop right now!*

23.4.3 When Have You Done Enough?

What is enough? It's the minimum needed to achieve project success. Don't ever do more than you have to, but invest any additional time and enthusiasm in doing a really exceptional job at building all the elements that are needed for success. It is much better to do what you said you were going to do well than it is to do more and risk the success of your project.

All kinds of opportunities will arise for expanding scope. Maybe the source system has more information than you require, but it might be useful some day. Don't forget that you have to maintain the data after it's in the database, or it will be garbage and you will spend more money cleaning it up than it's worth.

Sometimes, it will appear that if you expand the process scope just a little, you can really make a big impact. Beware: Almost every little process addition you encounter is really just the tip of a huge iceberg that will sink your project. Stay focused on the process that you identified and get it working right!

Sometimes, it seems like a great opportunity to resolve a major networking requirement or system hardware conversion as part of a new project. Resist this temptation. Sure, the business driver is a good incentive for IT investment, but the price tag could push your breakeven data so far in the future that it scares everyone away. Also, just getting all that new stuff up and running will probably take longer than your entire project. Do just enough to be successful. Your project can be the test case for some new technology, but just test your project requirements.

Many companies try to get support and buy-in by giving everyone an equal vote on all project decisions. This really doesn't work. Huge teams and committees are almost impossible to manage and keep on track. Have a small core team (more than four, but less than ten) whose members are responsible for making decisions based on input and involvement from their home organizations. They must have the authority to make decisions on behalf of their organizations.

During a project, don't gather every possible business requirement, just what's relevant to the project. Never analyze until you understand absolutely everything; you'll never get there anyway. Just do enough so that the team is comfortable with the approach and direction you've chosen. Do just enough that the team is confident in moving to the next step. Less really is more.

Finally, do not make CRM development a life-long career—at least not for the same company. There is no ideal CRM state that all companies must achieve. It depends on these factors:

- Your customers
- Your products
- Your competitors
- Your market
- Your company size

And on any number of other factors. Never start a new project without testing whether there is a good business reason for doing it. If you can't find one, don't do it.

23.5 Knowing How to Get Started

I'm guessing that most of you already know roughly what needs to be done. You didn't pick up this book because CRM is such a fascinating topic. More than likely, you're reading this book because you're faced with sponsoring, managing, or leading a critical CRM project for your company. You want to know what to expect, what to avoid, and what you can do to increase the likelihood that your project is successful. But maybe, most important of all, you want to know how to get started.

23.5.1 The First Step

That's a no brainer; the first step is to define your CRM strategy. Frankly, some of you may already have a project underway. Don't worry; it's not too late, and you don't have to bring everything to a screeching halt. But you do need to know if there are five other *competing* projects also underway in various parts of the business and what the general direction of the CRM program should be.

23.5.2 The Ten Commandments of CRM

These ten commandments, unlike the originals, were not written in stone on the top of a mountain. The CRM commandments summarize all the tools and tricks we've discussed during the previous 22 chapters. These are what you will follow to ensure that the Customer Relationship Management program you are building for your company is successful

1. Stop when you've done enough.
2. KISS (Keep It Simple, Sport).
3. Measure—everything—twice (before and after).
4. Manage the disconnects between organizational silos.
5. Take baby steps, and repeat as needed.

6. CRM is not a fairy tale; there is no sorcerer's stone.

7. There are *four* components; don't leave any out.

8. Use the framework: the CRM program life cycle.

9. It's the customer, really.

10. And above all things, you must make a profit!

My objective for this book was to give you the information, tools, and templates that will help deliver a successful CRM program for your company. But what's going to happen next?

23.6 So Where Will CRM Go from Here?

You probably can't wait for all the improvements anyway, so do the best with what's available now. We want to build a CRM infrastructure that is standard and open enough that you can just plug in the tools when they become available.

It's certainly important to keep your radar turned on for new tools, technologies, and information sources. We talked about a couple of fairly new tools earlier. The avatar discussed in Chapter 21 is one good example of a technology that is emerging to humanize the web site experience. New sources of customer information and new tools for analysis and data mining appear all the time. If you wait until all the breakthroughs are developed, you'll never get started. Design your CRM infrastructure for flexibility, and keep you options open. Look for—in fact, demand—options that are open and designed to work well with other products so you can protect and secure your customer information without sacrificing functionality and capabilities. This may be the eleventh CRM commandment!

So here's my wish list for what I hope becomes available as a product—and soon. The CRM industry needs a true customer reference database system that is designed to be independent of any application, but completely open and easily and efficiently accessible from any application. The database product could come empty or could contain data from one or more information suppliers. This dream product needs to include mapping and loading utilities and extensive quality assessment and data management tools. But someone just needs to start with some basics, and soon!

My family suggested that, instead of writing this concluding chapter, I should just tell you to get going.

So, why are you just sitting there reading?

Glossary of Terms

$\mathbf{T}$he glossary in Table A-1 summarizes the key CRM terms that were identified and defined throughout the text.

Table A-1   Glossary

Term	Definition	Chapter
assets	Everything a company owns that has significant value and can be sold to pay off debts.	20
brand	A pact between the company and its customers that makes promises, sets expectations, and defines agreements for their mutual benefit, which is symbolized by the "seal".	2
customer	A person (or group of persons) who influences or decides on the acquisition of one of your products or services or who uses one of these products or services.	1
customer company	An organization (public, private, non-profit, or governmental) that has characteristics which influence the group of people who work there.	1
customer lifecycle	The total time that the customer is engaged with your company from the customer's experience and viewpoint.	3
customer loyalty	A behavior, built on positive experiences and value, that causes a customer to buy our products, even when that may not appear to be the most rational decision.	1

Table A-1   Glossary (Continued)

Term	Definition	Chapter
customer relationship management (CRM)	The strategic use of *information, processes, technology,* and *people* to manage the customer's relationship with your company (marketing, sales, service, and support) across the whole customer life cycle.	3
customer segments	Groups of customers who *look like one.* You want to treat all group members the same, and all groups differently from other groups.	16
customer-centered company	A company that has an external point of view, making plans and decisions based on the anticipated impact on the customer.	2
data classes	High-level categories of stuff that is important to YOUR business.	10
data subjects	The stuff (people, places, things, or ideas) that is important to YOUR business *and about which you need to collect, store, and share certain facts.*	10
entities	The people, places, things, and ideas that are important to YOUR business. Entities have characteristics (attributes) that the business needs to collect, store, and share, and they have links (relationships) to other entities.	10
information component	Data in context.	10
people component	Changes in the way people function or operate.	13
process component	A series of work steps that lead to a specific result.	11
product-centered company	A company that makes plans and decisions based on an internal perspective (the impact inside the company).	2
program	The sum of all the work your company does to improve the customer experience and increase loyalty. Your program can be as long or short as appropriate to your business needs.	5
project	A well-defined effort with specific deliverables, due dates, and costs. To ensure success, a project must produce valuable and measurable results but must be small enough to complete within a business sponsor's attention span.	5
technology component	The computer tools (hardware, software, and networks) employed to manage the information and processes you use to deliver customer experiences.	12

Table A-1 Glossary (Continued)

Term	Definition	Chapter
touch points	The means (media) that you use to interact with your customers. Touch point interactions must be targeted to a specific customer or customer company, and they must allow for a response (a conversation, a transaction, a reply, and so on).	3

For more information about each term, please refer to the chapters referenced.

Tools and Templates

Using tools and templates is one of the best methods for achieving quick results and improving communication. If anything similar already exists within your company, you would be wise to use that. You'll have the advantage that the tools are already familiar within the company.

If your company doesn't currently use standards processes and forms, I hope you'll be able to take advantage of these and not have to waste time starting from scratch.

B.1 Putting Together a Strategic Plan

Data collection for the strategic planning phase is the cornerstone of your CRM program. It doesn't have to take years to gather enough information to get started, but *it has to be done*. The following templates are a great way to capture the basic information that most companies need to be ready to launch their first project.

B.1.1 Internal Strategic Interview

Table B-1 shows a sample internal strategic interview. You certainly will want to add some company-specific questions. But remember that the shorter and more direct the interview, the better the results are likely to be. Mix open-ended and close-ended questions.

Table B-1   Strategic Interview

Internal Strategic Interview				
Contact Information:				
Name		Phone		
Organization		Role/Title		
Date		Time		

XYZ has launched its company-wide CRM initiative with the objective **to make customer loyalty a competitive advantage for _____ using CRM methodologies and tools.** The purpose of this survey is to help us define our company vision and strategy for CRM – **quickly.**

I. Company Overall

What are the key business objectives/opportunities for ___ for next year?

1	
2	
3	

Biggest risks for ___ for next year?	**Three critical success factors (things that must go right)?**
1	
2	
3	

II Your organization	
What are the key business objectives/opportunities for your organization for next year?	
1	
2	
3	

Key business risks for your function?	**Three critical success factors (things that must go right)?**
1	
2	
3	

III. The Customer	
Who are the company's most important customer segments?	
	Segment (example customers)?	How do you recognize/classify them?
1		
2		

3		

What do these important customers expect from you (by segment if relevant)?

	Segment	Expectations
1		
2		
3		

IV. The CRM Initiative

What do you mean by "Customer Relationship Management (CRM)"?

For the purpose of the rest of this survey, we will define CRM as:

The strategic use of *information, processes, technology, and people* to manage the customer's relationship with your company (marketing, sales, service, and support) across the entire customer life cycle.

What will CRM do for your most important customers?

1	
2	

3	

What will CRM do for …

	The Company?	Your function?
1		
2		
3		

What touch points are most important to your company, and how do you compare to your competitors in these areas?

1	
2	
3	

Which CRM area or what projects should we tackle first?

1	
2	

3	

What are the biggest risks to a successful CRM initiative for the company (organizational, cultural, behavioral, etc.)?

1	
2	
3	

What CRM projects currently exist or are underway?

	Name/Owner/Organization	Purpose (marketing, support, sales, service)
1		
2		
3		

IV. Wrap-up

What are the three stupidest things that we currently do to our customers?

1	

2		
3		

Who do you think it's important that we interview?

	Name/Contact Info	Organization/Role
1		
2		
3		

Anything else you think that we need to know that we haven't already asked?

Some of XYZ's interview results are summarized in Chapter 8.

B.1.2   System Inventory

The system inventory is another important element impacting your strategic plan. You need to know what customer-related systems already exist and which are planned or under development in order to get an understanding of the scope of your company's CRM infrastructure. A sample systems inventory is shown in Table B 2.

Table B-2   Systems Inventory

System	Information	Technology
Name: Purpose: Business Unit: Contact Person: Location: Status: (live, development, planned)	__Customer ID (name/user ID) __Contact info (address/phone/e-mail/ __) __Company info (name, size, industry) __Owned products (ours/competitors) __Purchased service (ours/competitors) __Suspect/prospect/customer __Deals	Hardware Size (GB) Software/database Closed or open architecture Customer contact (e.g., web, phone)

The results of XYZ's systems inventory are shown in Chapter 8.

B.1.3   Customer Survey

The customer survey, shown in Table B-3, is intended to take a quick reading of how well your company is doing in the eyes of your customers. Find out what is important to customers in all your value segments.

Table B-3   Customer Survey

Touch point	Broadcast E-mail Systematic Internet	Mail Event Phone/fax Personal
Life Cycle Stage	Consider Awareness/interest Investigation	Set up Install Learn customize
	Purchase Evaluate/choose Order/purchase	Use Operate/maintain Upgrade/retire
Survey (replace the words in *italics* with one of the choices from the appropriate list above)	1. How important is ***touch point*** in helping you to accomplish ***life cycle stage***? **Very Somewhat Low** 2. How well does our ***touch point*** communication work for you/meet your ***life cycle stage*** needs? Not at all 1 2 3 4 5 Completely	

We saw some of XYZ's results in Chapter 8. By the way, it is also valuable to do a more in-depth survey of a few of your customers. You can modify the internal survey for this purpose, remembering to substitute their company name for yours, etc. Starting this type of survey with questions about the customer's goals and objectives sets the right customer-centered tone for the interview, making it more likely that you'll get honest answers about how you can (and do) impact your customer's success.

B.1.4   Competitive Assessment

The competitive assessment (shown in Table B-4) can (and should) be appended to the customer survey. Of course, this works only if you have an independent third party perform the survey and your company is anonymous.

Table B-4   Competitive Assessment

Company List	Create a list of three or four of the key competitors that you're interesting in comparing. Of course, you'll add your own company to the list.
Survey	1. What company's *touch point* has given you the best experience? Why was it best? 2. What company's *touch point* has given you the worst experience? Why was it the worst? 3. How well does *touch point* communication from *company* work for you/meet your *life cycle stage* needs? Not at all 1 2 3 4 5 Completely

Sample competitive results for XYZ are also illustrated in Chapter 8.

B.2   Choosing a Project and Its Duration and Scope

The next important step is to select and prepare for the first (or next) project.

B.2.1   Project Selection

The project selection scorecard allows you to compare a number of high-priority projects and select the one that has the highest chance of success. Table B-5 shows a sample project selection scorecard.

Table B-5 Project Selection Scorecard

	Project Scoring Characteristics	Target	System A		System B	
Size	Number of functions impacted by project	Few				
	Number of current systems impacted by project	Few				
	Complexity of business activity	Low				
	Number of data subjects	Few				
	Size: Do we completely understand project?	Small				
	Number of future systems on which this project depends	Low				
Impact	Importance: How meaningful is project to company? (Note: "no importance" scores 20.)	High				
	Critical: How critical is slippage/failure to the overall business goals?	Low				
	User commitment	High				
	Risk: How likely is it to be unsuccessful?	Low				
		TOTAL				
	Match Target Value = 1; partial match = 2; no match = 3					

The lowest score indicates the project that is the least risky and, therefore, has the best chance of success, while still providing visible company value.

B.2.2 Project Duration

The questions shown in Table B-6 will help you set realistic expectations for the length of each CRM projects. Based on your answers to Questions 1 and 2, plot your company's position on the chart shown in Question 3. This forms a guideline for the maximum size you should realistically target for each of your projects.

Table B-6 Estimating Your Maximum Project Size

1. What size is your company?	Number of employees _____ Number of locations _____ Number of countries where located _____
2. Describe your customer base.	a. Number of customers: Individuals _____ Companies _____ b. Type of customers: Consumers __ Business to Business __Both __ c. Industry breadth: Single industry: __Few __ Many/all __

3. Now find your situation on the following chart. You should limit the scope of each project such that you believe the entire project can be finished in no more than this amount of time.

		Company Size	
		Small/Local	Large/Global
Customer Base	Many/ Complex	5 months	9 months
	Few customers/ Industries	3 months	7 months

The benchmark project duration is six months or less, but you can see that, depending on the size and complexity of the company and its customer base, realistically you should expect some variation.

B.3 Setting the Project Scope

The project charter, which reflects a summary of all the decisions made during the project launch, is a key document and contains the fundamental agreements that govern the entire project effort. Table B-7 shows a sample project charter.

Table B-7   Project Charter

Project Title:		
Direction (issue/opportunity, critical success factors)		
Focus (business functions, target customers, customer offer)	• Functions: • Target audience: • Offer:	

Scope (what's in and what's out)

Component		Scope Is	Scope Is *Not*
Information	Categories		
	Sources		
Process			
Technology			
People			

Expected Deliverables

1.
2.
3.
4.

High Level Schedule

Milestone	Due	Actual	Owner	Approved
1. Launch/Plan completed				
2. Analysis completed				
3. Design completed				
4. Construction completed				
5. User Test completed				
6. Implementation				

Key Resources			
Role	**Assigned Individual**	**Percentage of time assigned**	**Duration**
Executive Sponsor			
Program Manager			
Project Manager			
Offer Manager			
Offer Response Manager			
IT analysts, designers, engineers			
Project Tradeoff Matrix			
	Deliverables	**Schedule**	**Resources**
Constrain (least flexible)			
Optimize			
Accept (most flexible)			

By completing the tradeoff matrix you will have gotten team-wide agreement on the most and least flexible aspects of the project, so it will be easier to make decisions later on.

B.4 Executing the Infrastructure Development Project

These tools are the responsibility of the Project Manager and are used for two major purposes: to keep the project moving along on schedule and to manage exceptions and issues. They are also excellent means of communication with the extended project team and the company at large.

B.4.1 Project Plan

The project plan reflects the individual activities (all these individual activities form what is called a work breakdown structure) that must be accomplished, when each activity is due, and when each is actually completed.

It may seem out of order to predetermine the length of any project before a project plan has been put together. You're right; it is premature to make a total commitment before this step has been taken. Setting up a target project length can now be used to impact the scope and resource requirements of the project, or the time line can be expanded based on these estimates. These changes should be reflected in an updated project charter and broadly communicated.

A word of caution: Be very wary of tackling a project that goes much beyond six or eight months. The risk of failure increases exponentially based on length of project. The project plan template is shown in Table B-8.

Table B-8   Project Plan

Project Plan							
Project Name:					**Revision #**		
Planned Start:				**Actual Start:**			
Task#	**Priority**	**Milestone Task**	**Assigned to**	**Est. hours**	**Due**	**Done**	**Comments**
1		Analysis					
2		Design					
3		Construction					
3.1		Build					
3.2		Unit Test					
3.3		System Test					
3.4		User Test					
4		Implementation					
Assumed Resource Availability							
Team Member		**Role**	**Percentage of Time**	**Comments**			
		Project Manager	100				
		Analyst					

Note that the time line is based on planned and specified resource availability. Deviations from the assumptions will always have an impact on the project duration.

B.4.2   Weekly Status Report

The weekly status report is the primary means of communicating the current status of the project and for bringing issues to the attention of the project's executive sponsors and managers. Keep the status report as short as possible, but always make it clear. Highlight the weekly status and summarize the explanation at the top of every weekly report, as illustrated in Table B-9. This might be all that many people read!

Table B-9 Weekly Status Report

Weekly Status Report					
Project Name:				**Week Ending:**	
Status Key: Green = On-track *Yellow = Caution* <u>Red = Critical</u>					
Status: (use color) **Green/***Yellow***/<u>Red</u>**	**Explanation:**				
Task	**Milestone**	**Responsible**	**Scheduled**	**Completed**	**Comments**
(1)	(match project milestones)				
(2)					
(3)					
(4)					
(5)					
(6)					
Unplanned Activities		**Responsible**	**Scheduled**	**Completed**	**Comments**
Accomplishment(s) This Week		**Responsible**	**Scheduled**	**Completed**	**Comments**
Objective(s) Next Week		**Owner**	**Due**	**Comments**	
New This Week					
Issue/ chng	**Item**	**Reported by**	**Description**	**Comments**	
Iss					
chg					

Table B-9   Weekly Status Report (Continued)

Open Issues List			
Issue Item	**Description**	**Status/Resolution**	**Date Resolved**

This document should be prepared with a high-level perspective and the business and end-user community in mind. Technical details are best dealt with in more detail on a change or issue request and analysis document and the change or issue log.

B.4.3   Issue Log

The Issue Log, shown in Table B-10, is a list of all of the situations and roadblocks that unexpectedly arise to derail your project.

Table B-10 Issue Log

ISSUE LOG									
Project Name:								**Date:**	
Issue ID	**Category** Information Process Technology, People	**Severity** Critical, Serious, Medium, Low	**Descrip-tion**	**Reported by**	**Report Date**	**Owner**	**Resolution/ Plan for Resolution**	**Close Date**	
1									
2									

The owner, resolution/plan, and close date track how the resolution was resolved. Open issues should be kept visible until they have been resolved. Often issues cannot be resolved by the project team and must be referred to the program team or sponsor.

B.4.4   Change Log

The Change Request Log summarizes every request for a change to the agreed-upon scope of the project, much like a construction change order, as shown in Table B-11.

Table B-11 Change Request Log

CHANGE REQUEST LOG								
Project Name:							**Date:**	
Change ID	**Priority Critical, Serious, Medium, Low**	**Request By**	**Request Date**	**Description**	**Assign to**	**Assign Date**	**Status (open, in progress, closed)**	**Close Date**
1								
2								

If the change increases scope, either resources must be added or the schedule must be lengthened.

APPENDIX C

Self-Assessments

S ome simple methods are available to help your organization determine its readiness for CRM. You can work through these assessments in a group or team meeting or compile the results of a number of interviews or questionnaires that have been completed by various constituents.

As a first step, though, just fill them out yourself. Because you've read this book, you undoubtedly are familiar with your company's current CRM state. These tools will give you a quick benchmark for how likely it is that your company is really ready for CRM.

C.1 Organizational Self-Assessment

Start with the company itself. What is your company's primary way of relating to customers? What's your company's Value Discipline?

C.1.1 Company Value Discipline

Table C-1 illustrates some questions that can be used to establish how your company builds and maintains relationships with its customers. What is the primary value that your company offers?

Table C-1   Value Discipline

Assessment Question	Response		
	Operation Excellence	Product Leadership	Customer Intimacy
What is your company's value discipline focus? (Operational Excellence, Product Leadership, Customer Intimacy) Select your company's value discipline focus.			
How do you assess your performance in your primary discipline compared to your competition? Enter (Worse, At Par, Better)			
How do you assess your performance in the other two disciplines compared to your competition? Enter (Worse, At Par, Better)			

Chapter 1 provides an explanation of the three value disciplines and how they are impacted.

C.1.2   Company Focus

Where is the primary focus of your organizations and how are decisions made? How do you determine which segments your customers are engaged in? Table C-2 shows some good basic self-assessment questions.

Table C-2   Customer-Centered or Product-Centered?

Assessment Question	Response
Where is your company focused?	___product-centered ___customer-centered? How do you know:
How do you segment your customers into groups?	___ by product purchased ___ by customer characteristic Describe:
How do customers experience their interactions with your company?	___fragmented ___integrated Why:

Chapter 2 discusses the impact of company focus on CRM, and vice versa.

C.1.3 Functional Assessment

The questions in Table C-3 can help you document the organizational structure of your company's "CRM functions." These are the organizations that will be most impacted by your company's CRM program.

Table C-3   CRM Business Functions

Assessment Question	Response	
1. What are the functions in your company that directly interact with the customer, and where do they report?	Function	Reports To
2. At what level in the organization do these functions come together?		
3. What touch points do you currently employ, and which function(s) manage them?	Touch Points	Functional Ownership
	Broadcast	
	E-mail	
	Systematic	
	Internet	
	Mail	
	Event	
	Phone/Fax	
	Personal	

There is more to CRM than just understanding your own organization.

C.1.4   Customer Life Cycle

The customer life cycle is what the relationship with your company looks like to the customer. Use words that describe what the customer experience is – not what your company is doing. Table C-4 illustrates a standard life cycle framework. Use terms that are familiar to your industry, customers, and company.

Table C-4   Customer Life Cycle

Describe Your Customers' Life Cycle	
Consider (or)	1. 2. 3.
Purchase (or)	1. 2. 3.
Setup (or)	1. 2. 3.
Use (or)	1. 2. 3.

You will be able to verify your understanding of the customer life cycle(s) through both internal and customer interviews.

C.2   Internet Readiness

Is your company taking advantage of the tremendous opportunities available from moving customer interactions to the Internet? If not, is it even ready? The questions in Table C-5 will help clarify the answer.

The Internet can provide a tremendous opportunity for implementing extremely cost effective CRM processes. Are you ready to take advantage of it?

Table C-5 Internet Readiness

Assessment Question	Response
Does your company currently have a web presence?	___ Yes ___No
Is your web site integrated into your overall CRM initiative?	___ Yes ___No
Do you use it for building relationships (or just for information)?	___ Build relationships ___ Information only
Have you ever "been a customer" on your own web site? How do you rate the experience?	(Low) 1 2 3 4 5 (Hi) Why?
Have you ever "been a customer" on any of your competitors' web sites? How do you rate each experience (write competitor name and ranking)?	a. _____ (Low) 1 2 3 4 5 (High) Why? b. _____ (Low) 1 2 3 4 5 (High) Why? c. _____ (Low) 1 2 3 4 5 (High) Why? d. _____ (Low) 1 2 3 4 5 (High) Why? e. _____ (Low) 1 2 3 4 5 (High) Why?
7. How does each Internet change impact your customers? In each cell, indicate whether that change has High, Medium, or Low impact.	Access	Easier to compare and swap	Commoditization	Providing human contact
	Control	Always on	Broader choice, less differentiation	Interaction preference
	Speed	Process expectations	Products unique for shorter periods	Efficiency not loyalty
	Globalization	Language, localization	Localization of products	Unknown language, culture
	Automation	Process disconnects	Distance from customer needs	Loss of human memory, connection

C.3 Privacy Self-Assessment

This privacy self-assessment has been used by XYZ and many other clients to help them formulate their internal privacy policy as well as their online Privacy Notice. One person I ran into at a Direct Marketing conference a few months ago was nice enough to write in.

> Thanks so much for the information. We just revised our web site and didn't really have a privacy policy [before]. This info[rmation] helped me to write one, and we should have it up and on our site in a few days. I think the structure and content of this information is very useful, informative, and easy to read and comprehend.

The questions in Table C-6 are those that this company used to create its online privacy notices in just a few days.

Table C-6   Privacy Self-Assessment

Framework	Question	Checklist
1. What is your company's overall privacy position?	a. Do you capture and store any data about your customers that is personally identifiable (is linked to an individual person's identity)?	___ Yes ___ No (If your answer is no, you don't need to answer the rest of these questions.)
	b. What is your company's overall position regarding the importance of your customers' privacy and the safety of their data?	
	c. What is your company's overall position regarding appropriate uses of customer data and who can access it?	
	d. What options do your customers have if they are not comfortable with your customer information practices?	
	e. When was the last time that your privacy policy and/or privacy statement was modified?	

Table C-6   Privacy Self-Assessment (Continued)

Framework	Question	Checklist
2. What do you collect and what do you do with data you collect (**Notice**)?	a. What types of data does your company collect from or about your customers?	Personal identification data: ___ Name ___ Street address ___ Phone (home, work, fax, cell) ___ E-mail Sensitive data: ___ Credit cards ___ Bank and financial information ___ Social security number ___ Driver's license number ___ Medical data ___ Educational data Transaction data ___Types of products ___Behavior (online activity, recency and frequency of purchase) ___Interests and preferences ___Feedback and complaints ___Service and support activity ___ Demographics and psychographics ___ Business employment data ___ Product ownership data ___ Credit and financial data
	b. How do you use the information you collect from your customers? (Check all that apply.)	___ Only to complete the transaction itself ___To reach customers in case of recalls or other product/service issues ___To validate the warranty or service contract ___To personalize and improve the customer's experience at our web site ___To monitor and improve our web site performance
	c. With whom do you share your customers' information? (Check all that apply.)	___Authorized individuals with business needs within our company ___Third parties who need the information to complete the transaction (e.g., a shipping company) ___ Third parties who offer products or services that we think would be of interest to the customer ___ We sell and/or lease our database to unrelated third-party organizations.

Table C-6   Privacy Self-Assessment (Continued)

Framework	Question	Checklist
	d. Does your company target children?	___Yes ___No. If you answered yes, how do you meet COPPA requirements? How do you ensure you have parental approval before accepting information from children under the age of 13? What third-party data do you append to your customer data? How do you ensure you have parental authorization to take a credit card number online?
	e. Do you use cookies?	___Yes ___No If you answered yes: Can a customer turn them off? How? What will happen to the customer's web site experience or other future interactions if he turns cookies off?
2. What kinds of **Choice** do you give customers about how you use their data?		___We don't give our customers any options; we just use the data any way we want to. ___We can't give our customers any guarantee; our data is not consolidated into a single database, and we can't control it all. ___We give a customer an option, and we never contact him for marketing purposes if he answered NO (opt-out). ___We give a customer an option, and we never contact him for marketing purposes unless he explicitly answered YES (opt-in). ___We use opt-in for e-mail, but not for our other types of marketing.
3. How to you give customers **access** to their data and allow them to correct its **accuracy?**	a. How do you allow your customer to see what data you have collected?	___We allow the customer to review and access his personal information online. ___We send the customer a printed copy of the information we have captured and stored. ___We currently cannot give customers access to their personally identifiable information. ___We only allow access after validating the customer's security information.
	b. How do you allow changes to be made to the customer's data? (Check all that apply.)	___We don't/can't change data in our customer databases. ___We allow the customer to update his information directly online. ___We (the company) make the changes requested by the customer. ___We only allow updates after validating his security information.

Table C-6   Privacy Self-Assessment (Continued)

Framework	Question	Checklist
4. What kind of **Security** protection do you provide for to protect your customers' data?	What do you do while data is traveling to your site over the Internet?	___ Identification data ___ Sensitive data ___ Transaction data
	What have you done to ensure the security of the data once it's inside the company (electronic and physical storage)?	
	What management practices have you set up to ensure physical safety and protection from unauthorized users?	
5. What is your position on **oversight** and providing an independent recourse for your customers?	a. Do you have company contact information? What is it?	
	b. Do you monitor the site and respond to concerns? Who is responsible?	
	c. Have you received a third-party privacy seal?	___Yes ___No If you answered yes: Who was it awarded by? You can contact them at:

For more information about customer privacy, refer to Chapter 22.

Information: The Raw Material of CRM

$\mathbf{I}$nformation is the foundation on which all successful CRM programs are built, but it is often ignored because of the belief that information just happens after the system is up and running. The business functions think information is the job of Information Technology, and the IT department believes that its job is only technology. In fact, they share responsibility. The business team doesn't need to know how to build a database, just what information they need to run their business. On the other hand, it's not a programmer's responsibility to define what information needs to be collected; they are responsible for building the storage facility to contain and protect the value of the information that the business identified.

Because there is so little expertise or experience available in managing the information engineering process, we will take XYZ's Valencia project as an example and detail exactly the process the company went through for Valencia. Often, it is the Information Technology experts who facilitate this process, but the early steps require active participation and ownership from the business experts who need the information. Both sets of experts must work together closely, using a formal methodology to ensure good communication and to manage the transition of responsibility from the business team members to the IT team members. Much like designing a filing system such as the one shown in Figure D-1, you would never expect the file cabinet manufacturer to decide what to put into each folder or how to arrange the folders in the drawers.

Of course, you would expect that the manufacturer built a cabinet such that standard files would fit in the drawers, the cabinet was sturdy and secure, and the drawers worked properly.

Figure D-1 One filing system

D.1   Information Engineering

In Chapter 11, we discussed the Information Engineering methodology at a high level. The engineering steps for the information component (and all the other components) are based on the overall CRM program requirements identified during strategic planning.

D.1.1   Strategic Data Requirements Inventory

The overall business owner's expectations or "wish list" was, of course, completed during the strategic planning process. The team started with the list of issues, opportunities, and "stupid things we do to customers" that was generated during the strategic plan, and they merged duplicate statements. These are the four steps they followed to develop the first pass at XYZ's strategic information needs inventory:

1. Go through the list with a highlighter, and mark every *noun*. These are your candidate data classes.
2. Identify and eliminate duplicate data classes as well as any unrealistic or unreasonable data classes.

3. Write a definition of each of the remaining data classes on your list.
4. Organize into Global Data Classes for ease of communication.

We will follow each of the steps XYZ took during its strategic planning development effort.

Identify Candidate Data Classes

In Table D-2, we see the data classes that were generated from reviewing XYZ's summary business opportunities and issues. For expediency, we're using just this short list, but you will want to examine all the information and business "quotes" you gathered internally and from customers. Table D-1 shows a portion of XYZ's full list of issues, opportunities, and customer mistakes.

Table D-1   XYZ's Data Classes

Business Opportunity/Risk	Data Class Candidates (nouns_
New customer selling model: solutions, installed base, not just boxes	Customer, selling model, solutions, installed base, boxes
Execute on channel strategy	Channel, strategy
New vertical market product categories	Vertical market, product categories
Marketplace consolidation	Marketplace
Competitor price gouging	Competitor, price
Current infrastructure doesn't support order and revenue growth targets	Infrastructure, order growth, revenue growth, targets
Too internally/product focused	Product

Although XYZ's actual list of business issues and opportunities was more than twice this long, for expedience we will work with a shorter list here.

Eliminate Duplicates and Unnecessary Classes

On average, you'll find two to three nouns for each statement on your list, but again many of these can be eliminated. Starting with the data class candidates (nouns) on the right side of Table D-2, we'll eliminate both duplicates and unlikely candidates to end up with our strategic data classes as shown.

You'll want to add to this inventory any other major data classes that you know are important to your company's CRM efforts.

Table D-2   XYZ's Data Classes

Data Class Candidates (nouns)	Data Classes
Customer	CUSTOMERS
Selling model	~~Selling model~~ (not a topic about which XYZ needed to capture information)
Solutions	PRODUCT SOLUTIONS
Installed base	INSTALLED PRODUCTS
Boxes	PRODUCTS (hardware products)
Channel	CHANNELS
Strategy	~~Strategy~~ (XYZ didn't need separate strategic planning data for CRM)
Vertical markets	INDUSTRIES
Product categories	~~Product solutions~~ (duplicate)
Marketplace	MARKETPLACE
Competitor	COMPETITORS
Price	PRODUCT PRICES
Infrastructure	~~Infrastructure~~ (XYZ didn't need infrastructure data for CRM)
Order growth	ORDERS
Revenue growth	REVENUE
Targets	TARGETS
Product	~~Products~~ (duplicate)

Create Data Class Definitions

Now that we have developed a wish list that includes all these data classes, we need to take one more step. Common understanding is always one of the key objectives for any development project, so we need to define each of these data classes. Remember, this is just your wish list; the definitions, like the data classes, should be very high-level and need not be perfect or exhaustive. Table D-3 shows XYZ's 12 data classes and the high-level definitions that were developed for each one.

Table D-3   XYZ's High-Level Class Definitions

Data Class	Definition
CUSTOMERS	A customer is a person (or a group of persons) who influences or decides on the acquisition of one of our products or services, or who uses one of these products or services
PRODUCTS	A single unit or service that we sell
INSTALLED PRODUCTS	Products and services owned or used by customers
PRODUCT SOLUTIONS	A group of products and services (which may not all be ours) that meets the customer's complete need
CHANNELS	The partner organizations we contract to help us market, sell, service and support products and services
INDUSTRIES	Groups of companies in the same line of business
MARKETPLACE	The environment in which we operate our business
COMPETITORS	Organizations that sell products and services that compete with our products and/or services
PRODUCT PRICES	Purchase amount for products and services
ORDERS	A transaction via which a customer acquires our products or services and agrees to a certain sales price
REVENUE	Gross income from sale of products and services
TARGETS	Expected goals for various financial measures such as orders and revenue

Now we're ready to start working on the Owner's View of information. But before we do that, we're going to do one more thing with our strategic data classes.

Organize into Global Data Classes

It's a very helpful to organize your data classes into logical groups: a few very high-level global data classes. We want our information needs inventory to be widely recognized and understood across the entire organization. People have a much easier time absorbing and remembering a few ideas at a time (from three to seven). Global data classes provide a very useful representation that supports understanding, recognition, and recall.

The CRM team at XYZ came up with a just four global data classes because they decided to be successful they really only needed to know four things:

- We need to know who our customers are.
- We need to understand the marketplace in which we operate.
- We need to be able to track our investments.
- We need to measure the returns we get from those investments.

One of their 12 data classes (MARKETPLACE) became a global data class. The remaining 11 data classes (which were really more like 30 at this point) were organized into the four global data classes, as shown in Figure D-2.

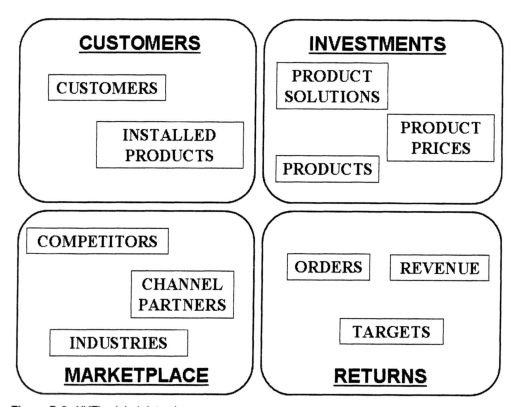

Figure D-2   XYZ's global data classes

The six information engineering views are all developed as part of the work on a specific project.

D.1.2   Engineering Information

The information engineering methodology is reviewed in Table D-4. XYZ completed all the steps of the framework just for the subset of data classes that were relevant to Valencia.

Table D-4   The Information Component

Business View	Data (System) View	File Cabinet View
Owner's Wants View	Data classes	File drawer labels
Owner's Needs View	Business subjects	Hanging file labels
Designer's View	Entity and relationship model	Individual folders
Builder's View	Physical data model	Document formats
Detailed Representation	Database: tables, columns, rows	Individual documents
Functioning System	Populated database	Filled filing cabinet

Let's look at all these views and the work performed by XYZ's Valencia project team to ensure that requirements were clearly defined and communicated so that the end result met expectations. XYZ's CRM team had decided to begin working on the first piece of their new customer identity system (El Cid). As you know the project team chose Valencia as the name for the first project.

D.2   Owner's Wants: Data Classes

After the Valencia project was selected, a project launch was scheduled to determine the objectives, time line, resource requirements, and specific scope of the four components. The project team began by selecting just the data classes that were relevant to Valencia's customer and product needs. The owner's wants view for the information component was defined during the project launch. At that time XYZ reviewed the list of strategic data classes and narrowed the scope to those that were relevant to Valencia. The team identified the two data classes shown in Table D-5.

Table D-5   Valencia Data Classes

Data Class	Definition
CUSTOMERS	A customer is a person (or a group of persons) who influences or decides on the acquisition of one of our products or services, or who uses one of these products or services.
INSTALLED PRODUCTS	Products or services owned or used by a customer

Every view (after the owner's wants view which is based on the strategic plan) depends on the results from the previous view.

D.3   Owner's Needs: Business Subjects

In the owner's needs view, the business experts defined the major categories of "stuff" that XYZ needed to store in its filing cabinet. The team followed these steps:

1. Start with the data classes that were deemed to be relevant for this project.
2. Identify the major divisions (data subjects) for these data classes.
3. Write a definition of each data subject.

Let's continue following the path that the project team took during planning and execution of Valencia.

D.3.1   Select Relevant Data Classes

Of course, they started with the previous view results—the list of data classes. During strategic planning XYZ had identified 12 (really 30) of them for their overall CRM program. Next, they identified just what was needed to accomplish the Valencia project. After reviewing its class list, XYZ identified just two data classes that were relevant to Valencia (which was the first iteration of the customer database, El Cid).

El Cid will serve as a customer reference database so all customers can be consistently identified and recognized wherever they touch XYZ. Obviously, the data class CUSTOMER was the starting point for Valencia. In addition, XYZ knew that an important part of *customer recognition* included knowing what products were owned by what customers. The INSTALLED PRODUCTS data class was the other one identified as relevant by the project team. Valencia involves only these two data classes. Other projects (like MyXYZ) would touch many data classes—one of the reasons we didn't select it, remember?

D.3.2   Identify Data Subjects

The data class (or file drawer) "Customer" represents just about anything we might decide to collect about a company or a person who owns one of our products or uses our services. This is a very conceptual level, which is easy to show on a diagram, but not useful in helping the IT team to understand what to build. Because building the information infrastructure is one of our goals, we'll keep working.

Subjects divide data classes into meaningful subsets that let us organize and store information in a way that it is useful for many different purposes. Subjects represent real things (including concepts like profit) that have characteristics that describe them. Their characteristics are usually different from those of any other subject. We have discussed that a customer can be a company or a person, so two obvious data subjects are company and people. These certainly have different characteristics, so they pass the test to be separate subjects.

Of course, XYZ also sells products to consumers, so should it separate consumers and company contacts? XYZ chose to have just one People subject because (at least for now) it needed the same basic information about all people (name, address, etc.) in either case. XYZ called these two subjects **Customer Company** and **Customer Contact.**

For the other data class, **INSTALLED PRODUCTS,** XYZ could not identify any meaningful subsets (at least for this project). The company decided to retain it as a data class, at least for now, and defined a subject **Installed Products** as its only subset. Later, XYZ might want to either find more data subjects for **INSTALLED PRODUCTS** or eliminate it as a data class and find another home for the **Installed Products** subject. The *right* model is the one that's right for XYZ's business. After they had identified the business data subjects for Valencia, the next step was to clearly define them all.

D.3.3   Create Data Subject Definitions

Just as we did for our data classes, we will create business definitions for each subject. Note that each definition is based on the data class definition so it took less time to create than if we started over (see Table D-6).

Table D-6   Data Subjects for Valencia

Data Subject	Definition
Customer Companies	Organizations that acquire at least one of our products or services
Customer Contacts	Persons who acquire at least one of our products or services
Installed Products	Products or services owned or used by a customer company or contact

These are the data subjects that XYZ needed to support its business **independent of any system that used them.** We never organize data around its uses, only on what the data actually is. XYZ's next step was to plan how to organize the facts it wanted to collect and store. "Company" is one thing, but what do we want to know about companies?

D.4   Designer's View: Entities and Relationships

The Designer's View is where the handoff between business knowledge and IT knowledge takes place. Let's review the process that XYZ used to identify the entities, attributes, and relationships for Valencia.

1. Develop a list of the characteristics (attributes) we want to collect and store about each of the project data subjects; identify and eliminate duplicates.

2. Assign each attribute to the data subject it describes; these are candidate entities.

3. Identify the KEY for each candidate entity.

4. Apply entity rules to determine whether all the related attributes can be stored in one entity or whether we need to define more than one.

5. Identify entity relationships.

6. Define entities, attributes, and relationships.

First, we will identify the facts that are important to XYZ's efforts to recognize customers consistently.

D.4.1   Develop Attribute List

We discussed that one of the best sources for understanding what your company needs is to look at what you already collect and use for reporting and other purposes. Figure D-3 is the example we saw in Chapter 10 of one of XYZ's early product registration cards.

We learned that each question on this card represents a characteristic or attribute of a single data entity. We just need to make a list of all these elements, and then assign them to the appropriate entity. Of course, we always start with the results of the previous step, the three data subjects: **Installed Products, Customer Contacts,** and **Customer Companies.**

XYZ Product Registration

Product Model _____   Serial # _____   Purchase Date_____

Where purchased (circle one)?   XYZ direct   XYZ online   XYZ catalog   Dealer/retailer

       If dealer/retailer: Store name_____   City_____   State_____

| Mr Mrs Ms |
| Last name _____   First Name _____   Gender: | M   F |

Title_____   Email address: _____

Street address _____   City _____   State ___ Zip_____

Is this your home or company address? | Home   Company | How many employees work here?_____

Company name _____   Total Employees _____   Revenue_____

Industry Code (see reverse): _____   Industry Description _____

This product will be used at | Office   Home   Both | for | Personal   Business   Travel   All |

What competitive products do you own/use? 1._____   2._____   3._____   4._____   5._____

May we contact you from time to time with information you might find interesting (circle one)? Yes   No

---

Figure D-3   XYZ's product registration card

D.4.2   Assign Attributes to Entities

To get started, XYZ first needed to define some entities. They didn't really know what all these should be at this point, so like previous steps, they used the data subjects from the previous view as candidate entities. The candidate entities then were Installed Product, Customer Contact, and Customer Company. By the way, a naming convention commonly used in information engineering uses the plural noun as names for the two highest level views (class and subject) and a singular form for the rest of the views. This book employs a convention for the hierarchy of views that for the "customer" is shown in Table D-7.

Table D-7   View Hierarchy Convention

Class	Subject	Entity	key	attribute
CUSTOMER	Customer Company Customer Contact	Customer Company Customer Contact		

The attribute assignment for each entity is the task that XYZ tackled next. Attributes were assigned to the entity it best described. The registration card asked for information about the product, the owner (customer contact person), and the customer company. XYZ had defined the data class **INSTALLED PRODUCTS** as "Products or services owned or used by a customer company or contact." The candidate entity of the same name carries has the same definition. The product information on the registration card describes products owned by customers, so that was the appropriate place to assign the product facts. XYZ assigned the rest of the information to the appropriate customer entity (contact person and company) as shown in Table D-8. I told you it was easy!

Well, I'm sorry; it's not quite *that* easy. If you were browsing through a file folder to check for a product warranty on a specific installed product, you'd probably sort through just the documents for the right product and then check each serial number. Product model and serial number uniquely identify a product (whether installed or not). These identifying attributes are called the "unique key." In a computer with its capacity for storing huge numbers of "forms," it would be impossible to browse through them one at a time. The *key* is how the computer recognizes and retrieves exactly the right information. XYZ's next task was to choose a unique key for each entity.

Table D-8   Attribute Assignments

Attribute	Candidate Entity (subject_	Attribute	Candidate Entity (subject)
1. product model	Installed Product	3. first name	Customer Contact (continued)
2. serial number		4. gender	
3. purchase date		5. title	
4. where purchased		6. e-mail address	
5. store name		7. street	
6. store city		8. city	
7. store state		9. state	
8. used for		10. postal code	
9. where used		11. company/home address	
10. competitive product 1		12. okay to contact?	
11. competitive product 2		1. employee count here	Customer Company
12. competitive product 3		2. company name	
13. competitive product 4		3. total employees	
14. competitive product 5		4. revenue	
1. address title	Customer Contact	5. industry code	
2. last name		6. industry description	

D.4.3   Develop Entity Keys

Every entity must have a unique key. The key identifies a specific real customer (or employee or product); the customer must always have the same key, and the key can never represent any other customer—even if the customer goes out of business. In other words, keys must remain stable over time, and each must uniquely identify only one customer (employee, product). A key is one or more attributes that, in combination, uniquely identify each instance of the entity.

Installed Product

Let's look at how XYZ handled the Installed Product entity shown in Table D-6. They had to decide which attribute(s) might uniquely identify a single Installed Product. Having just discussed this issue, we understand why XYZ identified product and serial number as the unique key identifier of a specific product installation. XYZ chose product model + serial number as the unique key for the Installed Product entity as shown in Table D-9, which also includes the other entity attributes of this entity.

Table D-9   Installed Product Keys

Candidate Entity (Subject)	Attribute
Installed Product	product model
	serial number
	purchase date
	where purchased
	store name
	store city
	store state
	used for
	where used
	competitive product 1
	competitive product 2
	competitive product 3
	competitive product 4
	competitive product 5

Next, XYZ did the same analysis for the other two candidate entities.

Customer Contact

At first glance, we might think a customer contact is identified by first and last name. But of course, names are not unique. However, XYZ decided that a name at a particular address (either street or e-mail address) was adequate to assume uniqueness for the purposes. (There is no right or wrong answer, just what makes sense for your situation—as long as it's unique, that is!)

But then the team thought of some problems. First, names and addresses are not stable; they change. Second, not all customers have e-mail addresses, and sometimes they don't want to give us their other information. A key must be complete (none of its elements can be blank), so this solution—while adequate in establishing uniqueness—is not sufficient for serving as the key. In this case, XYZ defined a new attribute, a random number that would be generated whenever a new name/address/e-mail combination was found by the system. They named this new key the *person identifier* because it is used to identify a specific individual based on name and addresses.

Customer Company

XYZ encountered a similar situation with the Customer Company entity. The company name might seem like the logical choice, but it too is neither unique nor unchanging. The company name and address are likely to be unique, but this has the same problems already discussed. XYZ defined a new attribute, *company identifier*, to act as the key.

The next step is polishing these entities so they are designed for optimum quality management, efficiency, and usability. To meet this end, we must apply the rules that govern entities to define more exactly what needs to be built.

D.4.4 Apply Entity Rules

This is the step where XYZ's IT team took over most of the responsibility for the project, and the business team members played more or less a review/approve role. Even so, there is benefit to understanding a little bit about how the other half lives. IT organizations have a rigorous process for developing entities (called **normalization**). IT experts (database designers or architects) use the **business rules** of the organization to drive the normalization process. According to Ronald G. Ross, one of the masters of business rule management, said in his white paper on the subject that business rules are the

> Units of business logic the company wishes to follow in its day to day operation.

All organizations have business rules, but often they are informal and undocumented. The business team's efforts during the early stages of each component development are aimed at formalizing the relevant business rules. Meaningful data definitions are essential because even though the normalization process is quite technical, all decisions are based on underlying business logic. Let's examine the normalization rules that Information Technology experts use in more detail so we have a clear understanding of why the business involvement and expertise is so important.

No Repeating Groups

Whenever there is data that can occur multiple times, you must create a separate entity. The reason behind this rule is that there is no way to decide the *right* number of repeated facts, such as competitive products that a customer might own. In a filing cabinet, if you learn about more products than the form allows for, you can just jot them in the margins or staple two forms together. That's not the way it works for databases.

XYZ had asked for five competitive products on the registration card—a nice round number. But XYZ found that customers often listed five products on the registration card, and then the company learned about more competitive installed products for this customer from other sources. In some early projects, XYZ built the database to store only five products and then it was stuck. Its choices were to invest in database redesign to add more competitive products ("How many?" you might well ask) or to throw the additional information away. Neither choice was very appealing. There are no business rules for the number of competitive products that a customer might have. Even if your company decided one, your customers aren't governed by it.

The right answer was the approach followed by the Valencia team. The "no repeating groups" rule allowed XYZ to avoid having to make this decision at all—it's like stapling an additional page to a form. The team defined a new entity, Competitive Installed Product, where they could store as much competitive product information as they came across. It no longer made sense to name the attributes "product 1" through "product 5" because the new entity would handle as many products as needed. XYZ renamed this attribute simply competitive product.

Next, XYZ realized that because it now had two entities, it had to use different names for each entity so there would be no confusion (and the computer loves uniqueness—as do paper files, if they're to be of any use). The data subject **Installed Product** contains two entities: Competitive-Installed Product and XYZ-Installed Product.

After XYZ had defined a new entity, it had to pick a key? We've already discussed that a product model by itself is hardly unique. The team knew they weren't likely to need (or get) serial numbers for competitive products, so that approach was out. The team knew that this entity was designed to capture all the competitive products owned/used by an XYZ customer. Did they know who the customer was for each of the installed products on the registration card? Of course they did. Let's bring the customer name fields over to help us create a key for this entity.

Is customer name (first plus last) enough to make a key? No, we know that a customer can own more than one product; that's why we created the Competitive-Installed Product entity in the first place! Well, how about combining customer and competitive product?

Sure, that works—unless a customer owns more than one of the same product; what then? Here's where XYZ's business knowledge and some common sense come into play again. They knew they wanted to know what installed equipment they were competing against, but that's about it. The most they might ever like to know is how many competitive products a customer owns, and that certainly wasn't unique either.

XYZ chose the customer plus competitive product to uniquely identify the Competitive-Installed Product entity. As we saw, the key that represents the customer contact name is the person identifier. The new key for Competitive-Installed Product is <u>person identifier + competitive</u> <u>product</u>. XYZ also added a new attribute, product quantity, which allows them to track the number of each competitive product the customer has. We now have two entities defined for the Installed Product subject area, as shown in Table D-10.

Table D-10 No Repeating Groups (First Normal Form)

Entity	Attribute
XYZ-Installed Product	<u>product model</u> <u>serial number</u>
	purchase date
	where purchased
	store name
	store city
	store state
	used for
	where used
Competitive-Installed Product	<u>person identifier</u> <u>competitive product</u>
	product quantity

Next, XYZ's team applied the second test—the one that helps reduce data redundancy and inconsistency.

No Repeated Data (Second and Third Normal Forms)

This rule requires that every attribute must depend completely on the entity key. The reason for this rule is that when data is repeated throughout a database, it's almost impossible to maintain accuracy and consistency. For example, storing the store name and address along with product purchased means that the all the address information would be repeated for every installed product purchased at the same store—even though the address was exactly the same. The Repeated Data rule means that every attribute in an entity must depend entirely on the key.

The question to ask for each attribute is "Does the value of this attribute describe the entity key and only the entity key?" Let's look at each attribute in the XYZ-Installed Base entity, just as they did (see Table D-11).

Table D-11 Dependence on the Key

Depend on Key?	Response
Does purchase date describe a specific physical product (identified by its *product + serial number*)?	Yes, it is the date the actual product was purchased.
What about where used and used for?	Yes, these describe where and how this product will be used.
Where purchased and store name?	Yes, these describe how and where the purchase of this product occurred.
How about store city and state?	No, the city and state would be the same for all products purchased at the same store; they describe the store not the product.

XYZ defined a new entity called Store where they could collect these elements. Of course, it needed a key. Similar to the reasons for developing a unique company identifier, independent of its name and address, XYZ defined a new attribute, *store identifier* as the logical key. But wait a second, how would XYZ know the actual store where this product was purchased if there is an entirely separate entity? The answer is that the database designer defined a link between XYZ-Installed Product and Store. These links are called relationships, which we'll look at next. For now, suffice to say that the IT experts will not lose track of these links.

One last question was asked: Is this new entity really related to the Installed Product subject area? No, it's not. Is it related to any of the subjects we've identified for the Valencia project (**Customer Companies, Customer Contacts,** and **Installed Products**)? No, it is not. But XYZ checked its strategic data class list and found a logical home subject for this entity: **Channel Partners**. XYZ had found some data that wasn't part of what it defined as the original project scope. At some point, the company would have to decide whether to expand the project to include the channel partner information, though strictly speaking it wasn't needed to satisfy the needs of Valencia.

For expedience, we won't go through the other two candidate entities step by step. All of XYZ's results from the Valencia project are shown in Table D-12.

The database designer added attributes where a unique field was needed to act as the key. She also added the attribute "country" to the Address entity because even though the company didn't specifically ask for it on these old cards, it definitely needed to know the country where a customer was located.

Table D-12 Valencia Entities and Attributes

Class	Subject	Entity	Attribute
INSTALLED PROD-UCTS	Installed Products	XYZ Installed Product	product model
			serial number
			purchase date
			where purchased
			primary use
			where used
		Competitive Installed Product	person identifier
			competitive product
			product quantity
CHANNEL PART-NERS	Stores	Store	store identifier
			store name
			store location city
			store location state
CUSTOMERS	Customer Contacts	Contact Person	person identifier
			person last name
			person first name
			person address title
			person business title
			person gender
			okay to contact?
	Customer Companies	Company Site	company identifier
			address identifier
			employee count here
		Company Organization	company identifier
			company name
			total employees
			revenue

Table D-12 Valencia Entities and Attributes (Continued)

Class	Subject	Entity	Attribute
LOCATERS	Locaters	Email Address	person identifier
			e-mail address
			e-mail inactive date
		Street Address	address identifier
			street
			city
			state
			postal code
			country
INDUSTRIES	Industries	Industry	industry code
			industry description

D.4.5 Identify Relationships

As we briefly discussed earlier, relationships are links that form connections between two entities. Early computer systems followed the file drawer method: Store everything in one big computer file. This approach had all the same inherent wasted space, inconsistency, and poor quality as a filing cabinet. Though computers are faster and bigger than filing cabinets, database software hadn't been designed to take advantage of the computer's potential. The early computer file designs forced programmers to "tie strings" between related files, as we discussed in Chapter 10 (see Figure D-4).

But that has changed. The database management systems most prevalent today (relational, object oriented) are designed to manage links between entities very efficiently. After these links are defined, the computer does the work of pulling everything together so it looks like one big form. The advantage is that we have also been able to eliminate all the repeated data required by the old method.

What Are Relationships?

Entity relationships have some specific technical characteristics that are important only to Information Technology. But let's get a quick overview. Relationships identify how two (and only two) entities interact with each other. From the business perspective, relationships are represented by a line connecting the two entities. In a physical database, a relationship is represented by including the key from one entity in the other entity. (Think of a U.S. Income Tax Form 1040. It has a line that represents all the information from Schedule A, Itemized Deductions.)

Figure D-4 Filing cabinet "relationships"

- Relationships have names that describe the role that each entity plays with the other: A person *owns* an installed product; an installed product *is owned by* a person.
- Relationships have cardinality that tells us the how many of one entity relates to how many of the other. Each end of the relationship has a lower limit and an upper limit.

Table D-13 shows the possible cardinalities for each end of the relationship. Zero as a possible lower limit means the relationship is optional. A relationship may have any of these four possible cardinalities on each end of the line.

Table D-13 Relationship Cardinality

Lower Limit	Upper Limit			
	One		Many	
Zero	zero or one		zero or many	
One	one and only one		one or many	

There are more complex conventions available and used by many database designers, but these four are the basics. We will discuss more about what these mean in section D-5.

All entities within a project must be linked (not necessarily directly), or it makes no sense to have them as part of the project at all. Of course, we worry about only the relationships between the entities that are part of the project.

XYZ actually got a head start while defining the Valencia project entities and assigning attributes. In real life, the company started documenting relationships as new entities that were created to meet the normalization rules, but which needed to be linked to the original candidate entity. For clarity, we're taking these steps sequentially in practice.

Any entity whose key includes the key from another entity has a dependent relationship with that entity. XYZ started by quickly drawing the relationships between Contact Person and both E-mail Address and Competitive Product. It also drew links between Company Organization and Company Site, and Street Address and Company Site. It had already identified the minimum required relationships for six of the nine entities!

Let's look at the other three. Earlier, we discussed that XYZ identified a link between Industry and Company Organization. It also knew that Store described where an Installed Product was purchased, so that was another link. At this point, XYZ had created a preliminary entity relationship diagram that looks like the one in Figure D-5.

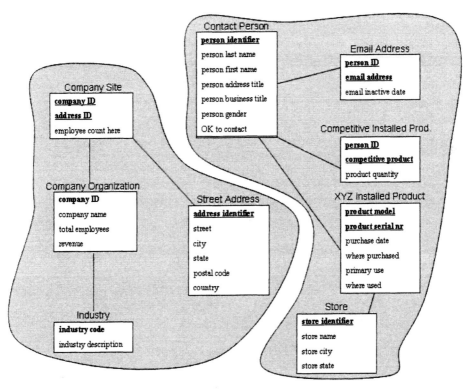

Figure D-5 Missing link?

But XYZ still had two separate groups with no link between them, and that's not allowed. There was a connection missing between the contact person and the address he gave. One question on the registration card asked whether the address was a home or business address. XYZ initially made this an attribute of Address. But sometimes, the address can be used for both home and business.

For business addresses, XYZ identified a link to Company Site (which we've already drawn). If it's a home address, the link is directly to Contact Person, representing XYZ's consumer customers. Business customers are linked to the Company Site where they work.

Finally, we must name the relationship and identify cardinalities. IT put all this together using a Computer Aided Software Engineering (CASE) tool (trust me, graphics software is NOT the way), and we got the entity relationship diagram for Valencia (and El Cid as well because Valencia was the first project) as shown in Figure D-6.

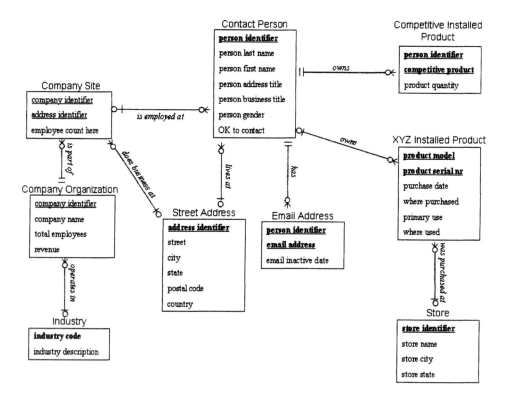

Figure D-6 The entity relationship diagram for Valencia

The relationships between XYZ's Valencia project entities can be "read" directly off this diagram. As an example, consider the relationship between Contact Person and Company Site:

- A Contact Person is employed at zero or one Company Sites. (The Contact Person may be a consumer.)
- Conversely, a Company Site employs zero to many Customer Contacts. (We may not know any of the contacts who work there, but we know the site exists.)

Next, the IT experts began constructing the physical computer "storage file" for this information.

The process takes some practice, but it's logical and consistent, and it follows step by step **as long as you use a methodology.** Because we normally work with only a small number of entities at a time, this really isn't all that difficult. And of course, lots of the relationships have already been identified by the time we've finished assigning attributes to entities.

D.4.6   Define Entities, Attributes, and Relationships

The business team has to worry about the business name and definition of each entity and attribute and relationship.

Entity

We saw how XYZ created the definitions for classes and subjects. Defining entities is just the same, so we won't go through that process again. Just remember that you can build off the subject definitions to help create the entity definitions. You don't have to start with a blank slate.

Attribute

When defining each of the attributes, XYZ had to do more than just give a business definition. IT takes over after the definitions are complete and identifies the size of the attribute, type of data being stored, and whether any special checks should be made on the value of each. Information Technology needs to be able to count on business participation to get this right. I have seen too many projects that had to be re-written because the IT team didn't know, for example, that the company's product models could have up to 18 characters, even though they are not often that long. Table D-14 holds the attribute definitions for the Installed Product entity.

There are some related concepts that the IT team uses that make the communication with the business team easier. One such tool is using a standard naming convention and standard abbreviations to generate consistent physical data names from the business-defined names. This topic is discussed in section D-7.

Table D-14 Installed Product Attribute Definitions

Attribute	Definition	Size	Type	Values
product model	Name of the type of hardware or software product installed	18	Text	On product file
serial number	Unique number that identifies the specific physical hardware or software product	16	Integer	Greater than zero
purchase date	Date of purchase	8	Date	Valid date
where purchased	Sales channel of purchase	3	Text	1. Direct 2. Catalog 3. Retail/dealer
used for	Purpose for which product is used			
where used	Primary place where product is used	1	Text	Home, Office, Both

Relationship

Relationship definitions include the name, cardinality, optionality, and related entities, as we've just seen. Usually, these are defined using a data modeling tool and displayed as shown in the entity relationship diagram (refer to Figure D-6).

D.5 Completing the Information Component

We're going to look at the rest of the framework views just so we can trace how critical the business views at the beginning are in guiding Information Technology's efforts to build the right system. In the next step, the IT team turns the entity relationship diagram (ERD) into physical designs.

D.5.1 Builder's View: Physical Data Model

Just as in each preceding view, the IT team started with the entity relationship diagram. The team reviewed for technical performance issues and suggested some modifications to the logical model to support faster updates, retrievals, and sorting. Each modification recommendation was explained to the business team with pros and cons. Exceptions that were approved and implemented were included in the project documentation, along with the explanation of why it was needed. System performance is always improving; there may be a reason to go back to the original design some time in the future. The people who have to make that change need to know why the database looks the way it does.

Next, Information Technology had to create the technical backbone for implementing the relationships on the ERD. This was accomplished by carrying the key from the independent entity in the dependent entity (sometimes called a foreign key). Many customers may live (or work) at a single address. Because we don't want to store all the duplicate data to put the actual full address in each customer record, the unique identifier of the correct address is stored instead. Using the foreign key *address identifier*, we can easily find and access all the information about the person's address. And because the address itself is captured only once, if it changes, we just need to update it in one place!

The physical data model includes the physical characteristics of the data to be stored such as type of data (numbers, text) and size (how much space needs to be set aside). Fixed-length data characteristics are generally required for transaction processing and most decision support. There are also many excellent products that support storing formatted and variable-length text for quick retrieval, but this was not a requirement of Valencia.

D.5.2   Detailed Representation: Individual Tables, Rows, and Columns

Now the IT team is ready to actually build the database. XYZ's programmers reproduced the physical data model in a database management system by creating one table for each entity. The database table is made up of a series of columns, one for each attribute, as shown in Table D-15.

Table D-15 Model and Database Terms

Data Model	Physical Database
Entity	Data table
Attribute	Column
Entity instance	Row

The database is empty when it is first built, just like a new empty spreadsheet in which you have only the spreadsheet and a list of column headers.

D.5.3   Functioning System: Physical Working Database

Finally, IT will get the system up and running so that data can be loaded and retrieved. Each individual record (set of information about an entity instance) that is added creates a new row in the data table. A specific row is retrieved based on the value of its key. Once accessed, all the data for the entity instance is available whether it is physically in that table or linked by a foreign key.

D.6   Relationship Types

Our job, should we chose to accept it (and we must accept it), is to determine which entities have relationships with each other, the role or name of the relationship, and the cardinality of each end. Business rules provide the guidance that helps make these determinations.

A company may be engaged in only one industry, but an industry describes many companies. This is called a *one-to-many* relationship and is the most common. In this type of relationship, one entity is said to be dependent on the other because the correct entity instance is based on knowing the specific record from the other (independent) entity. We know that entities represent a group of attributes; a dependent entity represents a group of that all together may be used to describe another entity. If you know a company, you know its industry; the industry is said to be dependent on the specific company. The reverse is not true; knowing the industry does not help you recognize a specific company.

> **A one-to-many relationship:**

A *one-to-one* relationship, indicating a maximum of one on each end of the relationship, is used for sets of attributes that are optional and frequently blank. It's a way to save space. Why reserve space for information that, while interesting, is only rarely available? For example, if most of our customer contacts are consumers, we might decide to create a separate entity for person title, which is used only for business contacts. XYZ's business is about 50 percent consumer and 50 percent B2B, so the company decided that this attribute wasn't worth the effort of creating a new entity. Of course, this could change later on.

> **A one-to-one relationship:**

In some cases, the relationship may be two-way, and both entities are independent. For instance, while we know that many people can share the same address, it is also true that a single person could have multiple addresses. This means that knowing the person wouldn't help you identify a specific address, nor would knowing the address help find the right person. Of course, just because the real world looks this way doesn't mean you care about it. XYZ decided it only needed one address per person because even though more were possible, it only needed to know one. This type of relationship is a special case for IT that we won't study further, but we do need to recognize that these can occur and document them if we find them important. Only the business knows what's important; then IT knows what to do about it.

> **A many-to-many relationship:**

Each of the preceding three examples has been shown as *required* (minimum of one). Of course, if any were *optional* on either end, the one would be replaced by a zero as shown in the following example.

> **An optional one-to-many relationship:**

An example of an optional one-to-many relationship is reflected in the relationship between the customers and products. A customer may own zero (a prospect), one or many product. A product may be owned by zero (new product), one or many customers. Of course a relationship may be optional at only one end. An order must be placed by one and only one customer, but a customer may have placed zero, one or many orders.

D.7 Data Element Naming Standards

Another excellent practice for ensuring that the data context is clearly understood is to use standard data naming conventions. Standard names are most important in helping the business users and IT team communicate about the system effectively. Standards are important because they form data documentation for the system.

Data naming conventions require good business definitions as their basis. Because XYZ has already completed the planning phase, there are just three simple rules that XYZ's database designer followed in order to create clear and understandable data element names for Valencia.

D.7.1 Data Naming Conventions

There are a number of different naming conventions. It is not important which one your company chooses as long as there is one and it is followed rigorously throughout the IT department. It is really amazing how much easier it is to support and enhance a database or application in which the data element names give an indication of what information the elements hold.

Name Components

There are three components of all data element names:

1. Prime Word(s): The basic fact that is being named
2. Modifier(s): Descriptors that indicate more specifically which fact this is
3. Class Word: Standard code describing the type (class) of data being named

Some experts recommend various tweaks to this basic convention, but these are the basics.

Standard Class Words

Class words are used to identify the type of data to be stored in each data element. Usually, there is a class word for any data types commonly used by your organization's systems. Classes also may indicate the purpose for which data is used. In Table D-16, "name" and "text" are both non-numeric fields, but "name" is a text field with a special purpose.

Table D-16 Data Name Classes

Class Word	Class Code	Use
amount	am	data content describes how much
code	cd	data content points back to a standard code list
date	dt	data content is a calendar date
identifier	id	data content is a number that is uniquely assigned to each record
name	nm	data content is the name of the fact being described
number	nr	data content is numeric
quantity	qt	data content describes how many
text	tx	data content is non-numeric (captured as characters, not values)

As shown, class words should be abbreviated in a standard way. Again, there is no universal standard to follow; just be sure that your company has thought through the types of data that are important to the business. Don't create too many class words, or you'll just be complicating life.

Strictly speaking, most DBMS systems don't have limits to the length of names they allow. Still, you'll reduce the amount of typing required by keeping names as short as possible (without sacrificing clarity, of course). One way to do this is to abbreviate each word in the definition.

Standard Abbreviations

Some people feel that it is clearer for business users to use real words, but I have found that as long as you follow a standard, everyone quickly learns that CUST is the shorthand for customer (not custard). Of course, if some use CUST and some use CUSTMR and still others use CUS, the situation becomes quickly unmanageable.

Pick a single standard list of abbreviations, and use them consistently. At HP, we started with a list created by the American Chemical Society. Their standard abbreviation list, known as CAS, can be reviewed at http://www.cas.org/ONLINE/standards.html, although it looks even more technically aimed than I remember. Start with a list of your own, and keep adding new abbreviations as you need them. HP used several abbreviation rules to create an addition to the list:

• New abbreviations should be as short as possible and never longer than five characters.
• Plural nouns use the same abbreviation as the singular form.

• Duplicate abbreviations are okay because the full name usually gives clear context.

If anyone is working on a standard abbreviations list (or better yet, knows of a good external standard that already exists), please get in touch with me. I'd love to collaborate.

D.7.2   Valencia Project

Data naming conventions require meaningful business definitions as their basis. Because we've seen the business definitions that XYZ developed for the Installed Base attributes, we will use them as examples. XYZ's database designer used these three rules to fill in the blanks and create a name for each attribute.

1. The prime word is generally the subject of the definition.
2. The adjectives that describe the subject are the modifiers.
3. The class word is the type or purpose of the data fact.

In Table D-17, you can see how the Valencia database designer followed these three rules and developed standard data names for the Installed Base entity.

Table D-17 Valencia Data Names

Attribute	Definition	Modifier(s) (descriptor)	Prime Word (fact)	Class Word (type)	Attribute Name (Data Element Name)
product model	Name that identifies the type of hardware or software product installed	installed	product	identifier	installed product identifier (instl_prod_id)
serial number	Unique number that identifies the specific physical hardware or software product	installed product	serial number	number	installed product serial number (number) (instl_prod_ser_nr)
purchase date	Date of purchase	installed product	purchase	date	installed product purchase date (instl_prod_purch_ dt)
where purchased	Sales channel where purchase	installed product purchase	sales channel	code	installed product purchase sales channel code (instl_prod_purch_sls_chan_cd)

Table D-17 Valencia Data Names

Attribute	Definition	Modifier(s) (descriptor)	Prime Word (fact)	Class Word (type)	Attribute Name (Data Element Name)
used for	Purpose for which product is used	installed product	use	code	installed product use code (instl_prod_use_cd)
where used	Primary location where product is used	installed product	location	code	installed product location code (instl_prod_loc_cd)

As you have seen, even the names of the physical database fields are completely determined by the business definition that was created by the business experts. The names are recognizable, meaningful, and sharable/reusable.

INDEX

inform IT

www.informit.com

YOUR GUIDE TO IT REFERENCE

Articles

Keep your edge with thousands of free articles, in-depth features, interviews, and IT reference recommendations – all written by experts you know and trust.

Online Books

Answers in an instant from **InformIT Online Book's** 600+ fully searchable on line books. Sign up now and get your first 14 days **free.**

POWERED BY

Catalog

Review online sample chapters, author biographies and customer rankings and choose exactly the right book from a selection of over 5,000 titles.

 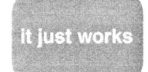

HP's world-class education and training offers hands on education solutions including:

- Linux
- HP-UX System and Network Administration
- Advanced HP-UX System Administration
- IT Service Management using advanced Internet technologies
- Microsoft Windows NT/2000
- Internet/Intranet
- MPE/iX
- Database Administration
- Software Development

HP's new IT Professional Certification program provides rigorous technical qualification for specific IT job roles including HP-UX System Administration, Network Management, Unix/NT Servers and Applications Management, and IT Service Management.

http://education.hp.com

fulfill your needs

Want to know about new products, services and solutions from Hewlett-Packard Company — as soon as they're invented?

Need information about new HP services to help you implement new or existing products?

Looking for HP's newest solution to a specific challenge in your business?

HP Computer News features the latest from HP!

4 easy ways to subscribe, and it's FREE:

- **fax** complete and fax the form below to (651) 430-3388, or

- **online** sign up online at www.hp.com/go/compnews, or

- **email** complete the information below and send to hporders@earthlink.net, or

- **mail** complete and mail the form below to:

Twin Cities Fulfillment Center
Hewlett-Packard Company
P.O. Box 408
Stillwater, MN 55082

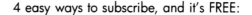

invent

reply now to receive the first year FREE!

name _____ title _____

company _____ dept./mail stop _____

address _____

city _____ state _____ zip _____

email _____ signature _____ date _____

please indicate your industry below:

☐ accounting   ☐ healthcare/medical   ☐ online services   ☐ telecommunications
☐ education   ☐ legal   ☐ real estate   ☐ transport and travel
☐ financial services   ☐ manufacturing   ☐ retail/wholesale distrib   ☐ utilities
☐ government   ☐ publishing/printing   ☐ technical   ☐ other: _____